MELCHIOR HOFFMAN

MELCHIOR HOF-MAN
van STRASBURG

Kaltenhof. f. Gottingae 1758.

Melchior Hoffman in prison at Strasbourg

MELCHIOR HOFFMAN

SOCIAL UNREST AND APOCALYPTIC VISIONS
IN THE AGE OF REFORMATION

KLAUS DEPPERMANN

Translated by

MALCOLM WREN

Edited by

BENJAMIN DREWERY

T. & T. CLARK
EDINBURGH

Translation © T. & T. Clark, 1987.

Originally published under the title
*Melchior Hoffman: Soziale Unruhen und apokalyptische Visionen im
Zeitalter der Reformation* by Vandenhoeck & Ruprecht, Göttingen,
1979

Printed and bound by OUP Printing House, Oxford,

for

T. & T. CLARK LTD,
59, George Street, Edinburgh EH2 2LQ,

First printed in Great Britain by T. & T. Clark Ltd., 1987.

British Library Cataloguing in Publication Data:

Deppermann, Klaus
Melchior Hoffman: social unrest and
apocalyptic visions in the Age of Reformation.
1. Hoffman, Melchior   2. Anabaptists—Biography
I. Title   II. Drewery, Benjamin
284'.3'0924   BX4946.H6/
ISBN: 0–567–09338–7

CONTENTS

Acknowledgements   vi

Introduction   1

1 Hoffman and the Iconoclastic Movement in
   Livonia.   35

2 The Stockholm Interlude (1526-1527).   89

3 Hoffman in Schleswig-Holstein: The Break With
   Lutheranism.   95

4 Hoffman's First Period in Eastern Frisia
   (April-June 1529).   153

5 Hoffman in Strasbourg: The Fusion of
   Apocalypticism, Spiritualism and Anabaptism.   160

6 Hoffman's Theology After His Break With
   Luther.   220

7 The Climax and Turning-Point of the Anabaptist
   Movement in Strasbourg: Apocalyptic
   Excitement Around 1530, the Synod of 1533
   and the End of the City Council's Policy of
   Tolerance.   268

8 Hoffman's Return to Eastern Frisia
   (May-November 1530).   312

9 Hoffman's Relationship With Anabaptism in the
   Netherlands and Westphalia, 1530-1535.   321

10   The Decline of the Melchiorite Movement.   349

11   Conclusion   381

     Bibliography   392

     Abbreviations   419

     List of illustrations   420

     Index   422

     Map   At end

QUOTATIONS FROM COPYRIGHT MATERIAL

RSV

Luther's Works – American Edition – Fortress Press, Philadelphia; G.H. Williams and A.M. Mergal (ed.), *Spiritual and Anabaptist Writers* (Library of Christian Classics) – SCM; G.W. Bromiley (ed.), *Zwingli and Bullinger* (Library of Christian Classics) – SCM; J.C. Olin (ed.), *A Reformation Debate* – Harper and Row, New York.

INTRODUCTION

The Issues at Stake and Research so far.

1. "Evangelical Anabaptism": Its Claim to be Sole Embodiment of the Movement.

"The rehabilitation (of the Anabaptists) is now so complete that we shall see a turn of the tide within the next ten years".[1] Since Heinold Fast made this prediction in 1967 the tide has turned.[2] Fast's prediction was made at a time when, under the influence of the Ecumenical Movement, the theological differences between the Reformers and the Anabaptists had been played down so much that they were no longer apparent.[3] The works of Bender, Blanke, Littell, Yoder and Bauman[4] had made it

[1] *MGB*, NF. 19 (1967), p. 25.

[2] On this cf. A. Friesen, "Social Revolution or Religious Reform? Some Salient Aspects of Anabaptist Historiography" in *Umstrittenes Täufertum 1525-1975. Neue Forschungen.* Edited by H.-J. Goertz, (Göttingen, 1975), pp. 223-243 and J.M. Stayer, W. Packull and K. Deppermann, "From Monogenesis to Polygenesis: The Historical Discussion of Anabaptist Origins" in *MQR* 49 (1975), pp. 83-122.

[3] There had certainly always been scholars during the time of the predominance of "Mennonite historiography" who *had* pointed out the theological differences between the Reformers and the Anabaptists, e.g. W. Maurer, *Luther und die Schwärmer* 1952 (Schriften des Theol. Konvents Augsburg. Bekenntnisses VI); K.G. Steck, *Luther und die Schwärmer* (Zollikon and Zurich, 1955); J.S. Oyer, *Lutheran Reformers against Anabaptists* (The Hague, 1965).

[4] H.S. Bender, *Conrad Grebel (c. 1498-1526): The Founder of the Swiss Brethren* (Goshen, Indiana, 1950); F. Blanke, *Brüder in Christo* (Zurich, 1955); F.H. Littell, *The Anabaptist view of the Church* 2nd ed. (Boston, 1958); J.H. Yoder, *Täufertum und Reformation in der Schweiz: I. Die Gespräche zwischen Täufern und Reformatoren, 1523–1538.* (Karlsruhe, 1962), *II. Täufertum und Reformation im Gespräch. Dogmengeschichtliche Untersuchung der frühen Gespräche zwischen schweizerischen Täufern und Reformatoren* (Zurich, 1968); C. Bauman, *Gewaltlosigkeit im Täufertum* (Leiden, 1968) (Studies in the History of Christian Thought 3).

1

appear that the 'original, genuine, normative, true or evangelical' Anabaptists had stood firmly inside the Reformation fold. It
appeared that they had intended to restore early Christianity in
its purest form, being more faithful to Scripture and more
consistent, and, as well, more radical, than either Zwingli or
Luther, who had both compromised with an unchristian world.
It was claimed that their establishment of a politically independent, voluntary and pacifist community of sincere Christians
had issued from an evangelical commitment to the imitation of
Christ in the believer's life.[5] It was the Reformers of Wittenberg
and Zürich, not the Anabaptists, who had been unfaithful to
their own great work of renewal on the basis of the New
Testament.[6]

Whereas the Reformers had retained the medieval *corpus
christianum* (and defended it with the theologically questionable
instruments of infant baptism and the persecution of heretics),
the 'evangelical' Anabaptists were seen as much more modern
because of their championing of freedom of conscience and their
separation of Church and state.[7] Ernst Troeltsch had already
seen the significance of the Anabaptists in this respect.[8] Their
pacifism also had a great attraction in the light of the pointless
slaughter of millions of people in two world wars; it appeared to
be a sensible Christian alternative to the self-destructive drives of
a mad world.

This idealised image of the Anabaptists as precursors of
modern developments could only come about by making a

[5] It was primarily Robert Friedmann who presented the idea of an
imitation of Christ as the essence of Anabaptist theology: cf. his essay
"Das Täuferische Glaubensgut" in *ARG* 55 (1964) pp. 145-161 and his
The Theology of Anabaptism (Scottdale, Pennsylvania, 1975).

[6] J.H. Yoder, "The Turning Point in the Zwinglian Reformation" in
MQR 32 (1958), pp. 128-140; R.C. Walton, "Was there a Turning Point
in the Zwinglian Reformation?" in *MQR* 42 (1968), pp. 45-56; J.H.
Yoder "The Evolution of the Zwinglian Reformation" in *MQR* 43
(1969), pp. 95-122.

[7] Cf. H.S. Bender "The Anabaptists and Religious Liberty in the
16th Century" in *ARG* 44 (1953), pp. 32-51.

[8] E. Troeltsch *The Social Teaching of the Christian Churches* (1912), *ET*
London and New York, 1931. Vol.2, pp. 691-706 (especially pp. 695-6,
698 and 704).

distinction between the "true" Anabaptists and their misguided relatives. Counted amongst the latter were the social-revolutionary "Enthusiasts" (Müntzer, Karlstadt, the Zwickau prophets, Melchior Rinck, Hoffman, Rothmann, Jan Matthijs and Jan van Leiden), to an extent also Balthasar Hubmaier (who formulated an apologia for self-defence) and also the spiritualists Ludwig Hätzer and Hans Denck, who placed the 'inner Word' of the conscience higher than the 'outer Word' of Scripture.[9] The representatives of social-revolutionary and of spiritualising Anabaptism appeared either as insignificant marginal figures[10] or as dangerous tempters[11] with whom, however, the mainstream Anabaptist movement had been able to deal. By 1550, at the latest, the original spirit, which, it was claimed, had vivified the earliest Swiss Anabaptists (and which could be seen documented in Grebel's letter to Müntzer of 1524 and in the Schleitheim Confession of 1527), broke through again to direct all the major Anabaptist groups (viz. the Swiss Brethren, the Mennonites and the Hutterites). This became the historical justification for the idea that 'true' Anabaptism was "evangelical, peace-loving and tolerant."

From the very beginning this highly evaluative style of historiography was bound up with the typological method of the sociology of religion that had been developed by Max Weber and Ernst Troeltsch. For Troeltsch, Swiss Anabaptism had embodied the 'Sect Type' in an unusually pure form, and it was his work in particular which encouraged "Mennonite historiography" to present its own case in an idealised light and as a normative example. Not even the objections of Karl Holl could prevail against this.[12] George Huntston Williams, in his 'magnum opus' *The Radical Reformation* (Philadelphia, 1962) further refined the typology that had been developed by the Heidelberg

---

[9] Cf. eg. Heinold Fast's rigid distinction between the Anabaptists, the 'Spiritualists' and the 'Enthusiasts' in his edition of source-texts, *Der linke Flügel der Reformation* Bremen, 1962 (Klassiker des Protestantismus 4).

[10] H.S. Bender, "Die Zwickauer Propheten, Thomas Müntzer und die Täufer" in *Theologische Zeitschrift* (Basel) 8 (1952) pp. 262-278.

[11] F.H. Littell, *The Anabaptist View of the Church* p. 24.

[12] K. Holl, "Luther und die Schwärmer" in *Gesammelte Aufsätze zur Kirchengeschichte.I:Luther* Tübingen 1932, pp. 420-467.

sociologists of religion, and from it created an instrument with which to impose order upon and allow an overview of the tangled growth of the movements which had sprung up along with the Reformation. But this meticulously constructed typological presentation of intellectual history had one major, inescapable weakness: it gave scarcely any consideration to the social and political context from which the ideas had grown. But since the beginning of the seventies scholars have begun to challenge the claim that "evangelical Anabaptists" were exclusively representative of the movement.[13] We can list the main objections to the dominant line of Anabaptist research as:

1. Its vision of the Anabaptist movement is restricted. Whilst scholars concentrate on the 'good seed' (in particular those 'typical' Anabaptists, the Swiss Brethren) they ignore the 'tares' (or at least leave them to the Marxists[14]). In the worst cases some 'tares' (e.g. Hans Hut) are wrongly counted amongst the 'good seed'.[15]

2. It wrongly underestimates the intimate relationships between the various groups that made up the 'left wing' of the Reformation (e.g. the connections between Müntzer, Karlstadt and Jakob Strauss on the one hand and Grebel's circle on the other, or between the revolutionary Melchiorites and the pacifist Mennonites).

3. It projects the later stages of a historical process back into a period when various developments would still have been possible (e.g. the attitude of mind behind the Schleitheim Confession of 1527 is attributed to the earliest Anabaptists in and around Zürich in 1523-4, and the majority of Melchiorites in

---

[13] Cf. the works of J.M. Stayer, C.P. Clasen and Gottfried Seebass, all of which appeared in 1972.

[14] The most important works on Anabaptism written from a Marxist standpoint are those of Gerhard Zschäbitz (*Zur mitteldeutschen Wiedertäuferbewegung nach dem Grossen Bauernkrieg*, Berlin, 1958) and of Gerhard Brendler (*Das Täuferreich zu Münster 1534/35*. Berlin, 1966). A.F. Mellink, *De Wederdopers in de Noordelijke Nederlanden* Groningen, 1953, arrives at similar conclusions – based on empirical evidence – as some Marxists, but his studies are not basically written from a Marxist standpoint.

[15] H. Klassen, "The Life and Teachings of Hans Hut" in *MQR* 33 (1959) pp. 171-205;267-304.

1534 are said to have shared the pacifist opinions of the
Mennonites of six years later).

4. The tendency to idealise and typify Anabaptist history
(especially the history of the "evangelical Anabaptists") means
that historical enquiry gives way to normative theology. This
means that it pays no attention to the tangible social conditions
which contributed substantially to the growth of nonconformity
in the sixteenth century.

5. To regard the Anabaptists' social revolutionary tendencies
as insignificant and harmless marginal phenomena means
conversely to demonize the authorities' reaction to the movement.

2. The Rejection of the Normative-Typological Approach, or the Return to the Historical Critical Method in Anabaptist Research.

a) *The beginning of Swiss Anabaptism*
Studies by Goeters, Stayer and Haas[16] have, it is generally
agreed, shown that the original intention of the group which
eventually became the Swiss Brethren had not been to establish
an independent and pacifist Free Church founded on the
principles of the Sermon on the Mount; they had wanted to
institute a radical reformation of the whole church and community. Amongst other things, they had aimed at establishing
the autonomy of individual congregations, at giving the
members of the congregation the free right to elect their
minister, at a restructuring of the tithe system, at abolishing
ecclesiastical sinecures, at forbidding religious images and at
introducing the 'evangelical Eucharist' without delay, if necessary in the face of official opposition. This is why Zwingli had

[16] J.F. Gerhard Goeters, "Die Vorgeschichte de Täufertums in
Zürich" in *Studien zur Geschichte und Theologie der Reformation. Festschrift
für Ernst Bizer* Neukirchen, 1969, pp. 239-281; J.M. Stayer, "Die
Anfänge des schweizerischen Täufertums im reformierten Kongrega-
tionalismus" in H.J. Goertz (ed.), *Umstrittenes Täufertum*, pp. 19-49; M.
Haas, "Der Weg der Täufer in die Absonderung" in H.J. Goertz (ed.),
Umstrittenes Täufertum pp. 50-78.

broken with his radical friends, who later became Anabaptists. Adult baptism represented only one relatively late and insignificant point of contention in this dispute.

Since several of their aims were identical with those fought for in the Peasants' War, the Anabaptists in Grüningen, in Eastern Switzerland (Hallau and St.Gallen) and in Waldshut joined with the insurgent peasants (under Simon Stumpf, Reublin, Brötli, Hubmaier and Krüsi). Whole congregations espoused Anabaptism. The idea of the Church as a group of separated and suffering true believers, which had already grown up before the Peasants' War within the circle around Grebel and Mantz in Zürich, was in no sense common to the whole movement; it most certainly does not represent the attitude of the rural congregations sympathetic to Anabaptism. Such a programme of separation and independence could only gain ground in Switzerland after the failure of the Peasants' War when Anabaptism lost its appeal to the peasants and the lesser artisans.

Thus the origins of Swiss Anabaptism became rooted again in the general social problems of the early Reformation. Differences from, and similarities to, other nonconformist movements (including the 'Wittenberg Movement', Müntzer and Karlstadt as well as later social-revolutionary Anabaptist movements) again take on significance. It is no longer possible to make an absolute distinction between those 'normative' evangelical Anabaptists, the Swiss Brethren, and the other similar movements which emerged from the Reformation.

b) *The problem of the continuity of medieval traditions within Anabaptism*

Hans J. Hillerbrand, in his article, "The Origins of Sixteenth Century Anabaptism: Another Look",[17] questioned the idea that the Anabaptist movement in Zürich could be understood simply as a radical version of early Zwinglianism. He showed that Erasmus, Karlstadt and Müntzer, as well as Luther and Zwingli, had left their marks on the Zürich radicals. Two years earlier Hillerbrand's essay, "Anabaptism and the Reformation: Another

---

[17] *ARG* 53 (1962), pp. 152-180.

Look", [18] had already concluded that Anabaptism because of its Pelagianism, legalism and perfectionism had more theological affinities with the Catholicism of the Middle Ages than with the Reformation. He thus re-opened the debate about the medieval origin of Anabaptism. This line of research was given further support when Hans-Jürgen Goertz brought forward evidence that Müntzer's theology had been more dependent on Tauler, Meister Eckhardt and the *Theologia Deutsch* than on Luther. [19] G.H. Williams also investigated the influence of mysticism and nominalism on Anabaptism. In his article 'Popularized German Mysticism as a Factor in the Rise of Anabaptist Communism'[20] he showed that the mystical doctrine of the mortification of the individual will had supplied the theological foundation for Hutterite collective ownership. Hans von Schubert had already suggested that the roots of communistic ideas lay in medieval mysticism. [21] In "Sanctification in the Testimony of Several So-Called Schwärmer"[22] Williams revealed the theological links between Denck and Hubmaier and the medieval concept of *iustificatio* (which was understood as an inseparable unity of justification and sanctification). This implies both the notion of cooperation of God and man in the attainment of salvation as well as the mystical idea that man's spirit or the 'divine spark' has not been totally corrupted by the Fall. Finally Williams showed that a considerable number of Anabaptists had followed the Mystic Path, whereby purification by suffering led on to 'enlightenment' from the 'Inner Word' and thence to the *unio mystica* and man's divinisation. [23]

Stephen E. Ozment analysed the social consequences of the revival of mysticism amongst the 16th century nonconformists

---

[18] *Church History* 29 (1960) pp. 404-424.

[19] H.J. Goertz, *Innere und Äussere Ordnung in der Theologie Thomas Müntzers* Leiden 1967 (Studies in the History of Christian Thought 2).

[20] In: *Glaube, Geist, Geschichte: Festschrift für Ernst Benz*. Edited by G. Müller and W. Zeller. Leiden, 1967, pp. 290-312.

[21] *Der Kommunismus der Wiedertäufer in Münster und seine Quellen* Heidelberg, 1919.

[22] In *MQR* 42 (1968), pp. 5-25.

[23] G.H. Williams, "German Mysticism in the Polarization of Ethical Behavior in Luther and the Anabaptists" in *MQR* 48 (1974), pp. 275-304.

(including Hut and Denck from amongst the Anabaptists).[24] In the *unio mystica* the individual is raised above all external authorities; the 'divinised man' can acknowledge only himself as the final authority and is thus always a potential revolutionary. Finally Kenneth R. Davis portrayed the Anabaptists as heirs of the medieval ascetic-monastic traditions, most notably of the *Devotio Moderna*.[25] He claims that the 'evangelical Anabaptists' inherited the spirituality of this movement from Erasmus, but this begs the question, 'How typical of the *Devotio Moderna* was Erasmus himself?'

The whole question of the relationship between the Hussites and the Anabaptists is still largely unexplained. Siegfried Hoyer began to tackle this problem by tracing the continuity of Hussite criticisms of the church in the Hanseatic towns of North-Eastern Germany and within Karlstadt's circle. These studies are of particular significance in respect to Melchior Hoffman, who frequently referred to Hus as his model.[26]

From these studies it has become apparent that the theological differences between the Reformers and the Anabaptists came about as a result of varying levels of attachment to medieval traditions. Whereas the influence of the mystics declined in the course of the Reformers' development, many Anabaptists retained much of the mystical and apocalyptic (as well as the ascetic) heritage of the Middle Ages. This does not mean that we should revert to thinking of Anabaptism as in any sense a clearly-defined or unified system. The enormously disparate nature of Anabaptism remains, even if we do acknowledge that the majority of Anabaptist leaders were more firmly rooted in the apocalyptic and mystical traditions of the Middle Ages than were the official Reformers.

[24] *Mysticism and Dissent. Religious Ideology and Social Protest in the Sixteenth Century* (New Haven and London, 1973).

[25] K.R. Davis, *Anabaptism and Asceticism* (Scottdale, Pennsylvania, 1974).

[26] S. Hoyer, *Häresien zwischen Hus und Luther*, MS Thesis, Leipzig, 1966; "Martin Reinhard und der erste Druck hussitischer Artikel in Deutschland" in ZfG 18 (1970), pp. 1597-1615; "Nicolaus Rutze und die Verbreitung hussitischer Gedanken im Hanseraum" in *Neue Hansische Studien*. Edited by K. Fritze, E. Müller-Mertens *et al.* (Berlin, 1970), pp. 157-170.

c) *The understanding of social revolutionary movements and of the social history of Anabaptism in non-Marxist research*

In 1972 three important works appeared simultaneously all dealing with the long-neglected social revolutionary and social historical aspects of Anabaptism. They were Gottfried Seebass' Erlangen thesis on Hans Hut, James M. Stayer's study of the Anabaptist attitude concerning "the Sword", and Claus-Peter Clasen's general social history of Anabaptism.[27] All three works share the conviction that the typological division of the Anabaptist movement formulated by G.H. Williams and Heinold Fast is unfruitful and apologetic. For them "Anabaptists" are all those religious communities based on adult baptism; the Swiss Brethren, the South German Anabaptists who followed Hans Denck, Hut's followers, Marbeck's circle, the Hutterites, the Thuringian Anabaptists and the Melchiorites/ Mennonites.

Gottfried Seebass shows that Hut's Anabaptism was firmly built on theological foundations laid by Müntzer and Karlstadt, with elements of the German mystical tradition and of late medieval apocalypticism. He sees in the movement that this instituted a metamorphosis of the revolutionary forces that had erupted in the Peasants' War. Seebass refutes the argument that Hut had at one point been a pacifist Anabaptist; he shows that he hung on to Müntzer's revolutionary aims even if he was prepared to leave his sword sheathed for a while, waiting for God's specific command until he drew it out. This type of Anabaptism had little in common with Grebel's "Swiss Brethren". Seebass thus concludes that it is justified to speak of a double origin for Anabaptism. Although he regards the Anabaptists of Zürich as a "genuine outgrowth" of the Reformation he sees Hut's type of Anabaptism as a fruit of the Middle Ages, mediated by the Zwickau Prophets, Müntzer and Karlstadt. Its roots are in Thuringia and Saxony.

James M. Stayer's analysis of all the Anabaptist groups contradicts the pious legend that before 1560 there had been a

---

[27] G. Seebass, *Müntzers Erbe. Werk, Leben und Theologie des Hans Hut* MS Thesis. (Erlangen, 1972); J.M. Stayer, *Anabaptists and the Sword*, (Lawrence, Kansas, 1972); C.P. Clasen, *Anabaptism. A Social History, 1525-1618* (Ithaca and London, 1972).

consensus amongst the Anabaptists on the question of the acceptance of official positions and of the use of force. Pilgram Marbeck, Melchior Hoffman and Menno Simons used Luther's doctrine of the two kingdoms and permitted Christians to accept offical positions in order to maintain general order. But they rejected the use of force in matters of faith. Hans Hut and the Anabaptists of Münster on the other hand followed the example of Thomas Müntzer; they wanted to establish the Kingdom of God on earth by force. Stayer finds only one example (Hubmaier) of Zwingli's pragmatic concept, which did not rule out the use of force in the course of a restoration of the Church though admitting that any enforcement of divine justice on earth can only be partial in this life. Over against this Konrad Grebel and Michael Sattler demanded that the Christian should renounce any use of force and forbad their followers to take up any official posts, although they recognized the necessity of secular authorities within the world. Since Stayer measures the Anabaptists by the yardstick of Zwingli's *Realpolitik*, he feels that neither the crusading spirit of the Anabaptists of Münster nor the pacifism of the later 'Swiss Brethren' offered practical solutions to the social conflicts of the age.

Claus-Peter Clasen uses extensive archive material to answer, with the help of statistics, questions concerning the social structure, the geographical expansion and the absolute strength of the Anabaptist movement in Central and Southern Germany. He analyses the Anabaptists' doctrines, organizational structures and practical procedures to see whether this movement of social protest offered a sensible and viable alternative to the existing social structure of the 16th century. His conclusion is that it did not.

According to Clasen the most significant factor in the rise of Anabaptism was the extensive period of religious uncertainty in those regions where Protestantism had made inroads but had not been adopted as the official state religion. The resulting atmosphere in which many were unsure about their salvation meant that even members of the upper social groups became susceptible to radical ideas.[28] With the development of the

---

[28] C.P. Clasen, *Anabaptism*, pp. 300-301.

Reformation came a closer correlation of economic interests and religious convictions. Although he repudiates the thesis that Anabaptism was simply the ideology of the poor, Clasen makes it clear that the majority of Anabaptists did come from the lower classes, on the one hand because the poor made up the majority of the population and on the other because Anabaptist doctrines had a much more direct appeal to the needs of the destitutes than to those of the nobility or the higher *bourgeoisie*. Clasen rejects the Marxist view of the Anabaptists as the victims of the emergence of capitalism. Those who joined the Anabaptists were on the whole employed in established and less skilled jobs and not artisans working in new and highly specialized fields (although these were subject to booms and slumps).[29] The proportion of peasants during the first five years of the movement, according to Clasen, was between 33% and 53%, but it rose after 1550 (when Anabaptism had spread to the villages) to between 77% and 84%.

Clasen's conclusion on the basis of his figures (there were on the average 3,000 converts in ten years, which means their proportion of the population was only 0.1%) is that the Anabaptist movement consisted of little more than an insignificant group of naïve sectarians. It hardly deserves the name of a reform-movement.[30]

Clasen's feeling is that the ineffectiveness of the Anabaptists was fortunate; if more people had joined them German society would have fallen into chaos. This negative view also applies to the pacifist and separatist Anabaptists. By denouncing secular authorities as 'unchristian', by their refusal to take up arms, by their contempt for higher culture and by their primitive economic ethics "they threatened to destroy sixteenth century society altogether."[31]

Clasen's statistical conclusions, based on the figures in the judicial records, are less convincing. A high proportion of the records has been lost and, in any case, only a fraction of the Anabaptists was known to the authorities. The Anabaptists in

[29] *Ibid.* p.319.
[30] *Ibid.* p.427.
[31] *Ibid.* p.208.

eastern Switzerland, Augsburg and Strasbourg were a disruptive minority throughout the whole of the population, while in Holland they caused such a mass movement that they substantially contributed to the establishment of the Reformation. Anabaptism developed an amazing impetus within its first ten years which was not halted until the harsh persecutions of 1528 to 1536.

Even if we share Clasen's conviction that Anabaptists offered no viable basis for social reform in the 16th century, we should recognise their role as a protest movement. They were justified in their protest against an inefficient "reform of living conditions", in their objections to ceaseless warfare and brutal punishments, in their condemnation of usury, pre-emption, sinecures and the tithe system, and in their opposition to the suppression of the autonomy of congregations and to the rising sacramentalism of Lutheran orthodoxy. Nor did the ideas which spread from a few Anabaptist groups concerning pacifism, morality as the hallmark of a Christian church and congregational democracy, disappear from European history without trace; we need only think of Calvin's concept of the holy community, which he developed out of his dealings with Anabaptism in Strasbourg, or of the radical wing of English Puritanism, which would have been unthinkable without continental Anabaptism.[32]

d) *The Marxist view of Anabaptism*

Marxist writers universally portray the Anabaptist movement as the final sectarian phase of the "early bourgeois revolution", which had already been paralysed by the opiate of religious mysticism.[33] They see it as the rallying-point of the disappointed

---

[32] Cf. I.B. Horst, *The Radical Brethren. Anabaptism and the English Reformation to 1558* (Nieuwkoop, 1972) and also W. Balke, *Calvijn en de Doperse Radikalen* Amsterdam, 1973 (with a summary in English).

[33] G. Zschäbitz, "Die Stellung der Täuferbewegung im Spannungsbogen der deutschen frühbürgerlichen Revolution", in G. Brendler (ed.), *Die Frühbürgerliche Revolution in Deutschland* (Berlin, 1961, pp. 152-162); A. Friesen, "The Marxist Interpretation of Anabaptism", in C.S. Meyer (ed.) *Sixteenth Century Essays and Studies.* Vol. I. (St. Louis, Missouri, 1970), pp. 17-34.

masses who were satisfied neither with the semi-success of a moderate or radical bourgeois Reformation (i.e. the Wittenberg and Zürich wings of the Reformation) nor with their defeat in the Peasants' War. The latent potential of the masses to rise in rebellion was mobilized by an appropriation of older heretical traditions (of the Waldensians and the Taborites) and an acceptance of chiliastic ideas. Their main interest thus centres on the revolutionary Anabaptists: Hans Hut, the Dutch Melchiorites and the Anabaptists of Münster.[34] They specify the economic cause of the Anabaptist movement as the increase of the original accumulation of capital at the beginning of the sixteenth century. The poorer craftsmen who had lost their economic independence were subjected to extensive expropriation by the wholesale dealers who provided them with raw material and sold their products ("Verlagssystem") as production developed for a supra-regional market with an expanding monetary economy.[35] Thus the Anabaptist movement, particularly in its first generation, appears to have been a movement of social protest by the impoverished artisans who had been caught in the wheels of early capitalism.

Brendler and Steinmetz[36] see an additional factor in the development of Anabaptism in north-western Germany and Holland: the delay in the implementing of Reformation caused by the policies of the bishops, the Emperor and the established council-oligarchies. The Reformation was forced to develop in this area as a popular movement independent of the authorities: this encouraged the rise of more radical forces. Against the background of their political aims (i.e. to destroy the episcopal government) Brendler explains why the Anabaptists of Münster succeeded in overcoming class barriers originally inherent in this movement and in winning over some of the merchants and members of the ruling class.

[34] Cf. n.14 above.

[35] A.N. Tschistoswonow has dealt with this aspect particularly. Cf. his article, "Die soziale Basis und der historische Ort des revolutionären Täufertums" in *Wiss. Zeitschr. d. Karl-Marx-Uni.*, Leipzig, Gesellschaftswiss. u. sprachwiss. Reihe 14 (1965), pp.407-418.

[36] G. Brendler, *Das Täuferreich zu Münster*, p. 73, pp.113-115; M. Steinmetz, *Deutschland von 1476 bis 1648*, (Berlin, 1967), pp. 168-169 (Lehrbuch der deutschen Geschichte (Beiträge) 3).

The 'early capitalism' thesis has been applied to the textile workers of Augsburg and Holland who inclined towards Anabaptism. The frequent objections of the Anabaptists to usury and their demand for property sharing (or at least for a Christian attitude towards private property) can certainly be understood as a protest against the dark side of the growth of early capitalism. Yet the same thesis cannot explain how the peasants or those artisans who had not been affected by the dynamism of the growth of capitalism (such as tailors, smiths, bakers and millers) seem to form such a high proportion of the Anabaptist population.

Added to this are the arguments of Plümper who explains the origins of the Hutterite community in terms of the reactionary cliquishness and anticapitalist economics of the guilds; their retention of outdated methods of production, the denial of rights to apprentices and journeymen and the rigorous limitation of the positions of masters encouraged the spread of Anabaptism amongst their ranks.[37]

But the Marxist view of the Anabaptists as pace-setters as well as victims of the growth of bourgeois capitalism is unconvincing. Rather the demands of the radical Anabaptists (the Hutterites and the Anabaptists of Münster) for the abolition of interest payment, private property and the family unit, and their contempt for scholarship and universities indicate much more a yearning for a lost paradise of simple social structures than a desire to bring about a modern bourgeois society.

3. The Problem of "Chiliasm" in the Sixteenth Century.

a) *The interpretations of messianic movements in non-Marxist research*

Since Hoffman appeared first of all as an apocalyptic prophet, and even after he had joined the Anabaptists, the message of the

---

[37] H.D. Plümper, *Die Gütergemeinschaft bei den Täufern des 16. Jahrhunderts* Göppingen, 1972. On this cf. also W. Treue, "Wirtschafts-und Sozialgeschichte vom 16. bis zum 18. Jahrhundert" in B. Gebhardt, *Handbuch der deutschen Geschichte* Edited by H. Grundmann, 8th ed. Vol. 2. 1955, pp. 380-383.

imminent establishment of the kingdom of God on earth stood at the heart of his preaching, we shall give here a brief account of the state of research into the messianic movements of the sixteenth century.

The most important recent studies of sixteenth century "chiliasm", whether written by "bourgeois" or Marxist authors, share the same approach; they are concerned more with evaluating the phenomenon than with analysing the circumstances in which it originated and developed. This "involved" approach is probably due to the alleged or real relationship between the apocalyptic "enthusiasts" and 20th-century political theologies.

Norman Cohn connects apocalyptic Anabaptism with the heretical movements of the Middle Ages.[38] His sole concern is thus to trace the universal constants which cause a millenarian movement to rise and fall. Such constants which recur amongst the chiliastic Anabaptists are:

1. The decline in the power and authority of the leading religious institution which had hitherto regulated the relationship between the human and the divine (in this case, the papacy). This was brought about by the failure of the clergy themselves who fell into *luxuria* and *avaritia* rather than keeping to the principles they preached.

2. The rise of stronger movements of social protest with limited aims from whom the radical apocalypticists with their utopian programmes could profit parasitically (in this case, the Peasants' War and the revolts aimed at deposing the prelates in the episcopal principalities).

3. The presence of an unstable mass of unemployed or economically insecure groups who had no organization that could legally protect their interests (in this case, the proletariat of artisans who had suffered social disintegration with the rise of early capitalism and who had lost the protection of a functioning guild system).

4. The appearance of a charismatic "prophet" (usually a semi-educated cleric or artisan) who claims absolute sanctity or

---

[38] N. Cohn, *The Pursuit of the Millenium*, Revised edition. (London, 1970).

infallibility and who appeals to the uprooted masses by claiming that they are the "chosen people" who will fulfil the purposes of history (in this case, the Zwickau Prophets, Müntzer, Hut and Hoffman).

The standard course of a millenarian movement, according to Cohn, runs as follows: First of all it posits "redemption" which is communal and will be practicable in this world. This "redemption" is seen to be directly at hand; the quality of life will be suddenly perfected by the intervention of heavenly powers (the descent of the Holy Spirit or the return of Christ). The group that has collected around the charismatic leader separates itself from its "evil" environment; opponents are branded as the "godless" who are to be annihilated. The apocalyptic excitement intensifies when the authorities begin to persecute; their action increases the danger of the outbreak of the revolt which it intended to suppress. Since the ridiculously inflated aims of the charismatic prophets can never be achieved on earth the millenarian movement will inevitably fail, resulting in the worst cases (such as Münster) in a bloody catastrophe.

Wilhelm E. Mühlmann is even more damning than Cohn in his assessment of millenarian movements.[39] For him the chiliastic Anabaptist movement forms a link in the chain of revolutions which runs throughout world history connecting the apocalyptic of late Judaism to the Russian October Revolution. The concept of "permanent revolution" adopted by Christian chiliasm produced in every case (even in its secularized form) a domination by a terrorist minority which regarded itself as the sole guardian of truth. Whilst their self-styled élite judged its followers according to the strictest moral standards, its members justified each of their own criminal activities as means towards their holy ends. Thus in place of the promised "eternal kingdom of peace" there inevitably arose a state of slavery and despotism. Periodically scapegoats had to be found to blame for the ensuing misery; they would then be removed in a process of "purification". The chiliasts' ideas about the future, as Mühl-

---

[39] W.E. Mühlmann, *Chiliasmus und Nativismus*, 2nd ed. (Berlin, 1964).

mann sees them, are a product of the "fantastic cravings" of the poor.[40]

In his phenomenological description of chiliasm Mühlmann lists the following structural components which also came into play during the millenarian movements of the 16th century: the claim to universality made by the various groups, which produced the need for a world mission; the promise of a future society free of conflict run on an anarchic-egalitarian system by the authoritarian leaders of the rising itself; the mythology of "the world turned upside down" ("The first will be last"); blind faith in a Redeemer-King or prophet and the mindless acceptance of the "messianic débâcle" as a necessary prelude to eternal peace ("from darkness to light"). A recurrent feature in the development of millenarian groups according to Mühlmann is the move from passive expectation to revolutionary activity, from pacifism to violence and from asceticism to libertinism.

Mühlmann explains the rise of chiliastic movements as a reaction on the part of the lower classes to a sudden change in the general social situation, which produced amongst some groups a relative economic deterioration, social disintegration and the loss of their spiritual orientation. Viewed in this light, chiliasm appears to be an act of protest by groups of socially disorientated people against a threatened loss of their individuality. He sees an analogy between these old European sectarian movements, the 'spirit-dance' movement of the North American Indians in the 19th century and the cargo-cults in present day New Guinea. This means that the yardstick Mühlmann uses to assess every appearance of 'chiliasm and nativism' is the concept of normality of the European *haute bourgeoisie*. As a result he generally sees chiliastic movements as irrational attempts made by semi-literate psychopathic demagogues to provide a 'total solution'; their fantastic promises therefore led the masses into misery. Mühlmann accounts for the susceptibility of the simple folk to chiliasm on the basis of the questionable premise of the congruence of psychical and social states. According to him the head and reason are predominant in the upper classes, whereas

[40] *Ibid.* p. 302.

the lower classes are ruled by the "subcortical urges".[41] This makes them more capable of being carried off to ecstasy or destruction.

Rüdiger Landfester[42] has taken up Mühlmann's comparative approach but has distanced himself from the negative judgments, the anthropological generalizations and the exaggerated importance his predecessor had granted to individual prophets. Landfester sees both colonial protest-cults and the millenarian sectarian movements of early modern Europe as "fitting and justifiable reactions" to the destruction of their environments by external forces and as "interesting experiments in finding alternative solutions." Their defeat is brought about not by moral superiority but by military strength. Their victorious opponents are always the same: modernising strategies motivated by profit maximization.

Undoubtedly there are many typological parallels between colonial protest-cults and the millenarian movements of early modern Europe. But it is questionable whether the impact of colonization by modern Europe on the primitive cultures of Africa, America and Asia is comparable with the economic and social changes which took place within European society between the 15th and the 17th centuries. There is a qualitative distinction between changes emerging out of a disintegrating society on the one hand and, on the other, an externally imposed acculturation accompanied by military occupation, the establishment of a foreign domination, economic plunder and the imposition of a new religion by forced conversion. Landfester questions his own research method when he makes the pertinent point that there is, as yet, no assured consensus concerning the social consequences of so-called "early capitalism" or the results of the price revolution in the 16th century (p. 125), whereas the devastating effects of colonialism are obvious in the third world. Comparing similar results involves the danger of overlooking divergent causes. Furthermore Landfester overlooks the fact that the Anabaptists were protesting first and foremost against the

---

[41] *Ibid.* p. 369-371.
[42] *Frühneuzeitliche Häresien und koloniale Protestkulte: Möglichkeiten eines historisch-komparativen Zugangs* in *ARG* 67 (1976), pp. 117-153.

Zwinglian and Lutheran Reformations, which already represented a divergence from traditional conformity, though they were not radical enough for them. Thus the Anabaptists used ideas and concepts which the "nonconformist" Reformers had used in their battle against the Catholic Church.

Nevertheless Mühlmann's suggestion that there is a connection between popular chiliastic movements and economic crises or cultural disintegration remains a fruitful hypothesis to which we shall return when we consider the Reformation as a fundamental break-down of established structures.

Günther List has investigated the significance of chiliasm within the history of utopian thought.[43] He defines "chiliasm" in its narrowest sense (following Revelation 20 it is the belief in an earthly reign of Christ and his saints for 1000 years before the Last Judgment) as an extreme case of utopianism in which the *passive* expectations of a social revolutionary movement find fulfilment.[44] It arises either before the stage of utopian revolutionary conflict has been reached, or after it has failed. Chiliastic fantasies also point to the impossibility of achieving 'utopian' aims by direct political action. According to List, chiliasm is a means of escape and of diverting people's attention from the problems of a hopeless situation.

However, this concept of chiliasm developed by List in the systematic section of his book plays little part in the main historical section where he investigates the 'utopian' movements of the 16th century. After analysing the leading representatives of apocalyptic thought, List comes to the conclusion that the idea of a millenial kingdom featured only in Augustin Bader, a few followers of Hans Hut and the final stages of the Anabaptist kingdom in Münster. List thus fails to provide any impressive historical evidence of his concept of 'chiliastic utopia', and in particular his categorization of the spiritual development of the Münsterite Anabaptists, who allegedly had no concept of utopian chiliasm during their successful revolutionary phase, lacks conviction.[45]

---

[43] G. List, *Chiliastische Utopie*, (Munich, 1973).
[44] *Ibid.* p. 115, also pp. 112, 117.
[45] *Ibid.* p. 201.

Readiness to indulge in revolutionary activity could on.ly have come about in the late Middle Ages or early modern periods if the spiritualization of the Millenial Reign (enforced by the official church) had been dispensed with and been replaced by a concept of an "earthly reign of Christ" either to be established directly by Christ himself or to be ushered in by a preliminary punishment of the sinful world. On these terms Hut, Hoffman in later life, Rothmann and Jan Matthijs were all indubitably "chiliasts", even if they did not keep to the fine details of Revelation 20 and even if, like Hoffman, they believed that the Millenium described there had already happened. List's conceptual system bears no relation to the varied forms which make up the historical reality. In most of the 'utopian' movements of the 16th century there is a disparate mixture of visions from the Book of Revelation, apocalyptic images from the Synoptic Gospels, predictions of Old Testament prophets as well as personal hopes and desires. There was rarely a precise correlation between the objective situation, subjective willingness to take action and pertinent apocalyptic concepts.

b) *Marxist interpretation of Chiliasm*

In his book on Thomas Müntzer Ernst Bloch celebrates the Anabaptists' chiliasm as a "column of fire" which symbolizes the "beginning of freedom for the Children of God" and the "breakthrough of the kingdom." "Man has never desired or experienced anything more profound than the aims of such a form of Anabaptism – yearning for a mystical democracy."[46] To Bloch's mind economic factors played only a secondary role in bringing about the chiliastic visions of the Anabaptists, "because the economic element, although certainly the most necessary and most constant, is neither the only, nor the longest lasting, nor the strongest, nor the most intrinsic motivation of the human soul."[47] To Bloch the "day dream image of an Anti-wolf", the "brotherly Kingdom of the last days", the

[46] E. Bloch, *Thomas Münzer als Theologe der Revolution* 2nd ed. (Frankfurt, 1963), p. 72 (Bibliothek Suhrkamp 77).
[47] *Ibid.* p. 61.

"ecstasy of man's upright posture" or the "impatient rebellious, resolute yearning for paradise" are not the superstructure of material despair; they embody the power of a primary longing which "derives from an original point of the soul where values are received and given out."[48] This apotheosis of Müntzer and the Anabaptists was decisively rejected by Georg Lukácz. For him there is a "dark and empty abyss", a *hiatus irrationalis*, between the actions and the utopian religious doctrine of the social revolutionary apocalypticists.[49] The exclusively subjective and undialectical utopia envisaged by the sectarians could provide the exploited masses with neither concrete aims nor practical means of achieving them. According to Lukácz any revolution that is taken seriously can only be directed towards a sensible transformation of real life. The radical sects with all their apocalypticism made no contribution to this task; they neither were in any position properly to appreciate their own historical situation nor did they have the will to inculcate class-consciousness amongst the peasants and urban proletariat, which is decisive in any potentially revolutionary movement. The utopian ideal of the true man as a saintly ascetic, which thereby denies true humanity to the majority of men, who cannot attain this goal, is simply a reproduction of the inhumanity of class structure on a religious level; it results in social stratification even if the classes often seem to have been reversed.[50]

The Marxist Leo Kofler has raised similar objections to Chiliasm in his history of bourgeois society.[51] But in contrast to Lukácz, Kofler acknowledges a rational core in the radical sects' criticisms of church and society, although apocalyptic expectations always ensured that it was smothered by "a dreamy

---

[48] *Ibid.* p.63.
[49] G. Lukácz, *Geschichte und Klassenbewusstsein* 2nd ed. (Neuwied and Berlin, 1970), p. 331 (Sammlung Luchterhand 11).
[50] *Ibid.* p. 329.
[51] L. Kofler, *Zur Geschichte der bürgerlichen Gesellschaft* 4th ed. (Neuwied and Berlin, 1971), pp. 203–215 (particularly p. 208), pp. 240–248; pp. 276–279 (Soziologische Texte, 28). Cf. also K. Ebert, *Theologie und politisches Handeln. Thomas Müntzer als Modell*, (Stuttgart, 1973), pp. 34–48 (Urban-Taschenbücher 602).

transcendence" of reality. Kofler feels that it was in principle impossible to develop a practical revolutionary programme which would lead to a classless society because of the limited productivity at that time. With the exception of Bloch's appraisal the general attitude to chiliasm resulting from historiography and cultural anthropology is thoroughly negative. Whether sympathy or antipathy is shown to the followers of the millenarian movement, who are doomed to failure in any case, depends on the author's political standpoint.

4. The State of Research on Melchior Hoffman.

Previous research has paid scant attention to Melchior Hoffman despite his importance as the founder of Anabaptism in north west Germany and Holland. Superficially this is due to the scattered and almost inaccessible nature of the sources, which are partly written in Low German or Middle Netherlandish. But Hoffman's omission from the historical recollections of the Mennonites is due mainly to his ambivalent position in respect to the events at Münster. He has been regarded on the one hand as responsible for the most serious crisis in the history of Anabaptism, since his apocalyptic prophecies produced a rebellious atmosphere which Jan Matthijs was able to harness as revolutionary activity. But on the other hand it was known that Hoffman himself had warned his followers against taking up the sword.[52] The Mennonites were thus faced with a dilemma: they could neither fully identify with Hoffman nor could they clearly distance themselves from him. The result was that they forgot him. In his place Menno Simons came to be regarded as the sole founder of Anabaptism in north-western Europe.

The work of Barthold Nikolaus Krohn was the beginning of

---

[52] For these two aspects of Hoffman's reputation in the 16th century: Obbe Philips, *Bekenntnisse* (written before 1565) in *BRN* 7 (1910), pp. 121-138 and Nikolaus Blesdijk (Blesdikius), *Historia Vitae, doctrinae ac rerum gestarum Davidis Georgii Haeresiarchae* (Deventer, 1642), pp. 4-7 (Blesdijk's biography of Joris was written in 1559-1560).

research into Hoffman.[53] At the time when he wrote his biography Krohn was still a trainee preacher at Hamburg under the supervision of Melchior Götze (notorious for his literary feud with Lessing). The book was aimed at winning back to Lutheranism the group of Mennonites established in the tolerant enclave of Altona by laying before them their miserable historical origins. Krohn's missionary zeal thus led him to make the false claims that Hoffman had recanted all his errors in 1539 and had died fully reconciled with the evangelical church of Strasbourg.[54] Although he made some faults in tracing Hoffman's movements and confused a number of characters, Krohn is still used up to the present day because of his extensive knowledge of the primary material, much of which he quoted at length or paraphrased. Krohn had more than a little sympathy for Hoffman's theologically uneducated naivety. He praised his genuine (even if unenlightened) desire to be a "Zwinglian lay missionary"(!) and explicitly dissociated him from Jan Matthijs.[55] Krohn stressed the fact that Hoffman had a Lutheran attitude to the use of force and that he did not share the attitudes of the 'Swiss Brethren' or of the revolutionary Melchiorites in respect to secular authorities. Yet Krohn had no understanding of the specific causes of the conflict between Hoffman and the reformers. He felt that his break from Lutheranism could have been avoided if Hoffman (an opinionated furrier) had not been so wrapped up in his apocalyptic fantasies and if his opponents Amsdorf and Bugenhagen had not treated him like a stupid ass.[56]

Although Carl Adolf Cornelius portrayed Hoffman as a precursor of the Anabaptist kingdom of Münster (1534–35) in 1860[57], it was not until 1881 that scholars were encouraged to turn their attention to the most influential lay preacher of the

---

[53] B.N. Krohn, *Geschichte der fanatischen und enthusiastischen Wiedertäufer, vornehmlich in Niederdeutschland. Melchior Hofmann und die Sekte der Hofmannianer* (Leipzig, 1758).

[54] *Ibid.* p. 381.

[55] *Ibid.* p. 301.

[56] *Ibid.* pp. 10-14.

[57] C.A. Cornelius, *Geschichte des Münsterschen Aufruhrs*, Vol. 2, 1860.

Reformation because of a competition organized by "Teylers Godgeleerd Genootschap." Of the two prize-winning works ᵗhe first to be published was a study of Hoffman by W. J. Leendertz, written in Dutch.[58] This was followed in 1885 by Friedrich Otto zur Linden's biography.[59] Both authors were involved in the Revival movement and were thus prepared to defend Hoffman in spite of some criticisms of details. Leendertz was particularly interested in the religious sources Hoffman had drawn upon. He laid great stress on the influence of Hus, Karlstadt and Clemens Ziegler. By placing Hoffman's apocalyptic prophecies in the context of the eschatological expectations of the 16th century he relieved him of the reputation of being singularly eccentric. Leendertz attributed both Hoffman's success and his failure to the fact that he filled in a general apocalyptic framework with explicit references to particular times, places and people. Leendertz could trace no original ideas in Hoffman's thought. It was not he but Jan Matthijs who was responsible for the tragedy at Münster. Leendertz thus presented Hoffman as an innocent though rather fantastic lay missionary who despite his erroneous teachings had "led many men to God by his call to repentance."[60]

In comparison with Leendertz, Friedrich Otto zur Linden was prepared to look critically at his hero. Unlike him he admitted Hoffman's responsibility for the rise of the militant Anabaptist kingdom of Münster.[61] Zur Linden presented Hoffman as part of the "great spiritualist opposition party" directed against the Reformation, which replaced Luther's doctrine of justification with the gospel of the imitation of Christ. This party wanted a democratically-controlled church of the people rather than a politically-based ecclesiastical institution, and rejected the Reformation for having failed to bring about a renewal of society. Zur Linden looked to medieval Mysticism for the origins of this opposition. He thus stressed the changes in Hoffman's thinking,

---

[58] W.J. Leendertz, *Melchior Hofmann* (Haarlem, 1883).

[59] F.O. zur Linden, *Melchior Hofmann, ein Prophet der Wiedertäufer*, (Haarlem, 1885).

[60] W.J. Leendertz, *Hofmann*, p. 337.

[61] F.O. zur Linden, *Hofmann*, pp. 349-366.

i.e. his development from Lutheranism via "Sacramentarianism" to Anabaptism. It was in Strasbourg under the influence of Hans Denck that Hoffman rejected the most important elements of his Lutheran heritage – the Wittenberg doctrines of predestination and justification. Zur Linden had a high regard for these doctrines, whereas he regarded Hoffman's apocalyptic dreams as deplorable errors. In the field of dogma Hoffman's ideas insofar as they were acceptable were unoriginal.[62] Nevertheless zur Linden's general assessment of Hoffman was favourable. His significance lay in the foundations he established for the later remarkable development in Germany, Holland, England and America of an ascetic view of life which was characterised by a stress on the inner experience of faith, practical Christianity and the holiness of the church. It was as a founding father of Puritanism and Pietism that zur Linden granted Hoffman an honourable place in the history of the church.

Both Leendertz's and zur Linden's biographies shared one fault: they presented Hoffman's life in isolation from his ideas and made no attempt to understand the connection between them. Thus in 1952 "Teylers Godgeleerd Genootschap" again explicitly commissioned a study of Hoffman's theology. The winner was Peter Kawerau, whose dissertation was published in 1954.[63]

Kawerau saw the sole key to Hoffman's thought not in his apocalypticism but in his spiritualism. He thus investigated the relationships between 'the letter and the spirit', 'man and the spirit', 'history and the spirit' in Hoffman's thinking. He also established the ruling principles of Hoffman's hermeneutics by a close study of the source material. Despite sparse criticism he made it clear that he regarded Hoffman's system to have been an expression of subjective arbitrary choice which inevitably aroused the enmity of the Lutheran theologians.

However useful Kawerau's work remains, through its bibliographical research and its presentation of unknown primary

---

[62] *Ibid.* p. 421.
[63] P. Kawerau, *Melchior Hoffman als religiöser Denker*, (Haarlem, 1954).

sources, it cannot satisfy a specifically historical interest in Hoffman for the following reasons:

1. Kawerau presents Hoffman's theology as an unchanging and unified system; he alleges that one cannot draw a distinction between the Lutheran and the Anabaptist stages of his thought.[64] Since Kawerau brings together in a single thought-structure different ideas from two stages of Hoffman's development, his ideas appear even more confused than they otherwise would. Kawerau paid as little attention to the profound change that came over Hoffman's apocalyptic ideas because of the influence of the Strasbourg prophets as he did to the changes in his doctrine produced by his encounter with Denck's theology.

2. Negative as well as positive attitudes can play a decisive role in life and thought. Yet Kawerau regards Hoffman's most important negative stance – his battle against sacramentalism – as thoroughly secondary. Since Hoffman rejected the idea of God's real presence in earthly elements because of his spiritualism, Kawerau dismissed all his quotations relating to Baptism and the Eucharist to an appendix at the end of his study, commenting that "the Eucharist is in a special way *secondary to* Hoffman's basic ideas."[65] Rather than standing outside of his basic spiritualist approach, Hoffman's doctrine of the Eucharist, which only acknowledged a real presence of Christ in the words of forgiveness, was a necessary consequence of it. What is more, it was the Eucharistic controversy which brought about one of the most significant incidents in Hoffman's career – his irreparable break with Lutheranism.

3. Kawerau pays no attention to the inner connections between Hoffman's spiritualist Eucharistic doctrine and his monophysite Christology, between his rejection of sacramentalism and his doctrine of the impossibility of forgiveness for sins committed after conversion, and between his pelagian perfectionist doctrine of justification and his revolutionary apocalypticism.

---

[64] *Ibid.* pp. 18-19 and p. 12 n.10.
[65] *Ibid.* p. 115.

4. Kawerau does not deal with Hoffman's thought in context. We are not told who Hoffman's followers were or under what social and political conditions he was able to achieve his short-lived success. He at no point indicates the historical effects of Hoffman's work; he rather presents us with an abstract system, which bears no relationship to the actual reality.

Until now the relationship between the religious movements instigated by Hoffman and their corresponding social environment has been studied only in the context of a limited period of his career. Joachim Kuhles has attempted to apply a Marxist interpretation to the situation in the Baltic countries.[66] He sees a division of society into well-to-do bourgeois, radical bourgeois and revolutionary plebeians; Hoffman acted as spokesman for the urban proletariat and the serfs.

Like Smirin in his portrait of Müntzer, Kuhles presents Hoffman as a class-conscious opponent of every form of oppression, old or new. He battled against Catholic bishops and evangelical clergy, against the established Catholic structure of Germany and against the new protestant city-magistrates. Kuhles praises him for his proclamation of a communistic concept of equality and for his early stance in favour of the abolition of private property. He had also been aware, according to Kuhles, that it was only the poor who could embody the "socialist ideal" or make any form of progress.[67]

Such an approach meant that Kuhles would be blind to Hoffman's true significance. Characteristic of Hoffman's whole career, up until the end of his life, was his attempt to implement his ideas about society and the true church with the help of the established authorities (for example in Livonia he appealed to the Wittenberg Reformers and to the city magistrates). Thus in his letter to the Livonian congregations of 1525 he categorically ruled out any attempted rebellion. Hoffman never proposed the

---

[66] J. Kuhles, *Studien zur sozialen Lage der Volksmassen und zu den Volksbewegungen zur Zeit der Reformation in Livland*, MS Thesis, (Leipzig, 1966).
[67] *Ibid.* pp. 109, 120.

abolition of private property,[68] and the 'poor' were only blessed, according to him, if they were the 'poor in spirit'. Like Kawerau Kuhles gives the impression that Hoffman's views never changed; in order to illustrate his attitude whilst in Livonia Kuhles thinks nothing of quoting from writings Hoffman produced some four to seven years after his time there.

In contrast to this there is M. Schwarz-Lausten's excellent study of Hoffman in Schleswig-Holstein.[69] This presents Hoffman's religious struggle in Schleswig-Holstein within the context of the conservative social and religious policies of the Crown Prince (who later became King Christian III).

A. F. Mellink has argued that the growth of the Melchiorite movement in the Netherlands is largely attributable to the region's economic crisis of 1529-1536. He brings convincing evidence to show that up until late in 1534 most of the Melchiorites were prepared to indulge in a revolutionary uprising.[70]

One of the most controversial issues in research about Hoffman is his spiritual responsibility for the Anabaptist Kingdom of Münster. W. J. Kühler argued that because Hoffman's eschatological visions show no trace of vindictiveness (!) he could have

---

[68] Cf. Kuhles ch. VI n.17. The decisive passage for Hoffman's alleged communism is the following from his commentary on Romans, "O eternal God, how blessed I would be if I could receive such grace that I could give up my freedom to enter the realm of your spirit and then I could give up all that is mine" (*Römerbrief* Q 8a/b). Kuhles relied on a mistranslation by Kawerau (. . . that I could give up all my *property*" p. 63) This passage is not concerned with the abolition of material *property* but with the renunciation of individual *particularity*; the suppression of individual freedom in order to share the universality of the Spirit of God. Kuhles has published the gist of his argument in "Zur ideologischen Differenzierung der reformatorischen Bewegung im Ostbaltikum" in *Weltwirkung der Reformation* (Berlin, 1969), Vol. 2. pp. 377-390.

[69] M. Schwarz-Lausten, *Melchior Hoffman og de lutherske praedikanten i Sleswig-Holstein 1527-1529* (Kirkehistoriske Samlinger. 7:5) 1963-1964.

[70] A.F. Mellink, *De Wederdopers in de Noordelijke Nederlande* (Groningen, 1953), and "Das niederländisch-westfälische Täufertum im 16. Jahrhundert" in H.J. Goertz, *Umstrittenes Täufertum*, pp. 206-222.

had absolutely nothing to do with Münster. He had expected a "reign of love and justice" which would be established by a supernatural intervention by God.[71] Cornelius Krahn shares Kühler's view of the difference between Hoffman and the Münsterites. In Hoffman's theology it was the Sermon on the Mount which was always normative, whereas for the Anabaptists of Münster it was the Old Testament; their aim was to establish a purely judaic theocracy rather than to restore the primitive church.[72] James M. Stayer has dealt with this problem in more depth. He sees the divergent wings of the Dutch Melchiorite movement (pacifist and militant) as a product of the ambiguity within Hoffman's apocalyptic preaching. He used a genuinely Lutheran understanding of secular authority to denounce all crusading ideas, and up until the last he always warned his followers against indulging in rebellion. Yet on the other hand he never stopped speaking of a day of vengeance when the 'priests' would be slaughtered. What is more he elevated perfected saints to a position above the law. Hoffman's true line of descent was in fact that of the pacifist Anabaptists, Obbe Philips and Menno Simons, but he also fathered another family (although a "bastard-line"), to which belong Jan Matthijs, Jan van Leiden and Jan van Batenburg.[73]

5. The Issues to be Tackled.

The present study takes up the unsolved problems of Hoffman research and attempts to deal with the following issues:

1. Hoffman's ideas must be presented within the context of

---

[71] W.J. Kühler, *Geschiedenis der Nederlandschen Doopsgezinden in de zestiende eeuw*, (Haarlem, 1932), pp. 62, 78.

[72] C. Krahn, *Dutch Anabaptism. Origin, Life and Thought. 1450-1600*. (The Hague, 1968).

[73] J.M. Stayer, *Anabaptists and the Sword*, pp. 211-226. In the introduction ("Reflections and Retractions") to the second revised edition of this book (Lawrence, Kansas, 1976), Stayer accepts my argument that Hoffman should be counted as a genuine ideological precursor of the militant Anabaptist kingdom.

the general religious, political and social environments of the regions in which he was active.

We do *not* start with the hypothesis that religious ideas derive exclusively from the social context in which they appear. Ideas and meanings may arise as responses to the social problems men face, and these responses may be passed on to the individual by society to a great extent, but very often they stem from spiritual traditions which originated in the social conditions of a long-past age as well as from individual experience and personal moral decisions. The ideas propagated by Hoffman will be considered as a source as well as a reflection of social processes: not just as conditioned, but also of conditioning factors.

But on the other hand the success or failure of religious ideas which are aimed at transforming the world, is dependent on the social context to which those ideas apply. We can only assess their historical significance if we understand their acceptance by society or the use to which they were put by social groups. Thus it comes about (and this can often be demonstrated in Hoffman's case) that the ideas and intentions of a particular prophet need not be the same as what his followers understand or expect. Since Hoffman's following was so heterogeneous it must be expected that his message was understood in many different ways.[74]

In particular the following questions arise:

a) From which social groups did the Melchiorites draw the most recruits? What was their social and economic situation? What were their hopes for the future? What did they make of Hoffman's message?

b) On what grounds did legally established political authorities (the Councils of the Livonian towns and of Stockholm, King Frederick I of Denmark, the East Frisian Chancellor Ulrich von Dornum, and the local magistrates in the Dutch towns) first tolerate, indeed actively encourage, Hoffman and then let him down? We can ask the same question of Luther and Bucer, the

---

[74] On this cf. the basic reflections by Quentin Skinner, "Meaning and Understanding in the History of Ideas" in *History and Theory* 7 (1969), pp. 3-53.

official Reformers, who for a period regarded Hoffman as a fellow-in-arms and later damned him as a false prophet.

c) What were the effects of the movements instigated by Hoffman on the further course of the Reformation in the regions in which he had been active?

2. In contrast to Kawerau's unified and ahistorical system, we shall present here the developments and changes in Hoffman's thought.

We do not consider it the role of a commentator to construct a single principle out of a man's thoughts, or to even out contradictions in them on some higher level. We are prepared to admit the possibility that a man's thought can contain irreconcilable contradictions. Melchior Hoffman was self-educated and had no religious training; he thus belonged to that group of semi-educated people who are overpowered by the abundance of ideas around them and who are in no position fully to understand the meaning or consequences of ideas which they themselves propound. But even taking this into account we are left with the following problems: to what extent were his views inherently consistent and how far did they remain coherent in the course of his development? What was static and what changed; which was the *cantus firmus* and which the variations? We must trace those ideas which Hoffman retained unchanged up to the end of his career, those which (although he at one time held them with vigour) he rejected, and those which he took up again in the course of time. Of particular significance in this respect are the ideas which brought about his breach with Lutheranism, the movement in which he had originally set out on his missionary work. We must also investigate the impact made on Hoffman's dogma and apocalypticism by his encounters with Denck's theology and the Strasbourg prophets as well as his conversion to Anabaptism. Finally we have to ask which of Hoffman's views formed the basis of the division of the Melchiorite movement into pacifist and militant wings, and how it was that Hoffman involuntarily became a spiritual precursor of the Anabaptist Kingdom of Münster.[75]

---

[75] Landfester (in *ARG* 67 (1976), p. 126 n. 32) is wrong in saying that I have attempted to produce an "unacceptable harmonization of the dis-

It is not our intention here to turn Melchior Hoffman into a "great man" of the Reformation period. He was a wandering preacher who can only be counted as a historically "great man" (in the sense of Jakob Burckhardt) insofar as he combined varying reforming and heretical streams of the late Middle Ages and Reformation, and in that his identification with the causes he espoused was such that he was prepared to die for them. In this he excelled the average man.

We shall limit our consideration of Hoffman's influence to those movements he directly instigated. We shall not deal with his wider influence on Menno Simons, Dirk Philips or the development of English separatism, particularly since there have been other recent studies in this field.[76]

Another justification for a complete new biography of Hoffman is the fact that no less than eight of his tracts, hitherto regarded as lost or totally unknown, have reappeared since the Second World War.[77] Because of these writings we can be much more precise in our presentation of Hoffman's ideas and the various stages in his development.

I am grateful to Dr. Heinold Fast of Emden who first encouraged me to undertake this study by making me aware of our widespread ignorance of Hoffman's thinking. Dr. Josef Benzing of Budenheim identified the printers of Hoffman's later

---

[76] C. Bornhäuser, *Leben und Lehre Menno Simons'* (Neukirchen-Vluyn, 1973) (Beiträge zur Geschichte und Lehre der Reformierten Kirche. 35); J. ten Doornkaat Koolman, *Dirk Philips, Vriend en Medewerker van Menno Simons* (Haarlem, 1964); I.B. Horst, *The Radical Brethren*, (cf. above n. 32).

[77] We are indebted to F. Husner for the discovery of the Commentaries on James and Jude. E.W. Kohls found the *Sendbrief an Wachter*

---

note 75 continued

parate elements within Hoffman" or to construct "a process of self-discovery or maturation." There is no question of this. Nor have I in any way exaggerated the originality of Hoffman's thought. I have been concerned much more to point out the divisions within his character and to trace which contradictions were ironed out in the course of his development and which remained. One is quite justified in investigating the consistency of someone's thought: only by assuming the possibility of consistency can any inconsistency become apparent.

works for me. Herr Helmuth Domizlaff of Munich very kindly made available to me two formerly unknown tracts by Hoffman. I am particularly grateful to Dr. Hans-Georg Rott of Strasbourg, the editor of the Anabaptist documents of Alsace, and to Dr. Hans-Jürgen Goertz of Hamburg, who have provided stimulating ideas and constructive criticism. I would also like to thank Professors Gottfried Seebass (Heidelberg), James M. Stayer (Queen's University, Kingston, Canada) and Gottfried Schramm (Freiburg). Last, but not least, I would like to express my gratitude to Mrs. Eileen Schwan (Denzlingen) and to Mrs. Sheila Scheer (Kirchzarten-Burg), who assisted us in the difficult problem of turning the German original into readable English.

A two-and-a-half year grant from the "Deutschen Forschungsgemeinschaft" made it possible for me to concentrate on the work necessary for this biography.

note 77 continued
and Calvin Pater brought to light the commentary on the Song of Songs. I discovered the Commentary on Daniel (undoubtedly the most important work) in the University Library at Hamburg. *Das ware trostliche . . Evangelion* was released by Trinity College, Dublin. I was informed of two further tracts by Herr Domizlaff of Munich, who has them in his private collection. (Van der waren hochprachtlichen cynigen *magestadt gottes* and *Een waraftyge tuchenisse*). Cf. F. Husner, "Zwei unbekannte Wiedertäuferdrucke" in *Stultifera Navis* 3 (1946), pp. 84–88; E.W. Kohls (ed), "Ein Sendbrieff Melchior Hofmanns aus dem Jahre 1534" in *Theologische Zeitschrift* 17 (1961), pp. 356–365; Calvin A. Pater, "Melchior Hoffman's Explication of the Songs (*sic*) of Songs" in *ARG* 68 (1977), pp. 173–191.

Chapter One

Hoffman and the Iconoclastic Movement in Livonia.

Melchior Hoffman the furrier and lay preacher, according to his own account, came originally from Schwäbisch-Hall. All that we know about his family is that in 1534 one of his sisters lived in Schwäbisch-Hall and another lived in Heilbronn.[1] The sources provide no clear evidence concerning where he was born, his education, his religious knowledge or the religious and spiritual influences to which he had been subjected before his arrival in Livonia.[2] In 1523 he turned up in Wolmar, one of the Teutonic Order's cities in Livonia, in order to work towards the victory of Luther's cause. As a lay preacher who kept up his activity as an artisan he saw himself as following in the footsteps of Paul the Apostle. This conformed with the advice of Karlstadt, who had been living a peasant life as "Brother Andrew" in Orlamünde since 1523 in an attempt to combine spiritual with physical labour. Livonia seemed to be an ideal place to undertake such a double task; there was a prosperous fur trade and the Reformation had only just begun in the region. A missionary in such an uncultivated field could thus expect a rich harvest. Hoffman's action was in no sense unique; one can think

---

[1] M. Krebs and H.G. Rott (ed.) *Quellen zur Geschichte der Täufer. VIII. Elsass, II* 1960, (hereinafter *TAE* II) No. 364, p. 14, also No. 610, p. 389, cf. also Hoffman's and Karlstadt's anonymously published *Dialogus* 1529, p. A2a.

[2] Gerd Wunder speculates about Hoffman's family in "Über die Verwandtschaft des Wiedertäufers Melchior Hofmann" in *Der Haalquell. Blätter für Heimatkunde des Haller Landes* 23, 6 (April 1971), pp. 21-23. Wunder is convinced that Hoffman was a cousin of Margarete Graeter who married Johannes Brenz, the reformer of Schwäbisch-Hall.

of Clemens Ziegler, Hans Hut, Hans Krüsi, Johannes Brötli or
Melchior Rinck, who all worked as popular missionaries whilst
retaining their secular jobs. In fact, there was usually an
opportunity for the lay preachers to work like this in these
regions only at the very beginning of the Reformation movement. By 1530, after the consolidation of the Reformation, the
phenomenon of the lay preacher involved in popular missionary
work had disappeared altogether. Such preachers were forced
'underground' into heretical movements.

Hoffman's message in Livonia was a confirmation of Luther's
proclamation of justification by faith with the threat of an
imminent divine judgment directed against those who still
trusted in justification by works. He preached against ecclesiastical princes, knights of the Order and monks, (whom he called
"crows of the night, owls and bats") and against the nuns and
beguines (who for him were "brides of the devil and whores of
heaven"). He fulminated against the "spectre of the requiem
mass with all its clashings, swishings and hootings" and, last but
not least, against the "painted dummies", the images of the
saints.[3] Because of his preaching Wolter von Plettenberg, the
Grand Master of the Teutonic Order, threw him into prison and
eventually banished him from Wolmar. Hoffman had to flee to
Dorpat, where he managed to build up a large following. When
Johannes Blankenfeld, the Archbishop of Riga, tried to arrest
him here he unleashed the most violent iconoclastic outburst of
the Livonian Reformation. The authorities in Dorpat, who had
at first shown toleration to Hoffman's preaching, became uneasy
in the face of this expression of popular rage. They stipulated
that the furrier could only carry on with his mission if the
Wittenberg reformers would testify to his orthodoxy. Hoffman
did manage to obtain a reference from Luther personally, but
soon after his return from Saxony he became enmeshed in an
implacable controversy with the evangelical clergy and the city
authorities, first of all in Dorpat and then (after his expulsion) in
Reval. He was finally forced to leave Livonia in 1526.

---

[3] Cf. his Commentary on Daniel Ch. 12.

We shall be mostly concerned in the following study to trace the interaction between Hoffman's mystical and apocalyptic thinking and the social and political tensions of Livonian society. The interaction will be investigated by consideration of the following questions:

a) What were the political and social realities which created a breeding-ground for anti-Catholic radicalism that contributed so much to Hoffman's mass-appeal?

b) From which social strata were the Hoffmanites recruited?

c) What was Hoffman's role in the iconoclastic movement in Dorpat?

d) What was the effect of the urban uprisings and peasant unrest on the development of the Reformation in Livonia?

e) What factors led to Hoffman's conflict with the Lutheran clergy?

f) Was Hoffman (as he himself unquestionably believed) in essence a Lutheran?

1. The Situation in Livonia at the Beginning of the Reformation: Social Tensions and External Threat.

When Hoffman arrived in Livonia the sword of Damocles was suspended over it in the form of a threatened invasion by Russia. Despite the defeat of the Russians at Pskov in 1502 by Wolter von Plettenberg, the Czar was not prepared to withdraw his claims to authority over Livonia. Rather than signing a peace he had only agreed to a ceasefire which came up for renewal every ten years. The emergent large states which were beginning to consolidate themselves around Livonia (Russia, Poland and Sweden) felt the need to terminate the trade-monopoly of the Livonian cities, which obtained their wealth from transit trade of the Hanseatic League. Helped by their introduction of demesne farming these eastern states were able to increase their productivity and became capable of producing more corn for the West European market. They waited to take advantage of the profits that could be gained from trade with the west but found the

Hanseatic monopoly a constraint on the growth of their economies.[4]

Their external pressure made the problem of an inner restructuring of the country all the more urgent. At the beginning of the Reformation Livonia was still divided into five ecclesiastical principalities under the bishops of Reval, Ösel-Wiek, Kurland, Dorpat and the Archbishop of Riga as well as the territory of the Teutonic Order. For more than a hundred years the three major cities had been vainly attempting to break free from the control of the Prelates. After the Treaty of Kirchholm in 1452 Riga was subjected to the double dominion of the Archbishop and the Grand Master of the Teutonic Order.

In the Reformation the cities saw an opportunity of throwing off the domination of the ecclesiastical princes. Of the six territories into which the country had been divided they wanted to create a unified, secular duchy, which, if allied with the Empire, would stand a good chance of survival in any conflict with Russia. Johannes Lohmüller, the leading political figure of the Livonian cities, tried to win over Wolter von Plettenberg to the cause of secularization. He wrote to Johannes Platter, the Provincial Marshal of the Teutonic Order, arguing that God had ordained a division between secular and spiritual authorities. Men in religious positions should use only the sword of the spirit; the worldly sword belongs in the hands of secular men.[5]

Popes and bishops (who are "neither fish nor fowl") have confused the two realms. They use spiritual weapons (excommunication) to attack their secular opponents and fight spiritual enemies with a worldly sword. The Pope, in confusing these two orders, has become Antichrist. By "sitting in the midst of the Temple and thinking himself to be God" he has rebelled

---

[4] W. Czaplinski, "Le problème baltique aux XVIe et au XVIIe siècles" in *XIᵉ Congrès International des Sciences Historiques. Stockholm 1960. Rapports*, 4 (Uppsala, 1960), pp. 25-47; W. Küttler, *Patriziat, Bürgeropposition und Volksbewegungen in Riga in der zweiten Hälfte des 16. Jahrhunderts*. MS Thesis (Leipzig, 1966), pp. 29, 32, 44, 50-57.

[5] *Das Bapst, Bischove und geistlich Stand kein Land und Leute besitzen, vorstehen und regieren mugen, aus der heiligen Schrift verfasset* (1525). Reprinted in *ARG* 36 (1939) pp. 59-67.

against God. What is more, he has humiliated rightful secular rulers by forcing them to kiss his "mangy, diseased and gout-ridden feet." We must now begin to cleanse the Temple. God will be overjoyed if the "obdurate and godless crowd" of bishops, who are the representatives of the great Antichrist in Rome, are removed. Plettenberg should take total control of Livonia and secularize the Teutonic Order.

Probably without intending to do so Lohmüller, with his call for the removal of the Prelates, encouraged the spread of apocalyptic ideas. According to Paul's prophecy (2 Thess. 2:3-4) the unmasking of Antichrist (i.e. the bishops) and the cleansing of the Temple will usher in the Last Judgment.

But nothing could shake Plettenberg's loyalty to the Catholic Church. The fate of Livonia's political and religious reform thus depended on whether the city magistrates could manage to win over the landed gentry to their scheme.

At the beginning of the Reformation the prospects for such co-operation were not unfavourable since there was a clash of interests between the knights of the ecclesiastical territories of Riga, Dorpat and Ösel-Wiek, and the bishops. The nobles in these areas were pressing for guarantees to be given to defend "Jungingen's privilege". This had been granted to the nobles of Harrien-Wierland (which belonged to the Teutonic Order) by the Grand Master, Konrad von Jungingen, in 1397. It established rights of succession for both sexes and, if there were no direct heirs, for cousins up to five times removed.[6]

Thus it was almost impossible for fiefdoms to revert to the Master of the Teutonic Order. But in the bishoprics there was still an agreement that all fiefdoms would return to the bishop if there was no male heir. Another of the nobility's grievances against the bishops was the "duty of giving the first offer ("upbedinge")". By this no fiefdom, or any part of it, could be sold or mortgaged until it had been offered, either as a sale or a loan, to the feudal lord. In fact, Archbishop Silvester Stodewescher had extended the privileges of the knights of Harrien-

[6] L. Arbusov *Grundriss der Geschichte Liv-, Est-, und Kurlands* (Riga, 1908), p. 64.

Wierland to those of Riga in 1457 ("Silvester's Privilege"), and shortly before he died (on 28th December, 1523) Archbishop Jasper Linde revoked the "duty of giving the first offer."[7] But Linde's successor as Archbishop of Riga, Johannes Blankenfeld, (who had been Bishop of Dorpat since 1518) took a dim view of this alienation of feudal rights. Along with Johannes IV Kievel, the Bishop of Ösel-Wiek, he wanted to tighten the reins of feudal control. He wanted to restrict the nobility's rights in terms of succession as well as to restore the "duty of giving the first offer". After their enthronements at Ösel (in 1515) and Dorpat (in 1518) both bishops refused to give confirmation of the knights' privileges.[8]

But the chances of the nobles and townsmen agreeing on a common policy directed against the Prelates were seriously threatened by their dispute over the so-called "deserter question". The point at issue was what to do about peasants who had run away from the dominion of their landlords.

The changeover from a natural to a money economy in Livonia brought with it the introduction of demesne-farming. More compulsory work was demanded of the peasants in order to raise the production of corn for the West European market. At the beginning of the sixteenth century the nobility began to tie the "Hakenbauern", i.e. the respected peasants living from the yields of their farms, to the land.[9] This resulted in many peasants fleeing to the towns. This desertion caused the nobles to tie members of even lower orders to the land. They laid this imposition on the so-called "Einfüßlinge" (small peasants with no share in the village's crop rotation system who cultivated poor land), on the "Lostreiber" (farm labourers with no land at all who changed their jobs frequently), and on "Mietknechte" (farm labourers on permanent hire).[10] Throughout the Middle Ages this rural proletariat had had unrestricted mobility. It was

<hr>

[7] AR III, No. 143, §11.

[8] AR III, No. 135 §24, No. 150 §8a. cf. L. Arbusov, Grundriss, p. 132.

[9] H. Bosse, "Der livländische Bauer am Ausgang der Ordenszeit" in Mitteilungen aus der livländischen Geschichte 24 (1933), pp. 421–428, 450–453.

[10] H. Bosse, op. cit. p. 332.

from this group of people that the towns could recruit cheap labour, particularly to work as porters in the harbours. On this "deserter question" the cities said that they would refuse asylum to the "Hakenbauern", i.e. the serfs who were regular peasants, but not to any "Einfüßlinge, "Lostreiber" or "Mietknechte".[11] Another point of contention was whether a "Hakenbauer" who had fled to the town could become a free citizen after "a year and a day" as the Law of Lübeck prescribed, or (as the nobles demanded) only after a period of thirty years.[12]

There were numerous other issues which continued to influence relations between the knights and the merchants: the towns' trading monopoly, the refusal to grant the nobility free use of the harbours, the prohibition of direct commerce between the knights and foreign merchants and the pre-emption carried out by the towns in their rural hinterlands.[13] We can gather the strength of feeling on the part of the "Kraut-knights" against the "pepper sacks" from a song they sang in a loud voice through the streets of Reval:

"The burghers' heads we'll slash and beat,
Their blood will pour out down the street".[14]

The nobility's economic policy was directed towards two aims; they wanted to take advantage of the new economic system of early capitalism while retaining the benefits of traditional feudalism. They directed their struggle for unrestricted property and free trade against the feudal rights of the

[11] *AR* III No 63 §2. B. Russow, *Chronica der Provintz Lyfflandt* 1584 (Reprinted Riga and Leipzig 1848, Scriptores Rerum Livonicarum 2), p. 37; V. Niitemaa, *Die undeutsche Frage in der Politik der livländischen Städte im Mittelalter* (Helsinki, 1949), p. 149.
[12] *AR* III No. 62 §1, No. 63 §2.
[13] *AR* III No. 62 §5, No. 231 §96. B. Russow, *Chronica*, p. 35; V. Niitemaa, *Der Binnenhandel in der Politik der livländischen Städte im Mittelalter* (Helsinki, 1952), pp. 192–195; W. Küttler, *Patriziat, Bürgeropposition und Volksbewegung*, p. 176.
[14] Wij willen de Börger up de Köppe slaan, dat blodt schall up de straaten stahn. C. Kelch, *Liefländische Historia bis aufs 1690. Jahr.* Reval 1695, p. 184.

Prelates and against the medieval trading privileges of the merchants. But at the same time they themselves were tightening the thumbscrews of feudalism by tying peasants to the land and demanding more compulsory service. The rural nobility's main question about the Reformation was whether it could favour one of their aims (unrestricted property) without threatening the other (the tightening of the fetters of feudalism on the peasants). Their attitude to Lutheranism depended, in the last analysis, on the solution of this problem.

The social tensions of Livonian society were made more acute because of the issue of nationality. In the countryside, over against the great mass of non-German enthralled peasants, there was the governing class: a thin stratum of German nobility. There were hardly any German peasants in Livonia because none of the peasants in north-western Germany wanted to travel by ship. In all the Livonian cities it was the Germans who made up the governing class and controlled the councils. Germans formed a proportion of the middle class whilst the petty bourgeoisie and proletariat was made up of Latvians, Estonians, and Courlanders. Thus Germans constituted a third of Reval's total population of about 5,000 (half were Estonians and a sixth Swedes). In Riga (c. 10,000 inhabitants) half of the population was German. We do not have any particular information about the social or national make-up of Dorpat's population (which was about 5,000) but there are specific figures for Reval. There the upper class (18% of the population – the merchants) was 100% German; in the middle class (22% of the inhabitants – shopkeepers and artisans affiliated to guilds) the Germans were still predominant (59% Germans, 23% Swedish, 18% Estonian), whilst most of the lower class (60% of the population – harbour workers, artisans not affiliated to the guilds and peddlars) was Estonian (73% Estonians, 25% Swedes, 2% Germans).[15]

Ever since the great Estonian uprising in 1343 all the

---

[15] H. zur Mühlen, "Versuch einer soziologischen Erfassung der Bevölkerung Revals im Spätmittelalter" in *Hansische Geschichtsblätter* 75 (1957), pp. 48-69.

"non-Germans" in the cities possessed only minimal rights.[16] Because of their nationality they could not belong to the "Great Guild"; this meant that from the end of the 16th century they were excluded from all magisterial positions and prevented from becoming merchants. In 1469 they were forbidden from acquiring property in the towns.[17] Thus in every town there was a completely unintegrated group of townsmen – the "non-Germans". Not even the artisans' guilds (with the exceptions of the goldsmiths, furriers, blacksmiths and journeyman smiths) would accept "non-Germans" as members.[18] One reason amongst others for these exceptions was the strength of the local jewellery and fur industries.

There was a further group which stood apart from the common townsfolk in the cities: the "Black-Headed Guild". This was an organization of journeyman merchants (either unmarried local men or foreigners from Germany) who spent the winter in Livonia when the Baltic was frozen over. Although the "Black-Heads" had no rights as townsmen, they were a highly respected and well-to-do guild; they used the same Council Chambers as the "Great Guild". No hired men or "non-Germans" (except journeyman smiths and sailors) could join the "Black-Heads".[19] Yet the German journeyman merchants from abroad did not feel very much attached to the social environment of Livonia. They brought the latest religious ideas to the area and in general they acted as propagators of the Reformation.

It is not easy to estimate the extent of the social tension within the cities. We can say with certainty that it was not as great as in the countryside, otherwise the peasants would not have flocked to the towns. To a certain extent the "Great Guild" made conditions favourable for the social improvement of the

---

[16] Russians, Swedes, Lithuanians and Poles did not count as "non-Germans".

[17] W. Küttler, *op. cit.* p. 64.

[18] C.E. Napiersky, *Rigas ältere Geschichte in Übersicht* (Riga and Leipzig, 1844) (Monumenta Livoniae Antiquae 4); W. Stieden and C. Mettig, *Schragen der Gilden und Ämter der Stadt Riga bis 1621* (Riga, 1896).

[19] C.E. Napiersky, *op cit.*, p. ccxvi.

"non-Germans". They allowed Germans to marry "non-Germans" and, despite the opposition of the "Little Guild" (the association of artisans), they ordered that all newly created guilds must accept "non-Germans" as members.[20] There was obviously never a rapprochement of the urban "semi-Germans" with the peasants, who remained untouched by German influence, since the urban "non-German" proletariat remained loyal to the German patriciate during the Livonian Peasants' Revolt in 1560.[21] However, there was still a latent potential for social unrest in the Livonian cities, because the "non-Germans" did not possess any civil rights, and this could be activated by an attack on the institutions of the Catholic Church. This was of more importance than the conflict between the "Great Guild" and the "Little Guild". The disputes between merchants and artisans in the first half of the 16th century were not over the great questions of political power; they were concerned with secondary issues like the artisans' trading or brewing-rights or dress-regulations. Behind these there was obviously a dispute over prestige and status.[22]

There were also considerable tensions between each of the Livonian cities. Dorpat and Narva entered a difficult period when the trading-post of the Hanseatic League in Novgorod was closed in 1494. Things were made worse by the opening of the road to Marienburg which linked Riga and Pskov but by-passed Dorpat. By 1525 Dorpat was on the verge of economic collapse. Petitions were sent to the Livonian Diet to close the road, but to no avail. Nor was any attention paid to the protests of Narva and Dorpat against the policy pursued by Reval and Riga of giving Russian merchants the rights to acquire property in their towns and of providing them with more favourable trading conditions.[23]

The advance of the Reformation threatened to leave the whole country in a state of chaos by setting loose the latent conflicts

---

[20] V. Niitemaa, *Die undeutsche Frage*, pp. 193-194, 197, 205.

[21] *Ibid.*, p. 210.

[22] B. Russow, *Chronica*, p. 38; W. Küttler, *op cit.* p. 188.

[23] *AR* III, No. 207 §43, 230 §8, 231 §97; Niitemaa, *Binnenhandel*. pp. 333, 357, 360.

within its complex and largely outdated social and political structure. The prospects soon seemed to become much bleaker with the expectations aroused by the Reformation that produced in many people a feeling of inevitable catastrophe. This feeling was to find expression in apocalyptic fantasies.[24]

2. The Development of the Movement for Radical Religious Reform in Livonia up to the Iconoclastic Outburst in Dorpat.

Hoffman's vehement attack on the Catholic Church at Wolmar in 1523 was part of a major reforming movement which gripped the whole of Livonia. In June, 1522 the magistrates had brought about a disputation at Riga aimed at enforcing the introduction of the Reformation. The leading spokesman for the Lutherans was Andreas Knopken, the Chaplain of St. Peter's Church and a former colleague of Bugenhagen in the school at Treptow.[25] Knopken was later described as a gentle man who "like his mentor Luther felt that idols should be removed from the heart before being removed from the churches."[26] But the 24 theses he propounded at the disputation in 1522 show him to have been a radical reformer, many of whose demands went much further than those of Luther. Thus, for example, he regarded the veneration of images as a form of madness (thesis 3), and he placed the role of the church in question by claiming that the unction of the Holy Spirit was more important than external consecration. The Pope was Antichrist who, because of his curse on the Emperor, deserved God's punishment (theses 18 and 22). Like Lohmüller

---

[24] Cf. B. Russow, *Chronica*, pp. 34–43 which sees the breakdown of Livonia as a divine punishment for widespread immorality and for the cities' thirst for quarrel; cf. also the conclusion to an article by R. Wittram: "Die Reformation in Livland" in R. Wittram (ed), *Baltische Kirchengeschichte* (Göttingen, 1956), pp. 35–36.

[25] Cf. Johannes Lohmüller's letter of 20th August 1522, *WA Br* 2:952

[26] C. Kelch, *Liefländische Historia*, p. 168.

he rejected the political structure of Livonia as ungodly because of its confusion of the spiritual and secular orders (thesis 20). Knopken accused the clergy of devouring the wealth of the church whilst doing nothing for the poor (thesis 13). Thus the Reformation was presented as a comprehensive programme for religious, political and social renewal.[27]

Riga's second evangelical preacher, Sylvester Tegetmeier, was reputed to be even more radical than Knopken. "He went much further and amazed the common people by punishing the papists' blasphemy and removing the images".[28] Tegetmeier was very probably a follower of Karlstadt during the first years of his activity as a preacher. Some notes in his diary support this idea. In 1519 he remarked that "Karlstadt disputed his propositions in Lipsick (Leipzig)". In 1525 he indicated that he was preaching daily in Dorpat on the book of Malachi, on which Karlstadt had written a commentary in 1522.[29]

But most important of all was that evangelical worship was conducted in Riga in the most extreme form imaginable – on the basis of Karlstadt's "Wittenberg Ordinance" of 1521-1522. Because there was no Latin liturgy or vestments, those in the community who held firm to the former practices complained that "they are handling the holy sacrament just as if it was a piece of ham or beef and making a mockery of it. The priest stands at the altar, approaching the sacrament just as if he was a smith's apprentice or a cobbler".[30] Tegetmeier, like his model Karlstadt, also wanted to remove all images from the churches.

Karlstadt based his opposition to images on the Old Testament's prohibition in Exodus 20:4, which, he felt, had not been superseded by the New Testament "because Christ did not

[27] Knopken's theses are printed in O. Pohrt, *Reformationsgeschichte Livlands* (1928), pp. 114-125 (Schriften des Vereins für Reformationsgeschichte, 46/2).

[28] From a contemporary chronicle by Bartholomaeus Grefenthal (Edited by F.G. v. Bunge, Riga and Leipzig, 1847), p. 48.

[29] F. Bienemann, "Sylvester Tegetmeier: Tagebuch" in *Mitteilungen aus dem Gebiet der Geschichte Liv-,Est-, und Kurlands*, Vol 12 (Riga 1880), p. 503-504.

[30] Cf. E. Sehling, *Die evangelischen Kirchenordnungen des 16. Jahrhunderts*, Vol. 5. 1913, pp. 13–14.

break down the tiniest jot or tittle in Moses". But the idea that God as a pure spirit could only be worshipped in the Spirit was more important than the biblical argument. Images bind men to the material level; for Karlstadt they could not carry a religious message. "Images point to nothing other than crude and empty flesh, which is of no avail".[31] To Karlstadt the assault on images was also a protest against the church's failure to care for the poor. The money spent on dead images would be much better used if it was given to the poor, who are the living images of God. The presence of beggars in a town is a sure sign that it has no Christian inhabitants.

The magisterial authority in Riga took up the cause of the Reformation in October-November, 1522 and appointed Knopken as preacher in St. Peter's and Tegetmeier as preacher in St. James'. But the Archbishop and Cathedral Chapter opposed these appointments and from then on refused to pay the preachers their stipends. They were supported both by voluntary contributions from their congregations and by two endowments established by the "Black-Headed Guild".[32]

Johannes Blankenfeld's planned reaction to these developments only opened the floodgates of iconoclasm. He sent two Franciscan monks (Antonius Bomhower and Burckhard Waldis) to Rome in order to urge the Pope to impose an interdict on the town of Riga and to order it to pay a fine of several thousand ducats. The Franciscans in fact did not achieve anything in Rome (where Pope Hadrian VI had died and Clement VII had not yet been elected), but Bomhower was careless enough to reveal the archbishop's schemes against Riga in a letter to Wilhelm von Isenbroeck, a Teutonic Knight and Custodian of the Franciscan brothers in Livonia. The letter was intercepted and Bomhower was imprisoned on his return to Riga.[33] The fury that erupted in

---

[31] A. Karlstadt, *Von abtuhung der Bylder/und das keyn Bettler unter den Christen sey* (Wittenberg 1522), D II.

[32] L. Arbusov, *Die Einführung der Reformation in Livland, Estland und Kurland* (2nd ed., 1964) p. 242.

[33] *AR* III, No. 150 §19; L. Arbusow, "Die Aktion der Rigaischen Franziskaner gegen das Vordringen des Luthertums und ihre Folgen" in *Sitzungsberichte der Gesellschaft für Geschichte und Alterthumskunde der Ostseeprovinzen Russlands aus dem Jahre 1913* (Riga 1914), pp. 21-70.

the town because of this betrayal by Blankenfeld and the Franciscans led to the first outbreak of iconoclasm on 10th March, 1524. Hermann Hoyte, the Teutonic Order's captain in charge of the castle, sounded the signal to begin by sending a knotted whip to a meeting of the "Black-Heads" along with this command: "If you want peace use this scourge against the priests and the monks".[34] The "Black-Heads" decided to remove the altarpiece they themselves had endowed to St. Peter's, since it had proved to be based "not on true and divine scripture but on a blasphemous abuse of Christ's holy testament".[35] Veneration of Mary and the saints now seemed to them to be incompatible with a saving faith in Christ alone. Until then the Madonna had been at the heart of the cult of images in Livonia, for the whole country had been dedicated to her in the days of Innocent III. Before the guild-members chosen by the church elders to remove the altar were able to set about it in an orderly way, "the whole group of the young guild-members took it into their stupid and dim heads to break into the church, causing a great disturbance, and to destroy the Black-Heads' altar".[36] The leadership of the Black-Heads had probably already lost control of the Guild. As a separate society within the guild they celebrated their feast-days, not with the younger members but with the "Great Guild". The resulting social isolation thus found expression in this act of public disobedience.[37]

Six days later, on 16th March, 1524, a great crowd burst into the two parish churches (St. Peter's and St. James') and shattered everything that still smacked of the Catholic cult. An entry in the records of the Latvian Guild of Beer-Carriers indicates that it was the lower class of "non-Germans" who were responsible for

[34] J.H. Arndt, *Liefländische Chronik* (Halle 1753), p. 186.

[35] C. Mettig, "Materialien zu einer Geschichte der reformatorischen Bewegung in Riga" in *SB d. Gesell. f. Geschichte u. Alterthumskunde d. Ostseeprovinzen Russlands a.d. J. 1890* (Riga 1891) pp. 65-71.

[36] H.J. Bothführ, "Einige Bemerkungen zu Sylvester Tegetmeiers Tagebuch" in *Mitteilungen a.d. Geschichte Liv-, Est- und Kurlands*, 13 (1886), p. 66.

[37] H. Spliet, "Die Schwarzen Häupter in ihrem Verhältnis zur deutschen kolonialen Ständegeschichte in Livland" in *Zeitschrift für Ostforschung*, 3 (1954), p. 242.

this action. "Item: in the year XXIIII during the mid-week fast after Passion Sunday (i.e. 16th March, 1524) the Lutherans brought to fruition a wonderful work within Riga. The blind saw, the dumb spoke, the lame walked and idols were destroyed. This took place when they broke into both churches, St. Peter's and St. James', and destroyed every image, cross, madonna or whatever was there. Item: they removed the relics of the saints, smashed them and threw them out. They broke whatever was in the church. That evening when they had done all this, they sang 'This Easter Day' (Haec dies paschalis) and some psalms. Then they listened to a sermon in which he (Tegetmeier) said they had acted properly because it was right to destroy idolatry".[38] This was a celebration of the iconoclastic outburst as an act of human liberation, releasing man from the magic of the image. Men were blind, dumb and lame (like wooden statues) before the Reformation, paralysed by the power of the images. Clearly some people must still have regarded images as real vehicles of supernatural power or identified them with the saints themselves. Lutheran preaching, by revealing the images to be a devilish deceit, gave believers the courage to liberate themselves from a paralysing servility. The iconoclasts experienced a rebirth by destroying "Satan's masks" and could thus sing the paschal hymn (eleven days before Easter) as a celebration of the conquest of death and the devil. Ten days later Tegetmeier went into the Cathedral at Riga with a band of followers where he demolished the altarpiece and reconsecrated the font.[39]

The church treasures that had not been plundered or destroyed (including expensive monstrances and chalices) were sold for the benefit of the poor. The fund that had paid for private masses was also used for social welfare.[40]

Because of the popular movement that spread out from Riga, most of the Livonian city authorities (such as Revel, Dorpat,

[38] H.J. Bothführ, *op. cit.* pp. 66–67.
[39] O. Pohrt, *Reformationsgeschichte*, p. 37; L. Arbusov, *Einführung der Reformation*, p. 297.
[40] C. Mettig, *op.cit.*

Narva and Kokenhusen) appointed evangelical ministers in the first half of 1524.[41]

The victory of the Reformation appeared to be almost at hand at the Diet of Reval between 17th and 23rd July, 1524. Because of the absence of the Prelates and the Master of the Order the three cities and the knights were able to transform the alliance they had had since 1522 into a vehicle to bring in the Reformation. Riga, Reval and Dorpat promised to support each other if there was ever a need to "protect the holy Gospel". The knights swore to "commit their bodies and worldly goods to God's Word as contained in the New and the Old Testaments". All the Estates guaranteed support for Riga against Johannes Blankenfeld, its new archbishop. Admittedly they made no explicit commitment to Luther's cause, but they did agree that the next Provincial Diet in Wolmar would hold a disputation to settle the religious issue for the whole of Livonia. In case the bishops refused to agree to this procedure any estate would be able to decide freely for itself whether or not it wanted to accept the new teaching. For their part the towns promised to support the knights of the episcopal domains in their battle against "the duty of giving the first offer" and the restrictions on heritage rights.[42]

Putting its trust in this alliance Riga informed Johannes Blankenfeld, the new archbishop, in August, 1524 that the town would no longer submit to his authority, and invited the Master of the Order to take sole responsibility for the protection of the city. The knights in the episcopal domain of Ösel-Wiek refused to pay their rents to the church in the form of a corn tax.[43] The peasants in these regions also began to rebel and, with the support of the nobility, they refused to pay their tithes to the church.[44] It appeared that the collapse of the Catholic Church was inevitable.

[41] O. Pohrt, *Reformationsgeschichte* p. 37; F. Bienemann, *Aus Livlands Luthertagen* (Reval 1883).
[42] *AR* III, No. 150 §8, 13, 14, 16a, No. 151 §16.
[43] *AR* III, No. 163, No. 165.
[44] *AR* III, No. 160 §7.

3. The Crisis of the Livonian Reformation (September 1524 – June 1525).

Faced with the threatened collapse of his church, Blankenfeld decided to break the united ranks of his opponents by making material concessions to the knights in his domain. He was not as yet prepared to come to an understanding on the issue of the faith. It was on 29th September, 1524 that Blankenfeld granted a new privilege to the knights in the Archbishopric of Riga. He withdrew his claim to escheat where there was no direct heir, revoked the "duty of giving the first offer" and refrained from introducing Roman Law, to which the nobles objected.[45] He even did something for the peasants by responding to the knights' request for him to withdraw the new ox-tax. The same concessions were granted to the knights in Dorpat on the 19th October, 1524. He also made a tiny gesture of coming to terms with the city of Dorpat and showed his willingness to compromise. He gave up his fish-tax and said that he was prepared to have the gates to the cathedral precinct walled up (this unbarred entrance had been abused by the clergy – they used it for smuggling).[46] Strong pressure from Wolter von Plettenberg finally caused the bishop of Ösel-Wiek to make concessions even more far-reaching than those of Blankenfeld. Not only did he renounce the "duty of giving the first offer" and his claims to escheat, but he also made the Cathedral Chapter's election of the bishop dependent on the approval of the nobility. But in future people would be regarded as nobility only if all four of their grand-parents were of pure blue blood. This stipulation reveals the overall political aim of separating the knights from the towns, for it meant that knights did not in practice have unrestricted rights to inherit fiefs if they were descended from townsmen.[47]

The Prelates issued a downright condemnation of the Reformation. "There will be no compromises or changes which

[45] AR III, No. 162 §10, 11, 7.
[46] AR III, No. 166 §2, 4, 13, 9.
[47] AR III, No. 169 §1, 2, 5, 6, 14.

will break down the church."[48] Blankenfeld swore that he was determined to banish Hermann Marsow, the evangelical preacher appointed by the Council of Dorpat, "even if he had to lose five, or even all ten fingers to do so".[49] Marsow had to leave Dorpat and escape to Reval.

Hoffman arrived in Dorpat in March, 1525. Economically the town was almost bankrupt. There was an undercurrent of popular antipathy to its unscrupulous and violent prince. Hoffman set up secret assemblies in burghers' homes, taking his following mainly from amongst the younger members of the "Black-Headed Guild", i.e. the same group that had been behind the iconoclastic outburst in Riga.[50]

Under orders from Blankenfeld, Peter Stackelberg, the town bailiff in charge of the castle, attempted to arrest this unlicensed wandering preacher on 10th January, 1525. He took a band of soldiers into the lower town (where matters of public order were in the hands of the Council) and there fought with a group of Germans (who were citizens enjoying full political privileges), Estonians and Black-Heads who tried to prevent Hoffman being arrested. Stackelberg and his men withdrew to the Cathedral precinct, which was situated in the centre of the town and was "quite unmarked and not protected by walls."[51] The townspeople followed the soldiers, swearing at them, but they did obey Stackelberg's order to clear the precinct. Then the soldiers took up their pikes again and ran after the retreating band of Hoffman's friends, making provocative cries of "Turn back!" When they were back in the lower town for the second time some of the burghers turned round and faced the attack. Stackelberg's men pressed hard. They killed two Germans and two non-Germans as well as seriously injuring about twenty other people. All of this bloodshed had taken place in the lower town where the bailiff was only allowed to enter with the

---

[48] *AR* III, No. 166 §10.

[49] *AR* III, No. 150 §13.

[50] T. Bredenbach, *Belli Livonici nova et memorabilis historia* Cologne, 1564, f.18: "He seduced many of the younger merchants from Catholicism by the new teachings".

[51] *AR* III No. 231 §14.

express permission of the Council. Because of this serious violation of the law the alarm bells were rung, the whole of the townsfolk armed themselves and broke into the Cathedral precinct. Stackelberg retreated to the castle and prepared it for a siege. Whilst some of the townspeople laid siege to the castle the rest stormed the Cathedral and the nearby homes of the canons, as well as the two city churches of St. Mary and St. John. Every image and altarpiece was thrown on a bonfire and burnt. Some fanatics even shattered the gravestones of former bishops. Even the Russian Orthodox Church of St. Nicholas (used by the merchants from Moscow and Pskov) fell victim to the icono-clasts – an unbelievably rash undertaking, since it gave the Czar the opportunity of sending an expedition against Dorpat to avenge the spoliation of the church.[52] The crowd finally turned its fury on the cloisters. The Dominicans were expelled first of all; they were left with nothing but their prayer books. They then drove the Franciscans and the Tertiaries out of their houses. The only cloister not to be affected by this popular outburst was that of the Cistercian nuns, where the daughters of the nobility lived.

Faced with a strong barrage directed against the castle, Stackelberg offered to surrender on condition that his men were allowed to walk out freely. The town agreed to this. The council appealed to Riga and Reval for help in protecting Dorpat against any future attack from Blankenfeld. The company from Reval reached Dorpat unhindered but the men from Riga were cut off by the Master of the Teutonic Order.[53]

After this battle the Council decided that the Reformation should be established officially in Dorpat. Sylvester Tegetmeier from Riga was entrusted with all the necessary ecclesiastical powers, and he led the process of Reformation in Dorpat between 1st and 28th February, 1525.

The Council asked for evidence of Melchior Hoffman's orthodoxy before it allowed him to preach openly. Hoffman thus set off for Riga and there obtained the necessary references

---

[52] C. Kelch, *Livländische Historia* p. 174.
[53] *AR* III No. 175.

from Knopken and Tegetmeier.[54] But the Council still had its doubts about this self-appointed missionary whose friends consisted mainly of non-Germans and young "foreign" German merchants who had no burghers' rights. The Council was also worried about the fact that he had aroused such exceptional passions during the uprising. To make quite certain they asked for an assurance of Hoffman's orthodoxy from no less a person than Martin Luther himself. Early in 1525 Hoffman set off on the long journey to Wittenberg in order to obtain Luther's approval for his work and his preaching.

On hearing the news of the iconoclastic uprising in Dorpat Plettenberg expressed his concern that the "barbarous" Russians might take advantage of the incident to invade the country.[55] He reminded every group of the dangerous external situation with which Livonia was faced and urged everyone (including the hated archbishop) to protect his rights.[56]

With the loss of his two cities, Dorpat and Riga, Blankenfeld was left in a desperate position. He now took the most insidious step possible for a German prince in Livonia – he used his bailiff, Gerhard Ringenberg, to negotiate a secret treaty with the Czar, encouraging him to intervene in Livonia to protect the established church structure. The city of Dorpat got wind of the scheme and by 14th February, 1525 was accusing Blankenfeld of high treason in front of the Master of the Order.[57] Blankenfeld denied that he had made any alliance with the Russians, but so much evidence of his complicity had accumulated by December, 1525 that the knights of his episcopal domain arrested him in Ronneburg a few days before Christmas.[58] There was a deafening cry of outrage throughout the land. People regarded this conspiracy with the national enemy as a "horrific and

---

[54] M. Hoffman, *Jhesus* in *WA* 18 p. 429, n. 23.

[55] The most important sources of our knowledge of the iconoclastic movement in Dorpat are: *AR* III No. 173, 179, 194, 196, 198, 207 §1, 22, 37 and 213; M. Hoffman, *An de gelöfighen vorsambling…* 1526 A 5a-b; Hoffman and Karlstadt, *Dialogus* A 2b and Tegetmeier's diary.

[56] *AR* III No. 172 and 173.

[57] *AR* III No. 180.

[58] *AR* III No. 218a.

careless" attempt to subject Livonia to "an unchristian and barbarous nation, leading her out from her highest freedom, into an endless servitude."[59] The towns demanded the archbishop's execution.[60] Blankenfeld saved his neck by swearing fealty and obedience to the Master of the Teutonic Order, as his vassal.[61] But as soon as he obtained his freedom he naturally claimed that he had sworn the oath of allegiance under duress and that it was hence invalid.

But the towns' hopes that they would finally be able to win over the knights to the cause of the Reformation by exposing Blankenfeld's treachery were not realised. The knights were led to change their attitudes by the growth of social revolutionary disturbances amongst their rural subjects.

In Harrien-Wierland, where demesne-farming was not firmly established, there were signs of peasant unrest from the beginning of 1524 onwards. This was due to the activity of the evangelical preachers, who were censured by the Council of Reval in March, 1524 for having encouraged peasants to disobey their masters.[62] The bailiff of Wesenberg made a similar complaint to the Master of the Order about the evangelical preachers in Narva.[63] In addition, the evangelical merchants from the towns who did trade in the countryside incited the peasants to what the knights would call rebellion.[64]

Hoffman, too, is implicated in the peasant unrest in a Livonian chronicle of 1610 by Dionysius Fabricius. According to this he had got to know a local weaver who spoke Latvian and sent him to the peasants in order to spread his doctrines out into the countryside. At Eastertide this weaver had given a mass absolution to the peasants after they had made a nominal confession, and he had then celebrated the Eucharist for them, in which he used slices of radish for the host. One peasant had cried

---

[59] *AR* III No. 223 §3; 225 §3.

[60] *AR* III No. 231 §37.

[61] *AR* III No. 239.

[62] G. von Hannen, *Aus baltischer Vergangenheit. Miscellaneen aus dem Revaler Stadtarchiv* Reval, 1894, pp. 123-125.

[63] L. Arbusov. *Einführung der Reformation* p. 323.

[64] *AR* III No. 207 §53, 54, 55; 242 §8.

out in amazement, "O sweet Jesus, why have you become so bitter?" The weaver had also granted absolution to a peasant who had stolen his master's ox, but he had not requested him to return the animal to its owner. The peasant was overjoyed at this new style of confession and immediately proceeded to steal another ox. But on doing this he was arrested and then condemned to death. On the scaffold the simple-minded thief had blamed his confessor for his fate in that he had not forced him to return the first ox.

We have every right, in view of the way this story has come to us, to doubt the details of such an episode. But the anecdote probably does reflect Hoffman's position as minister for the sick in Reval, where he had connections with the non-German peasants and introduced them to his criticisms of the secular authorities, of auricular confession and of both the Catholic and Lutheran views of the Eucharist.[65]

Because of the concessions made by the Prelates early in 1525 the Livonian nobles had in effect achieved all the material aims they had originally hoped for in supporting the Reformation. They recognised that if the Reformation took a more radical turn, as indicated in the Peasants' War and the iconoclastic outbursts in the cities, then all that had been achieved with its aid would be destroyed.

It was the nobility of Harrien-Wierland who gave the signal to give up the cause of the Reformation. In March, 1525 the knights complained to the town of Reval about the eviction of the Dominicans from the Black Cloister, where they used to lodge and were provided for on their visits to the city. They complained about the destruction and confiscation of the Church property they had donated and cried out about the

---

[65] D. Fabricius, *Livonicae historiae compendiosa series, edito secundo* Edited by G. Bergmann (Riga and Leipzig, 1884), pp. 467-470; F. Amelung, "Melchior Hoffman in Livland und die Einführung der Re-formation in dem Kirchspielen Dorpat und Nüggen im Jahre 1525" in *Sitzungsberichte der Gelehrten Estnischen Gesellschaft* Dorpat 1901-1902. p. 208. The story first appears in 1610 in Fabricius, who names Bredenbach as the chief witness. But there is no trace of the incident in Bredenbach's writings.

scandalous situation allowed by the city whereby nobly-born nuns could leave the cloisters and marry ordinary townsmen.[66] But above all they complained that the burghers of Reval had incorporated their former serfs by giving them rights of asylum and by lodging them *en masse* in plundered cloisters. The worst of all was that "they teach the lower classes that peasants need not obey their masters. They make them think they are as good as their masters and give them meat to eat on Fridays and other (fast-)days.... Whenever peasants come home from town they ought to be obedient to their superiors and masters, but we cannot make them behave so. If the peasants are punished they leave for the towns, where they are gladly received."[67]

The Diet of Wolmar (29th June – 10th July, 1525) set the seal on the nobles' decision to oppose the Reformation. The towns had hoped that this Diet would take a decision in favour of accepting Luther's doctrine, but the proceedings were overshadowed by the German Peasants' War which made clear the social-revolutionary implications of the Reformation. Rather than attempting to pour oil on the troubled waters, the towns made an unbelievably tactless error: they chose Tegetmeier, the iconoclast, to act as the leader of the Reformation movement. He was expected to appear in a disputation and win over to the evangelical cause those groups that were still undecided. But such a disputation (whose outcome would be decided by the Diet) was ruled out from the start by the bishops, the princes and even the knights. Tegetmeier was simply given permission to give a public sermon, but he finally destroyed any chance of making Luther's cause acceptable to the undecided groups by choosing to preach a radical sermon on Matt. 21:13, "My house shall be called a house of prayer; but you have made it a den of robbers". After this tirade against the Catholic church's ceremonies and image-cult, Plettenberg told Tegetmeier that he should not start any uprising because one could see very well that the peasants were already rising against their masters. When

[66] *AR* III No. 184 §8; 185 §8, 9; 244 §1; L. Arbusov, *Einführung der Reformation* pp. 352–357.
[67] *AR* III No. 242 §8.

an argument arose between Tegetmeier and a Dominican monk, who was trying to stop him entering his pulpit, the nobles of Harrien-Wierland intervened. They threatened Tegetmeier with knives and with their fists and shouted, "Traitor! Swindler! You're trying to deprive us of our land as well as of our belongings. We'll deal with your roguery." After this, Plettenberg forbad Tegetmeier to preach. Tegetmeier complied with this command, because on the same day his storm troopers, the Black-Heads, were holding a convention.[68]

The knights of Harrien-Wierland, who were most threatened by peasant unrest and iconoclasm, worked behind the backs of the towns to bring about an alliance of all the socially conservative forces. After the knights of the episcopal domains, the Teutonic Order and the bishops had all come together, they

---

[68] Cf. Tegetmeier's diary: "The Black-Heads were holding an assembly, so that nothing could be done about it". J.G. Arndt, *Livländische Chronik* p. 190, L. Arbusov, *Einführung der Reformation* pp. 438–444. The fact that Tegetmeier, the radical, rather than Knopken, the moderate, was chosen by the town councils to represent the Reformation at the Diet of Wolmar argues against Joachim Kuhles' formulation of the situation (cf. "Zur ideologischen Differenzierung der reformatorischen Bewegung im Ostbaltikum' in *Weltwirkung der Reformation* (Berlin, 1969) Vol.2. pp. 377-390). According to this Knopken represented a moderate, official Reformation as required by the "Great Guild", Tegetmeier represented the radical, petty bourgeois opposition and Hoffman was the spokesman of the plebeian lower classes. Undoubtedly the three preachers differed in their degree of radicalism on the ecclesiastical issue, but it is difficult to assess their attitudes to the secular authorities. The relationship between social environment and religious ideology is also much more complicated than Kuhles makes it seem. Tegetmeier was related to members of the "Great Guild" (he married the daughter of Hermann K. Mels, the merchant, and was related by marriage to the Schleper family, which provided council members) (cf. L. Arbusov, *Einführung der Reformation*, p. 565). It was Tegetmeier, not the conservative Knopken, who was Hoffman's archopponent in Livonia. He said that Hoffman's doctrines would result in death and slaughter (cf. *An de gelöfighen vorsambling* A5b) After his expulsion from Livonia Hoffman still spoke of Knopken as a "faithful shepherd". He was also concerned to convince the authorities that he rejected any kind of uprising. Furthermore the Black-Heads, who were Hoffman's strongest supporters, were certainly not members of the plebeian lower classes.

Plate 1: John Bugenhagen

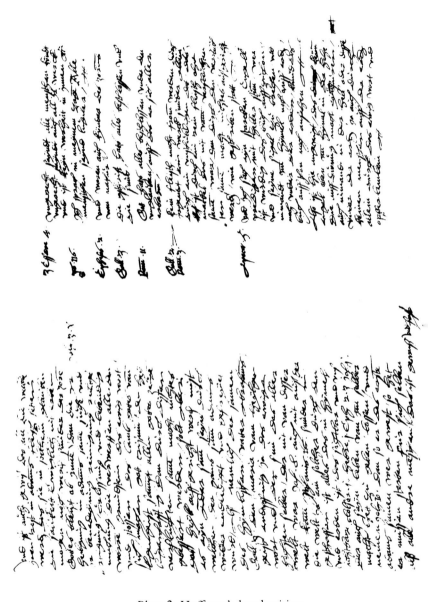

Plate 2: Hoffman's handwriting

submitted the following proposals to the astonished town councils for their approval: all the Estates in Livonia were to guarantee each other's rights and possessions (the status quo was to be maintained). Whatever decisions had been taken by the town in terms of ecclesiastical reforms, they had to be considered as merely provisional, subject to a reversal by a final decree of a general church council. But from then on, until a general Church Council gave the go-ahead, there were to be no more church reforms. The cloisters that were still functioning were to be left unmolested. Nuns who had run away must be sent back to their abbesses. Anybody marrying a nun would be mercilessly punished. Treasures belonging to ransacked churches were to be looked after by the magistrates until the Estates decided what to do with them.[69] The towns said these proposals were "evil, godless and unchristian." They refused to sign the decree, but the other Estates validated it nevertheless.

Even the complaints against the "godless and wrongly-called Lord Archbishop, Johannes Blankenfeld" fell on deaf ears amongst the knights of the episcopal domains and the Knights of the Order. Dorpat was forced to hand over the town's castle to the Cathedral Chapter and the knights of the domain. Plettenberg refused to be the sole protector of Riga.[70]

The three Livonian towns now had to accept the bitter fact that the iconoclastic uprisings and the ferment amongst the peasants had cost them their hoped-for alliance with the nobility. These two movements had re-united the broken front of the old feudal power (the bishops, the Order and the rural nobility).

In order to win back the trust of the nobility (which they needed if they were to achieve their political aims), the towns decided amongst themselves that they would no longer tolerate any iconoclasm in the cities and that they would put a stop to the merchants, preachers and Black-Heads encouraging peasants to rebel against their masters.[71] The three towns assured each other of support to suppress any further disturbances. The Hanseatic

---

[69] *AR* III No. 207 §34 section 1, 2, 3, 9, 10, 11.
[70] *AR* III No. 207 §34 section 7; no. 208 §5; no. 211.
[71] *AR* III No. 207 §50, 53-55.

Diet in Lübeck (7th – 29th July, 1525) ordered the Livonian towns no longer to tolerate any evangelical preachers who used the preaching of the pure Word of God as an excuse to "speak to the common people of achieving worldly freedom, which can only lead to the overthrow of authority and the downfall of the city."[72]

4. Hoffman visits Luther and Bugenhagen in Wittenberg (June, 1525).

Hoffman arrived in Wittenberg in June, 1525. Luther and Bugenhagen testified to his orthodoxy as requested. They then sent a letter in both their names, but subdivided into their individual contributions, to the evangelical congregations in Livonia. From their letter it appears that Hoffman had painted an unvarnished picture of the Livonian situation for his teachers in Wittenberg.[73] He must have explained that the major problems of the Reformation there were: a) the disputes between the evangelicals themselves concerning the new forms of worship, particularly about the form of the Eucharist and whether auricular confession was a necessary preliminary to eating at the Lord's Table; b) the question of good works as the fruit of the new faith, a particularly acute question in the light of the merchants' involvement in usury and taxation and in view of Livonia's national scandal – drunkenness;[74] c) the problem of armed rebellion against the mastery of prelates and nobles.

Luther's letter urged all his followers not to let themselves fall into error by divisions in their own ranks. Controversies had to arise so that the truth could come to light; they would have to be

[72] D. Schäfer and F. Techen (ed), *Hanserezesse von 1477-1530* Part 3 Vol 9. 1913, No. 132 §120-121. The significance of the Reformation for the disputes between the Livonian Estates is also considered by W. Küttler, "Sozialer Inhalt and politische Triebkräfte der Reformation im Ostbaltikum" in *Weltwirkung der Reformation* Vol. 2, 1969, pp. 367–376.

[73] *WA* 18:417–430. Luther's letter is translated in *LW* 53:45–50.

[74] The same problems are dealt with in Hoffman's Commentary on Daniel (usury-e3b, drunkenness-12a, auricular confession-n3a-o4b).

able to deal with conflicts and not put their trust in military solutions or in the proclamations of Councils. What really mattered was to concentrate on Christianity's main points: on justification by faith, on the need for brotherly love and on being prepared to follow in the way of the cross. External ordinances were free and variable, but consideration of one's neighbours meant that what was needed as a form of worship was something which appeared to be "an improvement and acceptable" to the majority of the congregation.

Bugenhagen's letter dealt in particular with the situation of the evangelical preachers. Auricular confession was a matter of evangelical freedom, not a divine command. It was aimed at giving comfort to those that were afraid, not at tormenting troubled consciences. Thus it should not be a compulsory requirement before anyone could receive the sacrament; the only precondition for admission to the Eucharist should be the communicant's faith. Concerning the unlawfulness of usury and taxation, Bugenhagen referred to Luther's book on the subject.[75] He censured the excessive drunkenness in Livonia as a hindrance to the entry of the Gospel into the heart, but also condemned those overzealous preachers who were prepared to give over all these thirsty souls to the flames of hell.

In his first tract, *Jhesus*, (dedicated to his congregation in Dorpat) Hoffman reminds his followers of the imminence of the Day of Judgment, which is "closer than we think." We can only be properly prepared for this by trusting not in our own works but in the justification brought about by the merits of Christ. Faith itself is not an acceptable human work, it is a gift of God's grace. He sees an incident from the story of the Fall as a "figure" of this "divine pull" (as opposed to human striving): "Just as God made fur clothing for Adam and Eve, so we must be clad with the Lamb Jesus Christ, by God, our Father."[76]

The gist of his tract is to encourage peace and unity "that there may be no more disputes between you, as unfortunately there have been in the past." This is a warning to those "enthusiasts"

---

[75] *Von Kaufmannshandlung und Wucher* 1524.
[76] *WA* 18:427.

amongst them who, by appealing to Ezekiel 29:3-5 and
Revelation 19:17-21, claimed to be already involved in enforcing
God's judgment in that they had taken the role of the birds who
partake of the Great Eucharist by eating "the flesh of kings and
the flesh of captains" (Rev. 19:18). "Alas, there are many such
birds in Livonia – avoid them as you would the plague."
Hoffman states more precisely that these "birds" are those
"unscrupulous men who fight against human and heavenly
images – without Christ, having faith only in their big
mouths,"[77] – i.e. the iconoclasts who do not have true
evangelical faith but who use attacks on the old church to give
vent to their personal anger. Although God's wrath is now
falling on "princes, lords and godless men" and "sin will be
punished with sin," the Christian does not participate in this
judgment by using the sword. His job is not to avenge evil, he
must leave vengeance to the Lord. "For Christ does not shine
forth where there is malice, hatred, division, anger or rebellion;
the sun has set there and there is no light."[78]

Since Luther himself had an apocalyptic outlook during this
period of the last stages of the Peasants' War,[79] Hoffman's
eschatological speculations were also an expression of the views
of the Wittenberg Reformers. Hoffman's work clearly stressed
all of Luther's most important ideas: justification by faith alone,
faith as a gift of divine grace, the need for the Christian to
renounce the use of force and any vengeful desires. There were
thus no grounds on which the Reformers could have refused to
testify to Hoffman's orthodoxy.

5. Hoffman's Early Theology. The Controversy with the Lutheran Clergy of Livonia.

Hoffman returned to Livonia in the autumn of 1525 with
increased self-confidence. But the situation to which he returned

[77] *WA* 18:428.
[78] *WA* 18:428.
[79] M. Greschat, "Luthers Haltung im Bauernkrieg" in *ARG* 56
(1965) pp. 31-47.

was radically altered. The knights of the episcopal domain had reverted to Catholicism, the evangelical magistrates were determined to tolerate no further disturbances, revolutionary ferment had died down in the cities and the triumphal progress of the Reformation had been halted. Only in the countryside was there any remaining social unrest.[80]

During the six months of Hoffman's absence Tegetmeier had divided the Dorpat congregation into two parties – opponents and supporters of the lay missionary.[81] This controversy had its origins in the ambitions and power struggles of the two opponents. Hoffman considered Tegetmeier to be an "inflated spirit", who thought he understood something about "divine wisdom" simply because he had a knowledge of the three ancient languages.[82] Since their disagreements involved such fundamental issues as the relationship between "prophets" and ministers, divine inspiration and wisdom derived from texts, the rights of the congregations in comparison with those of their ministers, the interpretation of the Eucharist and eschatology, the remaining Livonian clergy (and in the end the magistrates in the cities) were eventually drawn into the controversy. It is to this dispute that we owe Hoffman's "To the Livonian assembly"[83] and his commentary on Daniel, Chapter 12.[84] He wrote to keep his followers true to his doctrine after his departure from Livonia and in order to defend himself against a polemic work by Tegetmeier (which has since been lost).[85]

a) Prophet versus scholar

The controversy brought into the open the conflicting claims

---

[80] The first peasant uprising in Samland took place in September 1525: W.C. Schütz, *Historia Rerum Prussicarum. Continuatio durch David Chyträus* Eisleben 1599 f.505-506, and *AR* III No. 242 (a complaint by the knights of Harrien-Wierland against Reval charging the town of instigating the peasants against their feudal lords, March 1527).

[81] *An de gelöfighen vorsambling* A5a.

[82] *Ibid* A4b.

[83] *An de gelöfighen vorsambling inn Liflandt ein korte formaninghe* 1526 (Reprint ed. by A. Buchholtz in *Festschrift für M.D. Taube* Riga, 1856)

[84] *Das XII Capitel des propheten Daniels aussgelegt . . .* (Stockholm: Royal printers) 1526.

[85] *Daniel* 1a; *An de gelöfighen vorsambling* A5a.

to spiritual authority propounded by the self-appointed prophets on the one hand and the elected clergy on the other. Hoffman demanded that the "power of human reason" be put aside when dealing with the exposition of the Bible.[86] Human reason is Satan's doctrine, if it conflicts with divine wisdom. "Our most respected schools are not fountains of divine teaching", but go to make up part of the devilish trinity of Pope, Emperor and false doctors.[87] The equation "poor in body – rich in spirit" has always been valid. "Thus God's wisdom cannot be perceived with (the) bodily eyes but only with the eyes of the spirit which look neither at the outer person nor at his social rank."[88] "Thus the true scholar is not he who is knowledgeable in books but he whose knowledge is of the spirit."[89]

The "over-weening" book-scholars laugh at Hoffman because he is an artisan.[90] They think it impossible for "a layman or a furrier to be able to expound God's word as truly as their own scribblings, because they have been taught Scripture since childhood. A furrier should have spent the same amount of time in study as a Cathedral priest or monk (if he is to preach)".[91]

Hoffman considered that his battle against the "scholarly servants of the belly" was a stance on behalf of the poor and the oppressed who, according to the promise of the prophet Joel (Joel 2:28–30), would now at the end of time receive the Holy Spirit. "Those accounted wise will be found empty of wisdom and sterile but the barren will be made fruitful and filled with the wisdom of God."[92] As it was at the time of Jesus' birth so it is again; the shepherds and their flocks went off to the manger in Bethlehem whilst the priests and pharisees stayed at home, "and so it will happen now: the 'big-wigs' will pay no attention to Christ and they will not find Him within their spirits, but the

---

[86] *Daniel* a2a-b.
[87] *Daniel* f4b.
[88] *Daniel* f1b.
[89] *Daniel* d4a.
[90] *Daniel* IIb, i2a.
[91] *Daniel* n3a.
[92] *Daniel* d4a.

simple and unlearned will seek for Him and follow Him... and share in His spiritual Eucharist."[93]

The language of nature teaches us the following law: the higher a mountain rises the colder and more barren it is. "Thus the higher men reach in terms of nobility, power and worldly wisdom, so much less can they be warmed by the bright sun of Christ or by the wisdom of God... But the deeper the valleys are, the more fertile do they become and the warmer does the sun shine in them – thus it is also with men."[94]

Poverty and humiliation, however, offer no guarantees that somebody is God's child. Only God's elect inherit His Kingdom, even if He should whip them into it.[95] Signs of being elected are – besides poverty – the fear of God; freedom from fear of man, delight in God's law, and the humble, battered heart which in suffering has become open and prepared for the entry of the heavenly bridegroom.[96]

b) The spirit and the letter

Human wisdom can only grasp the literal meaning of the text of Scripture, yet this is not in fact the true meaning. A spiritual meaning lies hidden beneath the literal text which can only be revealed to prophets who are filled with the Spirit of God.[97] Hoffman uses the four symbols of the evangelists to distinguish between the four different forms of God's Word, three of them figurative and one explicit. The "figures" of the lion and the ox were dominant in the Old Testament. The "lion" symbolizes the letter of the Law of Moses and the "ox" (clumsy and ludicrous in its movements) represents the symbols and prefigurations in the Old Testament which (often so coarsely or comically) point forward to the later fulfilment of salvation history. In the New Testament the "human face" (a symbol of the simple parables of Jesus, which the human mind finds so easy to understand) and the "eagle" take over. The "eagle" symbolises the unmasked Spirit of God. The "eagle" ("whom God's children feel in their

---

[93] *Daniel* f2a.
[94] *Daniel* d1a.
[95] *Daniel* c3a, d1a.
[96] *Daniel* a3b, a4a, b1a, f1b, h2b.
[97] *Daniel* a2a-b.

hearts") must thus be discovered within the other three forms of God's Word, for it lies "covered up" beneath them.[98] Hence a second spiritual realm is uncovered underneath the first "fleshly" one. The eyes of the spirit can thus reveal that in the Bible "heaven" can also mean the soul of man that is filled with God and that "stars or angels" can refer to the teachers of the people. The movement of the planets described in the Synoptic Gospels (Mark 13:25, Matt. 24:29) is an allegory for the crowding together of the clergy at the Last Judgment, and the "fall of the stars" refers to the fall of the preachers away from the truth.[99] With the help of "spiritual" interpretation Hoffman was able to change cosmic and miraculous events into historical and psychological events. The biblical past could come to life as a prefiguration of future happenings. But the biblical text loses some of its simple meaning and becomes illustrative material for the prophet's imagination.

c) The minister and the congregation

If the authority for preaching comes not from scholarship but from possessing the Spirit of God, and if the Spirit is given primarily to the "poor and simple," then a new understanding of the congregation is called for. Scripture says that all pastors, elders and deacons are to be elected from amongst the congregation.[100] Hoffman dismissed the objection that there were not necessarily learned people in every congregation; at the time of the apostles, he said, all of the leaders were unlearned. There are no princes or lords in a Christian congregation, just brothers and sisters.

"For in spiritual matters they are directed by no head but Christ, the Saviour. Thus it should be that all teachers are only servants."[101]

Yet in the whole of Livonia not a single pastor was elected by the congregation as prescribed by Scripture;[102] they were all appointed by the secular authorities. Hoffman nevertheless

---

[98] *An de gelöfighen vorsambling* a1b–a2a.
[99] *Daniel* a1b–a2a, a3a, b1a, k2b–k3a, *An de gelöfighen vorsambling* a3a.
[100] *Daniel* l3b.
[101] *Daniel* c1b.
[102] *Daniel* l2b, *An de gelöfighen vorsambling* a4a.

would have been prepared to accept this situation if it did not mean "that the teachers became masters, feathering their own nests and living in comfort, mixing only with other teachers in despising the congregation like Hagar despised her mistress Sarah."[103] They deny the simple members of the congregation their right to preach and prophesy. Their motto is:

"We alone are right and strong;
What we decree goes for the throng."[104]

They are thus setting themselves up in opposition to the present age, which is marked by the outpouring of the spirit on the unlearned, and to the early church's idea of the congregation as described by St. Paul in I Corinthians 14. Everyone must be allowed to speak in the assembly, and if there is contention over a prophecy people must accept the decision of the whole congregation concerning its correct interpretation.[105]

The suppression of the congregation will lead to the spiritual death of the new church. The teachers are out for profit and their thinking is "according to the flesh" whilst the "man in the pew" is sleeping his deep spiritual sleep in the pastor's church. The actions of both deny true faith.[106] Inflated prices and usury govern public life whilst private life is dominated by the vice of drunkenness. [107]

Hoffman, like Müntzer and the Anabaptists, sees the church as a charismatic community in which all inspired people have an equal authority. This led Hoffman later on to begin some of his tracts with a text from Revelation (1:6): Christ has made believers "kings and priests before God."[108]

It was not until 1530 that Hoffman drew from this doctrine the practical conclusion that true believers and people possessed of the Holy Spirit should be separated from the common mass of the "godless." It should be remembered that it was not until

[103] Daniel 13b, An de gelöfighen vorsambling a4a.
[104] "Wij heben recht und macht allein; watt wij setten, dat gilt gemein" An de gelöfighen vorsambling a4a.
[105] Daniel 14a, An de gelöfighen vorsambling a4a-b.
[106] Daniel IIa, 13b-14a.
[107] Daniel 12a, e3b.
[108] Cf. eg. his commentary on Revelation, Prophetische Gesicht and Weissagung (all from 1530).

1527 (i.e. after the Schleitheim Confession) that the Swiss Anabaptists finally moved towards separation, though they had initially wanted to establish a non-separatist, congregationalist system. Even Grebel and Mantz, who (unlike the Anabaptist leaders in the rural Swiss congregations) veered towards separatism as early as the autumn of 1524, had first (in 1523) attempted to bring about a radical and far-reaching reform of the church, state and society by means of new elections for the Zürich Council.[109]

Hoffman's recommendations are obviously consonant with Luther's doctrine of the priesthood of all believers and his thesis of 1523 "that a Christian assembly or congregation has the power to judge all doctrine and to elect, establish and dismiss teachers." [110] But the impact of the Peasants' War meant that the Wittenberg Reformers began to qualify the principles they had been preaching. Luther explained that the priesthood of all believers was no warrant to give anyone the right to speak in public or celebrate the sacraments.[111] Preachers had to be elected, but in such a way that the congregation's right was, in practice, reduced to the "ius praesentandi" of the "noblest members" of the church, i.e. the feudal lords, patricians and princes. There was no longer any question of giving congregations the right to judge doctrine. This role was taken by the church government of the princely territories, which – in co-operation with the consistories – enforced a uniform doctrine throughout the territory in order to scotch dissension and the uproar of "the rabble". [112]

As against this, between 1521 and 1524 Karlstadt had been

[109] Cf. J.M. Stayer "Die Anfänge des Schweizerischen Täufertums im reformierten Kongregationalismus" and M. Haas, "Der Weg der Täufer in die Absonderung", both in H.-J. Goertz (ed), *Umstrittenes Täufertum* 2nd ed. Göttingen 1977, pp. 19 – 78.

[110] *WA* 11:408-416.

[111] *WA* 31(i):211.

[112] cf. Luther, *Instruction for the Visitors of Parish Pastors in Electoral Saxony* 1528, *LW* 40:269-320, *WA* 26: 195, 200. Luther's theory was that there was no conflict between the priesthood of all believers and this advice for the Christian princes and magistrates to act as members of the church who represented the congregations. But in practice the congregations lost their autonomy.

radicalizing Luther's doctrine of the priesthood of all believers. In contrast to Luther he felt that the "simple children of God" (i.e. the peasants and the craftsmen) were superior to the "crowned doctors and masters of Scripture" in matters of divine wisdom. Because of this he anticipated Hoffman in pressing for a restoration of the constitution of the Christian congregation as it was in primitive Christianity (I Cor. 14). He supported the right of congregations to present their own interpretations of the faith and to contradict their preachers. [113] We should almost certainly conclude that Hoffman was influenced by Karlstadt on this issue.

d) The tyranny of auricular confession

Hoffman had already had a sharp disagreement with Tegetmeier about auricular confession before his journey to Wittenberg. Hoffman had released his congregation in Dorpat from the duty of making a confession but Tegetmeier wanted to restore it since, he said, he had never seen a faith strong enough to make anyone able to receive communion without a confession first. A doctor had to see a wound before he can heal it. [114] For Hoffman the continuation of auricular confession was the strongest indication that the priests had a lust for power, they wanted to "investigate the inner secrets of the heart." Their supremacy was reinforced by the system whereby everyone was bound to a particular priest as his confessor. But Hoffman's proposed solution – to allow people to make what was an essentially general confession individually, found no favour. Even Bugenhagen's intervention on behalf of Hoffman's approach to this question could not shift the Livonian clergy from their stubborn opposition. [115]

Hoffman also saw auricular confession as another example of the rejection of the New Testament view of the congregation. In the early church people received communion because of their faith, not because they had made their confession. [116]

Hoffman allowed three forms of confession:

[113] A. Karlstadt, *Eyn Frage ob auch yemand möge selig werden on die fürbitte Marie* Wittenberg 1524, C3a.
[114] *Daniel* n2a.
[115] *Daniel* o2b.
[116] *Daniel* n3b.

1. The private confession of the sinner to God,
2. Confession to the person the sinner had wronged,
3. The confession of a tormented heart to a man experienced in spiritual things if one has not found peace by private repentance to God or by a confession to those he has wronged. This third type of confession should never be compulsory but left to the free choice of the disturbed person.

The congregation, and not just the minister, should have the right to exclude someone from the Eucharist because of his immoral life (but only if he had refused to repent after three warnings).[117]

Andrew Karlstadt was probably Hoffman's source for these ideas, too. In a tract on auricular confession published in 1524[118] he had argued that faith, not confession, makes someone worthy to receive communion, that the church's power to "bind and loose" belongs to the whole congregation (and this only applies in connection with public sin) and finally that a man's feelings of guilt should attract him to the Lord's Table, not cut him off from it.

e) The Eucharistic controversy

It appears that Hoffman accepted the Lutheran doctrine of the Eucharist, for he says that Paul and the evangelists would have agreed with the following statement: "Whoever eats of the bread eats of the Lord's body and whoever drinks of the cup drinks of the Lord's blood."[119] But if we enquire what "eat" and "drink" mean in this context we find that there is little sign of the Lutheran doctrine of Christ's real presence in the Eucharistic elements. According to Hoffman's interpretation the Eucharist is a purely spiritual communion of the believer with Christ.

The "eating" in the Eucharist has a double meaning for him. Firstly Christ must eat us so that we become one with him. Man is "slain" by the sword of God's Word, and Christ "eats" men daily through his preachers and the proclamation of the Law and the Gospel. But the believer also "eats" Christ, in that in the

---

[117] *Daniel* n4a-b, o4a.
[118] *Ayn Sermon ob dye Orenbeicht oder der Glaub allain oder was den menschen zu wirdiger empfahung des heiligen Sacraments geschickt macht* 1524.
[119] *Daniel* m2b.

Eucharist he thinks of Christ's death for him and realises that only this faith can redeem him. Anyone trusting in his own works cannot receive the Eucharist. "Wherever the Lord's Supper is to take place there must be a believing heart. There must be an open door and an empty home within so that Christ can enter there... Thus in the hearts of all disbelievers Christ's body is *not* received and Christ's blood is *not* drunk."[120] "This simply is what Christians believe about entering the body and drinking the blood of Christ Jesus; he eats them and they eat him, as stated above. He eats their bodies by His word and by His preachers. They eat His body and drink His blood by faith."[121]

Thus the union of Christ with the soul can only come about in the spirit by the Word and by faith.[122] Whoever believes the Word has eaten Christ's body and drunk his blood. Thus the elect no longer look towards the "flesh," which is of "no avail" (John 6:63).[123] Hoffman drew the following conclusions from these principles:

1. Since there is no real presence of Christ in the Eucharistic elements it is meaningless to keep the host in a monstrance in the belief that God is present in it.[124]

2. Since God should only be worshipped in spirit, the elevation of the cup and its accompanying veneration in the form of genuflections is an abuse which must be abolished.[125]

Although Hoffman did not explicitly attack Luther's Eucharistic doctrine in his commentary on Daniel, he did prepare the ground here for a later confrontation. Hoffman totally agrees with Karlstadt in his belief that the participant in the Eucharist can only be united to Christ by faith.[126] Karlstadt's main reason for rejecting the real presence of Christ in the bread and the wine was his conviction that it repudiated the uniqueness of Christ's

---

[120] *Daniel* m3a-b, m4b.
[121] *Daniel* n2a.
[122] *Daniel* m4a.
[123] *Daniel* n1b-n2a.
[124] *Daniel* n1a.
[125] *Daniel* n1b.
[126] A. Karlstadt, *Ob man mit heyliger geschrifft erweysen möge/das Christus mit leyb/ blut/ und sele in sacrament sey* 1524, f2b–f4a.

sacrifice on the cross. Karlstadt argued against the elevation of the cup on the same grounds. To him elevation was a symbol of sacrifice because sacrificial offerings in the Old Testament were raised up in the same way.[127]

Hoffman appears then in his view of the congregation and in his doctrines of auricular confession and of the Eucharist to have been a disciple of Karlstadt.

f) The apocalyptic interpretation of the age

Hoffman was most violently criticised by the evangelical preachers for his doctrine that the Last Judgment was imminent.[128] He saw his own age as the time when people were being for the last time invited to the Supper of the Lamb.[129] In particular he envisaged the following eschatological process:

In the Reformation God has replaced his wrath with his grace.[130] The Holy Spirit is again being poured out on all peoples and God's messengers proclaim the Gospel throughout the whole earth.[131] No violence will be needed to spread the new faith; its preachers should use only the word of God as a weapon, not the sword of the secular powers. "The sword will be used solely against evil-doers. The only force used by the shepherds will be the preaching of God's word and the punishment of sinners. No one is to be intimidated by violence."[132] Despite this renunciation of force, this first phase of the apocalyptic tumult is a time of fear and trembling for the godless. They will be squeezed in the press of God's Law. The good days are over for the priests and their concubines.[133] The Pope will be seen to be a corrupter and Antichrist, because he has put himself in the place of Christ and because he has suppressed God's Word with his lies and false laws. It is already common knowledge that the "merciful dispenser of grace" in

---

[127] A. Karlstadt, *Wider die alte und neue papistische Messen* 1524, A2b–A3a.
[128] *Daniel* II b, IIIa.
[129] *Daniel* c2a–b.
[130] *Daniel* a3a.
[131] *Daniel* d3b.
[132] *Daniel* b1b.
[133] *Daniel* b2b–b3a, F2b.

Rome has used his usurped power of the keys only in order to make money and to persecute "God's saints," such as, in former times, Jan Hus.[134]

The climax will be reached when the world will receive its punishment at the appearance of the "two witnesses" (Rev. 11). They are reincarnations of the prophets Elijah and Enoch and will remove the Pope from the inner sanctuary of the saints. They will visit vengeance upon the godless for either 1,260 (Rev. 11:3) or 1,290 (Daniel 12:11) days. The two witnesses are already alive, but are not yet known.[135] The Pope and the world will suffer great persecution and will call on the Emperor Charles V, "the highest man in Christendom," for help. Hoffman identifies him with the "red dragon" of the Book of Revelation.[136] The dragon will persecute God's saints and at the end of the first period of three and a half years he will slay the two witnesses.[137]

With this begins the second phase of the eschaton which will last for another three and a half years (or perhaps 1,335 days – Rev. 11:2, 12:14, Daniel 12:7, 12:12).[138] All Christians will have to escape into the wilderness during this period, and it will be forbidden to preach God's Word in public. As "faith's sun" sets in the world "faith's moon" will rise in the hearts of believers,[139] who will be taught directly by God. Here (in the commentary on Daniel) spiritualism has a very specific role in history; it is the particular form of faith in the last age. Later Hoffman will come to see the reception of the Holy Spirit as the goal of spiritual growth for all men.

During the messianic disturbances the common people will be confused by "powerful errors" and a third of all preachers will fall away from the true faith.[140] But two pious kings will give temporary protection to the true church (symbolised by the

---

[134] *Daniel* b3b, F2b.
[135] *Daniel* f4a, g1a.
[136] *Daniel* a3b.
[137] *Daniel* g1b.
[138] *Daniel* i1a.
[139] *Daniel* g1b, g2a.
[140] *Daniel* i4b; *An de gelöfighen vorsambling* a3a.

"woman clothed with the sun" in Rev. 12), thus saving it from destruction.[141] During the persecution of the believers Duke George of Saxony, "the bloodhound of Meissen," and King Sigismund of Poland, will grow in power and by their scheming lead many of their colleagues to imitate their cruelty.[142] The spiritual turmoil will come to a head in a great council in which there will be a futile exchange between true and false ideas. The worst is still to come: the pagan people of Gog and Magog will knock down the newly built spiritual temple and destroy the godly people. Then the sign of the Son of Man will appear in the sky and the elect will have to take up the cross. And then when night has finally fallen on earth, Christ will appear in the clouds of heaven. He will redeem the elect and judge the world according to the principle "What you have done to the least of these, you have done to me."[143]

When will all this happen? Hoffman's clear reply in the commentary on Daniel, is "now."[144] Hoffman says the following about the date of the "sixth trumpet": "The sixth trumpet is being sounded *now* (1526). It is a fine sound, a cry of Christ and God's Word to the false shepherds and to Antichrist and his followers." The age of the sixth trumpet, the time when all falsehood will be revealed, lasts for only three and a half years. Then we will hear the evil sound of the seventh trumpet. "As soon as the seventh trumpet sounds and the sixth is past, all things will be fulfilled in the time of the seventh... the trumpet will sound and the Antichrist will only have three and a half years left to reign." [145] Thus there will only be seven years between the time of writing of the commentary (1526) and the

---

[141] *Daniel* g2a-b.

[142] *Daniel* k2b.

[143] *Daniel* g3a.

[144] *Against* P. Kawerau, *op. cit.* p. 100. Kawerau concluded that Hoffman had not specified a date because he only knew the commentary on Daniel from the passages printed by Krohn and because he accepted Hoffman's claim that he had not specified "a day or hour" (in his polemical work against Amsdorf, *Das Nicholas Amsdorff*, 1528, a2a). In the Commentary on Daniel (f1a) on the other hand, Hoffman said that "the hour and the day is not the same as the time and the year", which we can know.

[145] *Daniel* g1b-g2a.

Last Judgment. Christ will return in Judgment in 1533. Hoffman makes this clear again in the following passages: "Some say if we tell them that there are only seven years left on earth before the Last Judgment they will stop working."[146]

For Hoffman the proclamation of the imminence of the Last Judgment was the most important element of his preaching. His own self-confidence relied so much on this that he eventually (after 1530) saw himself in the role of *Elijah redivivus*. It was his message of the approaching end of the world which, when fused with anticlerical and anti-intellectual prejudices, gave Hoffman such a mass-appeal and won him such a following.

We shall now attempt to trace the literary sources Hoffman used for his apocalyptic doctrines. We shall then investigate the religious traditions and historical factors which favoured the spread of his eschatological ideas in Livonia and later throughout Germany.

The literary model for Hoffman's commentary on Daniel was Luther's exposition of the Gospel for the second Sunday in Advent (Luke 21:15-36) which he had published in the *Church Postills* of 1522.[147] It was from this that Hoffman derived the allegorical interpretations he gave to the cosmic events connected with the coming of the Last Judgment, e.g. the identification of the sun with Christ, of the stars with spiritual teachers, of the darkening of the sun with the prohibition of public preaching, of the fall of the stars with the apostasy of Christians and of the movement of the planets with the council of the spiritual tyrants.[148] Hoffman also took his most important proof of the imminence of the Last Judgment from Luther's exegesis. For Luther it was the conviction that the Pope was in fact Antichrist which formed the major reason for feeling that the Last Judgment was not far off: "This point more than any other makes me believe that Christ must come soon."[149] This

---

[146] *Daniel* g4a. But in order for Hoffman's programme to relate to *actual* conditions he also says that the world is not prepared to believe the day is so close (*Daniel* IIIa).

[147] *WA* 10(1, 2,): 93-120.

[148] *WA* 10(1, 2,): 118-120.

[149] *WA* 10(1, 2): 97.

idea clearly derives from Paul himself who taught that Christ would not return until Antichrist was revealed seated in the heart of the Temple (2 Thess. 2:3-4). Hoffman found Luther's other arguments for the imminence of doomsday (such as fearful constellations in the sky, eclipses of the sun and the moon, the appearance of miracles and monsters in nature) to be unconvincing.[150] The interpretation of the "signs of the times" was a matter for "prophets", not for "astronomers."[151] It is the Bible, not nature, that is our guide to the future.

Luther also anticipated Hoffman's projected scheme for the unfolding of the messianic cataclysm. The reformer himself had already applied the parable of the fig tree that bears leaves, but no fruit, to the Reformation. "I am worried that we will be left with nothing but leaves. We speak much of true faith, but do nothing."[152] Hoffman expressed the same idea in his image of the spring of the world. Spring had arrived because of the preaching of the Gospel, but it would turn to winter before the fruit ripened.[153] Luther clarified his position in later years; he said that after the unmasking of the Antichrist would come the triumph of the Epicureans and of the atheists. Godlessness, he predicted, would reach its height between the fall of the Pope and the appearance of Christ.[154] But what had been a vague feeling for Luther became Hoffman's firm conviction; to him the Reformation itself would fail and give way to a period of godlessness.

Finally, Hoffman's evaluation of the secular authorities was also essentially Lutheran. Hoffman saw their role as that of "servants of God, established to punish wickedness," even though the authorities often acted now "by using the sword to protect evildoers and to punish the just."[155] Yet we never find Hoffman propounding a theory that it might be incompatible with Christian faith to hold a magisterial office. But on the other

---

[150] *WA* 10(1, 2): 97-99, 104-105, 108; *WA Br* 3:464.
[151] *Daniel* III b.
[152] *WA* 10(1,2): 120.
[153] *Daniel* 11a-12b.
[154] *WA* 50: 119-120: *WA Br* 10: 335.
[155] *Daniel* a4a.

hand secular authorities should not be used as a means of violently enforcing God's truth.[156] This was also ruled out by Luther's doctrine of the divergent functions of the church and secular powers. Finally Hoffman also agreed with Luther that the princes had the right and duty to prevent the destruction of Christendom threatened by the Pope and the Emperor. On this basis Hoffman, as well as Luther, Zwingli and Calvin developed a new way of bringing together spiritual and secular power.

But despite these agreements about eschatology we must not overlook two important differences between Luther and Hoffman:

1. For Luther, being concerned with apocalyptic ideas was always a secondary matter. We can see from his preface to the Book of Revelation (1522) how little he was affected by apocalyptic speculation; he said that the work was neither apostolic nor prophetic and that his own interpretation was no more binding on his readers than that of anyone else.[157] Luther's "prophetic" playing about with figures never went far enough to make him specify a date in the immediate future at which Christ would return. In his exposition of Daniel chapter 12, dating from 1530, he interprets the 1,290 days and the 1,335 days as years which are already in the past (from the death of Christ to the Great Schism). He consequently states that the Last Judgment cannot be far off, but says that it will not be possible to understand all of the prophecies until they have been fulfilled.[158] In the *Supputatio Annorum Mundi* of 1540 Luther spoke of a 2,000 year reign of the Messiah after which would come the Last Judgment. [159]

2. What is more, in Luther there is no trace of the idea that the

---

[156] *Daniel* b2a.

[157] *WA DB* 7:404.

[158] *WA DB* 11(2): 12, 48.

[159] *WA* 53, 22. From the extensive literature on Luther's apocalyptic ideas the following stand out: W.A. Quanbeck, "Luther and the Apocalyptic" in V. Vajta (ed.), *Luther und Melanchthon* 1961, pp. 119–128 (Referate und Berichte des Zweiten Internationalen Kongresses für Lutherforschung); J.M. Headley, *Luther's View of Church History* (Yale 1963); U. Asendorf, *Eschatologie bei Luther* (Göttingen, 1967).

messianic cataclysm would also bring about compensation in the form of higher spiritual knowledge. He did not believe in a new outpouring of the Holy Spirit granted to "servants and maids" or in any "rising of the full moon within the Christian heart"[160] after the setting of the sun of the external Word and the ending of ordered preaching. Luther's apocalypticism has no relationship whatsoever with the idea of an underground church of directly inspired people which would dispense with sacraments and the external Word.

Hoffman was probably influenced by the followers of Hans Hut or by central German Anabaptist groups in his division of the end-time into two three-and-a-half-year periods, separated by the death of the two witnesses. But Hoffman did not take over the idea propounded by Hut that the Anabaptists, when given a sign by God, would exact vengeance on the godless.[161]

It was from the traditions of the Zwickau Prophets and Thomas Müntzer that Hoffman derived the concept of the elect, at the time of the separation of the wheat from the chaff, no longer relying on Scripture alone because "they will study the living Word of God directly from God's mouth."[162]

Although we are on firm ground in our analysis of Hoffman's various precursors and influences it is more difficult to assess the strength of the apocalyptic-heretical tradition in Livonia on which he was building. That such a tradition existed we can gather from the following evidence:

1. A commentary on the Book of Revelation by John Purvey (a disciple of John Wycliffe) was known in Livonia. Early in 1527 Johannes Briessmann, the reformer of Königsberg, sent a copy to Luther from Riga where he had discovered it. Luther published it with his own preface in 1528.[163] Even this commentary, written somewhere around 1390, identified the Pope with Antichrist. Purvey's prophecy was that the power of

---

[160] Hoffman, *Daniel* g2a.

[161] On Hut's connections with Hoffman and the Melchiorites of Strasbourg, cf. the section below on "The arrival of Hut's form of Anabaptism in Strasbourg".

[162] T. Müntzer, *Schriften und Briefe* (ed. G. Franz) 1968, p. 504.

[163] *WA* 26:121, 131; *WA Br* 4, No. 1103 p. 204.

the Roman Antichrist would soon be destroyed by the Word of Christ and by the sword of the Emperor.

2. In about 1470 Johannes Hilten issued a great deal of apocalyptic anti-papal propaganda in Dorpat. He was a *frater legens* for the Franciscans and was obviously familiar with the ideas of Franciscan spirituality. His commentaries on Daniel and Revelation predicted the fall of the papacy and the ending of the religious orders which would come about "around 1516" through an "irresistible" monk. Hilten was imprisoned at Eisenach in the cloister's jail in 1477.[164]

3. Nikolaus Rutze, a Master of Arts from Rostock, was spreading Hussite ideas throughout the eastern Hanseatic region (including Livonia) around 1500.[165] Rutze found asylum for a while in Livonia after his expulsion from Rostock. Rutze's heir, Hans Kaffmeister the younger, who inherited those tracts of Hus's that had been translated into Low German, also had Livonian connections. After he was forced to escape from Rostock in 1526 or 1527, he appeared in Riga. Whilst there he probably sought the help of his relative Heinrich Kaffmeister, a member of the Black-Headed Guild and a co-founder of Riga's first evangelical congregation (1521–1522).[166] It was from Hans Kaffmeister the younger, too, that Karlstadt's friend Martin Reinhart got hold of a tract containing the Hussites' "four Articles of Eger" dating from 25th July, 1430. These demanded (1) the dispossession of all priests including their renunciation of secular overlordship; (2) the duty of priests and the right of deacons to proclaim the gospel throughout the world as poor wandering preachers; (3) the moral perfection of bishops and the

---

[164] Cf. L. Arbusov, *Die Einführung der Reformation* pp. 159ff. Friedrich Myconius informed Luther of Hilten's prophecies in December 1529 and Luther applied them to himself, *WA Br* 5, No. 1501, *WA* 53:410.

[165] S. Hoyer, "Nikolaus Rutze und die Verbreitung hussitischer Gedanken im Hanseraum" in K. Fritze, E. Müller-Mertens and J. Schildhauer (ed.), *Neue Hansische Studien* 1970, pp. 157-170; K. Schmaltz, *Kirchengeschichte Mecklenburgs* Vol. 2, 1936, pp. 10-11; S. Hoyer, "Martin Reinhard und der erste Druck Hussitischer Artikel in Deutschland" in *ZfG* 18(1970), pp. 1597-1615.

[166] L. Arbusov, *Einführung der Reformation* p. 166.

imposition of excommunication to punish mortal sins; and (4) communion in both kinds for the laity. Martin Reinhart published this tract in 1524.

Hoffman's writings show that he was familiar with Hussite ideas. Jan Hus is the only figure in the whole of medieval church history he makes any reference to in his books. Hussite ideas appear as early as his commentary on Daniel.[167] In his later writings Hoffman presents the Hussite movement as the "third rise of the Holy Spirit" in the course of world history (the first two were the missions to the Jews and to the Gentiles). Hoffman also took over the Hussite concept of the "apostolic messengers" who are sent out with no possessions to proclaim the Gospel throughout the earth.[168] Hoffman's idea, already propounded in the commentary on Daniel, of the impossibility of forgiveness for sin committed after enlightenment, possibly also reflects the Hussite stress on moral rectitude.[169]

Amongst the "concrete factors" which first aroused despair and then apocalyptic fantasies is surely the role of the Catholic Prelates. On the one hand they were incapable of modernising the antiquated and hopelessly fractured political and social structure of Livonia, but on the other they still retained enough power to prevent any radical reforms. Another element present in Hoffman's commentary on Daniel is his disappointment over the outcome of the Reformation. Despite the doctrine of the priesthood of all believers it was apparent by 1526 that the Livonian laity was again being oppressed but now by the "ordained" evangelical theologians. Both experiences are reflected in his eschatological programme; the old church (of Antichrist) will not be totally defeated by the preaching of the Gospel, and he prophesies that the spiritual Temple of the new church will be destroyed before the old church is defeated.

---

[167] *Daniel* f2b. cf. also *Der leuchter des alten Testaments* 1530 A4a–b and the Commentary on Revelation, E8a, F52b–F53a, K4b, K6a, P7a–b.

[168] *TAE* II No. 368 p. 19 and Hoffman's commentary on Romans (1553), S7b.

[169] *Daniel* d1a.

Naturally apocalyptic convictions cannot be accounted for simply on the basis of the situation in Livonia. However, their particular violence here (and the iconoclastic uprisings associated with them) are probably due to the fact that ecclesiastical princes still held political power in the area. On the other hand, this apocalypticism is obviously related to a tradition of eschatological thinking that we find throughout the 15th century in various parts of Europe – amongst the Lollards in England, the Hussites in Bohemia, the Franciscan spiritualists and Savonarola's followers in Italy. What they had in common was the experience that Christ's representatives were preoccupied with building up the Church's power (no matter by what scandalous means) rather than concentrating their energies on introducing urgently needed reforms. All apocalyptic tracts denounce the Pope as Antichrist because he has confused secular power with spiritual authority. What is true of the Pope on one level, is true of the bishops on another. The discrepancy between what the church preached about the rejection of power and riches (the Sermon on the Mount) and what it practised, was so enormous that throughout Europe there developed the idea that the devil himself, in the person of the Pope, had established himself in the holy of holies.

Secular authorities used these ideas sometimes deliberately as propaganda to hasten the destruction of the Pope's power. In order to concentrate and enforce their authority princes and towns were no longer prepared to leave the clergy with unlimited control of the churches in their domains. Thus this propaganda against Antichrist was used to bring about a mixture of spiritual and secular power in a new form, viz, the caesaropapism of the territorial princes.

The disappointment over what the Reformation had in fact managed to achieve was as strong as the anger against the Pope and the Prelates at the beginning of the 16th century. The hoped-for transformation "from top to toe" of the whole of life did not materialize.

The Peasants' War had crushed this hope for the "common people" in the regions that had rebelled. And finally there was the increasing sense of doom brought about by the advance of the Turks in south-eastern Europe, who came to be identified with Gog and Magog, the apocalyptic figures of the last days.[170]

g) The divinisation of man

What is man to do when he realises that "we are in the devil's kingdom and subject to hell's vengeance"?[171] Hoffman's reply is: "Prepare to escape from this prison of death and hell in which you have lain so long like the people of Israel in Egypt, and be led out into the wilderness – the wilderness of the deity."[172] Salvation will not be achieved by armed battles against injustice as the German peasants and the Livonian "enthusiasts" seem to think, but by our inner preparation for the "day of the Lord" which alone can bring us complete liberation. There is no better preparation for this day than the exercise of the highest Christian virtue: *Gelassenheit* (self-surrender).[173] Man must leave behind the world and pride in his works and his tiny, self-centred ego in order to discover in the "wilderness of the deity" an indestructible and unchanging level of spiritual life. The man who achieves *Gelassenheit* finds his fulfilment by rejecting all striving after his own blessedness, yet in this he does find blessedness – "What a great thing it is and a wonderful sight to see a man so divinised in such a state of *Gelassenheit*, that he does not care how God deals with him. To him living or dying, the kingdoms of life and death, are all alike. . . . Even if such a divinised man knew that God were to damn him, indeed that God had created him for damnation, he would still magnify and praise Him just as highly."[174]

The divinised man is no longer concerned about the future. He serves his creator not in order to get to heaven out of self-interest, but out of sheer love. He lives without either hopes or fears. For Hoffman the way of *Gelassenheit* begins by rejecting any idea of justification by one's own works and submitting

---

[170] W.-E. Peuckert, *Die grosse Wende* Vol. 1. 1966, p. 167. The Turks were identified with Gog and Magog as early as 1474 in the pseudonymous tract, *Tractatus de Turcis.*

[171] Hoffman, *Jhesus* in *WA* 18:429.

[172] *Daniel IVa.*

[173] TRANSLATOR'S NOTE. A rough translation of this mystical term might be "self- emptying" but it implies more than this. Not only does the mystic "leave-go" of himself but he also "allows-in" the spirit; both of these elements are contained within the one German word.

oneself to the loving mercy of God as revealed in the sacrifice of Christ. After a man has become a new creature by means of this faith "it comes about that he hates the world and the world hates him. He is crucified to the world and the world is crucified to him."[175] On the path to divinisation man is tested and purified by suffering. In accepting suffering, the mystical and the apocalyptic are fused; the messianic disturbances have a role in leading men towards *Gelassenheit*. "A divinised man must be tried and tested like gold and silver in a furnace... he that the Lord does not punish by persecution or test by affliction is without doubt no child of God."[176] For anyone who cannot endure the testing, and who betrays the truth, it would be better if he had never come to know the way of righteousness, for apostasy from true knowledge into error cannot be made good by a second repentance.[177]

In the commentary on Daniel, Hoffman's theology shows various traces of the conflict between his mystical apocalyptic-ism and his Lutheran heritage. As against his doctrine of human divinisation he also says, like Luther, "that the old Adam will never die to the flesh until it is glorified. The mortal cloak which besmirches and fouls us seven times daily will always be cleansed and whitened by faith in the blood of the lamb."[178] The idea of the Christian as "both sinner and justified at the same time" does not tally with the concept of the divinised man. The idea of testing by means of suffering contradicts his belief in predestination. The doctrine of the unforgivable nature of post-conversion sins can be squared neither with the doctrine of justification by faith alone nor with the idea of election. In the midst of predominantly Lutheran ethics which even counts righteous princes as children of God, and which permits Christians to use the sword, there suddenly appears (well before the Swiss Brethren's Schleitheim Confession) an absolute

---

[174] *Daniel* c3a-b.
[175] *Daniel* h2a.
[176] *Daniel* h2b.
[177] *Daniel* d1a-b.
[178] *Daniel* e2a-b, cf. g3b: "For as long as man lives here the serpent of the old Adam will not die but continue to bite".

prohibition of taking oaths.[179] In view of these contradictions we must question whether Hoffman had properly understood the central point of Luther's doctrine – viz. that it is *sinners* who are accepted by God.

Hoffman, with his doctrine of the divinised man purified by suffering, is going back to the soteriology of medieval mysticism. His exaltation of *Gelassenheit*, of the man who has left behind all fear of punishment and all hope of reward can be found expressed in the same way in Chapter 10 of the *Theologia Deutsch* (the most widely read mystical tract during the whole Reformation period).[180] Karlstadt's writings of 1520–1524 may also have given Hoffman an awareness of some fundamental ideas of mystical piety. The idea Hoffman later put forward, that man has no right to complain to his creator about his fate, can certainly be found in Karlstadt, as can the idea that there is no better way of learning *Gelassenheit* than the experience of suffering.[181]

6. Hoffman's Expulsion from Livonia.

Early in 1526 Hoffman publicly accused the magistrate of Dorpat of embezzling confiscated church property. This put an end to whatever willingness there had been to tolerate him.

One of the burgomasters of Dorpat had had necklaces made for his wife and daughter using golden chalices, i.e. former church property. One day, whilst Hoffman was leading the public worship, the burgomaster's daughter, wearing her necklace, arrived at church a little late. Hoffman, who had a fine

---

[179] *Daniel* e2b–e3a.

[180] G. Baring, "Neues von der Theologia Deutsch und ihrer weltweiten Bedeutung" in *ARG* 48 (1957), pp. 1–10 and *Bibliographie der Ausgaben der Theologia Deutsch 1516–1961* 1963; S.E. Ozment *Mysticism and Dissent* (New Haven and London 1973), pp. 14–60.

[181] A. Karlstadt, *Was gesagt ist/'sich gelassen'/und was das wort gelassenheit bedeut (Augsburg, 1523)* F3a. cf. *Hoffman, Daniel* c3a–b; Karlstadt, *Missive von der allerhöchsten Tugend gelassenheit* 1520, A2b–3b, Hoffman, *Daniel* h2b.

feeling for an impressive stage effect, ordered the members of his congregation to kneel down, for that was the fitting greeting for the golden robe of our Lord Jesus. Because of this public insult to the burgomaster Hoffman was forced to flee the town.[182]

He then went to Reval where he looked after sick peasants in a hospice. Peasants had fled by the hundred to the city after two consecutive harvest failures (in 1524 and 1525) in Harrien-Wierland. The nobles had refused to give them any help; they would not even reduce their taxes.[183] But the magistrate felt that this close connection between the radical spiritualist and former serfs was too dangerous. "He was banished from the land by false brethren who claimed to be evangelicals."[184] Hoffman finally turned his back on Livonia after this third banishment.

After the revolutionary disturbances of 1524-1526 there was a conservative reaction in Livonia in the years after 1527. It was in that year that Johannes Briessmann, the reformer of Königsberg, was entrusted with establishing a new Ecclesiastical Ordinance. In order to dissociate himself unambiguously from both the despisers of the sacrament and the iconoclasts, he decreed that worship should be conducted "rather more reverently and elegantly." Catholic ceremonies were restored. The German services with the hymns were replaced by Latin masses. Priests again had to wear hoods, surplices and cassocks on high feast days. The elevation of the host and cup were to be accompanied by sanctuary bells.[185] Whereas the Ecclesiastical Ordinance of 1524 established that the leading pastor should be elected by both the Council and the congregation, it was decided by the cities at the Diet of Wolmar in 1533 that the ministers of each of the towns could be appointed or dismissed by the Council alone. The approval of the congregation was desirable but not necessary. Preaching by unofficial lay people was firmly forbidden. Official positions should only be given to reliable preachers whose orthodoxy could be attested, if possible by

---

[182] Bredenbach, *Bellum Livonicum* f.26.
[183] *AR* III No. 230 §5.
[184] Hoffman and Karlstadt, *Dialogus* A2b.
[185] E. Sehling, *Kirchenordnungen* Vol. 5 pp. 15-16.

Luther or Melanchthon.[186] Until 1557 the Riga Consistory, which administered the church and settled disputes over matters of faith, consisted exclusively of laymen.[187] Thus the Councils used their dispute with the "enthusiasts" in order to establish a church government controlled by the magistracy, in which there was no longer a trace of autonomy left to the congregations.

7. Conclusions (cf. p. 37).

a) Social disturbances became acute in Livonia during the first quarter of the sixteenth century because of the external threat from Russia and the introduction of demesne-farming. The cities saw the Reformation as an opportunity to end the country's political divisions and to establish a secular duchy by means of the secularisation of the Teutonic Order and the ecclesiastical principalities. The knights in the episcopal domains of Riga, Dorpat and Ösel-Wiek also wanted to deprive the Prelates of their power in order to extend their inheritance-rights and to free themselves from the "duty of giving the first offer." But at the same time the problems associated with the introduction of demesne-farming (the issue of peasant refugees and the nobles' demands to be allowed free access to the markets) created conflicts between the towns and the Junkers. The alliance of local nobility and the towns which had come about in 1522 in opposition to the bishops, was not based on secure foundations.

Demesne-farming had deepened the gulf between the non-German peasants and their German feudal lords, which was also due to national divisions. This brought about the danger of potential revolution, which could easily be set loose by radical evangelical preaching about "the freedom of the Christian man." Compared with the situation in the countryside the social disintegration in the towns was less serious in spite of the great

---

[186] *Ibid.* vol. V p. 40; *AR* III No. 321 §6, 4.
[187] E. Sehling, *Kirchenordnungen* Vol. 5 pp. 10, 19.

differences between the German ruling class and the non-German lower classes. The hatred of the masses was directed not against the German patricians but against the Prelates and monks, whom they damned as representatives of Antichrist. The anger felt towards these alleged parasites found expression in ten great iconoclastic uprisings which followed the introduction of the Reformation.

b) The Hoffmanites in Livonia came from two heterogeneous groups of the population, which were also involved in the iconoclastic movements. The first group was that of the younger German journeyman-merchants who as a rule came from well-to-do families, and who formed the highly respected "Black-Headed Guild." The second group was the non-German urban proletariat. The foreign merchants, who had no civil rights, felt excluded from the existing social order. The "non-Germans", who had only limited rights, were in a desperate position. This unsatisfactory level of social integration explains the readiness of both groups to incline towards radical thinking and activity.

c) The outbreak of iconoclasm in Dorpat was precipitated by an unlawful attempt to arrest Hoffman. Two German townsmen and two non-Germans were killed in the lower city whilst opposing this arrest. No blood was shed in the course of the iconoclastic outburst itself. There is no evidence that Hoffman had called for the destruction of churches or for the expulsion of the canons before his attempted arrest, even if psychologically he had prepared the way for iconoclasm.

d) In view of this iconoclasm and the peasant disturbances, which had been aggravated by the radical evangelical preachers, the nobles ended their agreement with the cities which they had entered into with the purpose of introducing the Reformation. At the height of the crisis, in the winter of 1524/1525, the bishops had renounced their claims to escheat and dispensed with the "duty of giving first offer". The political reform of Livonia urged by the towns never materialised. The radicalism of the iconoclastic movements had isolated the towns and healed the breach between the old feudal authorities. In order to win back the nobles to the cause of the Reformation and to restore calm in their own communities as well, the towns repressed all "enthusiasm" which had a socially critical tenor. Thus Hoffman was forced to leave Livonia in 1526.

e) Hoffman came into conflict with the Livonian clergy over his claim to be an inspired prophet who had the capacity of explaining the "spiritual meanings" that lay behind the literal text of the Bible. At the same time he fought for the rights of the simple laymen within the congregation, i.e. the rights to elect ministers and deacons, to teach and to "prophesy." He saw the church as a charismatic community of equal brothers, though it should not be cut off from the official church or from the rest of society. He opposed auricular confession because of the means of domination it provided to the priests. His Eucharistic doctrine had already diverged from Luther's doctrine of Christ's real presence in the bread and wine. Hoffman's prophecy of the imminence of the Last Judgment, which he said would occur in seven years' time (1533), was strongly opposed by the Livonian clergy. But Hoffman saw the messianic conflict as a time of testing for Christians, not as a prelude to social revolution. Hoffman's attack on a Dorpat Burgomaster, by accusing him of embezzling confiscated church property, eventually led to his own banishment from Livonia.

f) Hoffman regarded himself as a Lutheran up until the end of his time in Livonia. He explicitly confessed to holding the Lutheran doctrines of justification, predestination, and of secular authority.

Yet even at this time the seeds of his later estrangement were apparent. He claimed to be a prophet and to possess a higher knowledge than learned theologians. He used a "figurative" exegesis of the biblical text and believed in a new outpouring of the Holy Spirit, particularly on "servants and maids." He denied the real presence of Christ in the Eucharistic elements. Hoffman's doctrine of the "unforgivable sin" contradicts the idea of eternal election, and his concept of *Gelassenheit* does not fit with the view of the Christian as "both sinner and justified at the same time."

Chapter Two

The Stockholm Interlude (1526-1527).

After his expulsion from Reval Hoffman went next to Stockholm, the emporium of the east European fur trade. The population here was similar in constitution to that of the towns of Livonia; there were many Germans with full civil rights (merchants and artisans) as well as German journeyman merchants with no civil rights ("kopsvenner") and Swedes. The Germans and Swedes formed a single political and ecclesiastical community. Germans were in a majority in the city up until 1520.

After the rise to power of Gustavus I Wasa, the Germans began to feel discontented. Germans had been in a strong position in Stockholm under his predecessor, Christian II of Denmark, but the German population suffered heavy losses during Gustavus I Wasa's two-year long siege of the city (between 1521 and 1523). The number of tax-payers fell from 1,136 in 1520 to 308 in 1523.[1] After 1523 the new king instigated an influx of Swedes which threatened to reverse the proportion of the nationalities in the city. The king's new trading policies were even less favourable to the Germans: he attempted to cut Stockholm off from the Hanseatic League. The Germans' response was to invite Christian II to resume power and to enter into a conspiracy with Lübeck, which had suffered the most from the new trading policy.

The conflict of nationalities within the city was heightened by divergent religious movements. From the end of 1523 the minister of the Great Church of St. Nicholas was Nikolaus Stecker, a pupil of Luther's. Olavus Petri, the Swedish reformer, also often preached here. Petri (at that time still the town-clerk

---

[1] E. Schieche, *Die Anfänge der deutschen St. Gertruds-Gemeinde zu Stockholm im 16. Jahrhundert* (Münster and Cologne, 1952) p. 2.

of Stockholm) supported Stecker's aim of reforming the city on the lines of Wittenberg. But most of the Swedish townspeople opposed these developments. Stecker and Petri were driven from the pulpit by means of slippers, sticks and stones on more than one occasion. The marriage of Olavus Petri to Kristina Michaelsdotter on 12th February, 1525 aroused a particularly vehement protest; a cleric was here daring to marry a wife in public, and worst of all, daring to read the marriage service in Swedish![2] The peasants in the area around Stockholm also held firmly to Catholic traditions and complained about the ecclesiastical practices within the city.

The situation was even more complicated by the fact that Gustavus I Wasa's ecclesiastical policies satisfied neither the radical German merchants nor the conservative Swedish peasants or artisans. The King's reforms did not go far enough for the Germans but the Swedish peasants felt they were excessive. What the king in fact did was to strip the Prelates of their political power (they were forced to give up their castles and fortresses) and then take over their rights of control over church property. He used the church's money to make economic restitution to the nobility by restoring to them all their property which had been acquired by the church since 1454 and handing over to them the management of monastic property.[3] But he felt disinclined to introduce radical reforms of the liturgy or make any changes in the role of the bishops. At the Diet of Västerås (June, 1527) it was decided to retain the traditional liturgy, the celibacy of the priesthood and the monastic orders. Evangelical preaching was to be introduced as a new element within the established Catholic liturgy. The King probably moderated his religious reforms because of his intention to marry Hedwig, the daughter of the Catholic King Sigismund I of Poland.

---

[2] H. Holmquist, *Die schwedische Reformation 1523-1531* (Leipzig, 1925), p. 47. (Schriften des Vereins für Reformationgeschichte. 43, 2).

[3] Cf. G. Johannesson, "Die Kirchenreformation in den nordischen Ländern" in *XIe Congrès International des Sciences Historiques (Stockholm, 1960). Rapports* Vol 4, (Uppsala, 1960), pp. 48-61.

Ich weyß nichts dann Christum den gecreußigten/ 1.Cor.2.

Plate 3: Martin Bucer

Plate 4: Wolfgang Capito

Hoffman began preaching at the cloister of St. John's church in Stockholm in the late summer of 1526. He was supported here by the following German townsmen: Gorius Holst, a merchant and one of the richest men in Sweden, Hans Bokman, the churchwarden of St. Nicholas' church, Kort Piper, Lukas Bartscherer, Jürgen von Sotteren and Brand Schreiber.[4] It was presumably these rich townsmen who financed the high printing costs of the commentary on Daniel, which was published by the royal printer (who also published Olavus Petri's books).

Olavus Petri had begun to introduce liturgical reforms in 1525-1526 (he introduced communion in both kinds and a simplified form of baptism). But it seems that these reforms were accelerated under Hoffman's influence; hence there later developed the story of Hoffman's iconoclasm in Stockholm.[5] Although the chronicler Peder Swart, who related this story, does not seem to have invented it out of nothing, he does seem to have expanded the known facts to a remarkable extent. In the King's trial of Laurentius Andreae and Olavus Petri for high treason in 1539–1540, these two Swedish reformers were accused, along with the leading German merchants (Gorius Holst, Hans Bokman, Kort Piper, Jürgen von Sotteren) and a certain "preacher or furrier, one Balthasar" (presumably Hoffman), of plundering a church, in 1526. The gist of this story was probably an attempt, instigated by Hoffman, to remove the images from a Stockholm Church. The leaders of the Stockholm congregation decided to go ahead against the wishes of the King.[6] Whatever the truth of the story may have been, by the end of 1526 Hoffman was expecting to be arrested or banished from

[4] Cf. E. Schieche, op. cit. p. 14.

[5] K. B. Westman, Reformationens Genombrottsar I Sverige (Stockholm, 1918), pp. 320-322.

[6] Cf. Swart's Chronicle (ed. N. Eden, Stockholm, 1912). None of the details given by Swart can be confirmed. There is no mention of an iconoclastic outburst in Stockholm either in the Council minutes or the royal registers. Swart says the outbreak took place in 1524. But Hoffman was still in Livonia then. He says Hoffman's colleague was Bernd Knipperdolling, but Hoffman in fact never met this man (a later Anabaptist leader of Münster).

Sweden; in the preface to the commentary on Daniel he informs his followers in Livonia that he might not be able to write to them again from Sweden and that he reckoned "God is leading my affairs into a difficult place" (i.e. prison).[7] It was probably the royal secretary who denounced Hoffman to Gustavus I during the latter's absence from Stockholm at this period. On 13th January, 1527 the King forbad Hoffman from continuing to preach publicly with the following decree. "It appears from the experience of those who have heard his preaching that Hoffman has been very fantastical and that his words have been indiscreet. Thus he is ordered to stop his public preaching before the general populace."[8]

Since the peasants in Uppland were already complaining in 1526 about the ecclesiastical changes in Stockholm, the King was afraid that Hoffman would widen the division between the radical Germans and the conservative Swedes. The danger of a peasants' war became apparent when the peasants of Dalarne rioted over the introduction of the Swedish liturgy in 1527. Furthermore Hoffman's concept of democratic congregationalism did not suit the king, who still believed in an episcopal hierarchy. After three years of civil war, and because his authority was still not firmly established, Gustavus I Wasa wanted his country at peace; he could not allow further unrest caused by expectations of an imminent apocalypse. Soon after being forbidden to preach, Hoffman was banished from Sweden along with Nikolaus Stecker, the German minister of Stockholm.

But the conflict between the congregation of radical Germans and the ecclesiastically conservative King of Sweden did not die down. The German merchants seem to have kept in contact with Hoffman even after his expulsion, for in the royal archives at Stockholm there is the transcript (by Gorius Holst) of a letter concerning Hoffman dated 14th March, 1528 from Martin Luther to Pravest, the minister in Kiel.[9] The conflict between the

---

[7] Hoffman, *Daniel* IVa.
[8] Quoted in J. Weidling, *Geschichte der Reformation in Schweden* 1882, p. 187.
[9] E. Schieche, *op. cit.* p. 20.

King and the German merchants (who wanted Christian II to return to power) became increasingly bitter. In 1534 the King deposed the Stockholm Burgomaster, Björn Björnsen, on the grounds of treachery and "Anabaptism", and in 1535 he imprisoned Gorius Holst for high treason. In 1536 there came to light a plot by seven members of the German congregation aimed at blowing up the King during a church service. Amongst the plotters were two of Hoffman's former patrons, Hans Bokman and Brand Schreiber. Since Olavus Petri and Laurentius Andreae had known about the conspiracy but had not warned the King about it, they too were condemned to death in 1540, though they were later reprieved in view of their earlier services. For some time the King intended to banish all the Germans from Stockholm.

Hoffman in fact made no lasting impression on Olavus Petri, who inherited none of his apocalyptic ideas nor his belief in direct revelation. Neither was his view of the Eucharist based on that of Hoffman.[10]

We can draw the following conclusions from this Stockholm episode: in Sweden Hoffman's apocalyptic spiritualism was not the ideology of a suffering lower class but of a well-to-do, ruling national minority, whose economic and political power, however, was being threatened by the nationalist and trading policies of a new ruler.

Gustavus I Wasa in his moderate reform of the official church was steering a middle-course between the conservative tendencies of the Swedish peasants and the pressure for radical reforms from the German congregation of Stockholm. Above all he wanted to subject the church to the state. This intensified the enmity between the King and the German minority. The rich German merchants supported Hoffman's radical ideas as a protest against half-hearted religious reforms; they made a

---

[10] *Pace* J. Weidling, *op. cit.* pp. 189, 193, cf. K.B. Westman, *op. cit.* p. 324 and H. Sandblad, *De eskatologiska Forestellningarna I Sverige under Reformation och Motreformation* Uppsala, 1942, p. 55 Petri's dispute with the king had different causes from Hoffman's disagreement with him. Petri opposed the plan to subject the Swedish church to the oversight of a secular superintendent and to leave the diocese in lay control.

church available to him and printed his book. But the King saw Hoffman as a danger in that his apocalyptic spiritualism intensified the religious conflict between the Germans and the Swedes and also threatened his own ecclesiastical polity. But even after Hoffman had been expelled from Sweden in the winter of 1527, the German congregation continued in opposition to the King's trading policies and religious programme right up until 1536.

Chapter Three

Hoffman in Schleswig-Holstein: The Break with Lutheranism.

1. Hoffman's Banishment from Lübeck.

After being expelled from Sweden, Hoffman attempted to encourage the popular reformation movement in Lübeck. Since 1522 the "Martinists" amongst the secular clergy and the monks had had a considerable following from the townspeople of Lübeck. But the Cathedral Chapter and City Council were determined to protect the Catholic church and its privileges. Whereas the burghers saw the cathedral canons as "ignorant whoremongers and courtesans" the Council looked on them as "friends, uncles, kith and kin" since the Chapter often conferred vacant benefices on the sons of Council members.[1] Because of this nexus of interests Hoffman was no more successful in Lübeck than any of his "Martinist" predecessors, Ossenbrügge, Manhuss, Wilmsen and Walhof, who had all been imprisoned and banished by the Council. As soon as people in the Town Hall realised what a dangerous guest they were harbouring "the highest authorities in Lübeck roused themselves and cried out for his neck, his blood, his body, his life."[2] But he managed to escape from the town unrecognized during the winter of 1527.[3]

---

[1] F. Peterson (ed.), *Ausführliche Geschichte der Lübeckschen Kirchenreformation* (Lübeck, 1830), p. 78.

[2] Hoffman and Karlstadt, *Dialogus,* A2a.

[3] For the course of the Reformation in Lübeck cf. the splendid book by W. Jannasch, *Reformationsgeschichte Lübecks 1515-1530* (Lübeck, 1958).

2. The Controversy with Schuldorp, Amsdorf and Pravest.

Hoffman tells us about the next stage in his life in the *Dialogus*: "The same furrier arrived in the country of Holstein with his wife and child. There he was summoned to King Frederick of Denmark, who wanted to hear his sermons. As he rightly preached the Word of God, the King appointed him as his servant, giving him a letter and seal that permitted him to preach God's Word in the whole land of Holstein. The King loved him and established him as a preacher in Kiel and granted protection to all his possessions. He protected his wife, child and all he owned in a just and Christian way."[4]

How did a lay preacher, who had suffered banishment five times over, and who had a reputation for causing disturbances, obtain a royal letter of protection?

Frederick I of Denmark was undecided with whom he should take sides in the religious question because of the existing power structure around him. He owed his throne to a rebellion by the Danish Prelates and the nobles of Schleswig-Holstein against the government of his nephew Christian II, who had favoured the towns and the peasants. One of the main grievances of the nobles and Prelates against the deposed King was his patronage of the Lutheran heresy. Thus at his coronation in Copenhagen in 1524 Frederick I had to swear to fight the growth of Lutheranism in Denmark and to protect the rights of the Catholic church.

In fact, the nobility of Schleswig-Holstein had considerably less interest in the retention of the ecclesiastical *status quo* than had the Prelates. Therefore the king, to whom Schleswig-Holstein had come by inheritance, was able to follow his personal inclinations, and on 7th August, 1524 he issued an edict of toleration which ordered "that no-one's life, body or possessions be attacked on account of his religion whether papal or Lutheran, and that everyone follow his religion as he thinks he can justify his conduct before God the Almighty and his own

---

[4] *Dialogus* A2a-b. The quotation is taken from the first edition, printed in Strasbourg.

conscience."[5] He thus anticipated the decree of the first Diet of Speyer (1526) by two years.

The King had adherents of both the old and new faiths close to him. Amongst the "faithful sons" of the Catholic church there were Gottschalk von Ahlefeld, the Bishop of Schleswig and the King's personal friend, his own son Johann and the counsellor Wulf Pogwisch. But followers of Luther were gradually gaining the upper hand. Amongst their number were the Crown Prince, Christian (who had been won over to the new faith by Luther's steadfastness at the Diet of Worms in 1521), Johann von Rantzau, the steward who had accompanied the Crown Prince on all his journeys, the Chancellor, Wolfgang von Utenhoven, and the royal counsellors Peter Suave and Benedikt von Ahlefeld. The King's links with the evangelical cause were strengthened when his daughter Dorothea married Duke Albrecht of Prussia in 1526. In the August of that year Frederick I ignored the fasting regulations and took communion in both kinds, thus consummating his personal conversion to the new faith.[6]

The crown's financial crisis, the need to prepare for the imminent attack by the King's exiled predecessor and the nobles' desire to extend their own property at the expense of the Church all favoured an anti-Catholic policy: the Prelates' land and money were desperately needed.

In 1525 there was a clash between the knights and the Catholic Prelates. The knights demanded that the bishops stop trading the sacraments for cash, that they end the practice of excommunication and that they allow the Gospel rather than "obnoxious legends" to be preached. At the Diet of Kiel in the following year (1526) the royal counsellors told the Prelates that the King would only intervene to stop the growth of the evangelical movement amongst the peasants (who had been refusing to pay their tithes to the church) if the clergy handed over 80,000 Lübeck marks to the crown. At the same time the

[5] G. Waitz, *Schleswig-Holsteins Geschichte* Vol. 2/2. (Göttingen, 1852), p. 159.

[6] Cf. G. Johannesson, *Die Kirchenreformation in den nordischen Ländern* p. 56.

King was only asking the nobility for 30,000 marks and even less from the towns (10,000 marks). The clergy complained both about the size of the financial demand and about the extortionate methods to get it, but the bishop of Schleswig, Gottschalk von Ahlefeld, had no choice but to concede to the King's request in the name of the clergy, "his sad voice quivering with emotion." But the clergy's hoped-for reward was only half delivered. After their concession the counsellors declared that they were in no position to promise that anyone who wanted to preach the "pure Gospel" would be persecuted. However, they would certainly force the peasants to pay their tithes. We can gather the mood of the higher clergy as they left the Diet of Kiel from a conversation between Johannes Parper, Cathedral Canon of Lübeck, and Detlev Reventlov, Provost of the Reinbek Cloister near Hamburg. Reventlov said that it looked as if similar financial burdens would be laid on the church every year until the clergy were eventually bankrupted. His mother would have done better to drown him at birth rather than let him become a priest.[7] The indirect consequences of this policy outweighted its immediate effects; in order to raise the money the Prelates saw no alternative but to sell large parts of their land to the nobles and to the King.[8]

---

[7] *Archiv für Staats- und Kirchengeschichte der Herzogtümer Schleswig-Holstein-Lauenburg* Vol. 4, (Altona, 1840), pp. 479-480)

[8] Cf. H.A. Jensen and A.L.J. Michelsen, *Schleswig-Holsteinische Kirchengeschichte* Vol. 3. (Kiel, 1877), p. 28. In order to obtain 4,000 Lübeck marks the Bordesholm cloister had to sell off its marshland property by the River Stör to Johann von Rantzau, who founded his principality Breitenburg in this way. In 1527, in order to pay *his* way, the bishop of Schleswig mortgaged his property in Ulnis, Steinfeld, Kjus and Hesel to the neighbouring nobility. The nuns of the cloister of Reinbek sold their nunnery, and the land around it, under suspicious circumstances in 1528. The king gave them 12,000 Lübeck marks allegedly to pay for their debts. But Detlev Reventlov, the Provost of the cloister, knew nothing about the transaction. But it was not only his signature that was missing from the contract; so was that of the prioress Anna von Plesse (who was a Lutheran). Reventlov objected to the methods the king was using, saying he was still provost although his nuns had simply run away from the cloister. But Reventlov then came to the conclusion that the cause of the old church was lost. He was not

Frederick I solved the problem of undermining the polity of the old church without openly contradicting his own coronation oath by taking evangelical wandering preachers into his personal protection and commissioning them to proclaim the "pure Word of God" (a euphemism for Luther's doctrine). They could not be given benefices because these remained in the hands of Catholic priests as agreed. In October, 1526 Hans Tausen received a missionary charge and a letter of protection covering Denmark, and Hoffman was given the same privilege for Holstein in the first few months of 1527. There were some evangelical ministers in a few places who also enjoyed the personal protection of the King, e.g. Hermann Tast in Husum, Gert Stewert in Flensburg and Marquard Schuldorp in Schleswig.[9] Religious vagabonds like "mad Friedrich" in Schleswig and Johannes van Campen in Itzehoe were able to raise the populace against upholders of the Catholic church without hindrance. Neither the King nor the nobles had any objection to the Catholic clergy coming under pressure from below as well as from above.

The presence of divergent forms of worship within the same church created a further source of conflict. While the canons of Schleswig Cathedral were singing their Latin *horae* in the upper choir (St. Peter's), "mad Friedrich" was in St. Laurence's choir in the same church leading his burgher congregation in German hymns. This meant that the canons could not follow their own

---

[9] For the beginnings of the Reformation in Schleswig-Holstein cf. E. Feddersen, *Kirchengeschichte Schleswig-Holsteins* Vol.2, 1517-1721, 1938, pp. 25ff.

---

note 8 continued

prepared to drink the dregs of the cup of suffering as a Catholic Prelate and so became a Protestant. The king generously gave him his income as Provost of the "liquidated" cloister of Reinbek and eventually (in 1555) Reventlov became the evangelical bishop of Lübeck. Along with Rantzau he was one of the counsellors who turned against Hoffman at the Disputation of Flensburg in 1529. For the Reinbek cloister cf. A. Kasch, "Das Kloster in Reinbek. Versuch einer Chronik" in *Festschrift zur 700-Jahrfeier der Gemeinde Reinbek* 1938, pp. 101ff.

singing.[10] Sermons were interrupted by hecklers shouting "Liar!" or "Babbler!" People urinated into the holy-water stoups, and if they received episcopal letters of remonstration they would deal with them in the following way: "Item, if they received a letter they would wipe their backsides with it, and having dried their arses on it would seal it and send it back."[11] Catholic priests and monks were mobbed in the streets, assaulted by stones and cries of "Wolf! flesh-eaters! traitors of God! murderers of the soul! cutthroat firebugs!"

But the case of "mad Friedrich" also shows how easily radical feelings directed against the Prelates could turn against the secular authorities. "Mad Friedrich" lost the favour of his patron by questioning the right of a prince to dictate his subjects' religious allegiance and by criticizing the ecclesiastical policies of Wolfgang Utenhofen (probably a reference to his appropriation of church property). "Mad Friedrich" was also hated by many of his fellow evangelical preachers because he followed the example of St. Paul in living on voluntary donations and part-time manual work. Like Karlstadt he expressed his solidarity with the simple "laymen" by wearing a habit of coarse blue cloth. He was arrested by the King at Neumünster in 1527 and banished from the country.[12] The "mad Friedrich" incident in Schleswig was the prelude to the drama that was to befall Hoffman in Kiel.

The situation in the church of Kiel was as confused as that of any other city in Schleswig-Holstein at that time. The Franciscan "Grey Cloister" still existed on the outskirts of the town as

[10] J.A. Cypraeus, *Annales Episcoporum Slesvicensium*, (Cologne, 1634), pp. 418-419.

[11] This and the following examples are taken from a manuscript by Lütge Namann, a Franciscan of Flensburg, whose cloister was closed in 1528. The manuscript, which was written in about 1540, is in the Flensburg city archives.

[12] J.A. Cypraeus, *Annales* pp. 418-419. Both "papists" and "enthusiasts" agreed on this one point, viz. that the ecclesiastical policies of the King and the nobles, implied an assault on the congregations, particularly on the sick and the weak. Lütge Namann's manuscript contains a complaint about the destructive impact of the Reformation on hospices and hostels. cf. also J. Möller, *Cimbria Literata* Vol. 1. 1744, p. 604.

well as the brotherhoods.[13] After 1526 the head of St. Nicholas'
church, and thus of all Kiel's clergy, was Wilhelm Pravest from
the Bordesholm Cloister, a staunch supporter of the old church.
He celebrated the traditional Catholic mass at the altar of the
Twelve Apostles.[14] The Bordesholm Cloister and the City
Council both still shared the patronage of this, the most
important church of the town. Until October, 1528 the Council
(in collaboration with the monastery) was still obliged to choose
Kiel's leading clergyman from the ranks of the cloister's own
monks.[14] The priest's stipend came from the monastery, and in
all financial matters St. Nicholas' was incorporated into the
Bordesholm foundation until 1528.

Nevertheless, Marquard Schuldorp, a Lutheran, had become a
deacon of St. Nicholas' in 1526 and had preached against
papacy.[15] He had left Kiel to study theology at Wittenberg in
1521.[16] A personal friend of Luther and Amsdorf, he became a
leader of the Lutheran magisterial reformation movement in
Schleswig and Kiel. Early in 1527 Hoffman and Schuldorp
worked side by side at St. Nicholas' for a short time.[17] And even
after moving to Schleswig, where he was made evangelical
pastor in the St. Laurence Chapel of the Cathedral, Schuldorp
sometimes returned home to Kiel in order to hear his colleagues'
sermons and to see what was happening in his former sphere of
influence. Schuldorp's place as deacon of St. Nicholas' was taken
by Hermann Biestermann, who appeared at first to be a staunch

---

[13] The Grey Cloister was closed in 1530 on the King's orders and
handed over to the city. cf. E.J. v. Westphalen (ed.), *Monumenta inedita
Rerum Germanicarum, praecipue Cimbricarum*. Vol. 4. (Leipzig, 1745), col.
3335-3336.

[14] Landesarchiv Schleswig, *Urkunden der Stadt Kiel* No. 422, 423 (6th
and 10th October, 1528).

[15] M. Schuldorp, *Breef an de gelövyghen der Stadt Kyll*, 1528, B1a. (The
only copy of this pamphlet is in the Royal library in Copenhagen).

[16] T.O. Achelis, "Beiträge zur Reformationsgeschiche des Herzog-
tums Schleswig aus der Wittenberger Universitätsmatrikel 1502-1602"
in *Genealogie* Vol. 6, 3/11. 1962. The entry reads, "Marquardus
Schuldorff, ex keyl, dioc. Bremen, 1521, Vl. 13."

[17] Cf. Kiel, Stadtarchiv No. 1025 and Schuldorp's, *Breef*, B1b.

Lutheran but who later identified himself with Hoffman.[18] Thus by the beginning of 1527 there were three representatives of mutually incompatible religious positions within St. Nicholas': Wilhelm Pravest the Catholic, Marquard Schuldorp the Lutheran and Melchior Hoffman the radical apocalypticist.

At the very beginning of his activity in Kiel Hoffman became involved in a serious dispute with the City Council and Marquard Schuldorp, who disapproved of his attitude to secular authority. Hoffman said that the conflict came about because he had been "subjected to much persecution at the hands of the Kiel authorities, who were strongly opposed to divine truth and justice."[19] Schuldorp said that Hoffman had insulted all the members of the Council, denouncing them by name and saying that the whole Council was "full of scoundrels, who should be hanged by the neck on trees so that a new council can be appointed." He called them "robbers" behind their backs but could not substantiate this allegation. When the church organist had urged him to be more lenient towards the councillors he had replied, "You don't understand, they've got to be slaughtered."[20] Schuldorp said that Hoffman's followers were those "who were not prepared to show the least respect to the Council and the governors." Nor were they concerned with Hoffman's religious message; "they don't care if St. Paul's letter to the Romans or the Apocalypse is being preached, so long as they get hold of the 'poor man's penny' " (i.e. the alms collected for the support of the poor).[21] This statement is probably the key to understanding the dispute; it was a controversy over how to dispose of the property of doomed Catholic institutions. According to Schuldorp Hoffman's followers were made up of

---

[18] This change of attitude can be seen by comparing the comments of Schuldorp (*Breef* D3a) and the references collected by Nicolaus Hermann Schwarze (Edited by M.J.H. Fehse, Flensburg 1775), p. 136. On the beginnings of the Reformation in Kiel cf. also F. Volbehr, "Kieler Predigergeschichte seit der Reformation" in *Mitteilungen der Gesellschaft für Kieler Stadtgeschichte*, Vol. 6, Kiel, 1884, pp. 6–13.

[19] *Dialogus* A2b.

[20] Schuldorp, *Breef* B2a–B3b.

[21] *ibid* B1a.

those who objected to the confiscated property going to the Councillors, because they wanted it for themselves.[22]

The charge of usurping church property must have been a particularly inflammable social issue in such an oligarchical town as Kiel. The City Council was not elected by the townspeople, it simply co-opted members. The twelve councillors and three burgomasters were all "hereditary merchants" who owned freehold property. Artisans were not eligible for a seat on the council. The council also controlled the committee which disposed of church property; this was made up of two council members plus two other eminent townsmen. Neither the clergy nor the artisans were able to keep a check on the magistracy's administration of church property. Hence the charge of corruption cut very deep.[23]

Even if the administration of the church had not been thoroughly correct, Schuldorp felt that Hoffman should remember that: "If you accept only perfect men as rulers you will not find a single one who is up to your standard."[24]. It was the preacher's duty to strengthen the authority of the magistrate instead of weakening it by "slander, so that everybody should willingly obey his master, even if he is an odd fellow." This

---

[22] We have no clear information about this process, since the first explicit document relating to the acquisition of church property by the Kiel Council dates from 1553 (which is confirmed by a letter of Emperor Maximilian II dated 30th November, 1570). But it can be gathered that the process of appropriation began in 1434 (when the Council began to share patronage rights over St. Nicholas') and was accelerated by the Reformation.

The Kiel archives also show a drastic reduction in rent payments from townsmen to the Church between 1528 and 1531. Between 1524 and 1527 75% of debts were paid to the Church. This fell to 50% in 1528 but rose again with the consolidation of the church after 1534.

A similar process can be traced in Flensburg: cf. E. Hoffmann, "Flensburg von der Reformation bis zum Ende des Nordischen Krieges, 1721" in *Flensburg. Geschichte einer Grenzstadt* (Flensburg, 1966), pp. 81f.

[23] H. Eckhardt, *"Alt-Kiel in Wort und Bild* (Kiel, 1899); H. Landgraf, *Bevölkerung und Wirtschaft Kiels im 15. Jahrhundert* (Neumünster, 1959), p. 64.

[24] Schuldorp *Breef* B3a-b.

corresponded to St. Paul's doctrine of a well-ordered community, in which men and women, young and old, elders and priests, servants and masters, all had their fixed places in society which obliged them to mutual service, to obedience on one hand, and to protection and care on the other hand. But Hoffman's attitude to the authorities was ambiguous. Before the king and his counsellors, who had power over him, he preached obedience; in the presence of the simple folk and the Kiel magistrates, who could not harm him, he advocated disobedience. Schuldorp felt that Hoffman's attacks on the authorities were a hindrance to the spread of the Gospel in northern Germany, for on the basis of what was happening in Kiel, Luther's doctrine would be distorted to become simply an invitation to rebellion.

Schuldorp's vehement defence of the council against Hoffman was not a thoroughly disinterested move since he came from a family of Kiel councillors. His ancestors Hans Schuldorp and Marquard Schuldorp had been councillors from 1478-1499 and 1501-1515 respectively.[25]. Thus in rejecting Hoffman's attack he was defending his own social group. Schuldorp's concern to show submission to the authorities can be seen again on the occasion of his first sermon in Schleswig, in which he urged his congregation to reject the rebellious ideas that "mad Friedrich" had introduced amongst them.[26]

According to Schuldorp Hoffman's radical preaching was not limited to an instigation of the urban artisans to rebellion against the council; he also encouraged a "destruction of the state of peace" amongst the local rural peasants. He curried their favour by presenting himself as a "poor grey man" who, although unconsecrated and a layman like them, preached the Gospel, but, unlike the money-grabbing "belly-servers" (i.e. the holders of official benefices), asked no money for doing so.[27]. Then this world-famous furrier, who had come to them all the way from

---

[25] A. Bremer, *Chronicon Kiliense tragicum-curiosum* Ed. M. Stern, (Kiel, 1916) p. 516.

[26] J. Möller, *Cimbria Literata* Vol. 1, p. 604.

[27] Schuldorp, *Breef* B1b.

Livonia, and who had been enlightened directly by God, besotted the stunned peasants with his erroneous concoction of apocolyptic fantasies. His sermons in the town and the country thrilled the hearts of the mob, but "this minister sounded like a Müntzer."[28]. He should thus be regarded as a "dangerous deceiver of the ignorant"[29]. In short, Schuldorp regarded Hoffman as the successor to Thomas Müntzer.

Hoffman could not but increase his popularity in his Kiel congregation by his preaching against the nobility. Many nobles from Holstein owned houses in the city but paid no tax on them and did not accept other responsibilities as townsmen. At assemblies of the Holstein knights, and particularly at the "Kiel turn-over"("Kieler Umschlag") in the last week of January (at which all the Holstein nobility would come together in the city to fix accounts and trading deals), clashes between the knights and the townsmen inevitably arose. The knights' coarse jokes against the hated "pepper sacks" and "brood of tailors and glove-makers" would lead on to the breaking of window panes and bursting in to burghers' houses. There would be disturbances of the peace as the knights tried to urge the townsmen to drink, sing and make merry. Not even burgomasters or council members were spared this annual display of boorishness on the part of the nobility. The town tried in vain to move the venue of the "Kiel turn-over" to Rendsburg. Sometimes, when the nobility indulged in their excesses, the townsmen were forced to assemble under their leaders and to give the knights a good thrashing.[30]

These feelings of resentment in the city must have fortified Hoffman in his intention to encourage an anti-nobility uprising amongst the peasants. He could easily make contact with the

---

[28] "De muenthe smeckt recht na dem muenther" - Schuldorp's word-play, *Breef* B3b, C1a.

[29] *Ibid.*, C1b.

[30] A. Bremer, *Chronicon* pp. 25, 123, 139, 143. Also C.F. Fick, *Kleine Mitteilungen aus Kiels Vergangenheit* (Kiel, 1867), p. 8; H. Eckardt, *Alt-Kiel* p.24.

In 1530, one of the knights, Johann von Ahlefeld, was killed by a group of townsmen "for greatly provoking the burghers".

peasants on market-days when people came into town from the
countryside. (In 1527 Kiel had only 3,000 inhabitants and most of
its trade was with the surrounding countryside, not across the
sea.)[31] He had further opportunities to speak to the peasants on
his journeys through Schleswig-Holstein, which took him to
Schleswig and Husum.[32]

The peasants of eastern Holstein had enough grounds for
social discontent. The peasants in Kiel's immediate neighbourhood (in the hilly country of eastern Holstein) were socially
inferior to those in the heath and marshlands. Whereas the
peasants of western Holstein and Schleswig were personally
free, as they had retained their old Germanic status and rights,
the only rights of the peasants of eastern Holstein, who lived on
former colonial land, were rights of usufruct on manorial
property. With the introduction of demesne-farming in eastern
Holstein the number of days' compulsory service by the peasant
was raised from 10–15 annually (as usual in the fifteenth century)
to daily services in the course of the sixteenth century.[33] In
order to ensure that the peasants would carry out this service
their lords tied them to the land. Demesne-farming gradually
spread from eastern Holstein to old Holstein, and eventually,
after a considerable delay, even to Schleswig, though it never
included the whole region

The gradual process of reduction of the peasants' rights was
accelerated when Frederick I granted the nobility of Schleswig-
Holstein a privilege on 6th May, 1524 in recognition of the part
they had played in obtaining the Danish throne for him. [34] He
renounced his right to inflict capital punishment, and subjected
the peasants (as far as they lived outside of domains immediately
belonging to the prince) to the justice of the nobility, who were
even given the right to order the death penalty. By granting

---

[31] For the economic and social structure in Kiel cf. H. Landgraf, *op.
cit.*

[32] Schuldorp, *Breef* C1a; E. Weidensee, *Eyn underricht uth der hillighen
schryfft* 1529, C2a.

[33] On this cf. W. Prange, *Die Anfänge der grossen Agrarreform in
Schleswig-Holstein bis um 1771* (Neumünster, 1971), pp. 592–594.

[34] Cf. F. C. Jensen and D.H. Hegewisch, *Privilegien der Schleswig-
Holsteinischen Ritterschaft* (Kiel, 1797), pp. 140-150.

them judicial authority he also bestowed upon them the right to exact labour and to demand a payment of rent in kind (i.e. in corn). The judicial privileges were used by the noblemen to turn free peasants into serfs.[35] In the same privilege Frederick I removed the obligation on the nobles of Schleswig-Holstein to submit judicial issues of their own personal affairs or of their fiefs to the princely court, and to submit cases relating to their allodial estate to the "Lotding and Goding" (the court of aldermen coming from the villages). In future a knight had to submit his criminal or civil matters only to the judgment of his noble peers.

The extent of the discontent over Frederick's favouritism towards the nobility can be seen from the three-year long uprisings and the disputed succession that followed the King's death in 1533. The peasants of Jutland rebelled against their lords, the townsmen of Copenhagen and Malmö rose against the Prelates, and the "common folk" of Flensburg rebelled against the patrician governing council. In order to prevent the peasants' revolt in Jutland from spreading to Holstein, the Holstein nobility intervened in the battles in Jutland, but were defeated by the Danish peasants near Svenstrup on 15th October, 1533.

Schuldorp's second complaint against Hoffman concerned his religious preaching. Instead of expounding the saving doctrines of Christ and Paul from the Gospels and the Epistle to the Romans he confused his congregation with the dazzling Book of Revelation. He encouraged "useless gossip about the Day of Judgment" and used such extravagant exegesis that he even turned "the noble evangelist" Matthew into an apocalypticist.[36] We are able to examine Schuldorp's claim because we still have a fragment of Hoffman's exposition of Matthew Chapter I dating from this period.[37]

---

[35] J. Jessen "Die Entstehung und Entwicklung der Gutswirtschaft in Schleswig-Holstein bis zum Beginn der Agrarreformen" in *Zeitschrift der Gesellschaft für Schleswig-Holsteinische Geschichte* 51(1922), p. 24.

[36] Schuldorp, *Breef* C1a.

[37] Printed in J.M. Krafft, *Ein Zweyfaches Zweyhundert-Jähriges Jubel-Gedächtnis* (Hamburg, 1723), Beilage VIII, pp. 440-445. On typological and allegorical exegesis in Bible prefaces up until Luther cf. M.E. Schild, *Abendländische Bibelvorreden* 1970, pp. 112-134.

In his preface to the commentary on Matthew, Hoffman reverts to his favourite theme of the exegesis of the "four beasts" (Ezek. 1:10,Rev. 4:7). Whereas they were traditionally seen as symbols of the four evangelists, Hoffman saw them as ciphers for the four forms of the Word of God.

Developing his earlier ideas, Hoffman here links the four forms of the divine Word with the process of salvation undergone by the human soul. First of all man must be startled by the voice of the lion and the selfish man in him must be killed. This corresponds to the task attributed to the Old Testament law, the bitter north wind. The purifying water of the Law comes up to the ankles of the believer (a reference to Ezekiel's immersion into the life-giving Temple stream, Ezek. 47). He then turns to the prophecies and figures which point to Christ and to rebirth. They are sometimes "awkward and rather ridiculous," hence they are symbolised by the ox. But man finds them more acceptable than the harsh Law, and in this way they are like the west wind. But the figures and literal wisdom of the Old Testament are doomed to pass away. Spiritual understanding must take over with the New Testament. When this occurs the water of the justifying spirit comes up to the knees. With the precepts and parables of the New Testament, man experiences how mildly and fittingly God can speak to the human spirit. They are similar to the south wind or dawn in their gentleness. They prepare the way for a spiritual rebirth. This itself is symbolised by the human face, the angel or the third river of Paradise, which came up to the prophet's loins (Ezek. 47:4). Only when man has reached this point can the "clear, bright Word" burst forth from its darkness and hiddenness. This is the bright light of the sun, or the east wind. In its overwhelming force it is like the river that the prophet could not pass through. The further one steps into it, the deeper does it become; or, as one could say, the higher one flies on the wings of an eagle, the wider appears the horizon. Just as no bird can fly higher than the eagle so man, if he is not to be destroyed, can only experience the movement of the divine Spirit within his heart up to a certain point. "He must stop here. Just as he cannot look directly at the sun he cannot go on being filled with the spirit. The eagle is the example of this. There is no limit or end to the spirit we see in the Word."[38] Man, as a creature, must be satisfied with a limited knowledge of the spiritual heaven, with merely approaching the Holy of Holies.[39]

A further example of Hoffman's continued use of a medieval type of allegorical exegesis is his commentary on the Song of Songs,[40] which he dedicated to Queen Sophia of Denmark (a sign that he still hoped to be able to institute reform with the aid of the authorities). This work repeats the doctrinal and apocalyptic points made in his earlier writings, such as polemic on the issues of freewill and predestination, justification by Christ alone and the necessity of suffering. He illustrates the benefits derived from suffering by the example of the palm trees which grow higher the more weighed down (p.03a). He strikes a new chord when he speaks of a "true inner baptism of fire and the spirit" (p.H4a) which anticipates his later rejection of infant baptism. His inclination towards a new charismatic ecclesiology can also be seen when he says that God's power falls first of all on the "apostolic shepherds" who then pass it on to the assembly of the faithful (p.L1b).[41]

Schuldorp did not appreciate Hoffman's fantastic description of the process of salvation. He said that Hoffman's allegorization of "Moses' hut" – the tabernacle, the seven-branched candlestick on the ark of the covenant, the vestments of the High Priest (to Hoffman all of these were symbols of the stages of man's divinisation) – was "an empty juggling trick", attractive to people tired of faith and love but useless to a hungry or distressed heart that was searching for a way to live and to die.

---

[38] J.M. Krafft, *op. cit.,* p. 445.

[39] I disagree with Kawerau (op. cit. p. 35) who interprets this passage as meaning that man must remain on the third level of God's Word (the parables of the New Testament) and not attempt to move towards the Spirit directly. All of Hoffman's exegesis is concerned exclusively with discovering the "eagle" that is hidden in Scripture. The children of God should "taste him and feel him in their hearts" (cf. *An de gelöfighen vorsambling* A2a).

[40] *Dat Boeck Cantica Canticorum* 1529. Hoffman printed this work himself.

[41] Cf. C.A. Pater, "Melchior Hoffman's Explication of the Songs (*sic*) of Songs" in *ARG* 68(1977) pp. 173-191.

We should speak to these hearts, much more, of the Saviour's goodness and the joy he gives to believers, not because of their good works, but out of his mercy alone. We should show Christians how to express their gratitude in good works done for their neighbours. It is no good babbling on to a dying man about the spiritual meaning of the tabernacle. What we should be saying is, "Man, God is your father; through Christ you are His son. You should now follow in the footsteps of Jesus Christ which will lead you through death to eternal life. These are the words of life."[42] People should not be looking into the Holy of Holies in the Temple but into the fatherly heart of God's Majesty. Thus, according to the Lutheran Schuldorp, Hoffman ignored the central articles of faith and deceived his congregation with empty frippery. He urged his colleague to expound to his congregation the sound doctrine of the Pauline epistles and to keep his day-dreaming to himself. When Hoffman ignored this request, Schuldorp lodged a complaint about him with Luther and Amsdorf. Hoffman now saw that his position was seriously threatened. In order to prevent Luther condemning him, Hoffman set off for Wittenberg in person (accompanied, incidentally, by a royal chaplain).[43] He took along the text of his exposition of Matthew Chapter I in the hope that he would be able to convince Luther of his method of allegorical exegesis. He also informed Luther of his coming visit to Wittenberg so that he would not come out openly in support of Schuldorp before he had given Hoffman a hearing. He also intended to look up Amsdorf in Magdeburg because he had "suffered greatly" at his hands; when Schuldorp (a personal friend of Amsdorf's) had sent him a copy of Hoffman's commentary on Daniel, he had proceeded to encourage Schuldorp in his opposition to the "furrier."[44]

Since Luther had been informed of Hoffman's planned visit to Magdeburg, he warned Amsdorf against him in a letter dated

---

[42] Schuldorp, *Breef* B4a.

[43] It is not known who the chaplain was, but the term "royal chaplain" simply means that he had been appointed by the king.

[44] Nikolaus von Amsdorf, *Eine Vermanung an die von Magdeburg/das sie sich für falsche Propheten zu hüten wissen* (Magdeburg, 1527), A3.

17th May, 1527. He urged him to give a cool reception to the "Livonian prophet" because he despised rightful evangelical preachers. Luther bitterly regretted the certificate of orthodoxy he ("stultus et deceptus") had earlier granted him. He did not trust the man; he taught without authority and suffered from great follies. Amsdorf should urge him to return to his manual work and give up preaching.[45] Amsdorf followed Luther's advice. When Hoffman came to him in the summer of 1527 and asked the reason for his hostility Amsdorf sharply dismissed him with the remark that he could remember neither Hoffman's articles nor his own letter. Hoffman should take to heart the proverb which says, "Cobbler, stick to your last!" Hoffman could not keep silent at this insult. He turned to the chaplain who was with him and said of Amsdorf, to his face "You can see here the sort of puffed-up spirit that is all around."[46] Amsdorf was afraid that Hoffman would establish contact with his own congregation in Magdeburg and so, in order to warn them against him, he wrote A Warning to the Magdeburgers to beware of false prophets.[47] Here Hoffman is portrayed as a "black devil," because he spreads the following false doctrines:

1. "Dark and useless talk of the imminent Day of Judgement." He would neither state clearly when the seven years of the apocalyptic catastrophe had begun nor the identity of the two witnesses. Instead of speculating about the date and the hour of Christ's return, Christians should be always watchful for his appearance.

2. Hoffman is a self-proclaimed prophet who has assumed a teacher's role. But we can see from the example of Christ that possession of the Spirit is not sufficient justification to set about missionary preaching; people must be formally appointed to the task. In the rare cases where God does call someone to be a prophet directly and "without mediation", his role is to preach a particular new revelation or to censure people for their false

---

[45] WA Br 4:202.
[46] Hoffman, Das Niclas Amsdorff . . . ein lügenhafftiger falscher nasen-geist sey (Kiel, 1528), C1a.
[47] Cf. above n.44.

doctrine; but Hoffman preaches nothing new and does not punish heretics.

In Hoffman Amsdorf was in fact dealing with the shades of his own past. His visit opened up an old wound, viz. that he had allowed himself to be misled by the Zwickau prophets in 1521/22. Like Melanchthon, he had seen Nikolaus Storch and Markus Stübner as preachers of a new revelation and as heralds of the Last Judgment. On account of this, he had urged the Elector not to use force against the new prophets. In those days he had been convinced by the argument – later used by Hoffman – that the final stage of history had already begun since Antichrist had been revealed sitting amidst the Holiest of Holies. Together with Karlstadt he had supported a new church ordinance and the abolition of images in the churches of Wittenberg.[48]

But after the Peasants' War Amsdorf had become the most vigorous defender of the developing Lutheran orthodoxy. He restricted the right to expound Scripture to clergy officially appointed by the secular authorities. He identified the Word of God with the literal text of the Bible; to this the believer must always submit, whatever doubts he may have. Amsdorf easily lost his self-control if contradicted and would attack opponents with coarse insults (though they would usually pay him back in the same currency).

Despite this cold reception from Amsdorf, Hoffman was not deterred from travelling on to Wittenberg. Here he met Luther and Bugenhagen for a second time.[49] He presented them with his allegorical interpretation of Matthew Chapter I , "When I tried to explain my doctrines in Wittenberg and give a clear interpretation according to Scripture, they made me out to be a great sinner and thought I was a lunatic."[50] Luther and

---

[48] H. Stille, *Nikolaus von Amsdorf. Sein Leben bis zu seiner Einweisung als Bischof von Naumburg (1483-1542)* (Leipzig, 1937), p. 37; P. Wappler, *Thomas Müntzer in Zwickau und die Zwickauer Propheten* (Zwickau, 1908), p. 26; W.H. Neuser, *Die Abendmahlslehre Melanchthons in ihrer geschichtlichen Entwicklung (1519-1530)* (Neukirchen – Vluyn, 1968).

[49] E. Weidensee, *Eyn underricht uth der hillighen schryfft* 1529, A3b.

[50] J.M. Krafft, *op. cit.*, p. 445.

Bugenhagen intended to question Hoffman closely again because of the nonsense of his allegorical exegesis, but he himself decided to set off home.[51] On the way he was arrested in Magdeburg. The Council confiscated everything he had with him. Hoffman said he had witnesses to prove that it was Amsdorf who was responsible for this violation of the law by instigating the magistrates, though Amsdorf denied this. Hoffman was quite destitute when he returned to Holstein in the late summer of 1527. Ziegenhagen, the pastor of St. Nicholas' Church in Hamburg, gave him some money, which allowed him to travel on to Kiel.[52] Here Hoffman soon managed to amass enough capital to establish the town's first printing shop. He immediately put it to use on behalf of his dispute with the Lutheran preachers.

But it does not seem that he had as yet arrived at a total breakdown in his relationship with his former teachers in Wittenberg . He must have retained a certain level of trust in Luther, because at the end of 1527 he sent him a copy of Amsdorf's polemical tract along with his own annotations to it.[53] But Hoffman could not have expected any friendship from Luther because Schuldorp had been sending bitter accounts about Hoffman. Hoffman also attempted to reply to Amsdorf "with civility", as he understood the word, in a book, written in Low German, published in 1528.[54] In view of his new honour his name on the title-page is followed by the phrase, "Preacher

---

[51] E. Weidensee, op. cit., A3b.

[52] Acta (Minutes of the Flensburg Disputation, edited by Bugenhagen) N1b.

[53] Wa Br 4:311.

[54] Dat Nicolaus Amsdorff der Meydeburger Pastor/nicht weth/wat he setten/schreven edder swetzen schall/darmede he syne lögen bestedigen möge und seynen gruweliken anlop (Kiel, 1528). The term "with affection" occurs in Hoffman's second tract against Amsdorf (cf. above n. 46). It is possible, but not probable, that Hoffman also wrote another work against Amsdorf's first polemical tract which has since been lost. In any case (pace Kawerau, op. cit. p. 5) it is clear that Hoffman wrote the Low German work before the High German one, because the former includes an invitation to a disputation and the threat of a memorable "farewell" which he takes up in the High German book.

of Kiel, appointed by His Royal Majesty of Denmark." The
vignette on the same page depicts a rose (as in Luther's seal) but
in the place of the cross, usually in the heart of the rose, there is a
representation of Christ the Judge of the world. From his mouth
issues, to the left, a sword (symbol of judgment on the wicked)
and, to the right, a lily (symbol of peace for the just). The image
may mean that Hoffman still regarded himself as a Lutheran
apocalypticist.

In his book Hoffman requests Amsdorf to explain his own
exposition of the major biblical texts concerning the apocalypse
(Daniel 12, Joel 3, Matthew 24, Luke 21, 2 Thess.2 and
Revelation 11-12) and thus to justify his condemnation of
Hoffman's eschatological doctrines. According to Hoffman, it is
meaningless to extract biblical texts from their context and then
mix them up together in the way that Amsdorf links Paul's
command to watch and pray without ceasing, with the verse
about man not being able to know the date or the hour of
Christ's return. Paul has clearly described the signs whereby we
can tell that the Lord's appearance is at hand, viz. the revelation
of Antichrist. The apostle opposed those who said that we must
always expect the Day of the Lord. In comparison with his
commentary on Daniel, Hoffman is rather more careful here in
what he says about his doctrine of the two witnesses and the date
of the messianic turmoil. When he says that the two witnesses
are already alive it does not mean they have already begun to
preach.[55] Despite a few passages of invective against Amsdorf,
on the whole he retains a tone of condescending irony (e.g. "the
clever, scrummy hero of Magdeburg," "that fine marksman,"
"the valiant warrior," "that nice child"). But at the end, after
inviting him to a dispute about the imminence of the Last
Judgment, Hoffman pulls out all the stops: "But I would advise
you rather to stay at home with your stench, otherwise I shall
give you such a "Farewell" that people will say, "That's a real
'Farewell'!"[56]

But this threat did not deter Amsdorf from making a reply. It

[55] *Dat Nicolaus Amsdorff* A2a.
[56] *Ibid.* A4a.

was probably in 1528 that he went to Hamburg (against Luther's advice) to establish a reformed ecclesiastical ordinance at the invitation of the magistracy.[57] Since Amsdorf did not understand Low German, it seems that the Hamburgers were not satisfied with him; in any event they invited Bugenhagen to carry on with the work. It was probably during this time in Hamburg that Amsdorf wrote his second polemical work against Hoffman.[58]

He did not, as Hoffman had requested, expound the apocalyptic texts, but repeated his earlier arguments: Hoffman's eschatology is meaningless because he refuses to name the two witnesses or date the first of the seven years. His doctrines pass over the main points of Christianity, i.e. its teachings about faith and love. Hoffman's "profound understanding" of apocalyptic matters derives from "the great intelligence of Satan." But he, Amsdorf, remains satisfied with "the simple, straightforward teachings of Christ." Hoffman is a false prophet, who should not be allowed to teach for he is not officially licensed. Amsdorf did not think preaching by laymen could be justified on the grounds of the religious needs of a people suffering under the darkness of the papacy. ("Never mind religious needs! Only ordained ministers should be allowed to preach".) Obviously Amsdorf preferred to keep the Catholic structure intact rather than allow a spontaneous evangelical movement, which would more often than not involve iconoclasm, social unrest and attacks on the stipendiary clergy (the "belly-servers"). Finally he prided himself on his superiority to the "useless babbler."

Schuldorp took charge of the distribution of this book in Holstein.[59] Hoffman's reply to it was the coarsest of his pamphlets. He responded to Amsdorf's insistence on official ordination by referring to Christ's promise (Rev. 1:6) that all believers are "kings and priests" before God. What is more he, Hoffman, *had* been officially appointed, and that by a pious

[57] *WA Br* 4:474.

[58] *Das Melchior Hoffman ein falscher Prophet/und sein ler von Jüngsten Tag unrecht/falsch und widder Gott ist.* 1528.

[59] Hoffman, *Das Niclas Amsdorf . . . ein lügenhafftiger falscher nasengeist sey* C3b.

Christian king and his advisers, who had sent him to Kiel and established him there. It was Amsdorf, not he, who was the "fanatic" and the disruptive influence, for he was urging a Christian congregation to depose its officially appointed teacher.[60] In any case ordination was no guarantee of the truth of a teacher's doctrine: "If you are so keen on people having official appointments, why are you opposed to the Pope's mob – they have all been appointed properly?"[61] The true issue has nothing to do with ordination, it is the fact that an unlearned furrier has dared to become a preacher, "I know that if I had been ordained, and knew Latin and was not a furrier, that I would not have so much trouble from you people."[62] God commands us to relieve the burdens of our asses if they are weighed down, but even more important is the command to help another man who is weighed down with spiritual problems . Anyone who has come to a knowledge of the truth is called to liberate the people from the terrible burden of the papacy. Hoffman's reply to Amsdorf's accusation that his apocalyptic is worthless since he will not name the two witnesses or the specific year he refers to, is that by using this argument we could also maintain that all the prophecies of the Old Testament are meaningless because none of them specifies dates for the coming events.[63]

Hoffman's predicted 'Farewell' to Amsdorf takes the form of a set of variations on an insult: "rogue, rooster, crazy fool, greasy grub, coarse ass, evil gossiper and shameless belcher, robber of God's honour, riotous and murdering scoundrel and blasphemer against God's truth." His understanding of God's Word is like a cow's appreciation of Muscady wine. His colleagues in Holstein behave like the long-eared "hee-haw brothers". If one ass brays "hee-haw", they all start "hee-hawing".[64]

Hoffman's final attack on Schuldorp and Amsdorf was on a very tender spot: Schuldorp's marriage to his niece (his sister's daughter). Amsdorf had married them in Magdeburg on 13th

---

[60] *Ibid.* C2a.
[61] *Ibid.* B2a.
[62] *Ibid.* B1b.
[63] *Ibid.* A3a-b.
[64] *Ibid.* C3a.

September, 1525. This marriage, which was forbidden by both Canon and Imperial Law, aroused a scandal throughout the whole town. The Cathedral Canons of Magdeburg accused Amsdorf of breaking the law and Schuldorp of incest. Desperate for support, Schuldorp turned to Luther, who had already considerably reduced the number of forbidden relationships. In *The Babylonian Captivity of the Church* he had declared the marriage of uncles and nieces permissible,[65] and he had already sanctioned Schuldorp's matrimonial intentions before the wedding. He then advised him to hold on to his wife until she was forcibly taken away from him.[66] Early in 1526 Luther and Amsdorf published a joint defence of Schuldorp's action.[67] Referring to Leviticus 18:6ff, Luther explains that the Law does not forbid this marriage, in fact it sanctions it, for what is not forbidden by the Law the Christian can do with a clear conscience. The outcry by the papists was sheer hypocrisy because the Pope (that "great pimp") gave dispensations under the same circumstances if he was paid enough. Indeed, this anger on the part of the enemies of Christian freedom is a sign that Schuldorp is actually on the right path. Nor should he be worried by attacks from those who are weak in the faith. The assertion of Christian freedom takes precedence over appeasement of those who have scruples. He himself was quite willing to arouse further scandals on behalf of Christian freedom if he knew for certain what it was that pleased God and displeased men. It was mainly for this reason that he had married a nun.[68]

But this defence in no way put an end to the matter for Schuldorp. The upholders of Catholicism in Schleswig-Holstein revelled in the issue, arguing that the introduction of the Reformation meant the end of the natural and divine order of

---

[65] *WA* 6:555, *LW* 36:99.

[66] Letter of 12th December, 1525 *WA* 3:644–645.

[67] *Grund und orsake/worup Marquardus Schuldorp hefft syner suster dochter thor ehe genommen.*

[68] *WA Br* 4:9–10. The following passages in Luther deal with permissible relationships for marriage: *WA* 102: 263, 280f; 303: 205-248; *WA Br* 4:331; 5:214. (*LW* 45:7-9, 22ff) (*LW* 46:265-320).

things.[69] Schuldorp's marriage considerably diminished his authority in the community. If he censured drunkards they would reply by shouting "Incestuous swine!" when he passed them in the street.[70] Hoffman took up this issue to counter Schuldorp's charge that his incendiary preaching was impairing the spread of the Reformation in Catholic towns; he could now say that it was Schuldorp's marriage which was prejudicial to the cause of the Gospel.

Amsdorf's third book against Hoffman is couched in comparatively moderate language.[71] He challenges Hoffman to prove that the seven years of the apocalypse have already begun (by 1528) and to name the two witnesses. But since he is obviously incapable of doing this he would do better to remain silent and to remember Christ's words that no-one can know when the Son of Man will appear. Furthermore he begs the "false prophet" "to preach to sows and asses, not to men."

Eventually Luther and Melanchthon began to get worried about the increasingly venomous controversy between Amsdorf, Schuldorp and Hoffman. In fact they had got the impression from the title Hoffman had given himself ("preacher appointed by His Royal Majesty") that King Frederick I had made him his court preacher.[72] Luther warned the Crown Prince Christian against Hoffman on 24th July, 1528 and told him "not to give much room to such raving spirits" and, if possible, to stop him preaching, "until he knows more about it." At present he only teaches the figments of his own imagination. He says very little or almost nothing at all, about the main points of Christianity – faith in Christ and love of one's neighbour because of the cross.[73] On the same day Melanchthon wrote to Peter Suave, the King's Counsellor in Copenhagen.[74] He

[69] L. Namann, *Egenwillion – Evangelion Martini Luthers* 124a. and J.A. Cypraeus, *Annales* p. 425.

[70] Schuldorp, *Breef* D1b.

[71] N. Amsdorf, *Das Melchior Hoffman/nicht ein wort auff mein Büchlein geantwortet hat* s.l. 1528.

[72] *WA Tr* 5:No. 5797 p. 360.

[73] *WA Br* 4:503–504.

[74] *CR* 1:993.

expressed his fear that the King did not know of Hoffman's fanatical ideas and hoped that the King would surround himself with better company in the future. The Crown Prince replied that he could do nothing about Hoffman since he had been appointed by the King and he was thus outside his jurisdiction. After this reply it was expected in Wittenberg that Hoffman would win a significant triumph. Strangely enough, Luther rejected Amsdorf's appeal for him to contribute to the polemical literature.[75]

The Catholic Rector of St. Nicholas' church used the controversy amongst the evangelical preachers as an opportunity to expel Hoffman. With this aim he wrote to Luther on 21st February, 1528. After ambiguous praise of Luther's "admirable and unusual doctrine" ("admirabilis et insolita") he complained that these very ideas were being used to lay aside sacred and long-established aspects of church life such as the rite of baptism, the Latin Mass and even belief in the bodily presence of Christ in the Eucharist. Hoffman was replacing these with his dubious doctrine of the imminence of the Last Judgement.[76] Pravest had struck the right note. Luther replied as early as 14th March, 1528, assuring him that the Sacramentarians were worse than the Papists; he fought them harder than he did the Pope for they were more harmful. He (Luther) was not responsible for the vehemence of the iconoclasts; it was Karlstadt who had started all that. But now a genuine peace had been restored to the church in Wittenberg. All was as it had been in the olden days, with ritual, vestments, images and even the Mass in Latin. Only the words of institution in the Lord's Supper were spoken in German, and he had been pressured into agreeing to even this. Everybody should beware of Hoffman and, despite the royal letter of protection, the magistrate should expel him from the pulpit. He must be silenced since he is not ordained and is not fitted to teach. Pravest could inform the members of his congregation of this judgment in Luther's name.[77]

[75] *WA Br* 4:610.
[76] *WA Br* 4:381.
[77] *WA Br* 4:410-411.

But Pravest then made a mistake; he went around Kiel showing Luther's letter but also a satirical poem he had written against Luther. Konrad Wulff, a townsman of Kiel, informed Luther of Pravest's abuse of his name. Luther wrote to Pravest on 9th May, 1528 forbidding him to circulate his earlier letter against Hoffman, otherwise he would make known to the whole world the evil and injustice of the papist serpent (Pravest). If he had known Pravest was an enemy of the Gospel he would have attempted to stop his raging and storming against a servant of God's Word even if that servant (Hoffman) had caused a little disturbance himself.[78]

On the same day Luther wrote two further letters connected with the Pravest/Hoffman dispute, one to Paul Harge, Burgomaster of Kiel, and the other to his informant, Konrad Wulff. In them he moderated his earlier condemnation of Hoffman. Hoffman meant well but was too impatient to implement the Reformation. He should be urged "to use grace and style in preaching the Gospel rather than having recourse to onslaughts, fights and riots." If the heart is ruled by justice external injustice will in time disappear automatically.[79] There was no longer any question of Hoffman being dismissed. Pravest could not remain in Kiel after this débâcle, and returned to the Bordesholm cloister in October, 1528. But he played a final trick on the city – he took the whole inventory of the rectory with him. On 6th October, 1528 the Cloister said it was prepared to hand over the inventory if the Council chose another rector from amongst their own monks. But this was unacceptable to the town. They came to a new agreement three days later, which stipulated that the town could at any time choose whom it liked to be the rector of St. Nicholas; as before the leading pastor would receive all of the tithes and incomes from the benefice, but only so long as he continued to celebrate the Catholic Mass in the Choir of the Twelve Apostles.[80] Thus the first unexpected result of Hoff-

---

[78] WA Br 4:453–454.
[79] WA Br 4:454–455. cf. M.A. Noll, "Luther Defends Hoffman" in The Sixteenth Century Journal 4 (1973), pp. 47-60.
[80] Cf. above n. 14.

man's controversy with the preachers was the expulsion of the Catholic rector and the take-over of the patronage of St. Nicholas' church by the city authorities.

In the second half of 1528 Hoffman's controversy with the Lutheran preachers turned from a dispute over eschatology and biblical exegesis to the issue of the Eucharist. Hoffman dubbed his Lutheran colleagues "sacramental conjurers" since they claimed to be able to remove God from Heaven and fix Him in a physical piece of bread. At this Schuldorp put aside his former hesitancy and wrote a tract against Hoffman entitled *The Content of the Sacrament and Testament of the Body and Blood of Jesus Christ*,[81] which, according to Krohn aroused three ripostes from Hoffman.[82] Schuldorp replied to one of these three works with his letter to the believers in Kiel in 1529. Of all these tracts only the latter has survived.[83]

Hoffman's anti-Lutheran position on the Eucharistic question eventually lost him the trust he had hitherto enjoyed of King Frederick I. His fate in Schleswig-Holstein was sealed.

Political factors seem also to have played a significant role in this. In view of the threatened onslaught of Christian II (who intended to reclaim his throne) and his alliance with his brother-in-law, the Emperor Charles V, Denmark wanted to form an alliance with the Lutheran princes of northern Germany, in particular with Hesse and the Electorate of Saxony.[84] Before Saxony would co-operate in political or military matters it stipulated the removal of the hated "Sacramentarians" from Denmark. Thus Hoffman no longer fitted into the ecclesiastical policy of the Crown Prince Christian.

---

[81] *Inhalt vom Sakrament und Testament des Leibes und Blutes Jesu Christi.*

[82] *Inhalt und Bekenntnisse vom Sakrament und Testament des Leibes und Blutes Jesu Christi.– Sendebreef dat he nich bekennen könne dat een stück lyvlickes brods syn god sy* and *Beweis das Marquard Schuldorp in seinen Inhalt vom Sakrament und Testament ketzerisch und verführerisch geschrieben.* B.K. Krohn, *Geschichte der Fanatischen und Enthusiastischen Wiedertäufer.* (Leipzig, 1758), pp. 140, 144.

[83] Cf. above n. 15.

[84] H. Virck (ed.) *Politische Korrespondenz der Stadt Strassburg* Vol. 1 (Strasbourg, 1882) pp. 298, 427.

The Crown Prince had established the Reformation (on the Wittenberg model) in his own domains of Hadersleben and Törning (in Schleswig) in 1528. This Reformation was based on the instructions of the Saxon Visitation of 1528, which transferred the bishop's rights to control church property and his supervision of doctrine, preaching and clerical as well as lay morality, directly to the Elector's visitors. Christian appointed Eberhard Weidensee and Johann Wendt (Slavus) as his visitors in Hadersleben. Weidensee had collaborated with Amsdorf in 1524 in establishing the reformation in Magdeburg and remained his life-long friend. Weidensee summoned all of the church leaders of the two ducal domains to assemble at Hadersleben; here he instructed them in Lutheran theology and, after examining their beliefs, made them swear a new oath of loyalty. This committed the clergy to suppressing every doctrine of the Sacramentarians or the Anabaptists; they swore to avoid drunkenness and other vices and to be obedient to Prince Christian in all just matters.[85] In order to facilitate the consent of the supporters of the old church there were no polemical articles against the Catholic doctrine. The only enemies seemed to be those on Luther's left – Sacramentarians and Anabaptists.

The Ecclesiastical Ordinance of Hadersleben and Törning issued in the same year (1528) is even more insistent in its rejection of any reforms that go further than those of Luther.[86] This linked very conservative liturgical forms with the need to preach obedience. The German Mass could only be celebrated if the old liturgical vessels were used. If possible the Gloria, Sanctus and Agnus Dei were to be sung in Latin on high feasts. Anyone guilty of mortal sin or convicted of an offence was to be excluded from the Eucharist and no-one could approach the Lord's Table without first making an auricular confession. The elevation of the cup was to form part of the rite. Article XI obliged preachers to urge their congregations to keep the peace and to submit to the authorities (which included the payment of

---

[85] F.C. Jensen and D.H. Hegewisch, *Privilegien*, p. 29.
[86] *Articuli pro pastoribus ruralibus*. For text cf. *Schriften des Vereins für Schleswig-Holsteinische Kirchengeschichte* I, 18. 1934.

all tithes, duties and obligations as well as the ready fulfilment of compulsory service).

At the beginning of 1529 Duke Christian asked his adviser Weidensee to prepare an assessment of Hoffman's Eucharistic doctrine; Weidensee published his book in the same year.[87] Like his friend Amsdorf, Weidensee had undergone a change of heart on this matter. While he had been attempting to institute reforms in Magdeburg against the opposition of the Cathedral Chapter in 1524, he had taught that a minister was only properly appointed if he had been elected by his congregation, but there was no longer any question of this in the Ecclesiastical Ordinance of Hadersleben in 1528. Here the minister was accountable for his appointment to the secular authority alone. Before the Peasants' War Weidensee had written a polemical tract against the necessity of infant baptism for salvation, in which he said that a man was justified by his own faith, not by that of the congregation, or his parents or god-parents. But after the Peasants' War he justified the appropriateness of infant baptism with the argument that even the dumb could have faith in some mysterious way.[88] In Magdeburg, in 1524, he had mobilized the townspeople against the Cathedral Chapter and their claims to keep control of patronage rights. But now he said that one should never oppose princes or lords, even if they act unjustly; rebellious peasants cannot have a drop of Christian blood in their bodies.

After this change of heart Weidensee's attitude to Hoffman could be nothing but damning. This is apparent from the book's motto: "The Lord knows the way of the righteous, but the way of the wicked will perish" (Psalm 1:6). But in comparison to Amsdorf's pamphlets this book by Weidensee is precise and to the point. Hoffman's arguments are stated simply and apparently accurately, before he attempts to counter them. Weidensee clearly entertains no more hopes of winning Hoffman back to Lutheranism: "If Melchior is confronted with the Scriptures he

---

[87] *Eyn underricht uth der hillighen schrifft* cf. P. Tschackert, *Dr. Eberhard Weidensee, Leben und Schriften* (Berlin, 1911).

[88] P. Tschackert, *op.cit.*, p. 22-30.

will hear none of them, like the dog that barks when it is hit with a stick."[89] Weidensee limited himself to two problems in this tract: Hoffman's doctrine of the Eucharist and his incitement of the common people against the evangelical preachers.

1. According to Weidensee Hoffman used the following biblical arguments to deny Christ's real presence in the Eucharistic elements:

Luke 17:21 ("Behold, the kingdom of God is within you") as a prohibition of localising God in external things;

Isaiah 66:1 and Acts 7:49-50, which, according to Hoffman, assert that the finite is incapable of holding the infinite. God does not approach man in external things, nor can he be imprisoned in matter by a priest's words; rather, he is close to those who suffer, to those with a broken spirit and to those who fear him.[90]

Weidensee replies to this by saying that in Luke 17 Christ was not speaking of His body and blood, but of His Kingdom. Christ's humanity involves corporeality, which means that he appears in a concrete place. Thus Christ came into the world in the virginal shrine of Mary's womb, He lay in the manger and hung on the cross. Resurrected, He is present in His humanity in the Eucharist.[91] Indeed, the elements are not changed, but the bread and wine are so united with Christ's body in the Sacrament that they become an inseparable unity just like iron and fire in red-hot metal.[92] To deny the real presence in the Eucharist is to remove the kernel from the nutshell and to leave the communicant with an empty shell.[93] Isaiah 66:1 asserts rather than rejects the doctrine of the real presence. God is ubiquitous in all creatures; Christ ascended into Heaven so as to fulfil all things. Yet he is not bound or prescribed by them, for he is also outside all creation, above and around it as well as within.[94] Because of this bodily presence of Christ, unbelievers

---

[89] *Eyn underricht* A3b.
[90] *ibid.*, A3b, B3a-b.
[91] *ibid.*, C1a.
[92] *ibid.*, B2b.
[93] *ibid.*, B3a. Weidensee took both of these images from Luther, *WA* 11:437, *LW* 36: 282; *WA* 19: 501, *LW* 36:346.)
[94] *ibid.*, C1a.

also partake of the Lord's body and blood, but to their own damnation.[95] Hoffman's interpretation of the Eucharist as a contract between Christ and the soul, in which Christ the bridegroom gives the Eucharistic elements to his bride as a pledge of fidelity, is treated as a joke by Weidensee.

2. Weidensee then turns to Hoffman's role as an inciter of the mob. Not a single Lutheran preacher finds favour with him; he damns them all as "false prophets, robbers of God, magicians or belly-servers." "One fellow, Hoffman says, is avaricious, the other one supercilious, this shaveling wears a golden waistcoat, and that black-coat runs around in a cloak lined with the fur of foxes; another one is unbidden by his congregation, and yonder priest has intruded himself; this bastard has ravished his own blood, and that rogue is a hardened perjurer."[96] Weidensee's main complaint is that Hoffman's fantastic stories about the priests' incomes are arousing feelings of hatred in the mob. Hoffman says that he, Weidensee, gets 400 gulden a year from the Duke, and has already sent 1,000 gulden to Magdeburg. He receives "four small casks of wine" a day from the Duke's cellar. Since the world-famous Melchior (who is as unable to tell a lie as a dog is unable to limp) has been preaching this madness, the common people have turned away from the fine teachings of the evangelical preachers, believing them to be immoral.

The unassailed authority of the ministers, who were officials of the secular power, was an integral part of the princely church government. If someone like Hoffman made a sustained (and, in parts, unjustified) criticism of the ministers appointed by the ruler he was threatening one pillar of princely government. Thus the Crown Prince Christian decided to contrive Hoffman's downfall in a large public disputation, as Weidensee had earlier proposed.[97] Hoffman's prospects at this colloquy were clear from the start. Duke Christian invited Nikolaus von Amsdorf, Hoffman's arch-enemy, to act as Luther's representative. But

---

[95] *ibid.*, C1b.
[96] *ibid.*, C2a.
[97] *ibid.*, A2b.

Luther advised Amsdorf to turn down the Duke's request.[98] His place was taken (as earlier in Hamburg) by Johannes Bugenhagen. Bugenhagen was given such an extravagant welcome by Hoffman's enemies that it seemed God Almighty had come Himself, according to Hoffman's barbed comment. "All that mattered was Pomeranus and his words. If the Holy Ghost had been there He would not have had a chance to speak up." [99]

3. The Flensburg Disputation.

The disputation was to take place at the secularized Franciscan cloister in Flensburg and King Frederick I called for it to begin on 9th April, 1529.[100] The king took up residence in the castle at Flensburg but did not take part in the disputation. He appointed six solicitors to make minutes of the disputation, and on the basis of this record he wanted to make the final decision himself.[101] Duke Christian himself took the chair, and was supported in controlling the proceedings by Johann von Rantzau, the king's steward, and Detlev Reventlov, the provost of Reinbeck.[102] Invitations had been issued to the Lutheran preachers of Schleswig-Holstein (whose spokesman was Hermann Tast, the reformer of Husum[103]) and Holstein's two sacramentarians,

---

[98] Letter of 21st March, 1529, *WA Br* 5, No. 1398.

[99] Hoffman and Karlstadt, *Dialogus* A3a.

[100] J. Bugenhagen (ed.), *Acta* M1a.

[101] *Acta* D3b-D4a. They were Franciscus Strienius, royal chaplain; Dietrich Becker from Husum; Johann Francke from Wilster; Johann Wendt from Hadersleben and a colleague of Weidensee; Tesmarus Halebeke and Johann Benekendapff from Kiel. Hoffman felt that all the notaries were his enemies.

[102] *Acta* A2a, A4a. Hoffman confused the provost of Reinbek with the royal physician, Dr. Lyder Reventlov.

[103] Hoffman (*Dialogus* A1a) says that Schuldorp had also taken part and had begun to talk about old heretics, at which Johann von Rantzau had silenced him. But there is no record of this in the minutes.

Hoffman and Johannes van Campen (a former monk) along with Jakob Hegge, a minister from Danzig.[104]

The Lutherans of Schleswig-Holstein had called in a number of theologians from outside as advisors to support them in their stance. There were Nicolaus Boie, the reformer of Dithmarschen (a free peasants' republic) who came from Wesselburen and Stephan Kempe, the Hamburg reformer. Kempe was accompanied by Master Theophilus, rector of St John's in Hamburg and a friend of Marquard Schuldorp's.[105] The Duke had called in Boie as an impartial adviser, but he had chosen to declare himself openly on the side of the Lutherans from the very beginning. [106] The leading guest was Johannes Bugenhagen, who had been called in by the king to act as the senior spiritual authority and who had the task of summing up.

Hoffman had tried to get the support of Karlstadt. Karlstadt did promise to help and secretly escaped from Kemberg in Saxony where he was living in exile. But Frederick I refused Hoffman's request to give Karlstadt a safe-conduct. Karlstadt was thus forced to leave Holstein, though he had already met up with Hoffman there.[107] With such a prejudgment of the issue on the part of the king and with such an unfair balance of forces the outcome of the disputation could not be in doubt. It developed into something more like a cross-examination than an open religious discussion.

There were about 400 spectators, amongst whom Hoffman counted about 100 of his own supporters.[108] Nobles, townsmen and peasants thronged to this show in such numbers "that people were standing on top of each other. Nobody else could get in and the doors had to be left open."[109]

As for so many other places the pattern for this event had been set by the two disputations of Zürich in 1523. In both cases it

---

[104] *Dialogus* A8a; *Acta* A3b, C8b, D1b.
[105] *Acta* A3b.
[106] *Acta* M2b.
[107] *Dialogus* A3a; Acta M2a.
[108] *Dialogus* B3a.
[109] *Acta* M7b.

was the secular authorities that instituted the debate and who claimed competence to decide on religious problems.[110] Even before the start of the disputation Hoffman declared that he, like Luther, would not submit to the judgment of a majority or of a prince in matters of faith, but would remain faithful to the truth as he had come to know it.[111] The disputation of Flensburg had little in common with contemporary university disputations, for in this case the loser faced a punishment which might even take the form of banishment. Even in formal matters they did not keep to the rules of the academic game, with both parties attacking each other with total abandon. Meanwhile the "impartial" figures took up the Lutheran case and it was never clear from the beginning whether Hoffman had to defend himself against the Lutherans or vice-versa. Only Kempe and Bugenhagen observed the rules of the disputation in that they methodically summarized the arguments of their opponents before they countered them. Hoffman often interrupted his opponents since he had had no training in the refinements of academic custom.[112]

On the eve of the disputation Hoffman attempted to convince Duke Christian that he had gone no further than Luther's original position and thus could not be accounted heretical. He sent the Crown Prince one of Luther's books from 1523 "in which he explicitly and clearly puts forward the furrier's argument that the Lord's bread is received by the mouth as a seal and sign, and the Lord's word by the ear, the heart and soul".[113] Unfortunately Hoffman does not give the name of this book; Luther's *The Adoration of the Sacrament* written in 1523 shows that he was already turning against "signification" and an allegorical interpretation of the words of institution.[114] So it was

[110] B. Möller, "Zwinglis Disputationen" In ZSRG, KA 87 (1970) pp. 303ff. and O. Scheib, "Die Religionsgespräche in Norddeutschland und ihre Entwicklung" in *Jb. d. Gesellschaft f. Niedersächsische Kirchengeschichte* 75 (1977) p. 39–88.

[111] *Dialogus* A3b.

[112] For the style of the disputations cf. the chapter "Disputationen" in Georg Kaufmann: *Geschichte der Deutschen Universität.* Vol. 2, 2.A.(1958).

[113] Hoffman-Karlstadt: *Dialogus* A3b.

[114] *WA* 11:434–435, *LW* 36:279–28.

probably his tract *The Misuse of the Mass* of 1521 (but printed in a new edition in 1523) that Hoffman sent to the Duke. This assumption is supported by the examples Hoffman used in the disputation to show that God always united his promises with meaningful signs; almost all of these examples appear in Luther's work of 1521.[115]

After reading this book the Duke invited Hoffman to have a private discussion. The prince did not deal with the controversial question as to whether Hoffman had been more faithful to Luther's earlier stance than had Luther himself. But he attempted to make Hoffman recant voluntarily – i.e. to accept the view of the Eucharist Luther had propounded since his controversy with Karlstadt. Hoffman's persistent refusal strengthened his belief that the furrier was a dangerous instigator of the mob. He asked: "Melchior, if you can speak so harshly to me, what do you say to the common people?" Hoffman, following in Luther's footsteps, replied: "Even if all emperors, kings, princes, popes, bishops and cardinals got together in one place – in spite of all, we have to tell the truth".[116]

On the way to the conference hall on the morning of the disputation Bugenhagen asked Hoffman how he had come to hold his views. Hoffman attempted to remind him that they had been in agreement previously and said that at root there was no division between them. The argument was simply about whether the chaff (the sign) and the wheat (the word of forgiveness) were inextricably united or whether they could be seen as separate.[117] But before Bugenhagan could reply someone pulled him away from Hoffman. Probably no one on the Duke's side was interested in coming to an understanding with Hoffman.

Johann von Rantzau opened the disputation by asking why Hoffman had called all the preachers of Schleswig-Holstein "false prophets". The accused replied: "I called them false prophets because they pin Christ down to a particular spot. If anybody says that the bread is Christ he is pinning him down to a particular spot."[118] What this view of the limitation of God

---

[115] *WA* 8:516, *LW* 36:174, cf. *Acta* A8b.
[116] *Dialogus* A3b.
[117] *Dialogus* A4b.
[118] *Acta* A6b.

implied for Hoffman is seen more clearly in the *Dialogus* than in the minutes of the disputation: "Whoever claims that Christ is bound to physical bread and can be consecrated and distributed when and to whom he likes proves that he is a false prophet, because he is claiming to do something that is the prerogative of God and the Holy Spirit."[119] Thus the Lutheran doctrine of the Eucharist means that the priest is putting himself in the place of God and is exercising the mastery over the congregation that belongs to God. Hermann Tast then defended the position of the Lutheran preachers. The charge of being "false prophets" was a personal attack, which they did not mind, but what they should be concerned about was an attack on the holy gospel. For his group, too, it was the "spiritual eating and drinking of Christ" that was the decisive factor in the Eucharist.[120] But because of human weakness the Lord had instituted bread and wine as visible signs and had taught his followers that they were His body and blood. They were obedient disciples and believed their master's words of instruction. Hoffman then expounded the opposing view by distinguishing between the Word of God and the signs that are linked with it. God has united His promises with visible signs from the very beginning (e.g. the fur garment He gave Adam and Eve after the Fall, the rainbow for Noah, circumcision for the descendants of Abraham and the passover lamb). "What we perceive by faith is not that the Word unites the body of Christ with the bread but that the Word is spirit and life. This we receive by faith but what is received by the mouth is the seal and the sign."[121] Tast replied that what was at issue was simply whether the sign was any more than bread and wine. "We say no to this!" replied Hoffman, "The bread that we receive is figuratively and sacramentally, but not truly, the body of Christ. But I don't think that it is *just* bread because it acts as a remembrance for me".[122] Tast concluded from this that Hoffman saw the words of institution as "figurative words". But Hoffman vigorously denied this interpretation, "I didn't say it

---

[119] *Dialogus* A4b.
[120] *Acta* A6b.
[121] *Acta* B1a.
[122] *Acta* B2a.

was the *words* that are figurative, but the *bread*. The word is Christ Himself – that is why the word is powerful"[123] Thus for Hoffman Christ is really present in the word when the Eucharist is celebrated. It is in the word of forgiveness, symbolized by the Last Supper, that the actual reconciliation of God and man is brought about. Bread and wine are external signs of this "real" inner event. Neither of Hoffman's opponents could grasp all he said.[124] They could only detect that he was denying the real presence of Christ in the Eucharistic elements. His repeated assertion that only the elements, not the words, are figurative seemed to them to be pure sophistry. The Duke insisted that he explain whether, to him, the bread of the Lord's Supper was or was not the body of Christ.[125] Hoffman confessed, "No, I don't believe it is". The dispute then went on to the issue as to how far it was justified to translate the "is" of the words of institution as "means". Hoffman gave a whole list of examples where Jesus "spoke figuratively" and which would lead us to heresy or sheer meaninglessness if we understood them literally (John 3:14, 19:26, Luke 2:48). But Hoffman could not persuade his opponents to interpret the words of institution symbolically using this analogy. [126] Finally Hoffman attempted to show that the Lutheran doctrine of the Eucharist was not even compatible with common sense.

1. Sitting at the table, Christ could not have shared his body amongst the disciples at the Last Supper.[127]

2. If Christ has ascended to heaven and is seated at the right hand of God, he cannot be in the Sacrament at the same time unless he has several bodies.[128]

3. If the bread is also the body of Christ it would inevitably mean that the two distinct natures were sharing a single essence

---

[123] *Acta* B2b.
[124] Cf. W. Köhler, Zwingli und Luther. Ihr Streit über das Abendmahl. Vol. I 1924, pp. 556, 671.
[125] *Acta* C4a.
[126] *Acta* B3b.
[127] *Acta* C5a.
[128] *Acta* C7a.

(i.e. it would destroy the concept of identity and with it all logic).[129]

4. The Eucharist should not be linked with blasphemous cannibalistic ideas about eating Christ in such a physical way that we digest and process him like any other food.[130]

But to all of these ideas Hoffman's opponents (Tast, Boie, and Kempe) could only repeat the formula, "It is written: This is my body".

During the debate Hoffman often found himself in the difficult position of being cross-examined by three theologians (Tast, Boie and Kempe) and three noblemen at the same time. They took turns of throwing out questions or answers whilst he had constantly to argue with each of them without support from anyone else. Irritated by this constant pressure he made the mistake of saying, "We shall have to come to an agreement on this matter otherwise a lot of blood will be shed . . . and nobody would be more guilty (of causing bloodshed) than you, who teach it to the people in your sermons".[131] He was immediately interrupted by Bugenhagen and the King's counsellors who rejected the accusation and turned it against Hoffman and his party of sacramentarians. Soon after this the noblemen were prepared to put an end to the theological discussion. Johann von Rantzau declared that the issue had been discussed sufficiently. Duke Christian would inform the king about the course of the disputation.[132] Bugenhagen then took the opportunity to make a general critical assessment of Hoffman's doctrine. Without his contribution the Lutheran position would have appeared particularly narrow and spiritually arid because there had been hardly any attempt to argue from anything more than a literal interpretation of the words of institution. But Bugenhagen put the controversy into a greater context by making the following points.

Without a belief in the physical real presence of Christ in the Eucharistic elements it would be meaningless to say that

[129] *Acta* C2b.
[130] *Acta* C4a; C6b.
[131] *Acta* C5b.
[132] *Acta* C7b.

someone could share "unworthily" in Christ's body and blood to his own condemnation (I Cor. 11:27), for there could be no such thing as an unworthy "spiritual eating" of Christ; "to eat spiritually" means nothing other than "to have faith".[133] In response to Hoffman's objection that he could not believe that an unbeliever ate Christ in the Eucharist, Bugenhagen attenuated the new Lutheran tendency of regarding the Eucharist as an "opus operatum" by differentiating between "unbelievers" and "the unworthy." Christ is not present for Jews or Turks, who know nothing of Christ, even if they take part in the same celebration of the sacrament as believers, just as Christ is not present in the crumbs of consecrated bread that are nibbled by the mice. The "unworthy" at the Eucharist are those like the rich Corinthians, who believe in Christ but still go to the Lord's Table when drunk, or who allow their poor fellow-believers to go hungry even at an agape taken directly beforehand. Bugenhagen was thus again linking the "physical real presence of Christ" to the inner state of the recipients.[134]

Bugenhagen replied to Hoffman's rational arguments against the Lutheran doctrine of the Eucharist by saying that the mode of Christ's presence in the Sacrament is hidden from all reason. But Hoffman can be assured "that Christ is well able to protect Himself from having his ears bitten off."[135] The doctrine of Christ's sitting at God's right hand is in no way opposed to the doctrine of the presence of his body and blood on earth in the Sacrament because the term "seated at God's right hand" does not mean that Christ is "high up in a tiny corner of heaven" but that "He reigns like a king." This means that the "seat at God's right hand" is in fact that which makes possible his presence in the Sacrament.[136]

Bugenhagen then considered the consequences of the spiritualist and realist interpretations of the Eucharist for the relationship between God and men. "Yes, you say, He is with us in spirit, that is spiritually and not visibly. But what I say is,

[133] *Acta* D8a, G4a.
[134] *Acta* I4b, I5a, K1a.
[135] *Acta* K3a.
[136] *Acta* H5a-b.

what sort of Christ is it who is with us in spirit? Is He not God and man, who fills all things (Eph. 1)?" [137] He means by this that the sacramentarians are inclined towards dualism; they cut off the spiritual from the material and restrict what is divine to the spiritual realm. Bugenhagen responded to this by asserting Luther's doctrine of the Eucharist as an expression of the belief that God suffuses, rules and sanctifies the whole world, both spiritual and material.

In connection with the Eucharist Bugenhagen also raised the question as to what extent Christ's disciples have the power to forgive sins. Hoffman immediately retorted, "Nobody can forgive sins, that is for God alone" [138] to which Bugenhagen replied, "We, too, believe that, but this should not mean that we despise the minister's role like Müntzer and the heavenly prophets, who tried to do away with baptism and the sacrament, and who despised the external word." Bugenhagen saw the "sacramentarians" as false teachers in that they wanted to do away with the divine ordinance whereby God's power to bestow blessing is mediated by the work of the preachers, firstly in the proclamation of the Gospel and secondly in the distribution of the Lord's Supper, in which Christ himself is bodily present. To Bugenhagen's thinking we can only be assured of forgiveness by concrete experiences, by hearing the words of the preacher and by physically eating and drinking the bread and the wine.

At the end of the proceedings Hoffman's two companions, Hegge and van Campen, took the floor. Johann van Campen, a former monk, had found a post as preacher in the nunnery at Itzehoe (which was run by Johann von Rantzau's sister). He had then married one of the nuns in this cloister. "He went out of the gates of heaven with 200 Lübeck marks." The Rantzaus regarded him as "a desperate rogue". [139] Count Johann gave van Campen short shrift. He asked him if he agreed with Melchior's

---

[137] *Acta* H7b.

[138] *Acta* F3a.

[139] Cf. C.A. Cornelius, *Geschichte des Münsterschen Aufruhrs* pp. 301-303.

opinion, and he replied that he had reached the same view of the Eucharist as Hoffman, but independently of him. This was sufficient for the judges.[140] Jakob Hegge, a minister in Danzig, regarded it as an absurdity to say that "unbelievers" do not receive the Lord's body whereas the "unworthy", such as Judas do receive it. But he was not totally convinced about this matter and was willing to be instructed.[141] Bugenhagen consequently urged that Hegge be released, for a doubting conscience should never be damned. [142]

With this the disputation came to an end. But as the spectators were leaving the hall someone breathlessly burst through them. This was Johannes Barse, a supporter of Karlstadt. He had not been able to gain admittance but felt compelled to make a statement. Gesticulating frantically, he explained, "My argument is based on the Word of God which says 'This is my body.' The Wittenbergers object to this and make up new articles of faith such as 'My body is in the bread' or 'under the bread'." He had presumably taken up the interpretation of Karlstadt, according to which when Jesus said 'This is my body', he had pointed to his own body. Most people could not understand the point he was making and took him to be a fool and "they could not stop themselves from laughing".[143] In desperation Barse shouted out a phrase of Augustine's, "Believe and you have eaten!", but it was to no avail because Stephen Kempe informed him that in other places Augustine had taught the real bodily presence in the Eucharist.

On the following day King Frederick held counsel to decide on his judgment. The knights were divided. One group pressed for the death penalty because Hoffman was a "Müntzerite agitator" who had "publicly stated in the course of the disputation that much blood would have to be shed because the other preachers would not teach what he wanted them to about

---

[140] Johann van Campen is not the same as the antitrinitarian Johannes Campanus, who was a student in Wittenberg from 1527 to 1530.

[141] *Acta* D1b.

[142] *Acta* D2a.

[143] *Acta* D2a.

the Sacrament." The other group argued that he should be banished as a false teacher if he refused to recant.[144] The King sided with this latter group.

Johann von Rantzau proclaimed the King's decision on 11th April, 1529; Melchior Hoffman and Johann van Campen had to recant their doctrines otherwise they would have to leave the country, Hoffman within three days and van Campen within one. Neither did recant. Von Rantzau then asked Hegge if he had meanwhile accepted "the clear Word of God." He said he had not, and was banished.[145]

Despite the King's assurances Hoffman was robbed of all his possessions including his printing-press, which he estimated to be worth 1,000 gulden.[146] The printing-press was taken over by the city of Kiel, though they had to hand it over to the king in 1533. Rather than condemning this infringement of Hoffman's rights, Bugenhagen revelled in what had happened to the "poor little worm", who knew more about begging than any mendicant monk.[147] Bugenhagen himself was not badly off when he returned to Wittenberg. The Hamburg City Council, in gratitude for his work in setting up the Ecclesiastical Ordinance, granted him an honorary gift of 100 rhenish gulden and his wife received an extra 20 golden gulden.[148]

For Hoffman the Flensburg disputation revealed Lutheranism for what it truly was. He saw that the Wittenberg theologians were restoring the papacy in a new form. This could be seen in two things. In their doctrine of the Eucharist they made the same error as the Pope in confusing God with His creatures, though God could only be truly approached in spirit and in truth, and they used coarse secular power to deal with matters of conscience where questions of God's truth and ordinance

---

[144] *Acta* L8b.

[145] *Acta* L7b. A few weeks later Hegge did confess the Lutheran doctrine of the Eucharist in front of Bugenhagen.

[146] *Dialogus* B3b.

[147] *Acta* N2a.

[148] Cf. E. Feddersen, *Kirchengeschichte* p. 72 n. 7. Bugenhagen's partiality for monetary gifts was notorious. Lütge Namann (*op. cit.* fol. 128b) said he did not know how Bugenhagen would be able to explain to St. Peter at the gate of heaven why he had accepted so much money from Hamburg, Brunswick, Lübeck, Nuremberg etc. etc.

were at stake.[149] They locked God into material dust and usurped His control of spiritual affairs. Because of the unjust judgement against him Hoffman saw himself as joining the band of God's martyrs, which stretched from the Old Testament prophets, through Christ and up to Jan Hus and his followers.

Hoffman blamed only Bugenhagen and the Lutheran preachers for his disaster at Flensburg. He felt that the King and Duke were pawns of the evil priests.

At the end of the *Dialogus* he thinks back to Pilate and says that none of the secular rulers, neither the King nor Duke Christian, neither the royal counsellors nor the nobles, had had anything to do with his condemnation, "but Pomeranus and his cronies should be warned that they will have to answer for their bodies and souls on the Day of Judgment."[150]

Hoffman retained the amazing delusion that he had simply been the victim of the new Lutheran orthodoxy but not of the new princely church government. He still trusted Frederick I and after his banishment he dedicated the commentary on Revelation, his second major book, to the King. In this he presented Frederick as one of the two Christian kings who would protect the suffering church from annihilation at the hands of the beast (the Emperor) in the course of the apocalyptic disturbances.

Several factors seem to have brought about this misunderstanding: his previous gratitude for a letter of protection, the simple man's faith in the myth of the "good king" and his "wicked servants" and the divergent assessments a spiritualist would make of secular and religious authorities. Up to Gottfried Arnold it was more frequent for spiritualists to complain of the church's abuse of the "secular arm" than to cry out against the degradation of the church at the hands of the state.

This subjective view of Hoffman's cannot disguise the historical fact that his failure in Holstein was due primarily to the incompatibility of a spiritualist and socially-critical lay movement with the Prince's concept of an orthodox and submissive established state church.

---

[149] *Dialogus* B2b-B3a.
[150] *Dialogus* B2b.

4. Hoffman's Position in the Eucharistic Controversy of the Sixteenth Century.

Throughout his dispute with Bugenhagen and the Lutheran preachers of Schleswig-Holstein, Hoffman regarded himself as a disciple of Luther's. To his mind he had been faithful to the doctrines of the young Luther, although the latter had deviated from his purpose of bringing liberation from the papal yoke. Was Hoffman's assessment of himself, and of Luther, accurate?

Certainly Hoffman did take over the essentials of his Eucharistic doctrine from the early Luther, namely:

1. The distinction between the sign (the sacrament) and the promise of forgiveness (the testament).[151]

2. Luther's original elevation of the 'testament' above the 'sacrament'. In his *Sermon on the New Testament* of 1520 Luther wrote, "We thus see that the best and greater part of all sacraments and of the mass is the *word* and promise of God, without which the sacrament is dead and empty, just like a body without a soul."[152]

3. The dependence of the effect of the sacrament on the faith of the recipient.[153] Anyone who does not believe the promise has eaten and drunk to no effect. Luther and Hoffman also agreed that anyone firmly believing in the promise of forgiveness could be saved without partaking of the Sacrament.[154]

But there are also passages in Luther's early writings which oppose a reduction of the sacrament to a simple matter of the word. Thus in *The Misuse of the Mass* of 1521 he said that Christ

---

[151] *WA* 6:517-518, *LW* 36:43-44; *WA* 8:516, *LW* 36:174. cf. *Dialogus* A3b.

[152] *WA* 6:363 cf. *Dialogus* A4b.

[153] *WA* 6:516. *LW* 36:43 cf. Hoffman. *Daniel* M3b. M4a.

[154] Luther, *Sermon von dem neuen Testament* (1520),:

"For I can receive the sacrament of the mass daily so long as I take to heart that it is the testament, that is the word and promise of Christ, and use it to build up and strengthen my faith", *WA* 6:358.

cf. *WA* 11:433, *LW* 36:279 and Hoffman, *Daniel* N2b:

"Because whoever is unable to receive the sign or the seal, so long as he holds fast to the words, believes them, trusts and builds on them, he has still eaten Christ in all His power and life".

had hidden His true flesh and blood under the bread and wine and distributed it to believers.[155] In *The Babylonian Captivity* of 1520 he used the image of "burning iron" to describe the relationship between the Eucharistic elements and Christ's body. Just as there is an inseparable unity of fire and iron in red-hot metal, so a new power enters the elements in the Eucharist, namely the body of Christ, which suffuses them like fire, changing their effects but in no way altering their basic essence.[156] After the celebration the remaining bread and wine revert to being natural things, just as iron returns to its natural state when it cools down. Luther explicitly denied in *The Babylonian Captivity* that John 6:63 ("It is the spirit that gives life, the flesh is of no avail") refers to the body of Christ in the Eucharist, thus refuting in advance the later argument of the sacramentarians.[157]

Luther's disputes with the spiritualists (the Zwickau prophets and Thomas Müntzer) and the sacramentarians (Karlstadt and the evangelical preachers from the Netherlands), which began in 1522-1523, led him to reconsider his priorities with respect to his Eucharistic doctrine. Luther felt that these "enthusiasts" threatened the very core of Reformation doctrine, i.e. the certainty that salvation comes from God and reaches us by external concrete means – by audible preaching and an edible sacrament. The spiritualists reversed this divinely appointed structure by setting an inner transformation before the outward gifts; they taught that men must prepare for God's entry into the heart by "self-denial" (asceticism and meditative submission) and that only a purified inner disposition ("a receptive heart") could make them worthy to receive the external gifts of salvation. But Luther stressed that the Eucharist was first and foremost a sign given to troubled men to strengthen their faith and grant them assurance.[158] In the Eucharist man can experi-

---

[155] *WA* 8:516, *LW* 36:174.

[156] *WA* 6:510, *LW* 36:32.

[157] *WA* 6:502, *LW* 36:19, "The sixth chapter of John must be entirely excluded from this discussion".

[158] *WA* 18:135 ff., *LW* 40:146ff. On the significance of the "verbum externum" and the sacrament in Luther cf. K.-H. zur Mühlen, *Nos extra nos* (Tübingen, 1972), pp. 227-265.

ence God's "real" presence for him personally in a concrete way
and he sees God's willingness to deal with him although a sinner
and poor in faith.

The Eucharistic controversy of the 16th century brought
together theological, philosophical and social elements, which
need only be outlined here.

1. It dealt with the possibility of a concrete experience of the
divine within the world or, more precisely, with the way of
atonement of God with man. Two contradictory tendencies
came together here – the need to find a concrete assurance of
salvation in a chaotic world, and the tendency resulting from the
spread of rationalism to deprive the world of its "magic" (which
was a threat to man's desire for salvation). Following the
Protestants' objection to the idea of God's immanence in the
papal church, its sacraments, reliquaries and images, they said
that the holy was manifest in the here and now in Christ alone,
by means of the 'Word of God' (which was not identical with
the letter of Scripture), baptism, the Eucharist and the communion of believers (which was not to be identified with an
institution). The sacramentarians then went further in rationalis-
ing and individualising faith, and they almost allowed Christianity's objective foundations to disappear; God, according to
them, could only be present in the form of an "inner word."

They thus did away with all of the magical and juridical
elements of traditional Christianity. There was no longer any
"holy substance" which could be controlled by priests or given
(in certain circumstances) to individual believers. Faith became a
matter of a purely personal and spiritual relationship between
God and the individual soul. But was it still a relationship
between two beings, or was man now speaking only to himself?
This was Luther's question to the sacramentarians.[159]

What, to the sacramentarians, was the logical conclusion of
the Protestant principle of justification by faith alone, was for
Luther nothing but individualism. He attacked their view, on

---

[159] On this whole question cf. P. Tillich, *Protestantische Vision-
katholische Substanz-Sozialistische Entscheidung*, 1952, pp. 10f., and
"Protestantismus als Kritik" in *Gesammelte Werke* Vol. 7. pp. 106-109.

behalf of timorous man, in his *Against the Heavenly Prophets in the Matter of Images and Sacraments* (1525): "For in no place do they teach how we are to become free from our sins, obtain a good conscience, and win a peaceful and joyful heart before God."[160] He thus believed it vital to hold on to the external word and to the sacrament as mediators of the "inner word". It is they that guarantee God's commitment to man. Luther's opponents saw this as a hangover from papal sacramentalism. For the sacramentarians the divine word could only appear in one form, that is in the spirit. The question as to how the spirit was mediated was secondary for them; on the whole the spirit used the "external word" and sacraments but was in no way limited to these external means. Over and above these there was "unmediated revelation", and all that really mattered was that the "inner Word" be trusted.[161]

2. The sacramentarian view of the Lord's Supper was based on a dualistic world view, which separated the spiritual from the material and regarded the spiritual as the only realm of divine revelation. They found biblical support for this approach in the long discourse on the bread of life in John Chapter 6 (in particular v.27, "Do not labour for the food which perishes, but for the food which endures to eternal life" and v.63 "It is the spirit that gives life, the flesh is of no avail; the words that I have spoken to you are spirit and life"). Karlstadt considered that such an eternal food could only be the faith that looks to the crucified Christ; the flesh that is "of no avail" is a reference to the physical eating, "which chops with the teeth and jaws."[162] For Zwingli, John 6:63 was the unassailable rock on which he based his opposition to Luther. In his work on the Last Supper published in 1526 he concluded that faith has nothing to do with what is physical; it is not Christ's flesh and blood which have the power to give life, but his sacrificial death. We appropriate the benefits

---

[160] *WA 18:213, LW* 40:222-223.

[161] H. Kaminsky, "The Free Spirit in the Hussite Revolution" in S.L. Thrupp, *Millenial Dreams in Action* (The Hague, 1962), pp. 172 f.

[162] Karlstadt, *Dialogue*, English translation by C. Lindberg, "Karlstadt's *Dialogue* on the Lord's Supper" in *MQR* 53 (1979) pp. 35-77.

of this death by faith.[163] At the Colloquy of Marburg in 1529 Zwingli declared "flesh and spirit are opposed to each other" and all the arguments of the Swiss group were based on the idea that only man's *spirit* was capable of apprehending the divine.[164]

3. The identification of the divine with the spiritual led the sacramentarians to rationalize Christian faith. Luther had already said that such an attempt was doomed. For him revelation confronted human reason with enormous and imponderable facts, such as the virgin birth, Christ's atoning death, the resurrection of the body and the physical presence of Christ in the Sacrament. Luther insisted on these paradoxes and provoked his opponents at the Colloquy of Marburg by saying: "If He asked me to eat dung I would do it because I would know it would be a benefit for me. The servant should not ponder over his master's will. You just have to close your eyes." Zwingli's reply to this was: "God is light and truth, and does not lead us into obscurity. Thus when He says 'This is my body', He does not mean it essentially, actually or bodily, which would contradict the Scripture. Demons' oracles are obscure, but Christ's words are not. God does not act that way. The soul lives on spiritual things, it does not eat flesh. Spirit eats spirit."

4. Finally the sacramentarians saw in Luther's doctrine of the Eucharist the germ of a new division of believers into "laity" and "clergy." If the words of institution can only be uttered by priests, and if they bring about a real presence of Christ's body in the Eucharistic elements, then the evangelical clergy (particularly if they retained the power of the keys) would again dominate their congregations. Consequently it was the proud townspeople of the Netherlands, of the south German Imperial cities and of Switzerland, who were attracted to sacramentarian-

---

[163] H. Zwingli, *Eine klare unterrichtung vom Nachtmahl Christi* in *CR* 91: 789-862. English translation, "On the Lord's Supper" in G.W. Bromiley (ed), *Zwingli and Bullinger*, (Library of Christian Classics. Vol. 24.) pp. 185-238.

[164] Cf. the accounts of the colloquy of Marburg in *LW* Vol. 38 and W. Köhler, *Das Marburger Religionsgespräch. Versuch einer Rekonstruktion* 1929. Wilhelm Maurer (in *Luther und die Schwärmer*, 1952) felt that the dualism between spirit and flesh was the factor that brought Zwingli and the "enthusiasts" together in opposition to Luther.

ism. The social aspect of the Eucharistic issue had first emerged in the Hussite movement; the struggle of the Czech townsmen to achieve social equality with the priests found expression in their demand for communion in both kinds for the laity. The radical Taborites went further than this and argued that the dogma of Christ's real presence in the Eucharistic elements was incompatible with their concept of the church, for they believed that the laity should have the right to settle all matters of faith. It was a hundred years before Cornelis Hoen that the Bohemians had put forward the doctrine that only believers can receive Christ "spiritually" in the Eucharist.[165]

Luther's response to these sacramentarian tendencies (which had already emerged by 1523) was to reassess his earlier evaluation of 'sacrament' (the bread and the wine) and 'testament' (the word of forgiveness). In his first book against the sacramentarians, *The Adoration of the Sacrament*(1523), he still says that the words are more important than the sacrament, and that a man could live a blessed and devout life without the Eucharist,[166] but Luther already sees the "significatists" (i.e. those like Cornelis Hoen who interpreted the *est* in the words of institution to mean *significat*) as corruptors of Scripture and of Christian faith. The symbolical interpretation of the words of institution is an outrage against the clear Word of God, which does not allow for such an interpretation at this point. If people turned the allegorical method into a general hermeneutical principle they would deny the whole Scripture, for one could just as easily give a "symbolic" interpretation of the Virgin Birth or the Divinity of Christ.[167] Nobody should be prevented from raising the cup or from visibly expressing his devotion by kneeling if these things assured him of the presence of Christ's "natural body" in the Eucharistic elements. Although the Catholic doctrine of transubstantiation is false, "this error is not very important, provided the body and blood of Christ, together with the Word, are not taken away." Bugenhagen made a similar comment about the Catholics during the

---

[165] Cf. H. Kaminsky, *op. cit.* pp. 172-173.
[166] *WA* 11:433, *LW* 36:279.
[167] *WA* 11:434, *LW* 36:280.

Flensburg Disputation; to deny the real presence of Christ in the Eucharistic elements is more damnable than the Catholic doctrine of transubstantiation.[168] The only really damnable doctrine held by the Catholics, according to Luther and Bugenhagen, was their view of the Mass as a repetition of Christ's sacrifice, which into the bargain – and this is surely the height of blasphemy – is supposed to be a meritorious act whereby men can erase their own sins, or even the sins of the dead.

In his polemical masterpiece *Against the Heavenly Prophets* published in 1525, Luther argued the following points against the sacramentarians:

1. A symbolical interpretation of the Eucharistic elements opens the floodgates for general allegorical interpretation, but there is no criterion for assessing the validity of allegorical meanings. They belong to the realm of intuition; some find them fascinating and convincing whilst others find them senseless and incomprehensible – "spiritual juggling."[169] Hence true biblical exegesis must keep to the literal meaning wherever this makes sense. This principle demands that the "is" of the words of institution stands firm.

2. If we deny the bodily presence of Christ in the Eucharistic elements, the Holy Supper will be valid only for the believing recipient who is merely commemorating a historical event, the death of Christ.[170]

3. This erroneous process of spiritualising the means of grace leads to a new form of justification by the works of man, and sees Christ merely as a moral example. By claiming to "imitate

---

[168] *WA* 11:441, *LW* 36:287, cf. Bugenhagen in *Acta* F8b-G1a. In the same year (1529) Melanchthon wanted to invite the Catholics as a neutral party to the Colloquy of Marburg so as to strengthen the Lutherans' position against the Zwinglians. He also wanted the Lutheran estates at the second diet of Speyer (1529) to agree to a Catholic proposal of an anti-Zwinglian edict. (cf. M. Lenz (ed), *Briefwechsel Landgraf Philipps des Grossmütigen mit Bucer*, Vol. I (Leipzig, 1880), pp. 11, 14).

[169] *WA* 18:178-179, *LW* 40:187-189.

[170] *WA* 18:203, *LW* 40:213.

Christ" men are undertaking a new but doomed attempt to earn their own justification.[171]

4. Since none of the essential dogmas of the Christian faith can be illuminated by reason the Christian is not specially called upon to use reason in order to grasp this particular article of belief.[172]

But in his controversy with Zwingli and Bucer, Luther stressed the "realist" interpretation of the Supper to such an extent that he almost contradicted the value he had given to the ideas of 'testament' and 'sacrament' in *The Babylonian Captivity*. In *The Sacrament of the Body and Blood of Christ – Against the Fanatics* in 1526 he called the promise of forgiveness the "shell" (*sic*) and Christ's body and blood in the elements the "kernel" of the Eucharist. Whoever denies Christ's real presence in the elements makes the sacrament an empty shell.[173] The object of faith is thus not only the word of forgiveness but also the sacrament itself as the container of the whole person of Christ.

After this Luther turns to the ancient church's doctrine of the Eucharist as the medicine of immortality. In *That These Words of Christ 'This Is My Body' etc., Still Stand Firm Against the Fanatics* of 1527, Luther teaches that Christ's flesh, even before the resurrection, was qualitatively different from normal human flesh. Christ's flesh, unlike all ordinary flesh, is a "spiritual flesh", "deified flesh" and consequently a "spiritual food", which gives eternal life.[174] Death choked on this food, "for this food was too strong for death, and has devoured and digested its devourer."[175] Whoever eats Christ's immortal flesh in the Eucharist changes his own corruptible body into an eternal and blessed body.[176]

Luther then turned to an exposition of the paradoxical and "irrational" nature of his "doctrine of consubstantiation":

[171] *WA* 18:196, *LW* 40:207.
[172] *WA* 18:143, *LW* 40:153-154.
[173] *WA* 19:501, *LW* 36:346.
[174] *WA* 23:203, *LW* 37:99-100.
[175] *WA* 23:243; *LW* 37:124.
[176] *WA* 23:204, *LW* 37:101.

Christ's body is "sacramentally united" with the bread and the wine and is present in them bodily and concretely. But unlike normal bread this is not corruptible food for the stomach. The believer chews it with his teeth, yet it remains true that "no-one sees or grasps or eats or chews Christ's body in the way he visibly sees and chews any other flesh."[177] Christ dwells in heaven and in all places on earth where the Eucharist is properly celebrated. He is characterized by ubiquity and invisibility, and these characteristics relate as much to His divinity as to His humanity (*communicatio idiomatum*). In short: Christ's body is visible in the Eucharist but escapes all attempts to "limit" it there.

The concept of a physical eating of Christ (*manducatio oralis*) inevitably leads to the idea that the godless receive the Lord's body in the Supper (*manducatio impii*), but it brings them eternal death. Bugenhagen (unlike Luther) restricted the circle of those who receive the Lord's body to their own damnation, to the "unworthy" (*indigni*),[178] i.e. those who possess an element of true faith as members of the Christian community but who bring it into disrepute by their immoral lives. Luther himself did not accede to this restriction until Bucer urged him to do so in the "Wittenberg Concorde" of 1536. Thus the absolute objectivity was again broken in theory, but in actual fact the distinction between "unbelievers" and "the unworthy" was meaningless, for how many of the heathens, who have heard nothing of Christ, take part in the Lord's Supper?[179]

If Luther did occasionally put forward almost magical ideas in his later Eucharistic doctrine his aim in the last analysis was always to provide an assurance of the Lord's personal presence and of the beneficial validity of the sacrament irrespective of the recipient. He did not want to extol the Eucharist as some thaumaturgical substance. Finally, by identifying the divine body with the Eucharist elements, he wanted to stress that the

---

[177] *WA* 26:442, *LW* 37:300. cf. W. Köhler, *Dogmengeschichte als Geschichte des christlichen Selbstbewusstseins.* Vol. 2, 1951, pp. 306-316.
[178] *Acta* I 5a-I7b.
[179] W. Köhler, *Dogmengeschichte* Vol. 2, p. 313.

whole man, body and soul, and not just his spirit, was to be redeemed.[180]

Whereas the Wittenberg reformer reverted more towards the old church in the course of the controversy with Zwingli and Karlstadt (seeing the Catholics as a lesser danger than the "Enthusiasts"), Hoffman moved further towards the sacramentarians. It is not possible to trace exactly which points he took over from Cornelis Hoen, Karlstadt or Zwingli, for all three agreed on Eucharistic doctrine – whereby Zwingli was dependent on Hoen and Karlstadt for his symbolical view of the Eucharist.[181]

Hoen's letter on the Eucharist must have been decisive for Hoffman. Since we find Hoen's images and arguments repeated without alteration by Hoffman, it is probable that he had read one of the two German translations of Hoen, which had been published in 1525 and 1526.[182] He could not have taken them from Zwingli's writings, since the Zürich reformer had changed the arguments in important details. Hoffman took over four of Hoen's ideas:

1. The comparison of the Eucharist to the ring given by the bridegroom to his bride as a pledge of fidelity, and as a sign of the bride's commitment to be faithful and to reject all other suitors.[183] Thus for Hoen the Eucharist is not simply a human commemorative meal. Christ is the one who is active in it, committing himself to men. In giving bread and wine He is giving Himself to His believers.[184]

We know from Weidensee that Hoffman first used this image

[180] W. Joest, *Ontologie der Person bei Luther* (Göttingen, 1967), pp. 414-436.

[181] Cf. Zwingli's comments on Karlstadt, *CR* 90:323, 608.

[182] The first was printed in Strasbourg, the second in Augsburg. There is a photographic reprint of the original Latin in A. Eekhof (ed), *De avondmaalsbrief von Cornelis Hoen 1525*, s'Gravenhage, 1917 and an English translation in H.A. Oberman (ed.), *Forerunners of the Reformation. The Shapes of Late Medieval Thought* (London, 1967), pp. 268-278.

[183] Hoen, (in H.A. Oberman, ed., *op. cit.*) p. 268.

[184] Cf. H. Gollwitzer, "Zur Auslegung von Johannes 6 bei Luther und Zwingli" in *In Memoriam Ernst Lohmeyer*, (Stuttgart, 1957), p. 146.

in his last book on the Eucharist written in 1528: "Melchior brings up here the confusing image of the ring as a pledge given by the bridegroom to the bride; the bread of the Eucharist is not Christ's body but a seal given in the celebration of the sacrament."[185] Hoffman also used this image in later writings, particularly in *The Ordinance of God*, where the symbol of the ring has a dual function – it both demonstrates that Christ cannot be in the Sacrament bodily just as the ring cannot be identical with the bridegroom, and also underlines the commitment involved in the Eucharist. Here the firm covenant between God and individual man is fulfilled in the spiritual wedding of Christ with the soul.

Zwingli on the other hand, in his early writings on the Eucharist, turned this symbol of the union of the bride and bridegroom into a simple sign of remembrance left behind by someone when he leaves, "just as a faithful wife, whose husband has left her a ring as a keepsake, frequently refers to the ring as her husband, saying: This is my late husband, although what she means is that it recalls her husband."[186]

2. Hoen had used John 19:26 as a justification for using *significat* as an interpretation of *est* (Christ on the cross commits His mother to John, the beloved disciple, saying, "Woman, behold, this is your son"). Hoffman also used this verse to support a symbolic interpretation of the words of institution.[187]

3. Hoen used Luke 17:20-21 ("The kingdom of God is not coming with signs to be observed; nor will they say, 'Lo, here it is!' or 'There!'") to prove the impossibility of localizing God. Hoffman took this over in his arguments against any attempt to unite God with matter.[188]

4. Finally Hoen strengthened Hoffman's conviction that there was an inner connection between the *power* of the priesthood and belief in God's immanence, present within matter. Hoen demonstrated how the whole splendour of Catholic churches, beginning with expensive monstrances, going through lavishly

---

[185] Weidensee, *Eyn underricht* C1b.
[186] In G.W. Bromily (ed), *op. cit.*, p. 234; *CR* 1:856.
[187] Hoen, p. 270; *Acta* B3b.
[188] Hoen, p. 269; Weidensee, *op. cit.* A3b.

decorated church buildings and on to the priest's robes with their gold inlay, the "bleating of the monks" and the anointing of priests, was all built on the foundation of the Mass, i.e. on the superstition that the bread and wine are changed into Christ's body and blood by the consecration uttered by the priest. In order to protect this dominion and its attendant riches the priests withheld part of the Sacrament (the wine) from the laity. If belief in God's presence in the bread is discarded, the Pope's temple is destroyed. Hoen put these ideas at the service of the educated townsmen of the Netherlands in their struggle against the power and wealth of the Catholic priests.

Hoffman applied this idea to the doctrine of consubstantiation advocated by the Lutheran clergy, who claimed powers which belonged to God alone, so as to exercise *control* over their congregations.[189]

Karlstadt had already expounded these ideas in 1524. After Hoen it was he who was the most important of Hoffman's teachers on the Eucharistic issue.[190] It was from Karlstadt that Hoffman derived the argument that the historical context of the Last Supper, in which Christ was celebrating the Passover with his disciples, did not permit a 'realistic' understanding of the Eucharistic elements, because when Jesus shared out the broken bread his body had not yet been broken.[191] When Christ broke the bread this was a symbolic prefiguration of his death on the cross, just as when we break bread it is a symbolic imitation of

---

[189] Hoffmann and Karlstadt, *Dialogus* A4b.

[190] Karlstadt first rejected the physical real presence in *Vom Priestertum und Opfer Christi* as early as 1523. After his dispute with Luther at Jena in August 1524, when he undertook to challenge Luther's position in writing, he wrote seven tracts on the subject in six weeks. Capito wrote a pamphlet about the disagreement between Karlstadt and Luther to which Luther responded in his 'Letter to Strasbourg' (*WA* 15:380-377). *Against the Heavenly Prophets* was directed mainly against Karlstadt (*WA* 18:37-214, *LW* 40). Karlstadt wrote three replies to this. There are English translations of three of Karlstadt's Eucharistic tracts in R.J. Sider (ed) *Karlstadt's Battle with Luther: Documents in a Liberal-Radical Debate*, 1978. cf. also E.G. Rupp, *Patterns of Reformation*, (London, 1969), pp. 141-148.

[191] Cf. Hoffman in *Acta* C1b. Karlstadt, *Ob man mit heyliger geschrifft* C4; Zwingli in *CR* 90: 333.

his sacrifice in remembrance of him (the anticipatory and commemorative character of the Eucharist). Otherwise we would have to say that Christ was present at the Last Supper in two ways, first as an active person at the table and second as bread on the table. He would also have eaten himself. Karlstadt had only one concern in this argument, to hold on to Christ's unique, singular sacrifice. It was Christ himself, not the Sacrament, that suffered for us. Thus anyone believing in a real presence of Christ in the Eucharistic elements threatens the sanctity of the cross, "because it is as much as to say that Christ's suffering was not enough – Christ is still mortal and must be martyred for our sins in the Mass"[192] This idea recurs in Hoffman, "We have one Christ who suffered for us on the cross, not several Christs".[193] He, too, regarded Luther's sacramental doctrine as a limitation of the significance of Christ's death.

Karlstadt, Zwingli and Hoffman all considered Luther's doctrine of Christ being mauled by the teeth, resting in the stomach and following the natural course of digestion to be thoroughly barbaric and blasphemous. In particular Zwingli found this "cannibalism" incompatible with a sense of God's majesty and spirituality.[194] As a humanist it reminded him of pagan sacrificial meals and ancient ideas of eating the gods.

Zwingli also took from Karlstadt's *Dialogue* the argument that Christ could not be in heaven and in the Sacrament at one and the same time. Zwingli attempted to root the idea more firmly within his Christology. He stressed the distinction of the two natures, the divine and the human, in the person of Christ, a distinction which did not end with the resurrection. Christ's human nature was creaturely even after the Ascension, and so could not be infinite but must be limited to a particular place. Only in respect to his divine nature could he fill heaven and earth.[195] Following this view Hoffman said, "If He has ascended

---

[192] Karlstadt, *Wider die alte und neue papistische Messen*, 1524, A2.
[193] *Acta* C3b-C4a.
[194] *CR* 90:787, 789, cf. W. Köhler, *Zwingli und Luther* Vol. 1. 1924, pp. 89ff.
[195] Cf. Zwingli in G.W. Bromily (ed.) *op. cit*.pp. 212-217 and *CR* 90:535.

to heaven He cannot be in the Sacrament, otherwise He would have to have two bodies.[196]

For Karlstadt the Eucharist plays an essential part in the process of the mystical union of Christ with the soul because it conveys an "inner taste" of Christ's sufferings.[197] In it the communicant can come to know Christ "ardently and passionately", and it is from this knowledge that an individual derives the power to undergo a spiritual renewal. The purpose of the process is the transformation of the knower by the known life of Christ – a concrete discipleship. To Karlstadt the correct use of the Eucharist consists in becoming "conformable to Christ".[198]

Hoffman was closer to Karlstadt than to Zwingli in this view of the Eucharist as a power enabling man to become a new creature. Hoffman identifies Christ with the word of forgiveness which is spoken into the believer's soul.[199] This word possesses an overwhelming power for the hearer. For the believer it is "the true bread of heaven", the "eternal food", i.e. it takes on sacramental characteristics. It is not a sign pointing towards the thing signified (that is the task of the Eucharistic elements), but it is the thing itself: 'spirit', 'power', 'life', or (to move away from set phrases) the foundation-stone of redemption. Hoffman's image of the wedding-ring given by the bridegroom to his bride also stresses the priority of God's activity in the Eucharist. As against this, Zwingli's image of the widow's memorial ring places the believer at the centre, though Christ's spiritual presence is not excluded by that.

---

[196] Acta C7a. Luther on the other hand stressed the unity of the person of Christ, which can only come about if the two natures share each other's properties (communicatio idiomatum), and he also felt that Zwingli's Christology presented Christ's body as if it was a "cuckoo in a cage".

[197] Cf. Karlstadt's Dialogue above n. 162.

[198] Cf. Karlstadt in R.J. Sider (ed), *Karlstadt's Battle with Luther*, pp. 74-91. Also H. Barge, *Andreas Bodenstein von Carlstadt*, Vol. 2, 1905, p. 154 and F. Kriechbaum, *Grundzüge der Theologie Karlstadts* (Hamburg, 1967), p. 130.

[199] *Acta* B2b, C4b; Hoffman and Karlstadt, *Dialogus*, A4b, A5a.

Finally we must consider the relationship between the stages of Hoffman's development in Livonia and in Schleswig-Holstein. After his struggle in Livonia, where as a spiritualist he mainly attacked the veneration of images, it was natural that he would be led on to oppose the Lutheran doctrine of consubstantiation. To a spiritualist a mixture of the divine with bread and wine would appear even more blasphemous than the superstitious belief that pictures could convey an impression of the divine.

There is also a hidden connection between Hoffman's apocalypticism and his denial of the real presence – a connection which Hoffman had not been aware of. In the early church the non-appearance of the Parousia and the unfulfilled hopes of a total transformation of the world were compensated for by frequent repetitions of the Eucharist which mediated immortality to the individual.[200] The social consequence of sacramentalism was calming, for it concentrated men's hopes on their personal survival after death. There was thus no need to look forward to an imminent renewal of the world. Anyone who, like Hoffman, believed firmly in an imminent appearance of God and who was convinced of the unsatisfactory nature of the present structure of things, must have seen Lutheranism's established cult as an impediment to preparing the world for judgment and for the appearance of a new aeon, since it aroused the illusion that God was already present here and now in bread and wine as "the medicine of immortality."

[200] R. Bultmann, *Theology of the New Testament*, (English translation London, 1952-1955) Vol. 2. pp. 111-118.

Chapter Four

Hoffman's First Period in Eastern Frisia (April-June 1529).

In April, 1529, after being banished from Schleswig-Holstein, Hoffman (who was probably accompanied by Karlstadt) set off for Eastern Frisia. His aim here was to support the local "sacramentarians" in their battle against Lutheranism, which Count Enno II was attempting to impose on his subjects. Hoffman and Karlstadt were given the protection of Ulrich von Dornum, the influential counsellor and chancellor of Edzard the Great, the Imperial Count, who had died in the previous year.[1] Karlstadt's and Hoffman's defence of the symbolical view of the Eucharist was not in vain, for the Zwinglians succeeded in making advances in the economically more advanced regions in the west of the country. Hoffman's responsibility for this success cannot have been great since he had left Eastern Frisia by June, 1529. But he had such good memories of the country that after his conversion to Anabaptism and his consequent banishment from Strasbourg he returned there in May, 1530.

We shall investigate here the circumstances which led, despite the opposition of the Count, to the growth of Zwinglianism, and also what it was that favoured the development of radical Anabaptism out of sacramentarianism.

Eastern Frisia in the early 16th century was distinguished from its neighbours by its primitive feudal social and political structure. The prince could only govern his territory in co-operation with his vassals and the towns, because he was not more than a "primus inter pares".[2] Even the peasants had

---

[1] It was out of gratitude for this protection that Hoffman dedicated his next two books to Ulrich von Dornum *Weissagung.* . . . (1529) and *Prophezey.* . . . (1530).

[2] A. Koolman and H. Wiemann, *Ostfriesische Geschichte I,* (Leer, 1951), and H. Schmidt, *Politische Geschichte Ostfrieslands* (Leer, 1975).

succeeded in maintaining their personal freedom and their power of collective political action in the local councils ("mene meente"). The nobles of Eastern Frisia (except for those in the Harlingen district) had hardly begun to establish demesne-farming by the beginning of the Reformation. There were only a few insignificant duties of compulsory labour. In many villages the better-off peasants still possessed the right to elect their priests.[3] The East Frisian church was still close to the simple people in the decades before the Reformation, because usually only local men became priests in this region, who were expected to live with a woman all their lives ("priests pledged to one woman"). The peasants did not trust "unmarried" priests. "They would not tolerate priests without wives because they did not want the beds of other people to be soiled."[4]

Edzard I had not intervened in the religious development of his country before his death in 1528, though Lutheran ideas had been coming into the region since 1519. Edzard's children were brought up by Jürgen van der Daere (Aportanus), a "sacramentarian", though the Count's closest advisors, Wilhelm Ubben(a), who was chancellor for a while, and Poppo Maninga, provost of Emden, remained Catholics. Several congregations and nobles found no opposition from the Count when they appointed Dutch sacramentarian refugees as evangelical preachers. Hinne Rode, one of the first protagonists of the Eucharistic controversy, found asylum in Norden, and his fellow sacramentarians Johannes Oldeguil and Jacobus Canter from Groningen established themselves in Aurich and in Emden respectively. Amongst other "significatists" active in Marienhafe and in Leer were Regnerus Dagma, Gellius Faber de Bouma (of Leeuwarden), Thomas Bramus (of Zwolle) and Lübbert Canz (who had been expelled from Münster in 1525).

---

[3] W. Ebel, *Ostfriesische Bauernrechte*, (1964), H. Schmidt, "Die Reformation in Ostfriesland" in *Jahrbuch d. Gesell. für Niedersächsische Kirchengeschichte* 69(1971), p. 21, D. Kurze, *Pfarrerwahlen im Mittelalter*, (Cologne, 1966), pp. 181 ff.

[4] E. Beninga, *Cronica der Fresen* in H. Ramm (ed) *Quellen zur Geschichte Ostfrieslands* Vol. 4. (Aurich, 1961), p. 117.

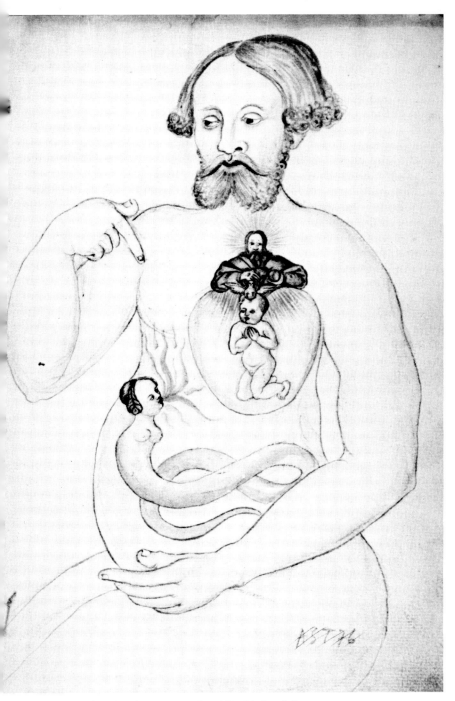

Plate 5: Clemens Ziegler: The birth of the new man

Plate 6: Clemens Ziegler: The struggle of the new man with the serpent

The sacramentarians found a reliable patron in Ulrich von Dornum, who called Zwingli his "alter ego".[5] The Zwinglians dominated the religious scene in Eastern Frisia up until 1530, more by their spiritual activity than by their numerical superiority.

Hinrich Rese, a former Dominican monk, put forward an openly radical Zwinglian confession of faith at the Colloquy of Norden on 1st January, 1527. His theses on the veneration of images, auricular confession and the Eucharist could have been derived from Melchior Hoffman.[6] The 48 articles on the Eucharist, which Jürgen van der Daere put before his congregation probably at the end of 1526, were fully in the spirit of Zwingli.[7]

Eastern Frisia's Lutheran neighbours found it intolerable to witness the development in the north of the Empire of an "ecclesia in verba Lutheri non iurata", a development brought about by the support of peasants and nobles and with the tacit acquiescence of the prince. On 11th September, 1528 Bugenhagen warned the Council of Bremen against the "despisers of the sacrament" on their own doorstep.[8] In order to arm themselves against such attacks the Zwinglians of Eastern Frisia published a confession of faith at the end of 1528.[9] These extremely spiritualist articles (which had probably been drawn up by Aportanus) rejected Luther's ideas of an indivisible unity of the outer and the inner word and of the actual presence of salvation within the Sacrament. All that matters for man's redemption is the invisible activity of the Holy Spirit within the human soul. The Spirit is bound neither to the external word

[5] H. Barge, *Andreas Bodenstein von Carlstadt* Vol. 2. p. 588.

[6] E. Meiners, *Oostvrieschlandts kerkelyke geschiedenisse* Vol. 2, Groningen 1739, p. 352–366.

[7] Aportanus' 48 articles on the Eucharist are reprinted in E. Meiners, *op. cit.*, p. 114–123.

[8] In *Bremische Jahrbücher* 2nd Series. Vol. I. (Bremen, 1885), pp. 262-268.

[9] E. Meiners, *op. cit.*, Vol. I. pp.53-64. It is clear from Article 21 ("I say") that there was a single author of these articles.

nor to the sacrament. "External things (viz. preaching and the sacraments) though they are useful, are only useful to men for other things," viz. for a public manifestation of faith and brotherly love, as well as for encouragement, guidance and punishment in earthly life. Every Christian is free to use or to reject "God's external works." But if anyone declares they are necessary for salvation it is essential that he be opposed and that external worship be done away with.

This probably unique confession of faith, in which a church declared its own redundancy, was signed by the Zwinglians of Emden, Norden, Aurich, Leer, Oldersum, Jemgum and Larrelt. The consequences for the congregations were devastating.[10] Encouraged by the clergy, the voices that had been hushed since the suppression of the peasants dared once more to make themselves heard. The words inspired by Thomas Müntzer that Luther had heard in the villages of Thuringia in 1524 were proclaimed in the streets of Eastern Frisia, "Bible, babble, Babylon-spirit! spirit! spirit! If you bring nothing, you get nothing. Beware of the sacrament as of a white horse (foreboding disaster)!"[11] In a letter of 25th March, 1530 Count Enno II wrote of the transformation of intense spiritualism into complete religious indifference. Peasants, he reported, even hold "impure" Eucharists at home using beer, water or wine. The louts in the villages blaspheme saying, the oblation "is nothing but a baked God, and it would be much better for a man to eat a thousand devils than to eat one sacrament." It was claimed that it was evil to baptise infants, and moreover people should follow Christ's example and undergo baptism at the age of 33. Preaching was said to be meaningless because God can give faith without the "external word." Prayer is equally pointless because everything is foreordained. Rather than respecting holy days they preferred working in the fields on a Sunday.[12]

---

[10] The confession was probably influenced by Karlstadt, cf. H. Barge, *op. cit.*, Vol. 2. pp. 82, 156-157, 161 and H. Reimers *Die Gestaltung der Reformation in Ostfriesland*, (1917), p. 25.

[11] E. Meiners, *op. cit.*, Vol. I, p. 46, cf. *WA*, 15:211.

[12] The letter is printed in C.A. Cornelius, *Der Antheil Ostfrieslands an der Reformation*, (Münster, 1852), pp. 57-59.

The Emperor Charles V and Duke Karl von Geldern (who controlled Groningen) regarded this disintegration of religious life as a welcome opportunity "to punish the Frisian heretics." In the event of an attack by the Catholic powers the Count could only count on the support of his Lutheran neighbours (Bremen, Hamburg, Oldenburg and Lüneburg) if the East Frisian church did not fall fully into the hands of the radical spiritualists. In the face of the difficult situation in 1529 Ulrich von Dornum (despite his personal conviction of the justice of Zwingli's and Karlstadt's positions) advised the Count to call in Bugenhagen in order to come to a compromise with Hinne Rode on the Eucharistic question.[13] But Bugenhagen felt no inclination to have another debate with the hated sacramentarians.[14] His place was taken by Johann Tiemann (Soetemelk) and Johann Pelt, the reformers of Bremen. Both were loyal Lutherans and attempted to impose the Wittenberg doctrine of the Eucharist, thereby arousing the opposition of the East Frisian congregations. When Tieman declared, in the course of his fourth sermon in Emden, that Christ's true body and blood were present in the Eucharist and were received in the mouth, the audience stormed the pulpit shouting, "kill the cannibal, strike him dead!" Tiemann only just made it into the sacristy. The attempt to convince the congregations of the higher truths of Lutheranism by means of preaching was a total failure.

This was the explosive situation into which Hoffman and Karlstadt entered on their arrival in Eastern Frisia. Their presence led to a sharp division of the parties in the area. Karlstadt was put under the protection not only of Ulrich von Dornum but also of other leaders – his brother Hero Omken of Witmund and Esen, Hicco Howerda of Uphusen and Jeltko Iderhoff, the bailiff of Berum. Karlstadt also won over the parish priests of Pilsen and Wirdum. On the other hand three evangelical preachers (Meinardus Hage in Uphusen, Heddo

---

[13] Ulrich's letter to Enno II, dated 14th February 1529, is printed in *Jahrbuch für bildende Kunst und vaterländische Altertümer zu Emden*, 7, 2. pp. 104f.

[14] Cf. Bugenhagen's letter of 8th March, 1529, *WA Br* 5:33.

Cankena in Berum and the leading Lutheran of Eastern Frisia, Johann Stevens of Norden) forbad Karlstadt from entering their churches.[15] But the two refugees did strengthen the opposition of the East Frisian nobility to a Lutheran state church. Ulrich von Dornum made contact with the reformers of Strasbourg, with Zwingli and with Oecolampadius, urging them to take up their pens and enter the controversy in Eastern Frisia.[16] It may have been Ulrich von Dornum who advised Hoffman to go to Strasbourg in June 1529, though we do not know the reason for this recommendation.

It was during his first stay in Eastern Frisia that Hoffman, together with Karlstadt, wrote his *Dialogus* about the Flensburg Disputation. But despite their agreement on the issue of the Eucharist and their opposition to Lutheranism, the two men did not conclude a permanent friendship. Karlstadt seems to have received very little from their relationship because he wanted to have nothing to do with those ideas that were peculiar to Hoffman, i.e. his apocalyptic speculations. Karlstadt had little respect for the biblical texts on which Hoffman founded his theology, Daniel, II Esdras, the Epistles of James and Jude, 2 Peter and Revelation. He believed large sections of Daniel and II Esdras to be uncanonical, that no-one should be forced to accept these passages. Karlstadt regarded Revelation as the most worthless book in the Bible. In contrast to Hoffman he felt that it was certainly not written by "John the Apostle", the author of the Fourth Gospel. It was full of obscure allegories and hidden allusions. It was not advisable to be concerned with this, the most obscure biblical text, more than with any other. He would have preferred to remove Revelation, "the lowest book in the

[15] F. Ritter (ed), "Henricus Ubbius' Beschreibung von Ostfriesland vom Jahre 1530" in *Jahrbuch der Gesellschaft für bildende Kunst und vaterländische Altertümer zu Emden* 18 (1913), p. 88.

[16] H. Barge, *op. cit.*, Vol. 2. pp. 587-588.

Bible", from the canon altogether.[17] Because of these differences the collaboration of the two men was only temporary.[18]

---

[17] A. Karlstadt, *Welche bücher heilig und biblisch sind* 1521, B2b-B3a; C26-C3a.

[18] There are few sources dealing with Hoffman's first period in Eastern Frisia. The most important is an anonymous letter to Bucer of 9th June, 1529 (printed in C.A. Cornelius, *Geschichte des Münsterschen Aufruhrs* Vol. 2. p. 292) saying that Karlstadt and Hoffman had joined the "Court of Emden". There they had written a book about the Flensburg Disputation and Bugenhagen's arguments.

J.E. Longhurst's idea (*Luther's Ghost in Spain* Lawrence, Kansas 1969, pp. 28-30) that Hoffman went to Valencia as an evangelical missionary in April, 1529 is quite improbable. The Flensburg Disputation took place on 9th April, 1529 and Hoffman was banished from Schleswig-Holstein on 12th April. He could hardly have been brought before the inquisition in Valencia for spreading anti-Catholic propaganda by 22nd April. Bucer's letter to Zwingli of 30th June, 1529 mentions Hoffman's arrival in Strasbourg; this must also argue against a trip to Spain (*TAE* I, No. 188 p. 240).

Chapter Five

Hoffman in Strasbourg:
The Fusion of Apocalypticism,
Spiritualism and Anabaptism.

After his two-month stay in Eastern Frisia, Hoffman moved
on to Strasbourg in June 1529. Here he was given a cordial
reception by Bucer, who greeted him as an ally in the campaign
against the "magic" of the Lutheran doctrine of the Eucharist.[1]
And here he was able to print the *Dialogus* (his account of the
Flensburg Disputation); Balthasar Beck was even able to sign as
printer, an indication that he had no fear of censorship. Relations
between Luther and Bucer were at their lowest ebb and
Hoffman enjoyed particular trust as an opponent of Luther.

But the friendship did not last long. When Hoffman claimed
to possess a higher knowledge, which gave him the right to
reveal the secrets of Scripture, the Strasbourgers gave him the
same advice as had Luther before them – to keep to his job as a
furrier, which he hopefully understood better than he did
theology.[2] Alienated now from the "Zwinglians" as well as the
Lutherans, Hoffman finally broke with the official evangelical
Reformation and entered the sphere of religious nonconformity.
He joined forces with the "Strasbourg Prophets", a circle of
enthusiasts centred around Lienhard and Ursula Jost. At the
same time he took over the doctrines of the universality of
divine grace and of the freedom of the human will from the
Strasbourg Anabaptists, who had come under the influence of
Hans Denck. He thus did away with two of the most important
Lutheran elements in his theology (Luther's doctrines of
justification and predestination) which had hitherto disturbed

---

[1] *TAE* I No. 188, p. 240.
[2] M. Bucer, *Handlung in dem öffentlichen gesprech zu Strassburg iungst
inn Synodo gehalten/gegen Melchior Hoffman* 1533, L6a.

the unity of his system. But he retained the Lutheran doctrine that subjects had a duty to obey their overlords. The synthesis of apocalypticism, visionary spiritualism and Denck's form of Anabaptism which came about in Strasbourg soon made Hoffman the undisputed leader of a type of Protestant nonconformity whose influence spread beyond the city boundaries as far as Holland and Hesse.

The sectarian movement in Strasbourg became increasingly powerful between 1529 and 1534. Hoffman's preaching gave it an apocalyptic tone, with the result that the evangelical preachers feared a general uprising. Hoffman's highest hopes related to the Imperial City itself; he believed that Strasbourg was called to be the "heavenly Jerusalem", the centre of a world-wide renewal. 144,000 "apostolic messengers" would go out from its gates to prepare the earth to receive the Son of God. Eventually (under the influence of the "Strasbourg Prophets") he came to see himself in the role of the second Elijah, the prophet of the last days.

But Strasbourg also became the scene of Hoffman's deepest disappointment. The Strasbourg Council, instead of setting up "the banner of divine justice" with Hoffman's help, imprisoned him for life in 1533 (despite his loyalty towards them). The anticipated revolt of the Melchiorites actually took place in Münster. It was undertaken without Hoffman's approval, and it failed. In Strasbourg the disturbances set off by Hoffman's activity resulted in a conservative backlash on the part of the evangelical preachers. The City Council established a formal confession of faith and implemented a general programme to suppress nonconformity.

In the following chapters we shall attempt to explain in particular how it came about that Strasbourg (although it was a hot-bed of the most radical ideas) possessed a social and political stability which was to be Hoffman's eventual undoing. We shall also analyse the changes in Hoffman's theological system brought about by the influence of Strasbourg nonconformity and the historical results of these theological changes.

1. The Political and Social Structure of Strasbourg around 1530.

One essential reason for Strasbourg's inner stability at the time of the Reformation was the unbloody transfer of political power to the guilds, which had taken place during the 15th century. After 1482 the guilds had a two-thirds majority in the Council and the standing committees, whereas the "Konstof-fler", the patricians whose power they had taken, had to be satisfied with a one-third representation. In the course of the following decades the old and new leaderships fused to make a homogeneous governing class.[3]

But the disappearance of the old antagonism between patricians and plebeians did have one side-effect; it built up an aristocracy within the guilds, which became alienated from the smaller masters and journeymen. The most important decisions were taken by the three "secret chambers". The members of the Chamber of XV were co-opted, whereas the members of the Chambers of XIII and of XXI were nominated by the Council. The 300 jurymen of the fifteen guilds, who elected the Council members for a two-year term of office, filled their vacancies by co-option and had a life-long term of office. Political initiative came from above, i.e. from the practically irremovable members of the "secret chambers". The small artisans, who had to make a living from their work, hardly stood a chance of breaking into this ruling class of well-to-do career politicians. Journeymen had no electoral or coalition rights, nor did they have the right to

[3] U. Crämer, *Die Verfassung und Verwaltung Strassburgs von der Reformationszeit bis zum Fall der Reichsstadt* (Frankfurt, 1931), pp. 21-28; W. Andreas, *Strassburg an der Wende vom Mittelalter zur Neuzeit* (Leipzig, 1940), p. 16; J. Rott, "Artisanat et mouvements sociaux autour de 1525" in *Artisans et ouvriers d'Alsace* (Strasbourg, 1965), pp. 140; M.U. Chrisman, *Strasbourg and the Reform* (New Haven, 1967), pp. 20-26; T.A. Brady, *Ruling class, Regime and Reformation at Strasbourg 1520-1555* (Leiden, 1978).

[4] G. Schanz, *Zur Geschichte der deutschen Gesellenverbände*, (Leipzig, 1877), pp. 246–249.

strike.[4] By 1530 the guilds had already lost their autonomy. It was the Council's Chamber of XV which laid down the rules of the guilds, and it was the Council, not the members of the guilds, who approved the appointment of guild-leaders and who chose some of their representatives.[5] By 1530 the co-operative nature of the city- and guild-administration had already vanished and had been replaced by a new governing aristocracy.

The clash of interests between the new guild aristocracy and the small townsmen came to a head in the conflicts about taxes, pre-emption and usurious interest payments which emerged alongside the violent rise of sectarian movements between 1520 and 1534. The artisans wanted a reduction of the levy on wine and food and in compensation a rise in stallage (i.e. property tax).[6] In 1528 and 1529 the jurymen of the guilds, the evangelical preachers, and the representatives of the Anabaptists appealed unanimously (in rare harmony) to the Council to take action against pre-emption and usurious interest, but they were unsuccessful.[7] The "Constitution" published by the Council in 1529 did not make any reference to this demand.[8] It was not until 1533, during a severe famine and financial crisis, that the Council decided to raise the property tax from two to three shillings (per 100 gulden of property) and to issue a mandate forbidding pre-emption of grain.[9]

Yet the social disturbances in the city during the decade that followed the introduction of the Reformation never took on the character of a real revolution. This was due, amongst other things, to the fact that the Council knew the limits of its own power. When the very existence of the town was at stake the new oligarchy was so concerned to win over a broad majority of the townspeople that they formally ceded the necessary decisions to the assembly of 300 jurors. This happened in 1525,

---

[5] G. Schmoller, *Die Strassburger Tucher-und Weberzunft*, (Strassburg, 1879), pp. 472-488.

[6] Cf. H. Virck (ed.), *Politische Korrespondenz* Vol. I. p. 153 and J. Rott, *op. cit.*, p. 142.

[7] *TAE* I. No. 172 p. 222, No. 178 p. 233, No. 245 p. 329.

[8] *TAE* I p. 233, n.1.

[9] Strasbourg archives, Sign R. 18, fol. 17.

when the city denied support for the insurgent peasants under the command of Erasmus Gerber, and again in 1529, when the Catholic Mass was abolished against the Emperor's will. The Council was also anxious not to exacerbate social antagonisms. It supported small masters by opposing attempts to establish monopolies and larger businesses, developments which threatened the poorer guild members.[10] It frequently supported the weaker party in disputes between masters and journeymen. So, for example, in 1526 the Council forced the master tailors to increase the weekly wage of their journeymen to compensate for the feast days which had been abolished.[11] In 1533 it ordered that journeyman-weavers should be paid half of the masters' net profits as wages although the masters only wanted to grant them a third.[12] The Council put up a ten-year long opposition to the plan of the master furriers to limit the number of their journeymen and apprentices to three (where previously there had been five) because so many journeymen were losing their jobs.[13]

The healthy economic structure of the city facilitated the maintenance of social order. Strasbourg's prosperity was based on the alliance between trade, commerce and farming. The city was surrounded by the best arable land in the Empire. Sebastian Franck extolled the fertility of the Strasbourg region "which feeds the gluttonous people in their endless feastings and makes it possible that nearly everybody can afford to drink wine".[14] There was essentially a much closer social connection between merchants and artisans than was the case in Augsburg, Frankfurt or Lübeck. Because external trade did not play such a central role in Strasbourg the city was not so subject to fluctuations in the market as were, for example, Augsburg or Nuremberg. Even the textile and weaving guilds were still expanding in Strasbourg after 1520, although in Holland, Flanders and Augsburg they

---

[10] U. Crämer, *op. cit.*, p. 81.
[11] J. Rott, *op. cit.*, 153.
[12] G. Schmoller, *op. cit.*, p. 133.
[13] G. Schanz, *op. cit.*, pp. 146ff.; J. Rott, *op. cit.*, p.155.
[14] S. Franck, *Weltbuch*, 1542, p. 62b.

formed the main source of social disturbance because of the periodical bursts of unemployment to which they were subjected. The better situation in Strasbourg was due in part to the control of the magistracy, which improved the quality of Strasbourg cloth.[15]

The city's social stability made it possible for the Council to extend hospitality and show tolerance to foreigners, "heretics" and lawbreakers. The town was particularly proud of its "freedom of access", a privilege granted by the Emperor which allowed the city to accept almost any stranger. "They do not care where anyone comes from, so long as he is law-abiding. Whilst he stays with them they welcome him and grant him all burgher's rights. In Strasbourg in particular no-one asks where anyone has come from, to whom he formerly belonged or how he left."[16] All that was necessary to obtain "lesser burgher rights" ("das kleine Bürgerrecht", which was a precondition for entry into the guilds but did not grant voting rights) was to pay half a gulden to the Bailiff, the bishop's representative in the town.[17] This "freedom of access", along with the city's generous provision for its poor, made Strasbourg a refuge for exiles and the indigent during the period of the great persecutions. In an average year (during the period 1500 – 1530), between 50 and 100 newcomers were granted "burgher rights" but in 1525 (the year of the Peasants' War) the number was 485 and in 1528 (at the beginning of the great persecution of the Anabaptists) it was 260.[18] The refugees brought their radical ideas along with them. With the exception of Clemens Ziegler all the nonconformist leaders in Strasbourg came to the city as refugees (Karlstadt, Hätzer, Denck, Cellarius, Sattler, Kautz, Reublin, Marbeck, Schwenckfeld, Franck, Bünderlin, Servetus, Hoffman). Since censorship was not very strict and since the printers in Alsace preferred to publish works by the exiles rather than by the orthodox evangelical preachers, Strasbourg became between 1522 and 1534 the centre in Europe where heretical writings

[15] G. Schmoller, op. cit., pp. 136-138, 513.

[16] S. Franck, op. cit., p. 64b.

[17] TAE II, No. 611, p. 390.

[18] C. Wittmer and J.C. Meyer, Le livre de Bourgeoisie de la Ville de Strasbourg, Vol I, 1954, p. XLVII.

were exchanged.[19] Until 1533 the Council contented itself with a short period of imprisonment followed by banishment as a punishment for heresy (with the single exception of Thomas Salzman, who was executed in 1527 for serious blasphemy). Sebastian Franck said that the general rule for penalties in Strasbourg was that "where elsewhere a man would be hanged, in Strasbourg he would be birched."[20] In an environment so torn by deep social and religious conflicts such a policy of toleration attracted radicals from all over Europe. This eventually forced the Council to introduce sterner measures against heresy.

Its tolerance was incomprehensible to Strasbourg's neighbours. Bucer disapproved of it, but he defended the Council from the charge of incompetence, saying it was rather a fine example of liberal humanity. He wrote in a letter to Schwebel in Zweibrücken dated 24th September, 1534, "You will know how it is with human inclinations, how easily they tend towards extremes. When sternness is needed we often produce violence. Friendliness often turns into compliance or cowardice. As far as I can tell, our leaders seek justice and equity, but they are frail human beings. They are convinced that it is better not to punish many criminals than to condemn a single innocent man."[21]

One community within Strasbourg did respond positively to the radical ideas of the refugees. This was the guild of the "gardeners", who despite their personal freedom were often dependent economically on the property owners from whom they had rented their land. With about 600 members they were numerically the strongest guild in Strasbourg.[22] During the Peasants' War only a few of the gardeners out of the whole urban

---

[19] Cf. Capito's letter of 1534 in T. Schiess (ed), *Briefwechsel der Brüder Thomas und Ambrosius Blaurer* Vol. I. 1908, p. 495; F. Rittler, "Elsässische Buchdrucker im Dienst der Strassburger Sektenbewegung zur Zeit der Reformation" in *Gutenberg-Jahrbuch*, 1962, pp. 225-333 and 1963, pp. 97-108 and Jakob Sturm's letter of 15th July, 1526 in *Politische Korrespondenz* Vol.I, No. 464, pp. 262-264.

[20] S. Franck, *Germaniae Chronicon*, (Augsburg, 1538), p. 283a.

[21] *TAE* II No. 611, p. 391.

[22] U. Crämer, *op. cit.*, pp. 90, 99.

population had publicly expressed their support for the rebels. Clemens Ziegler, the lay-preacher so popular with the gardeners of Ruprechtsau, along with a few guild members, actually joined the peasants' army for a short time. The gardeners of Krutenau demanded that the clergy who had fled to the city should be delivered up to the peasants, whereas all the other guilds decided to defend the city and everyone in it against the peasants. Indeed, most of the gardeners also accepted this decision.[23] The intransigence of the gardeners did not come suddenly to an end with the failure of the Peasants' War. In 1528 the gardeners of Ruprechtsau appointed Clemens Ziegler their preacher despite the opposition of the magistracy. When the Council refused to recognize Ziegler's election he nevertheless remained their real "spiritual father".[24]

2. The Development of a Radical Lay Spirituality in Strasbourg Before Hoffman's Arrival.

We can only understand Hoffman's development during his time in Strasbourg, his success with the population and his belief that this city had been chosen to be the "heavenly Jerusalem", against the background of the radical lay spirituality that had developed in the city before he arrived there. This spirituality was characterized by asceticism, spiritualism and tendencies towards social reform; it culminated in the idea of a regeneration of individual and social life. Many factors contributed to the development of this particular spiritual climate: the social appeal of the Reformation to Strasbourg's lower middle class, toleration by the Council, the incipient spiritualist tendencies of the Strasbourg reformers (particularly of Capito), the work of Clemens Ziegler, the foundation of a distinctly spiritualist Anabaptist community by Hans Denck and Jakob Kautz, the presence of Schwenckfeld and Sebastian Franck, the existence of a

---

[23] *Politische Korrespondenz*, Vol. I, No. 212, pp. 120–121, No. 274, pp 154–155.

[24] *TAE* I Nos. 118 and 119, pp. 145-147.

group of supporters of Lienhard and Ursula Jost and finally the flood of refugees who arrived in the city between 1528 and 1532, who avidly accepted the idea of a forthcoming revolution. Although Hoffman did not succeed in uniting the warring groups of nonconformists in Strasbourg he did absorb many of their ideas. His effect on the masses can be explained by the fact that he embodied the programme not just of a single party but of numerous religious movements. Certainly Hoffman did also criticize some ideas of the Strasbourg sectarians. In the following chapter we shall analyse the complex religious environment of Strasbourg in which Hoffman developed, to which in general he made a positive response, although he did react negatively in several instances.

a)   The toleration of religious radicalism on the part of the Strasbourg Reformers

Strasbourg's Reformation was established by a group of preachers (Zell, Firn, Hedio, Bucer, Capito) in association with the lower middle-class and a few intellectuals (Otto Brunfels, a doctor and botanist, Nikolaus Gerbel, a lawyer, Lukas Hackfurt and Johannes Schwebel, the masters of the Latin school). They enforced the admission of Protestant preaching by disregarding the bishop's supervisory rights and the patronage-privileges of the chapters. They appealed to the Council to appoint the preachers. The Council warily accepted these "burgher initiatives" and subsequently "legitimized" the illegal appointments of the evangelical preachers by church congregations, because the pressure from below had become too strong. The Council protected married clergy from persecution by the bishop, and despite the Edict of Worms it tolerated the propagation of Reformation writings. It was clearly in the Council's interest to create a single class of townsmen (as implied by the Reformation) and to have the right to appoint the clergy.[25] But the Council did not develop a clear ecclesiastical policy within the first years of the Reformation. It was prevented from coming out clearly in favour of the Reformation by the external threat from the Emperor as well as by an internal division between supporters

[25] M.U. Chrisman, *op. cit.*, pp. 132-149.

(Nikolaus Kniebis, Jakob Sturm, Mathis Pfarrer, Martin Herlin, Daniel Mueg, Bernhard Wurmser) and opponents of the Reformation (Martin Betschold, Konrad von Duntzenheim, Wolfgang Böcklin, Conrad and Friedrich von Gottesheim). On the other hand, the Strasbourg reformers, particularly Capito, made the Council members accountable for the salvation of the city. The magistracy was won over when it was convinced that inner peace would result from the establishment of religious unity based on evangelical principles.[26] It was not until 10th January, 1529 that the magistrates decided to forbid the Catholic Mass in the city.[27] Until that time the initiative in religious matters had been taken by the townsmen and the preachers. Because the Council had been concerned to keep the religious question "open" until 1529 it had unwittingly created an opportunity for the expansion of religious radicalism.

The evangelical preachers remembered for a long time to come that they owed their positions primarily to the support of the "man in the street." This was apparent in the period leading up to, and during the Peasants' War, when the Strasbourg reformers showed more understanding of the aspirations of the rebels than did their colleagues in Wittenberg. In two Cathedral sermons in 1524 Hedio urged the Catholic Prelates voluntarily to renounce tithing so that the tithes could be used according to "human justice" for the care of the poor and to pay the wages of evangelical preachers and "secular magistrates" (if they were serving the general good). The authorities were asked to make sure that the bishops and "priests of Baal" did not provide a comfortable life for themselves at the expense of the peasants.[28] But as soon as the peasants wanted to press their demands by means of force the preachers parted company with them. At the

---

[26] *Ibid.* p. 93 and J. Kittelson, "Wolfgang Capito, the Council and Reform in Strasbourg" in *ARG* 63 (1972), pp. 126-141.

[27] M.U. Chrisman, *op. cit.*, p. 173.

[28] C. Hedio, *Von dem zehenden zwo trefflicher predig*, 1524. Hedio agreed with Brunfels on this issue. Brunfels (who put forward Hussite ideas) went further than Hedio in denying the clergy any secular possessions, O. Brunfels, *Von dem Pfaffen zehenden/hundert und zwen und fyertzig Schlussreden* 1524.

height of the Peasant's War in April, 1525 Capito, Bucer and Zell tried to persuade Erasmus Gerber (the leader of the troops in Alsace) to send the insurgents home because Christians had no right to resist on secular issues. But the goodwill of the Strasbourg preachers ("who wanted to relieve the common man's burden") could not be doubted even though their attempted mediation together with the Strasbourg Council stood little chance of success from the outset.[29] After the defeat of the peasants in June, 1525 Capito wrote to Kniebis, at that time "Ammeister" (burgomaster), protesting against the "unheard-of persecution" of the peasants and urging his masters to have "fatherly compassion" on the vanquished. (Compare this with Luther's attitude).[30] On the other hand the bishop's advisors accused Capito and Zell of having instigated the rebellion by their preaching.[31]

In the following years the evangelical preachers continued to support the economic demands of the common people, but always appealing to the Council to institute reforms peaceably. At Bucer's suggestion Fridolin Meyger, a notary and one of Strasbourg's leading Anabaptists, wrote a book on usury at the end of 1528, which implicated members of the Council.[32] Meyger openly admitted that he had welcomed the Peasants' War; he had hoped God would rid the world of its usury and that, as in ancient Israel, He would "make every seventh year free" by remitting of debts and liberating debtors from prison. In particular he attacked the extortionate "wine-tax", which demanded an interest of 7.5% in addition to the borrowed capital. He also attacked the practice of demanding a security of double the value of the capital borrowed and the clause which

---

[29] *Politische Korrespondenz* Vol. I pp. 114–116.

[30] This letter is printed in J. Rott, "Un Recueil de Correspondances Strasbourgeoises du XVIe siècle à la Bibliothèque de Copenhague" in *Bulletin Philologique et Historique publié par la Ministère de L'Education Nationale 1968* (Paris, 1971), pp. 786–787.

[31] *Politische Korrespondenz* Vol. I. No. 334, p. 188.

[32] TAE I No. 172. The wine-tax imposed by the Strasbourg councillors was 7.5%, way above the normal rate of 5%. An Ohm of wine (46 liter = 18 pfennigs) had to be paid back in every normal year for a borrowed capital of two guilders (=240 pfennigs).

stipulated that even unforeseeable catastrophes like war or harvest failures were no excuse for not paying interest punctually. The preachers made a submission to the Council urging the magistrate to forbid the usurious interest of 7.5%, but naturally they had no success.[33] Two years later the evangelical preachers pressed for further measures against usury.[34] In 1532, in his commentary on the Psalms, Bucer condemned the practice of demanding a security of four times the value of the borrowed capital.[35]

However inadequate, outdated and half-hearted these well-meant attempts may have been, there can be no doubt that Capito and Bucer gave a great boost to religious radicalism by their spiritualistic tendencies in relation to baptism and the Eucharist. This led them into conflict with Luther, a conflict which developed into open enmity between 1527 and 1529.[36]

In the controversy about baptism, the Strasbourg reformers conceded in 1524 that the early church had practised adult baptism and that such a practice was more conformable to Scripture than was infant baptism.[37] But the dispute over the timing of baptism was irrelevant because "God has not stipulated any particular time."[38] If anyone wants to undergo adult baptism this request should be granted, so long as this does not result in a "destruction of the love and unity" of the town's population.[39] Thus they were prepared to allow believers' baptism, but not its logical outcome, i.e. the establishment of a separate community of "true Christians." Bucer distinguished between "John's baptism with water," which is administered by men, and the baptism in the spirit, which is a gift of Christ. Infant baptism does not bring the two together. Only the baptism in the spirit has any significance for salvation, for it purifies man's soul and brings

[33] TAE I No. 178, p. 233.
[34] TAE I No. 245, p. 329.
[35] M. Bucer, *Sacrorum Psalmorum libri quinque* 1532, pp.68b-69b.
[36] Cf. WA Br 4:508 (where Luther calls the Strasbourg reformers "monsters, vipers and panthers") and the accounts of the colloquy of Marburg at which Luther called Bucer a "windbag" and refused to testify to his orthodoxy.
[37] *WA Br* 3: 384.
[38] *TAE* I No. 22, p. 28.
[39] M. Bucer, *Deutsche Schriften* Vol. I. p. 262.

forgiveness for his sins. Since only God can elect men for salvation or damnation, baptism with water can in no way be a sign of God's gift of grace to man.[40] Hence Bucer at this early stage regarded infant baptism as simply a pedagogical act which committed parents and the community to raising children in the Christian faith.[41] Bucer's and Capito's main criticism of the Anabaptists before 1527 was that they associated salvation with baptism with water.[42]

The Strasbourg theologians sided with the sacramentarians on the issue of the Eucharist by again applying their fundamental spiritualist distinction between sign and thing signified, between the "inner" and the "outer Word". When the controversy about the real presence of Christ in the consecrated elements came into the open in the autumn of 1524 Bucer and Capito attempted to play down the significance of the issue, although they took Karlstadt's side against Luther.

Karlstadt won over Clemens Ziegler and Otto Brunfels during a four-day visit to Strasbourg at the beginning of October, 1524. Through these popular figures he influenced many people, and the Council began to mention a "sect which Karlstadt had founded amongst the common people because of the sacrament".[43] The Strasbourg reformers were not particularly happy about Karlstadt's visit and distanced themselves from him because of his legalism, his "judaizing", his impetuosity in the implementation of evangelical reform and his support of the iconoclasts who had no backing from the authorities.[44] But shortly afterwards when Hinne Rode arrived in the town in November, 1524 with Cornelius Hoen's tract on the Eucharist, Bucer and Capito did join forces with the sacramentarians and

[40] *Ibid.* p. 260.

[41] *TAE* I No. 86, pp. 99–101, No. 124, pp. 149–151. M. Bucer, *Enarratio in evangelion Johannis*, 1528, pp. 436–444.

[42] *TAE* I No. 36, p. 48, No. 37, p. 49.

[43] *TAE* I No. 30, p. 44, No. 24, pp. 30–36; *WA Br* 3, p. 382; H. Barge, *op. cit.*, vol 2, p. 212; F. Ritter, *op. cit.*, 1962, pp. 225-233. 11 of Karlstadt's tracts had been printed in Strasbourg and Schlettstadt even before his visit. cf. H.-W. Müsing, "Karlstadt und die Entstehung der Strassburger Täufergemeinde" in M. Lienhard (ed.) *The Origins and Characteristics of Anabaptism*, (The Hague, 1977), pp. 169-195.

[44] *TAE* I No. 36, p. 48.

Bucer even declared that he had never believed in the real presence of Christ in the bread and the wine.[45]

On the other side Nikolaus Gerbel, the lawyer, sided with Luther. It looked as if the Strasbourg Reformation movement might splinter into three factions: Lutherans, followers of Karlstadt, and supporters of Capito and Bucer.

The Strasbourg theologians complained bitterly about the hatred and dissension that were being aroused by the Eucharistic dispute amongst the evangelicals; the Eucharist should be a celebration of brotherly love.[46] Capito wrote a book in 1524 urging tolerance on both sides. Even then the main aim of the Strasbourgers was to bring about unity amongst the evangelicals, but this did not mean that they themselves took no stand on the issue. We can see where they stood in Capito's statement that we should acknowledge that "Christ is *internal* and *invisible* and is not bound to anything external". The essence of the Eucharist is "the contemplation and commemoration of Christ in order to restore our hope." Beyond this bread and wine are of no value; "we should feed only our faith with the Lord's bread and wine, and dismiss the rest."[47] This could have been written by Karlstadt. The Strasbourg theologians could not contemplate any idea of divine "impanation" or any concept of the holy being bound up with earthly elements.[48] In contrast to Zwingli they were only prepared to stress the spiritual presence of Christ in the Eucharistic liturgy and the appropriation of his benefits in the believing soul through the signs of bread and wine.[49] In a letter to Landgrave Philip of Hesse Bucer defined the problem which the Strasbourg theologians were attempting to solve right up to the Wittenberg Concorde of 1536. It was to find a formula, *in the interests of*

[45] Cf. R. Stupperich, "Strassburgs Stellung zu Beginn des Sakramentsstreites, 1524-1525" in *ARG* 38 (1941), pp. 254ff.

[46] M. Bucer, *Deutsche Schriften* Vol. I, pp. 242-243, 247-249, 252. J.M. Kittelson, "Martin Bucer and the Sacramentarian Controversy: the Origins of his Policy of Concord" in *ARG* 64 (1973) pp. 166-182.

[47] W. Capito, *Was man halten und Antwurtten soll/von der spaltung zwischen Martin Luther/und Andres Carolstadt*, (Strasbourg, 1524), B2b, B3a.

[48] Cf. J. Rott, "Bucer et les débuts de la querelle sacramentaire" in *Révue d'Histoire et de Philosophie religieuses* 4 (1954), pp. 247, 250.

[49] *TAE* I No. 329, p. 545.

evangelical unity, which would "keep to the true and certain presence of Christ in the Eucharist" but which would not sound "as if they were making Christ's body and the bread into one single object in any natural way or as if they were localizing the body in the bread. It should give us to understand that the true body and true blood of Christ are *presented* in the words of the sacrament and in the bread and wine, but are accepted and received in faith by the soul alone.[50] But because Luther insisted on the "oral eating" of Christ's body by both believers and unbelievers the Strasbourg theologians obviously became his despised enemies. The Strasbourgers greeted all opponents of Wittenberg as friends. Schwenckfeld found asylum in Strasbourg in May, 1529[51] and a month later Hoffman was given a warm welcome in the town.[52] Sebastian Franck and Bünderlin also attempted to find a home in Strasbourg. Finally the Strasbourg theologians committed Karlstadt to Zwingli's special care when the Council, for political reasons, felt it could no longer offer shelter to Luther's arch-enemy.[53] Thus, not least for its stand against Wittenberg in the Eucharistic controversy, Strasbourg had become the capital of the spiritualist outlook in Germany.

b)   Clemens Ziegler.

The most popular local representative of the spiritualism which led to criticism of church and society was Clemens Ziegler, the gardener and lay preacher.[54] Like Thomas Müntzer and the Zwickau prophets, he believed that the latter days were approaching when there would be a new outpouring of the Holy Spirit which would affect the "poor in spirit" amongst all peoples, classes and religions and which would unite all men as one flock under a single shepherd.[55] Like them he believed their

---

[50] M. Lenz (ed.), *Briefwechsel Landgraf Philipps des Grossmütigen von Hessen mit Bucer.* Vol. I, 1880, p. 23.

[51] *CR* 97:124-126.

[52] *CR* 97:182-184.

[53] *CR* 97:574ff.; *TAE* I No. 215, p. 263.

[54] R. Peter, "Le Maraîcher Clement Ziegler. L'homme et son oeuvre" in *Revue d'Histoire et de Philosophie religieuses,* 34 (1954), pp. 255-282. (This article is based on Peter's unpublished thesis, *Le Jardinier Clément Ziegler*).

[55] *TAE* I No. 24, p. 35.

faith was "power of the impossible"; faith makes men capable of fulfilling the Law and of creating a better social order. The church of the future would be a brotherly community with no popes or councils. His political ideal was a community run by its own members on the lines of the first Swiss cantons, without princes or tyrants. All the economic burdens which oppressed the lower classes such as tithes, usury and indissoluble tenancy agreements, would be abolished.[56]

At the beginning of his public ministry he laid great stress on two basic concepts of religious radicalism: the idea of the immediate nature of religious consciousness where the church has no role regarding salvation, and the idea of a universal reign of God on earth in an empire that would also embrace Jews and Turks. At the beginning of 1525 Ziegler, along with a few other Strasbourg gardeners, joined the rebellious peasants at Oberehnheim (today Obernai) and Molsheim. They had two aims: to support and clarify the peasants' demands and to warn them at the same time not to use violence.[57] When Erasmus Gerber, the leader of the Alsatian troops, rejected his advice and led a punitive expedition against the abbey of Altdorf, Ziegler left the peasant army. This was only a few weeks before its defeat at Zabern.

After the failure of the peasants, the spiritualist revolutionary turned into an ascetic visionary who had, deeply disillusioned, resigned himself to accepting the existing social structure. He was given the rights of a burgher and in 1526 became a tithe-collector in Ruprechtsau. In this post he collected "reformed" tithes, which were used to pay the clergy and feed the poor.[58] His yearning for human freedom within a brotherly community was "sublimated" into a new concept of man's self-redemption by means of asceticism and the new idea of universal redemption in the world to come.

Unlike Luther, Ziegler now postulated the idea of the universality of divine grace. The concepts of good and evil, damnation and salvation, should be used not to distinguish

[56] *TAE* I No. 25, p. 36, R. Peter, *Le Jardinier*, p. 128.
[57] *TAE* I No. 25, p. 38.
[58] *TAE* I No. 40, pp. 49-50.

between men but to describe the contradictory tendencies within
each man. The "children of God" and the "good seed" are
references to man's soul, whereas the "devil" should be seen as a
symbol of the "flesh". Ziegler, like Hoffman after him, saw the
idea of predestination in terms of men's varying roles and talents.
Since Christ's sacrifical death has liberated all men's wills, men
must collaborate in the process of redemption using their own
strength. "In so much as we do as we should, God will do as we
would."[59] The concept of "damnation" applies simply to the
sickness, poverty and death of the body, it cannot affect "the
noble soul of any man, which is God in us."[60]

Ziegler saw the conquest of the flesh as the path which leads to
man's perfection and deification, "for the created body has
become the devil's abode."[61] In the drawings illustrating a book
Ziegler presented to the Strasbourg Council 1532[62] in which he
described the way of salvation, the flesh appears as a serpent with a
woman's head and breasts. The serpent is tempting a man, within
whose heart there grows the "new man", symbolised by a small
child over whom hovers a dove (the Holy Spirit). In a second
illustration the man stands on the cross; he imitates Christ and
strangles the serpent, which now reveals its true nature – the
serpent turns into a dragon. The dove (the Holy Spirit) settles in
the heart of the "new man", who turns away from the woman.[63]
Ziegler was stressing the anti-sexual meaning of his ascetic
demands: the "flesh" which opposes the "spirit" is the lustful
temptation which emanates from women.

In about 1530 Ziegler added a fascination for dreams and
visions to his asceticism. His visions were the expression of a
profound anxiety which took concrete form in fears about the
Turks or the eventual failure of the Reformation. Thus he saw
"dark-skinned" mercenaries pouring into the Rhine valley and
devastating the country. In another dream he watched

---

[59] *TAE* I No. 350, p. 579, cf. *TAE* I No. 346, p. 567.
[60] *TAE* I No. 346, pp. 567-568.
[61] *TAE* I No. 350, p. 579.
[62] *Von der seligkeit aller menschen selen*, in Strasbourg, Thomas
Archive, No. 76 (45, 2).
[63] *TAE* I No. 350, pp. 578-583.

Strasbourg Cathedral being turned into a stable and the Catholic Mass celebrated in the presence of the burgomaster. On more than one occasion he saw the Emperor, though gravely ill, attempting to preach the Gospel but being prevented from doing so by his evil counsellors.[64]

Ziegler's spiritualism also influenced his Eucharistic and Christological doctrines. As with Schwenckfeld and Hoffman, these two doctrines were closely interrelated. In his books of 1524 and 1525,[65] Ziegler emphasized Christ's spirituality and his pre-existence before his earthly nativity. Christ, the Word of God, possessed his own body in the same way that the Holy Spirit had bodily form in the dove. During Jesus' earthly life *two distinct* bodies were untied in Christ – the mortal body that he had taken from the Virgin Mary and the immortal body which he had possessed before the creation of the world. Without this he could not have been resurrected.[66] It is this "divine and spiritual body of Christ" which believers receive in the Lord's Supper, as a pledge of atonement with God. If we are to win over the Jews and Turks, we must proclaim the eternal, omnipresent Christ, not the son of Mary who was born in Israel.[67]

Although very much courted, Ziegler never joined the Anabaptists. Yet he was the first local Strasbourger to doubt the biblical legitimation of infant baptism and to accept as scriptural a baptism conforming to St. Mark's principle of "believe first, then be baptized" (Mark 16:16). But he could not bring himself to accept the practice of adult baptism.[68] A major reason for this was his conviction that the élitist incapsulation of the Anabaptists which was implied in believers' baptism was unchristian. "They thereby condemn everyone who does not join them, which I cannot accept."[69]

---

[64] *TAE* II No. 486, pp. 257-259, R. Peter, "Le Maraîcher" pp. 276, 281.

[65] *Von der vermehlung Marie und Josephs* and *Ein fast schon buchlin-. . . von dem leib und blut Christi.*

[66] *TAE* I No. 7, pp. 11-13, No. 24, p. 34, R. Peter, *Le Jardinier*, pp. 36, 71-73.

[67] R. Peter, "Le Maraîcher" p. 270.

[68] *TAE* I No. 8, p. 13-14.

[69] *TAE* I No. 346, p. 573.

Despite distancing himself from the Anabaptists, Clemens Ziegler had a profound effect on the spiritual milieu of Strasbourg, the environment in which Hoffman's ideas were to change. Many of the elements of Hoffman's theology which first appeared during his time in Strasbourg are already present in Ziegler: the doctrine of the freedom of the will, the new interpretation of predestination in terms of "roles and gifts", the fascination with dreams and visions and the idea of a world-wide mission bound up with the idea of the conversion of the Jews. But Hoffman and Ziegler differed on the question of total forgiveness, on Mariology and on Christology. For Ziegler Mary was a "pure virgin" before and after Christ's birth, and she was the Lord's physical mother.[70] But Hoffman thought of her as a "sinful daughter of Adam" through whom Christ had passed like water through a pipe. But Ziegler did prepare the way for the development of Hoffman's monophysite speculations about Christ, at least in so far as he distinguished between Christ's two bodies and placed such one-sided stress on Christ's divine nature. To Ziegler the historical and concrete humanity of the Son of God as mediated by Mary was of no consequence. What matters for salvation is "Christ according to the spirit"; "Jesus according to the flesh" can be forgotten. Only one more step in this direction was needed (i.e. to deny Christ's second body, taken from Mary) in order to arrive at Hoffman's monophysite Christology. But this does not imply a direct dependence of Hoffman on Ziegler; we are concerned here simply with recognizing the atmosphere in which Hoffman's thought took shape.

c)   Anabaptism in Strasbourg: its Growth and Divisions

It appears that no permanent separatist Anabaptist community had been established in Strasbourg before 1526,[71] though the social context for such a development had been favourable since October, 1524. Capito mentions that in the late autumn of 1524 some townsmen "from amongst the common folk" were refusing to have their children baptized.[72] In a book published in

---

[70] *TAE* I No. 7, p. 10.
[71] *TAE* I No. 39, p. 49.
[72] *TAE* I No. 23, p. 29, No. 27, p. 40.

Strasbourg in July, 1525 Hubmaien turned Karlstadt's negative comments on infant baptism into a positive demand for adult believers' baptism.[73]

The actual beginning of the Anabaptist movement in Strasbourg can be dated to early 1526. In March of that year Wilhelm Reublin, the Zurich Anabaptist who had baptized Hubmaier arrived in the city. Like Hubmaier Reublin had been involved in the Peasant's War of 1525 (when he was in Hallau and Waldshut). But afterwards he had come to accept Grebel's call for Anabaptism to take a pacifist direction.[74] In Strasbourg he won over the tailor Jörg Ziegler (Clemens Ziegler's brother) to his views, and during the following years Ziegler's house in the Steinstrasse served as a focal point for the first Anabaptist community in Strasbourg; a community which was committed to the biblicism and pacifism propounded by Grebel, Reublin and Sattler.[75]

But whereas Reublin and Jörg Ziegler were unable (apart from a few discussions with Capito and Clemens Ziegler) to gain any spectacular following for their ideas, Hans Wolff, a weaver from Benfeld, caused great public excitement. Convinced that he was enlightened directly by the Holy Spirit, Wolff interrupted one of Zell's sermons in Strasbourg Cathedral and attempted to force him out of the chancel. He charged the evangelical preachers with being satisfied with abolishing a few papist ceremonies and not making sure that the Reformation brought about any fruits in the Christian's life. Under the new doctrine people were still bestial, adultery and prostitution abounded just as before, and usury and unjust taxes had not been abolished. Instead of mixing with the people in order to encourage and improve them, the learned preachers called themselves "doctors, masters and rabbis", isolating themselves from their congregations and looking after

---

[73] B. Hubmaier, *Von dem christlichen tauff der gläubigen*, *TAE* I No. 35, pp. 46-47. cf. also *WA Br* 3, No. 796, No. 797, *TAE* I No. 15, p. 23 and No. 21, p. 25.

[74] Cf. J. M. Stayer, "Die Anfänge des schweizerischen Täufertums im reformierten Kongregationalismus" in H.-J. Goertz (ed.) *Umstrittenes Täufertum*, 1975, p. 42.

[75] *CR* 95:557.

their own interests. They also erred seriously in matters of doctrine. Infant baptism was unscriptural, he claimed. It was false to teach eternal damnation in Hell; even the devil would be saved eventually. Wolff also denounced military service and said that holding magisterial office was incompatible with being a Christian. This frightful world would come to an end in seven years' time, on the stroke of noon on Ascension Day, 1533. The magistracy responded to Wolff's attack on the evangelical preachers by having him banished.

Wolff's message was one of the earliest examples of the fusion of apocalyptic spiritualism and Anabaptism – a fusion which was to be found again later in Hoffman. What is most remarkable is that both Wolff in Strasbourg and Hoffman in Stockholm predicted the same date for the end of the world (1533) at the same time (1526). These speculations may have derived from the calculations made by Hans Hut, who presented the messianic confusion as a seven-year-long process (which was divided into two periods of 3½ years each).[76] Like Hut, both Hoffman and Wolff were prepared to change the dates of the beginning and end of these periods.

The autumn of 1526 saw the arrival in Strasbourg of four important figures in Protestant radicalism: Hans Denck, Michael Sattler, Martin Cellarius (Borrhaus) and Ludwig Hätzer. They (and in particular Denck's missionary work) gave a great boost to nonconformity in the city, and only now did it become a serious

---

[76] On Hans Wolff, cf. TAE I No. 47-No. 55, pp. 52-77. For Hut the 7-year-long apocalyptic débâcle had begun with the revolutionary activity of Thomas Müntzer and Heinrich Pfeiffer (i.e. 1521-1522), whom he regarded as the two witnesses of the last days. The executions of Pfeiffer and Müntzer in May, 1525 brought the first 3½-year-period to an end. Thus Christ would return in another 3½ years, at the end of 1528. But since the Lord had promised to shorten the period of suffering for his elect, Pentecost of 1528 seemed to be the earliest possible date for the Parousia. Hoffman dissociated himself from these calculations. In December, 1537 he said: "The devil did everything he could to spoil the success of the two witnesses. Müntzer and Pfeiffer, who were beheaded in the rebellion in Saxony, pretended to be the two witnesses." For him the messianic disturbances probably began with his own battle with Lutheranism in Livonia (1526) and he thus arrived at 1533 as the date for Christ's return.

challenge to Strasbourg's official Reformation. A group of "Swiss Brethren" also made an appearance in the town. They were Jakob Gross, who had been banished from Waldshut because he had refused to fight in the Peasants' War, Wilhelm Echsel, a cobbler from Wallis and Mathis Hiller, a furrier from St. Gallen. Two Strasbourg townsmen joined forces with them: Jörg Tucher and Jörg Ziegler.[77]

These pacifist Anabaptists (with the exception of Sattler) were imprisoned immediately after they arrived. Bucer led the opposition. The decisive question was whether they were prepared to recognize secular authority as a Christian institution if it made use of the sword. When Gross gave an evasive answer but said he would refuse to kill an enemy or take an oath, Bucer told him to go to hell.[78] The concession made by these "Swiss Brethren" to undertake guard duties and to obey the magistrate in all just demands, did not help them at all. Bucer was aware that the idea of a separate community of saints who, in the name of the Sermon on the Mount, would not be prepared to fulfil their duties as citizens, was incompatible with the traditional structure of society (the *corpus christianum*) in which church and state complement and endorse one another. Bucer ensured that all of them (with the probable exception of Jörg Ziegler) were forced to leave the city in 1527.[79] In view of these events the Council decided to issue its first Anabaptist mandate. Anabaptists were forbidden to stay in the city, "because they do not acknowledge the authorities to be Christian" and because they found pretexts to avoid fulfilling their duties and obeying orders "designed to promote the general good and intended to encourage love, peace and unity." They thus "threaten the town with division and insult which attack a united and Christian structure."[80] It should be noted that this first Anabaptist mandate in Strasbourg was not

---

[77] *TAE* I No. 67. The term "Swiss Brethren", which applies to the pacifist Anabaptists of S.W. Germany and Switzerland, was not used until the end of the 1530's.

[78] *TAE* I No. 67, p. 64.

[79] *TAE* I No. 72.

[80] The mandate was approved on 31st December, 1526 but not issued until 27th July, 1527. *TAE* I Nos. 68 and 92.

based on a religious objection to doctrinal heresy, but on the political argument that a united city community was being threatened by them.[81]

The dispute between the Strasbourg Reformers and the Swiss Brethren reached its height during the final days of 1526 in the course of discussion between Bucer and Capito on the one side and Michael Sattler on the other. The outcome of these debates was Sattler's farewell letter to the Reformers and the "Schleitheim Confession," which he wrote shortly afterwards, in February, 1527. In this confession the Swiss Brethren dissociated themselves both from the official Protestant Reformation and also the revolutionary spiritualist Anabaptist communities (i.e. Hubmaier, the Eastern Swiss Anabaptist movement which had been involved in the Peasants' War in Hallau and Schaffhausen, Hans Denck and the spiritualist antinomians of St. Gallen and Appenzell).[82]

For Bucer and Capito the commandment to love is the sum of all God's commandments (1 Tim. 1:5). All other individual commandments are subordinate to this and can claim no absolute validity. But in relation to state and society this idea of love must be qualified by Luther's doctrine of God's two forms of governance. The individual is bound by the precept of the Sermon on the Mount not to resist evil. A Christian, if he is unjustly treated, should not defend himself, yet on the other hand, for love's sake, he must protect the rights of his neighbour (if he has been treated unjustly). In particular he must do this if God has entrusted him with secular power. In view of the power of evil which rules the world, the Christian is not fulfilling his duty to love if he refuses to appeal to the law on behalf of his neighbour, if he refuses to enforce the law or if he refuses to take

---

[81] For Bucer's concept of the *corpus christianum*, which was rooted in his social ethics cf. K. Deppermann, "Die Strassburger Reformatoren und die Krise des oberdeutschen Täufertums im Jahre 1527" in *MGB* 25 (1973) pp. 24-52. On the growth of the Swiss Brethren cf. J. M. Stayer in *MGB* 29 (1977), pp. 7-34.

[82] For Sattler's letter to Capito and Bucer, *TAE* I No. 70. For the Schleitheim Confession cf. B. Jenny (ed.), *Das Schleitheimer Bekenntnis 1527*, (1951), pp. 9-18.

up arms against domestic or foreign enemies. The Anabaptists make the Son (Christ) the Father's enemy in that they reject, in the Son's name, that which the Creator of the world has ordained for the benefit of fallen man, namely the power of the secular authorities.[83]

Michael Sattler saw in these doctrines an attempt to do away with Christ's true ordinances. He particularly attacked the thesis that the command to love overrode or limited God's other commandments, and the interpretation of this central command in terms of Luther's doctrine of the two modes of God's governance. For him God's commandment to love was unequivocal and given unique expression in the Sermon on the Mount. This shows that there are two fundamental and distinct ordinances: the ordinance of the world, "outside of Christ's perfection", in which, according to the will of God, the sword has to be used, and the ordinance of Christianity in which the most extreme means of force that can be used is excommunication. A man can belong to only one of these two ordinances. The pure community of Christ, which one enters voluntarily by believer's baptism and in which one is subjected by the brethren to a rigorous church discipline, has nothing to do with the state or its laws. The Christian lives "without external or worldly defences." His citizenship is in heaven, not on earth. He rejects every demand made by the state in terms of military service, law-enforcement and swearing oaths of allegiance. A Christian cannot hold an office. He must shun the "world" for it is the kingdom of darkness. The Christian must reject "papist" and "anti-papist" (Reformed) worship, and avoid public houses and worldly associations in unions and brotherhoods. He need not fulfil civil duties demanded by unbelievers. "To sum up: Christ and Belial have nothing in common."[84]

The rigid dualism lying behind this theology breaks down at one point when he says that "the sword is ordained by God

---

[83] M. Bucer: *Enarrationum in evangelia Mathaei, Marci et Lucae libri duo* 1527, 172a–178b and W. Capito, *In Hoseam prophetam . . . commentarius* (Strasbourg, 1528).

[84] *TAE* I No. 70, p. 69.

outside of Christ's perfection," but this concession is immediately nullified when he speaks of "the sword, harness and the like as devilish weapons of power."[85]

There was an unbridgeable gulf between this view of the world and Bucer's and Capito's idea of an undivided Christian community. So Sattler left Strasbourg voluntarily in January, 1527. He had asked in vain for mercy for his imprisoned colleagues (Gross, Hiller and Echsel). In spite of his pleas they had been banished.

Although the Strasbourg preachers condemned Sattler's dualistic legalism as the "start of a new monasticism", he made a profound impression on them as a man. After his cruel execution in Rottenburg they spoke of him as "a martyr for Christ" and "God's beloved friend". Capito even petitioned the council of Horb for the release of Sattler's imprisoned followers, but he was unsuccessful.[86]

In contrast, from the outset the Strasbourg reformers considered Hans Denck to be a sly hypocrite and dangerous deceiver of the people. It appears from the number of spectators at the disputation between Denck and Bucer (Gerbel speaks of 200, but the Council minutes record an audience of 400) that Denck had managed to arouse considerable interest in his doctrines amongst the educated artisans and the upper middle class. Those sympathetic to him included members of the Steltz Guild (which incorporated glaziers, goldsmiths, printers, painters and other self-employed workers) as well as Fridolin Meiger the notary and Friedrich Ingolt, merchant and member of the Council.[87] So as to suppress Denck's influence on the population Bucer went against the wishes of the Council and on 22nd December, 1526 held a disputation in which he and Denck debated the thesis of the latter's book, *On the Law of God*. Although Denck claimed that his doctrines were compatible in all points with those of the Strasbourg preachers, Bucer insisted that there was a fundamental

---

[85] B. Jenny (ed.), *op. cit,*p. 13.
[86] *TAE* I No. 86, p. 110; Nos. 88 and 84.
[87] *TAE* I No. 64 and 65.

difference between them. He made sure that Denck was banished on 25th December, 1526.[88] Nevertheless Denck had managed to win over a circle of followers in Strasbourg which continued to exist into the 1530s. It was led until about 1532 by Jakob Kautz, a preacher from Worms. Since it was under the influence of Denck that Hoffman renounced most of his Lutheran ideas, and since the Melchiorites in Strasbourg remained on friendly terms with Denck's followers, we shall give an indication here of Denck's own theology, insofar as it had significance for Hoffman.

The most important impulse behind Denck's theology was his disappointment at the practical results produced by the Reformation. He compared it to a barren tree which produced nothing but green leaves and crab apples.[89] He attributed the Reformation's alleged failure to renew individual and social life to Luther's doctrines of predestination and justification. Denck considered that the doctrine of predestination placed the source of evil within the Godhead and that it did away with man's accountability for his own sins.[90] The Lutheran doctrine of justification presented Christ as a heathen idol, to which men pay lip-service by relying on his "merits" in order to avoid following Christ in their lives.[91]

As against Luther's belief in predestination Denck argued for the universality of grace; God wishes all men to be saved.[92] His "inner Word" is manifested in every man's conscience. If anyone says that God has not called him to a devout life he is a liar.[93] This "inner Word" is "spirit, not letter, written without pen or paper, so that it cannot be erased. Thus salvation is *not* bound to Scripture".[94] But so that all men could have visible evidence of God's will and could have no excuse for remaining in darkness, the invisible Word became flesh in Jesus. Christ died for all men in

---

[88] *CR* 95:819.
[89] H. Denck, *Schriften* (ed. W. Fellmann), 1956, Vol. 2. p. 56.
[90] *ibid.*, Vol. 2, p. 41.
[91] *ibid.*, Vol. 2, pp. 52, 106.
[92] *ibid.*, Vol. 2, p. 38.
[93] *ibid.*, Vol. 2, 96.
[94] *ibid.*, Vol. 2, p. 106.

order to provide everyone with an example of complete love. God became man so that man could be divinised.[95]

Man cannot be forced into doing good either by his experience of the "inner Word" in his conscience or by the example given by Christ. These simply provide him with the "free choice" to do either good or evil.[96] Denck rejects the idea that God himself is the origin of evil: this is blasphemy. Since goodness is identical with God's nature, God cannot do other than good. God does not cause the sins committed by men – He rather lets them happen. Sin, which Denck as a mystic identifies with the addiction to creaturely things, derives from men's free will.[97]

The biblical cornerstone of the doctrine of predestination had always been Romans 9, in which Paul explains that God (in total freedom) had loved Jacob and hated Esau even before their birth. Denck's interpretation of this passage presented double election in terms of God's prescience. The Creator had foreseen that Jacob, unlike Esau, would not sin, although he was capable of sinning. Thus the election of Jacob did not contradict God's demand for justice. This interpretation of the Pauline doctrine of predestination made a great impact on other movements at the time of the Reformation. It was taken over almost word for word by Sebastian Franck and Melchior Hoffman.[98]

For Denck man's "justification" constituted a genuine renewal brought about by love of God. It is in love that real atonement takes place, for "love is a spiritual force in which men are united or in which they desire to be united with another person."[99] By love man can share in God's nature and "he approaches the divine form."[100] "Justification by faith" does not mean the opposite of "justification by works" but that inner perfection from which all

[95] *ibid.*, Vol. 2, p. 39.
[96] *ibid.*, Vol. 2, p. 35.
[97] *ibid.*, Vol. 2, p. 28.
[98] *ibid.*, Vol. 2, pp. 90–91; S. Franck, *Chronica*, 1543, p. 15, 9b; M. Hoffman, *Eyn waraftyghe tuchenisse unde gruntlyke verclarynge wo die worden tho den Ro. IX von deme Esau unde Jacob soldeen verstaen worden* 1531, cf. also his Commentary on Romans (1533) N4a-b.
[99] H. Denck, *Schriften*, Vol. 2, p. 76.
[100] *Ibid.*, Vol. 2, p. 37.

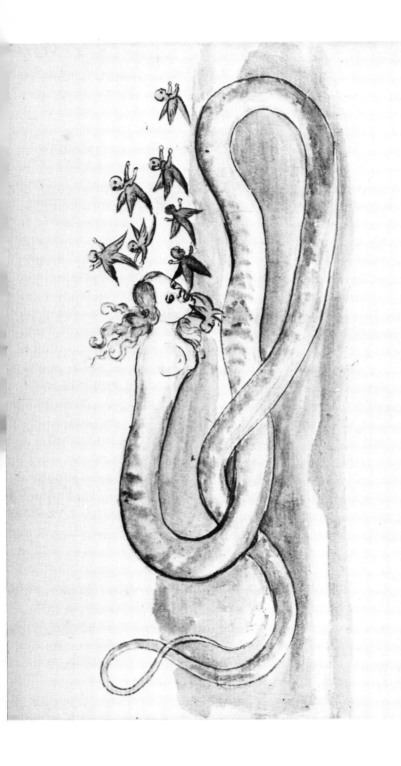

Plate 7: Clemens Ziegler: The woman as the serpent from which the angels of death go forth

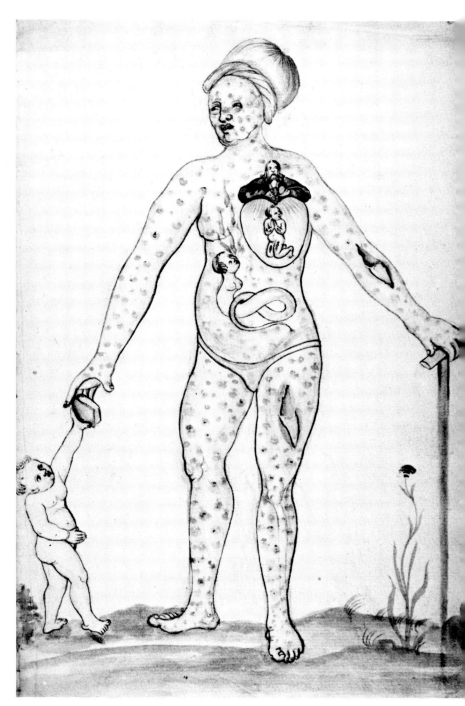

Plate 8: Clemens Ziegler: The old, ailing man

good acts flow. "For the justification by faith which God accepts should and must go beyond all works of the law, willingly renouncing all those things which – though they are permitted – are not perfect."[101] Thus fulfilment of the law is necessary for justification by faith. "Blessed is he who hears the Word of God and keeps to it. He who hears it but does not act accordingly behaves like a fool."[102]

Denck makes it clear in his writings that just as a servant who knowingly disobeys his master's orders is punished by death so, as a rule, those who fall away after having tasted eternal life, are doomed. However, merciful as God may be, there are only very few who return to a state of grace after sinning in full knowledge of the truth.[103] The Christian must as a rule take into account that sins committed after conversion will not be forgiven.[104]

Bucer and Capito felt that these doctrines struck at the very core of the Reformation. To them Denck's doctrine was a new attempt to teach justification by man's own works, because he made the alleged "divine spark in the soul" the motivating force in salvation and because he reduced the role of the historical Jesus to that of a prototype.[105]

After his banishment from Strasbourg Denck went to Worms where he won over two evangelical preachers, Kautz and Hilarius. Kautz took over the leadership of the Anabaptist community Denck had founded in Strasbourg. But he was mercilessly attacked: tracts were written against him, he was imprisoned in 1529 and refused rights of residence in 1532.[106] The controversy with him began while he was still in Worms, when he published his "Seven Articles" challenging the Lutheran preachers to a disputation. He was particularly attacked for his sixth article: "Jesus of Nazareth suffered for us and acted for us in no other way than that we stand in His footsteps and follow the

---

[101] *Ibid.*, Vol. 2, p. 79.
[102] *Ibid.*, Vol. 2, p. 43.
[103] *Ibid.*, Vol. 2, p. 56.
[104] *Ibid.*, Vol. 2, pp. 47, 107, 39.
[105] *CR* 95, pp. 800, 819, *CR* 96, p. 184.
[106] *TAE* I Nos. 340-343.

way that He has made."[107] The Strasbourg reformers thus accused him of making a "foul idol" of man's wretched will.[108]

The division amongst the Strasbourg Anabaptists between the supporters of Denck and the followers of Reublin and Sattler was already apparent by the winter of 1526–1527. From a warning letter written by the Strasbourg reformers against Kautz we can gather that Ludwig Hätzer (a friend and colleague of Denck's) had called Michael Sattler "a sly and evil rogue" and had praised the Strasbourg reformers for keeping the baptismal question open. What is more, Sattler, unlike Denck, had not erred in matters of the true faith concerning "redemption by Christ Jesus, on which everything depends."[109]

Altogether there were three main reasons for the division between the Anabaptists in Strasbourg:

1. Unlike Denck, Sattler retained the orthodox forensic doctrine of satisfaction regarding the sacrifice of Christ.

2. Denck agreed with the Strasbourg reformers rather than with Sattler in seeing love as the fulfilment of the law. "All commandments, traditions and laws that appear in the scriptures of the Old and New Testaments can be reduced for a true disciple of Christ to a single precept simply to love God. By this he knows which things he shall do or leave undone, even if he has no Scripture to go on."[110]

Sattler believed that the idea "that faith and love can do and suffer all things" was an invitation to give in "to the weakness and licentiousness of the flesh".[111] He insisted that the observance of particular laws and ceremonies (which he specified in the "Schleitheim Confession") was an obligation on the Christian community and necessary for the salvation of the individual Christian. Amongst these essentials were believers' baptism (an act of incorporation into the body of Christ), the Eucharist and excommunication (as a means of keeping the community pure

---

[107] M. Krebs (ed.), *Quellen zur Geschichte der Täufer. 4:Baden und Pfalz*, 1951, No. 129, pp. 113–114.

[108] *TAE* I No. 86, pp. 114, 110.

[109] *TAE* I No. 86, pp. 106, 107.

[110] H. Denck, *Schriften*, Vol. 2, pp. 63, 54.

[111] B. Jenny (ed.), *op. cit.*, p. 10.

and separate from the world), the refusal to use force and to swear oaths. For the spiritualist Denck all of these things were desirable but in no way necessary for salvation. It would not harm a man to have been baptised as a child, or even not to have been baptised at all, so long as he experienced an inner baptism, the baptism in the spirit.[112] Anyone who has overcome the old Adam within himself has no need for the external Eucharist, "for he drinks from an invisible cup that invisible wine which God has prepared from the beginning through His Son, through the Word."[113] Since the true church was scattered amongst all churches, and even amongst the Jews and the heathen, Denck eventually concluded towards the end of his life that the practice of "shunning" ("Meidung") should be limited to those tyrants who attempt to force particular beliefs onto their subjects.[114] Finally, anyone who speaks the truth can confidently call on God to witness his veracity. Oaths should be forbidden only in cases where men commit themselves to future undertakings over which they have no control.[115]

Sattler saw in Denck's spiritualism "a ruse of the flesh" aimed at avoiding the cross. In his farewell letter written shortly before his execution he referred to the coming persecution and urged his followers to hold firm and without deviation to the ordinance of Christ, which had been clearly expounded once and for all.[116]

3. Finally Denck and Sattler differed in their assessment of the Bible. Denck exalted the "invisible, inner word" of God far above the Scriptures. Man should accept "the outer word" only as far as it is confirmed by the inner witness of the Holy Spirit. Blind trust in the letter of the Bible is an abomination before God.[117] But Sattler rejected Denck's belief in immediate revelation because it removed man's dependence on Scripture, preaching and all historical revelation. In his farewell letter

---

[112] H. Denck, *Schriften*, Vol. 2, pp. 24, 80, 81, 109.

[113] *Ibid.*, Vol. 2, p. 25.

[114] *Ibid.*, Vol. 2, p. 108.

[115] *Ibid.*, Vol. 2, p. 110.

[116] The letter is printed in W. Köhler (ed.), *Flugschriften aus den ersten Jahren der Reformation*, Vol. 2. 1908, pp. 319ff.

[117] H. Denck, *Schriften*, Vol. 2, p. 22.

(which was directed against Denck and the spiritualists of Eastern Switzerland) Sattler wrote, "Never remove your destination which is imprinted by the *letter* of Holy Scripture and sealed by the blood of Christ and many eye-witnesses of Jesus. Do not listen to what they say about their father, for he is a liar; do not believe their spirit because it is immersed in the flesh."[118]

Thus there grew up within Strasbourg two totally distinct Anabaptist communities, the spiritualist Anabaptists under Kautz, Denck's disciple, and the legalist biblicists, who were led by Reublin after Sattler's death. But this division did not prevent the two communities from keeping a joint fund for the relief of the poor or from coming together to fight the Strasbourg reformers. Yet when Reublin and Kautz were imprisoned together in 1529 and wrote a joint confession of faith against the Strasbourg reformers, they were still conscious of their differences.[119] The reformers saw Kautz as their most dangerous opponent. "If Jacob Kautz is correct in his teaching, then all of the contents and teachings of Holy Scripture will have been done away with. Wilhelm Reublin does not agree in all points with Kautz, but he still says that we do not teach true Christian doctrine, that we are not the church of God and that we cannot bring forth fruit."[120]

Hoffman took two ideas from Denck's theology which contradicted his own previous teachings:

1. That God is not the source of evil and elects no one to damnation. He wants all men to be saved (the universality of grace).

2. That divine illumination, in co-operation with divine grace, enables every man to win his own salvation by good works (the doctrine of the freedom of will).

Denck's conviction that justification consists in regeneration confirmed the idea of human divinisation which Hoffman had already formulated in his commentary on Daniel. But the idea

---

[118] W. Köhler (ed.), *Flugschriften*, Vol. 2, p. 321.
[119] *TAE* I No. 168.
[120] *TAE* I No. 167.

that man remained both justified and a sinner (which he had retained in the commentary on Daniel) became meaningless for Hoffman under Denck's influence.

Because Denck's ideas were accepted, the Melchiorites remained on friendly terms with Kautz's circle, whereas the followers of Reublin and Marbeck opposed the Hoffmanites; the Strasbourg Anabaptists were thus divided into three groups.[121]

Some dogmatic differences between the Melchiorites and Kautz's circle, however, prevented the two groups from coming together as one community. Unlike Denck, Hoffman still believed in the historical mediation of God's grace. Grace comes to man by Christ's sacrificial death, which has freed all men from the curse of original sin, and by the preaching of the "apostolic messengers", which brings about the actual liberation of men's wills. In the early stages of the development of faith (literal belief) men are instructed by hearing the Gospel. Hoffman opposes Denck's mysticism, which had no place for the written word or history as mediators of divine truth, by saying, "Some preachers contest these fundamentals very foolishly by telling us that we should close our eyes and ears and just 'believe', but nobody knows what."[122] In fact Hoffman, like Denck, was convinced that immediate revelation was possible, but he felt that this could only occur in the second stage of the development of faith.

This difference resulted in divergent attitudes to missionary activity and evangelization. Whereas Denck and Kautz gave up any attempt to proselytize at the end of their lives (as much because of their mysticism as because of their disappointed hopes) Hoffman and his disciples wandered restlessly around the country in order to win men for their beliefs.

A second major difference between Denck and Hoffman concerned eschatology and eternal damnation. Denck had attacked Hut's apocalyptic speculations at the "Martyrs' Synod of Augsburg" in 1527, considering the proclamation of the

---

[121] *TAE* I No. 234, pp. 288-298, *TAE* II No. 533, p. 299, No. 370, p. 23. Abraham Hulshof was wrong in saying that Denck's party opposed Hoffman, (*Geschiedenis van de Doopsgezinden te Straatsburg 1525-1527*, Amsterdam, 1905, p. 115).

[122] Hoffman, *Römerbrief*, Q1b.

imminence of the Day of Judgment and the call to arms for the
saints to be a false prophecy. Eventually, in conversation but not
in print, Denck went further than this. He replaced the whole
idea of a final judgment which would separate the good from the
evil with the concept of universal forgiveness.[123] Denck had
already written that Being was identical with God and Goodness
and that Non-being was identical with Evil; sin and punishment
were pedagogical tools to educate mankind.[124] But Hoffman, on
the other hand, always held to the doctrine of merciless, eternal
wrath directed against the godless.

*d) Capito's Inclination towards Apocalyptic Spiritualism
(1527–1531)*

The growth of apocalypticist Anabaptism was encouraged
between 1527 and 1531 by Capito's acceptance of Martin
Cellarius's spiritualistic federal theology. Cellarius, who had once
been a member of the Zwickau Prophets, stayed with Capito for
several months in 1527 and impressed his host with his theology
of history, which postulated a historical progression towards an
increasingly spiritual form of communion between God and
man. According to Cellarius each historical epoch is marked out
by a particular covenant. The Old Testament covenants were
simply "figures" of later developments. As history progresses
material means of salvation give way to more spiritual forms.[125]
The New Testament, which began with the outpouring of the
Holy Spirit and its accompanying new awareness of God, has
now been interrupted by the rule of Antichrist, the papacy. But
this deviation will soon be corrected without recourse to human
violence. Present-day believers must follow the example of the

[123] There is incontrovertible evidence for this in the letter of Nicolaus
Thomae (Siegelpach) to Oecolampadius, dated 1st April, 1527, printed
in E. Staehelin (ed), *Briefe und Akten zum Leben Oekolampads* Vol. 2.
1927, No. 479, pp. 52–53.

[124] Denck, *Schriften* Vol. 2, pp. 29–30, cf. W. Klassen, "Was Hans
Denck a Universalist? in *MQR* 39 (1965), pp. 152–154. There is an
English translation of *Whether God Is the Cause of Evil* (*Schriften* Vol. 2,
pp. 27–47) in G.H. Williams and A.M. Mergal (ed), *Spiritual and
Anabaptist Writers* (Library of Christian Classics, 25, London, 1957), pp.
88–111.

[125] M. Cellarius, *De operibus Dei*, (Strasbourg, 1527), p. 59a.

Jews during the Babylonian captivity; instead of using the sword to fight spiritual and temporal tyrants, they must wait patiently for God to intervene.[126] Thus Cellarius was trying to keep the old hopes alive whilst rejecting Müntzer's call to revolution. According to Cellarius the people of Israel will also come to a true knowledge of God at the end of history; they will return to the land of Canaan and will rule the earth from there. Since the Holy Spirit will in future write the law into the hearts of the sons of God, peace, freedom, equality and justice will triumph among them.[127]

Capito wrote a preface recommending Cellarius's De operibus Dei[128] and then went on to write a commentary on Hosea on the basis of Cellarius's views.[129] Here he accepted the form of anticlerical apocalyptic spiritualism which had hitherto only been seen in nonconformist circles.

In particular Capito argued that the higher level of the knowledge of God which had been brought by Christ had already been relinquished by the end of the apostolic age. Jews, Muslims and Christians discarded their newly won spiritual freedom and reverted to a new legalism and revived ritualism. A modified form of justification by works had led men away from the true basis of Christian faith, i.e. simple trust in God's fatherly care.[130] But Capito hoped that in his century Christ would remove the Antichrist from his seat and again establish his kingdom.[131] Capito saw the Protestant martyrdom as a sign of the beginnings of the apocalyptic disturbances and the coming of a third period of the Spirit.[132] He predicted that Gog and Magog would shortly appear, along with Elijah Redivivus. This prophet of the latter days would finally destroy any trust in justification

---

[126] Ibid., pp. 72a-b, 74b.
[127] Ibid., pp. 80b, 84a-85b, 87b.
[128] TAE I No. 90, pp. 116-121.
[129] W. Capito, In Hoseam prophetam . . . commentarius, Strasbourg 1528. In my opinion James M. Kittelson (Wolfgang Capito, Leiden 1975, pp. 183f.) underestimates Capito's spiritualist tendency.
[130] W. Capito, In Hoseam, p. 78b.
[131] Ibid., p. 267b-268a, 79b.
[132] Ibid., p. 18a.

by man's own efforts and he would level out all social distinctions between men, since these result from the flesh, not the spirit.[133] The new Elijah would also lead the Jews back to a true knowledge of God.[134] They would recognize Christ as their King and return to Canaan to live there "in great brightness and deepest peace." There would be no more wars between nations, and along with wars all earthly kings and tyrants would disappear.[135]

In the future kingdom of peace, because of man's higher knowledge, the use of force will give way to admonition and instruction. All ceremonies, including baptism, the Eucharist and the keeping of the Lord's day, could then disappear.[136]

Enthralled by this spiritualist theology of history, Capito had also changed his attitudes to the "external word", to the sacraments, to the church, and last, but not least, to the Anabaptists.

Faith is based on God's "inner Word". Only an "inner purification" can enable man to solve the apparent contradictions in the Bible. The mystery of divine love can be experienced much more in the suffering of the cross than in the study of Scripture.[137] What constitutes a sign of election is the "pure fear of God", something which can also be found amongst Saracens and Turks. The Bible is the touchstone of faith, not its foundation.

The sacraments have no role in man's salvation. Catholics, Lutherans and Anabaptists all err in putting too much value on ceremonies, by limiting the gift of the Holy Spirit to baptism or by stressing Christ's real presence in the Eucharistic elements. In fact sacraments cannot mediate salvation, nor can they give comfort to the disturbed. In baptism what the Christian does is simply to commit himself (in the presence of his fellow-believers) to killing the flesh and following the guidance of the spirit.[138]

---

[133] *Ibid.*, p. 271a.
[134] *Ibid.*, p. 272a, 79a.
[135] *Ibid.*, p. 269b, 271a, 30b-31a, 74a.
[136] *Ibid.*, p. 3, 9.
[137] *Ibid.*, p. 3, 9.
[138] *Ibid.*, p. 273b.

Hence he must understand the Word before being baptised.[139]
This meant that Capito had come to accept the Anabaptist view
of believers' baptism. The church is no longer for him the
community of all those who were baptized as children, but a
union of adult Christians who have sworn to believe in God and
to love their neighbours.[140] But since it was predestination which
determined whether or not men belonged to the kingdom of
God, Capito did not regard baptism as necessary for salvation.

Capito now changed his attitude to the Anabaptists. The Swiss
Brethren's demand for an external separation of "believers" from
the "world" seemed to him to be a "judaistic" misunderstanding
of the kingdom of Christ. What mattered was "inner
separation".[141] Like Bucer he kept to Luther's doctrine of the two
forms of God's governance. In an evil world the Christian is
called upon, for the love of his neighbour, to take up offices, to use
weapons to protect the defenceless in a defensive war and to
testify to the truth by taking oaths.[142]

Whereas in the summer of 1527 Capito had labelled most of
the Anabaptists as "impostors, thieves, adulterers and disruptive
elements,"[143] in 1528 he admitted that most Anabaptists were
personally quite devout. Their criticisms of the church were
valuable; the people had become more cautious and the preachers
more watchful. They had also more scrupulously observed their
official duties.[144] In an undated memo (probably 1530) Capito
expressed amazement at the willingness of the Anabaptists to
subject themselves to the moral discipline of their fellow-
believers and at their readiness to die for their convictions, even
when these only related to insignificant ceremonies which were

---

[139] *Ibid.*, p. 241, 279b.
[140] Cf. J. Usteri, "Die Stellung der Strassburger Reformatoren Bucer
und Capito zur Tauffrage" in *Theologische Studien und Kritiken*, 57
(1884), p. 471.
[141] W. Capito, *In Hoseam*, 133a-b.
[142] *ibid.*, 18a-19b, 91, 95, 98b-99a.
[143] *CR* 96:171-172.
[144] W. Capito, *In Hoseam*, 177b, *TAE* I No. 126, p. 152.

not worth the effort. Morally, he felt, the Swiss Brethren were superior to his own church.[145]

Capito's sympathies for the Anabaptists led to a cooling-off of his friendship with Bucer. Bucer attacked Cellarius' "*De operibus Dei*", recommended by Capito, by taking a stand in favour of infant baptism in his commentary on the Gospel of St. John. Here he also rejected typological interpretation of the Old Testament and accused the Anabaptists of being followers of Thomas Müntzer and of being sexual libertines.[146]

Capito attempted to counter this charge in his commentary on Hosea, though without mentioning Bucer's name. At this Bucer mobilized their mutual friends Zwingli, Oecolampadius, Pellikan and Ambrosius Blaurer, urging them to prevent Capito from joining the Anabaptists as he was threatening to do. Their warnings against "Judaizers" and a spiritualistic dissolution of the church only succeeded in so far as Capito never publicly admitted his support for the Anabaptists.[147]

The estrangement between Bucer and Capito lasted until 1532. In 1531 Capito objected to Bucer's demand that the authorities should indiscriminately and rigorously persecute all Anabaptists by asking them either to renounce their faith or leave the city. Capito felt that this was unjust and perverse and that Bucer's plan to enforce infant baptism could not be supported by Scripture. The Council should be satisfied with assurances from the Anabaptists that they would not publicly refute the doctrines of the evangelical preachers, that they would not hold secret assemblies and that they would fulfil their civil obligations. No man is in any position to judge another's faith. There would be peace in the city if patient instruction was used to enlighten separatist conscience, yet the Anabaptists were instead being treated like secular criminals.[148] Capito urged his friends to recognize the distinction between military and pacifist

---

[145] *TAE* I No. 233, pp. 284-287.

[146] M. Bucer, *Enarratio in evangelion Johannis* 1528, 34–54, Excerpts in *TAE* I No. 124.

[147] *CR* 96:487-488, *TAE* I No. 140.

[148] *TAE* I No. 248, p. 331.

Anabaptists. He, too, was firmly opposed to those "insurgent fanatics" who wanted to wipe out the godless, restore Mosaic Law and bring about a total revolution.[149]

Taking up this balanced position Capito found himself fighting on two fronts. The Anabaptists expected him to draw the logical conclusion from the "truth" he had grasped, and join forces with them. When he refused to do so they regarded him as a coward who was only prepared to go half way for fear of the tyrants. When Hätzer left in January, 1527, he said that he wished Capito had even half the courage of Hubmaier.[150] The leaders of the Anabaptist circle avoided him "as a dog avoids snakes". Capito himself admitted that his own nature, inclined as it was to melancholy and lacking in inner strength or ambition, made him unsuitable for a role as a great leader in a religious underground-movement.[151]

Although Capito did not fulfil the hopes set in him he did play a significant role in the rise of the Anabaptist movement between 1528 and 1532. He was the senior and most eminent of the Strasbourg preachers, whose signature was always the first to be affixed to church letters. So long as he identified himself in so many points with the position of the spiritualist Anabaptism, it must have looked like an invitation to join them. Capito also discredited all Bucer's attempts to clamp down more firmly on all of the sectarian movements.

Capito's "middle way" was a failure in the sense that he neither managed to win back large groups of Anabaptists for the Strasbourg church nor to convince Bucer and Hedio of the rightness of his course. Bucer gradually took his place as the spiritual leader of Strasbourg's church government. These failures meant that Capito's depressions worsened and he began to imagine himself rejected by God and of no value for the church.[152]

[149] *TAE* I No. 151, p. 184.
[150] *TAE* I No. 74, p. 72.
[151] *CR*, 96:516.
[152] *TAE* I No. 310, p. 534.

e)   The Arrival of Hut's form of Anabaptism in Strasbourg.

When about a hundred Anabaptists fled from Augsburg to Strasbourg early in 1528, a revolutionary element was introduced to the formerly pacifist Anabaptism of Strasbourg.[153] Many, though by no means all, of the Anabaptist refugees from Augsburg had been influenced by Hans Hut, the man who had introduced Müntzer's heritage to the Anabaptist movement.[154]

Augsburg had been the capital of the Anabaptist movement in southern Germany until the end of 1527. C.P. Clasen's cautious estimate was that about 300 inhabitants of the town became Anabaptists between 1526 and 1529.[155] The rapid growth of the movement was encouraged by deep social divisions within the city. Social divisions deepened in the first quarter of the 16th century as the proletariat was growing at the expense of the lower middle-class. The number of propertyless households who did not need to pay property tax grew faster than the whole population between 1512 and 1526. In 1526, 54% of householders were "without property", whereas "only" 45% had been so in 1512.[156] Weavers and dyers constituted most of the Augsburg proletariat (there were 2,500 of them altogether).

---

[153] *TAE* I No. 176, p. 232.

[154] Cf. the crucially important thesis by G. Seebass, *Müntzers Erbe. Werke, Leben und Theologie des Hans Hut*, (Erlangen, 1972).

[155] C.P. Clasen, *Anabaptism. A Social History 1525-1618* (Ithaca and London, 1972), p. 324. According to F. Roth (*Augsburgs Reformationgeschichte* Vol. I, 1881, p. 180) there were 1,100 members of the Anabaptist community.

[156] Figures of householders in Augsburg:

		1512	1526
"Penniless"	(up to 20fl. tax)	2,476 (45.2%)	3,251 (54.1%)
Petty Bourgeoisie	(20fl.-100fl. tax)	2,857 (52.13%)	2,623 (43.04%)
Middle Class	(over 100fl. tax)	117 (2.12%)	143 (2.34%)
Grande bourgeoisie		29 (0.53%)	40 (0.65%)

Taken from J. Hartung, "Die augsburgische Vermögenssteuer und die Entwicklung der Besitzverhältnisse im 16. Jahrhundert" in *Jahrbuch für Gesetzgebung, Verwaltung und Volkswirtschaft im Deutschen Reich* 19 (1895), p. 869. Other figures, which compare Augsburg with the Hanse towns, can be found in H. Reincke, "Bevölkerungsprobleme der Hansestädte" in *Hansische Geschichtsblätter* 70 (1951), pp. 30-31.

Most of the small masters and journeymen in their professions were economically dependent on wholesale dealers. If they manufactured fustian, the cotton they imported from Cyprus and Crete was subject to enormous fluctuations in price. The supply of raw materials became erratic because of the wars in northern Italy (1521--1529), and more and more weavers lost their jobs. On top of all this two poor harvests in the Augsburg region led to meat shortages and price increases in 1526 and 1527.[157]

People accused the rich merchant guild of causing these economic difficulties. It was claimed that they controlled prices, abused monopolies and practised pre-emption and usury. "Fuggery" (the practices of the Fuggers in this guild) became another word for "usury".[158] It was in this situation that Anabaptism took hold.

But Anabaptism in Augsburg was not a uniform social or religious phenomenon. Between 1527 and 1529, 73% of the Anabaptists belonged to the lower classes,[159] yet we also find rich merchants and patricians (such as Haug Miller, Georg Regel and Eitelhans Langenmantel) amongst the earliest members of the movement. Indeed, two distinguished guild leaders and members of the Inner Council (Laux Fischer and Endris Widholz) were also Anabaptists. The heterogeneous ideas of Hätzer, Denck, Hut and Jakob Gross all circulated within the one congregation. There were clearly serious differences amongst them because a few of the rich members refused to meet with the poor in woods and quarries outside the town, as this smacked of conspiracy.[160]

Hans Hut's influence on the Anabaptists of Augsburg grew in the course of 1527 after Denck had been forced to leave the town in the previous autumn. After the failure of the Peasants' War (in which he had taken part), Hans Hut has distanced himself from the aims of the peasants, saying (like his mentor Thomas Müntzer)

---

[157] M.J. Elsas, *Umriss einer Geschichte der Preise und Löhne in Deutschland vom ausgehenden Mittelalter bis zum Beginn des 19. Jahrhunderts.* Vol. I. (Leiden, 1936), pp. 186f.

[158] TRANSLATOR'S NOTE. The Fuggers were the leading family of Augsburg. Their financial dealings had provided them with great wealth and much influence throughout the Empire.

[159] C.P. Clasen, *op. cit.*,p. 327, *TAE* I No. 148, pp. 180-182.

[160] C.P. Clasen, *op. cit.*, p. 326.

that the peasants were only concerned with their own interests and not with the glory of God. Yet he still retained the idea that the godless should be uprooted. In the light of the defeat in 1525 he urged his audience to wait for a sign from God before they unsheathed their swords.[161]

Hut regarded Müntzer and Pfeiffer as the reincarnation of the two apocalyptic witnesses, Enoch and Elijah, whose deaths would usher in the second $3\frac{1}{2}$-year period of the apocalypse. The Lord would not bring together his people or give them power to sit in judgement over sinners and wicked authorities until after a period of destruction, famine, plague and war.[162] Hut imagined that the climax of the apocalyptic débâcle would come with the invasion of the Turks. Rather than stay with their masters, Anabaptists should then set off for one or other of the two Mühlhausen (in Alsace and Thuringia) or hide in the forests. The Turks would then implement God's justice. "When the Turk comes those who do the will of the Father in Heaven will stand firm, but the princes and lords and all who do not do the will of the Father in Heaven will be struck dead."[163] After the departure of the Turks it would be left to the Anabaptists to kill any remaining tyrants. Finally Hans Hut would begin to reign as sole master of the earth, because even Charles V had to be strangled.[164] Hut reckoned that Christ would entrust the Anabaptists with the sword 3½ years after Müntzer's death. This calculation was based on Daniel 12:12. Since he also took into account the promised shortening of the time of tribulation (Matt. 24:22), he expected the great cataclysm to come early in 1528, at the latest by Whitsun of 1528. After the purifying storm the saints would spend calm days in a world restored to peace.[165] As during persecution, during

---

[161] C. Meyer, "Zur Geschichte der Wiedertäufer in Oberschwaben I. Die Anfänge des Wiedertäufertums in Augsburg" in *Zeitschrift des Historischen Vereins für Schwaben und Neuburg* I (1874), p. 242.

[162] C. Meyer, *op. cit.*, p. 239, P. Wappler, *Die Täuferbewegung in Thüringen*, 1913, No. 23, p. 282.

[163] P. Wappler, *op. cit.*, p. 242. cf. pp. 231, 235, 240, 244.

[164] *Ibid.*, p. 281.

[165] C. Meyer, *op. cit.*, pp. 239-242.

happier times, too, they would continue to share all their possessions with each other.[166]

Hut saw himself as the final preacher of repentance before the Last Judgment; he was offering the world its last chance to change its ways. His mission was to assemble the holy community of the latter days – the community which would survive the judgment. The baptism he bestowed would be a guarantee against the death of the apocalypse.

Hut's message was aimed primarily at the poor and the oppressed. His doctrine of a "threefold baptism" (the central feature of his theology) gave a meaning to their sufferings by seeing them as a necessary preparation for the reception of the Holy Spirit. "Water baptism", preceded by instruction (the beginning of "baptism in the spirit") leads men into suffering, and only after this (the baptism in suffering) can a true and justifying faith be born in a man's heart. For Hut, suffering is a necessary preliminary to regeneration; this is the "Gospel of all creatures" which is proclaimed by the whole of creation. Just as plants and animals fulfil their purpose in creation (to serve men) when they are cut down (i.e. tamed or slaughtered), so men come to see the meaning of their lives (the worship of God) only when their own wills are broken in the school of suffering. Creation, Scripture and the "inner Word" all point to the path of the cross as the way of salvation.[167]

Hut's promise of an imminent day of divine wrath gave a new sense of hope to the people defeated in the Peasants' War, and his declaration that God is revealed not only in the Bible but also in nature, dreams and visions strengthened the self-confidence of the "common man".[168]

---

[166] P. Wappler, *op. cit.*, p. 280. cf. K. Schornbaum (ed.), *Bayern I:Markgraftum Brandenburg, Quellen zur Geschichte der Wiedertäufer*, Vol. 2. (Leipzig, 1934), p. 188.

[167] Cf. H. Hut, *Von dem Geheimnis der Taufe*, in L. Müller, *Glaubenszeugnisse oberdeutscher Taufgesinnter*, Vol. I, 1938, pp. 10f.

[168] *Ibid.*, pp. 13-14. C. Meyer, *op. cit.*, p. 232. cf. G. Seebass, "Täufertum und Bauernkrieg in Franken" in *ZKG* 85 (1974), pp. 140-156.

Unlike the "Swiss Brethren", Hut did not want to establish a holy island in a sea of evil. He wanted to turn the whole earth into "the kingdom of God", even by violent means. Like Müntzer, he followed the medieval idea of the *corpus Christianum* to its logical conclusion, demanding the destruction of the godless. He did not condemn religious persecution itself, but simply the persecution of those he considered to be "the just".[169] Hut opposed the Schleitheim Confession by allowing his followers to take oaths and to undertake military service, so that they would not be detected by the authorities before the day of wrath.[170]

The Council of Augsburg decided in September, 1527 to put a stop to any further growth of the Anabaptist congregation. It imprisoned its leaders and some of their followers. Hut suffocated in prison on 6th December, 1527, after a fire broke out in his cell in circumstances which could not be ascertained.[171] In the spring of 1528 even more Anabaptists were imprisoned and eventually expelled from the city. The exiles found a new home in Strasbourg and in the underground there they created a spiritual climate in which Hoffman's ideas were to be transformed and be able to spread in modified form.

In late December, 1527 or early January, 1528 the Augsburg Council informed its colleagues in Strasbourg of the beliefs of the Anabaptists. The document they sent, "Articles to which the Augsburg Anabaptists have confessed under torture", listed the beliefs admitted to on the rack by the imprisoned Augsburg Anabaptists in the autumn of 1527.[172] Despite some distortions (it makes all the Augsburg Anabaptists appear as rebels and blasphemers), this document does reflect a remarkable mixture of the ideas of Hätzer, Denck and Hut.

After the arrival of the refugees from Augsburg Bucer, Hedio and Zell became even more convinced that there was no longer

---

[169] cf. G. Seebass, *Müntzers Erbe*, pp. 351-352.
[170] C. Meyer, *op. cit.*, pp. 227-228.
[171] *Ibid.*, pp. 219, 252-253.
[172] *TAE* I No. 116, pp. 138-142 (Column C).

any basis on which they would be able to come to an understanding with the Anabaptists. "Now they are bringing more serious errors in with them. Some do not admit that Christ was God and some will not accept the use of Scripture, but reject it, thinking that their own whims are the inspiration of the Holy Spirit. They also want to share all property and they are prepared to use the sword to force everybody else to accept their error. They also go against the Scripture in their attitude to marriage."[173] These Anabaptists derive their ideas not from "the simple teaching of Christ" but from the more obscure books of the Bible: Revelation and the apocryphal II Esdra: Alleged direct revelations played a great role for them: "Whatever they dream during the night it becomes a miracle of God in the morning."[174] Bucer was particularly angry about the claim of some Anabaptists from Augsburg that they were incapable of sinning since they had received the Holy Spirit.[175] He regarded Hans Hut as unquestionably a disciple of the devil and said that his followers were instigated by "the unbelievable power of Satan."[176] All of the Strasbourg reformers except Capito called for the death penalty for the revolutionary Anabaptists who followed Hut. They also demanded that all other Anabaptists (i.e. the pacifists) be banished.[177] Nevertheless the Council kept to banishment as its harshest sentence.[178]

3. Hoffman and the "Strasbourg Prophets".

When the Strasbourg theologians refused to recognize Hoffman as a lay missionary he decided "to stretch out (his) hand to the starving in spirit", because he preferred "to sit with God's prophets and prophetesses in filth and disgrace than to possess a full maggot-ridden belly with the blind leaders of the Lutherans

---

[173] *TAE* I No. 178, p. 233.
[174] *TAE* I No. 171, p. 219.
[175] *TAE* I No. 148, p. 181, No 149, pp. 182–183.
[176] *TAE* I No. 149, p. 183.
[177] *TAE* I No. 154, pp. 187-188.
[178] *TAE* I No. 155 pp. 188-189.

and Zwinglians."[179] Who were these prophets and prophetesses who were to have such a decisive impact on Hoffman's life and thought?

During his first period in Strasbourg (from June, 1529 to April, 1530) Hoffman lived in the house of Katharina Seid, the wife of Andreas Klaiber. It appears from the accounts of her interrogation in 1534 that she was not happy with the course of the Reformation in Strasbourg and that, trusting a prophecy of Zell's, was awaiting the arrival of preachers who would be "more truthful" than the Strasbourg reformers. She thus saw Hoffman as one of those witnesses to a higher knowledge as prophesied by Zell; she felt that he would "lead her out of the house of servility and on to salvation." Hoffman's wife regarded this admirer as a rival and refused to stay in Strasbourg. Because of the hospitality she had offered Hoffman, the Police Court of the "Seven" fined Katharina Seid two guilders. She did not have herself rebaptized until 1532, and even then she did not attach great significance to this ceremony. She did not see her role, if we can believe what she said at the trial, as a propagator of Anabaptist ideas; she simply wanted to love her neighbour in a practical sense and in particular, to care for the sick. She was banished from the city in April, 1534 as an "obstinate Anabaptist", because she would not recant, she would not betray her fellow-believers and she would not allow herself to be converted by the official preachers. She begged to be allowed to retain the truth as she had come to know it because no one else could live, die or believe for her. Katharina Seid's protestations suggest that she was a staunch and insistent woman who, whilst unwilling to yield in her convictions, wanted to establish during interrogation that she was not dangerous. On the other hand, she is said to have been highly excitable and to have suffered from epileptic fits. She did not obey her sentence; even after her banishment she often returned home in secret to visit friends in the city.[180]

The leading figures amongst the "Strasbourg Prophets" were

[179] M. Hoffman, *Van der waren hochprachtlichen eynigen magestadt gottes* 1532, A1b-A2a.
[180] *TAE* II No. 547, pp. 309-310.

Lienhard and Ursula Jost (a married couple) and Barbara Rebstock, "the great prophetess of the Kalbsgasse." Lienhard Jost hailed from Illkirch and was probably a butcher by trade. He was held in chains in the Strasbourg "madhouse" for many months in 1524 but was eventually released from spiritual and physical "captivity" and was able to return to his wife.[181] After a period of inward calm in 1526 and 1527, both Lienhard and Ursula Jost again went into visionary states at the turn of 1528 and 1529. Hans Rebstock, a weaver, and his wife Barbara had been expelled from Esslingen in February, 1529. The Anabaptist group in Esslingen had come under the influence of Hans Hut in 1527, after having been brought there by the Anabaptist leader Jörg Nespitzer and the refugees from Augsburg; this community lived in a world of apocalyptic expectations, trance and visions.[182] Two apostate Anabaptists, Hans Pfau of Heilbronn and Hans Zuber of Stuttgart, accused the Esslingen Anabaptists of plotting a violent rebellion which was to have taken place at Easter, 1528.[183] Although such a charge was probably grossly exaggerated, it contains a seed of truth in view of the chiliastic mood in Esslingen resulting from the influence of Hans Hut. After Ursula Jost's death, Barbara Rebstock became the "leading prophetess" of the Melchiorites. Hoffman was guided by her prophecies, because, as he said in November, 1534, "everything he had done so far had been inspired by the prophecies of others".[184] The news of the miracles allegedly performed by Barbara Rebstock had even reached the Netherlands.[185]

Other members of this circle of "Strasbourg Prophets" were

---

[181] *TAE* II No. 461, p. 213, M. Bucer, *Handlung in dem öffentlichen gesprech zu Strassburg* A4b, *TAE* II No. 402 pp. 113-114. On Jost's trade *TAE* II No. 665, p. 453 refers to him as a butcher, but according to *TAE* II No. 68, p. 468 he was a cobbler. But it is not certain that the "obstinate Anabaptist" under discussion is actually Jost.

[182] C.P. Clasen, *Die Wiedertäufer im Herzogtum Württemberg* 1965 pp. 69-80.

[183] J.M. Stayer, "Eine fanatische Täuferbewegung in Esslingen und Reutlingen?" in *Blätter für Württembergische Kirchengeschichte* 68-69 (1968-1969) pp. 53-59.

[184] *TAE* II No. 617, p. 393.

[185] *TAE* II No. 533, p. 300.

Valentin Dufft, a goldsmith; Valentin Nessel; Gertrud and Josef Lorenz; Wilhelm Blum the elder (an officer of the Lucerne Guild, an association of millers and corn and flax merchants) and his son Wilhelm Blum the younger, who was also a miller. After 1531 they were joined by Agnes Jost, Lienhard Jost's second wife, and her daughter Elizabeth, as well as the Dutchman Johannes Eisenburg, who was intellectually far superior to the others.[186]

The "Strasbourg Prophets" made up the solid core of Hoffman's followers, remaining loyal to him, even after his arrest, until 1538–1539. Hoffman saw in the appearance of these prophets evidence that the last days had in fact arrived. In 1530 he arranged for Balthasar Beck to print Lienhard and Ursula Jost's prophecies in Strasbourg in the hope that he would be able to turn the attention of his contemporaries from "stargazers, nature-worshippers and magicians" to the true prophets.[187] Hoffman wrote a preface and an epilogue for the edition of Ursula Jost's visions. Hoffman, Obbe Philips and Cornelis Polderman, all agree that the "visions" of the Josts and of Barbara Rebstock made a much greater impact on the Dutch Melchiorites than they did on Hoffman's followers in Strasbourg. The Dutch Hoffmanites interpreted the "figures" by seeing apocalyptic signs in actual happenings; the excitement heightened by the visions thus found a release in action.[188]

Ursula Jost's visions give us a very rare insight into the atmosphere surrounding the prophetic group in Strasbourg, an insight almost unparalleled in our knowledge of the early modern period. Of the 77 reported "visions" 58 occurred during

---

[186] Hoffman's list of the sixteen prophets: Thomas Archive No. 166 f. 198r. For Barbara Rebstock cf. *TAE* II No. 362 p. 13, No. 540 p. 304 and for Wilhelm Blum cf. *TAE* II No. 597 p. 375 n. 21.

[187] M. Hoffman (ed.), *Prophetische Gesicht* A1b-A2a. A second edition of Lienhard Jost's prophecies was published in 1532 cf. *TAE* I No. 210 p. 259, No. 343 p. 561.

[188] *TAE* II No. 461 p. 213, No. 617 p. 393. For O. Philips' account cf. p. 128. G.H. Williams and A.M. Mergal (ed.), *Spiritual and Anabaptist Writers* p. 211-212.

the Peasants' War. But there is only one single vision dating from the following three years of peace. In 1529, with the famine and the persecution of the Anabaptists, the number soars to 18. This relationship of the visions to the general social environment of the time from which they date indicates that they are the reactions of an unusually sensitive medium, who was able to express the hopes and fears of her environment in these fantastic images. But they were not all reflections of the contemporary scene; occasionally they reveal psychic states of universal significance.

Ursula Jost's "visions" were usually hallucinatory experiences. She says herself that she was quite conscious when she saw the images (Visions 28, 39, 51,52), having been woken from sleep by a bright light. In some cases the visions arrived unexpectedly at dawn or dusk, or even in the middle of the day, when she was always in a conscious state (Visions 15, 18, 22, 23). The authenticity of the experiences is supported by the fact that she felt fear and terror when she was faced with "the glory of the Lord", which was "an inexpressible brilliance, like the shining of the sun." She sweated with fear and tried to ignore the images but the visions "took hold of (her) face and turned it back to confront the light" (Vision 39).[189] But Ursula Jost's experiences were not totally involuntary. She says that she and her husband had prayed that God would show them His future miracles and the works of His wrath and judgment (Preface and Vision 4). Although she could only interpret a few of the images the prophetess was convinced from the very beginning that God was revealing Himself in them.

At the start of the visions she encountered the two-fold character of God as judge and liberator. An omnipotent father appeared to her on the first night. In his outstretched left hand he

---

[189] For the difference between prophetic visions and normal dreaming cf. A.F.C. Wallace, "Revitalization Movements" in *American Anthropologist* 58 (1956) p. 271, R. Otto, *The Idea of the Holy* E.T. pp. 5ff. Oxford 1923, and especially E. Benz, *Die Vision. Erfahrungsformen und Bilderwelt* Stuttgart 1969, pp. 83–149, 311–410.

held the globe and indicated that if he were to clench his fist all
men would be destroyed. On the following night she felt herself
to be in the hands of evil spirits who were attempting to pull her
down into an abyss. Only after her third cry of terror did the
demons let her go. Confronted with God's majesty, she felt
herself to be totally insignificant; she needed the help which had
come to her at the climax of the second vision. Visions of wrath
and destruction recur throughout this series of images: God
shooting burning arrows (38); the Saviour leading his people in
triumph but carrying a sharp rod as an instrument of chastise-
ment (35); a bird dropping a corner-stone, which kills many
people (50). The most impressive visions portray cosmic
catastrophes. Firmaments intermingle, headless men and animals run into each other in panic and suffocate in burning fumes
(52); rivers of blood fill the sky (67). In 1524 she saw corpses
floating in the waters (19); dead fish cover a parched landscape
with stray animals wandering across it (26). Water, fire, pitch
and brimstone rained down from heaven burning men and
leaving the earth in chaos (32). The great city played an
important role in these visions of destruction. In 1525 Ursula
Jost saw it totally destroyed as if razed by the wind (51) and in
1529 she saw it surrounded by enormous hostile dogs.

God's wrath is directed mostly against the prelates. She saw
the bishops as exploiters; they dragged people up hill and down
dale with ropes (9); they were idle parasites who sneered at the
hard-working tillers of the soil (14). Then she saw a bishop,
whose head had been riven, being pushed into a dark lake (21)
and the pope, with a rope around his neck, being dragged out
into the darkness (41). In contrast to this the oppressed
common-folk wore crowns and were depicted ascending into
heaven (9).

The Saviour (carrying a cross or a rod) usually appeared
together with a band of common people, marching at their head.
Knights who ride against him fall to the ground or are
obliterated (Visions 16, 23, 35, 39). The liberation of the people
is preceded by a period of suffering on "the blood-covered
Mount of Olives" (69) or in a dungeon (70) where the prisoners
are gagged and held under the feet of the tyrants.

Ursula Jost makes an appearance herself in the sixth vision. A troop of men are lying dead on a sun-baked heath. The figure of a woman stands in front of two stone troughs which are full of blood. She mixes the contents of the two troughs and sprinkles the blood over the bodies in order to bring them back to life. Suddenly there appears a band of knights who charge over the bodies, and thwart her attempt at resurrection and reconciliation.

The Turks appeared in her visions of 1529, the year of the first siege of Vienna (74), looking like black figures with a "bright light" shining from them. When she expresses amazement at this, it is "revealed" to her that this light signifies "the power of God". Like the Zwickau Prophets, Müntzer and Hut, she regarded the Turks as God's tool. But, on the other hand, she had no high regard for the refugees who had been flooding into Strasbourg since 1528. Although they included many Anabaptists, and although she first saw them "in supplication", she said that many of them were "rogues and treacherous ruffians" (75).

Images of destruction are interspersed with visions of renewal. Occasionally she would see a mother and child, and then the woman would turn into a bird (10, 13); then small children climbing up and down a sunbeam (49, 5, 70, 76); a group of young people being lifted up and hidden by a bright crystal (54). Renewal was brought to the world by men carrying books in their hands and sailing on a ship which was "carried along by swift, strong waters." She thought that these men were the Apostles proclaiming the imminence of God's judgment throughout the world. (20).

Her burning conviction that the final cataclysm was imminent and had already struck life's very core, but that thereafter the earth would rise again, was expressed in the following images: she saw a large spider running over the branch of a green tree (a symbol of the world), and a serpent was coiled around the tree-trunk, poisoning the tree with its venom (47). A rainbow (a symbol of the covenant between God and man) puts forth branches on which there are two knights who begin to fight one another, with blood eventually being spilt. A third, grey figure smiles maliciously at this. In the end the swordsmen cut the rainbow in two (77). Finally things are transformed: a spring emerges at the bottom of the tree-trunk. Two men dam the stream with a sod of turf. The water thereupon rises into the branches and drips out of thousands of green leaves. Finally a great band of people, "from amongst the general throng", run up and drink (34). The life-giving energy ascends, becomes spiritual and is then poured out on the "common man".

The visions also indicate that the dangers of a sinful life come not always from society outside but also from within. Some images deal with the conflict between ascetic morality and natural instincts. She sees a skull lying on a heath which turns into two animals lying one on top of the other. A man beats them both with a rod (15). She then sees the leader of a band of men whose face turns dark, whose body changes into a stick and whose head becomes merely an appendage to his belly. This sinister phallic hero is confronted with a young man with a cross in his hand (16). The same conflict occurs in the following vision (17). Two men are feasting at a table. They are joined by a third man who is vainly trying to shake a toad off his back. Suddenly the man and the toad fuse together and become a single giant frog which proceeds to turn into a sow and then into a puffed-up black bear. A fire-breathing lion attacks the "frog-king" and burns the loathsome company to cinders. In the 11th vision she sees Jesus in his Father's bosom. The dove of the Holy Spirit hovers above them. Then immediately afterwards she sees a contrasting image: a house with men squatting row upon row on its roof. The uppermost figure then turns into "half a he-goat", with two horns, one pink and one white, though its abdomen is still human. A boy dressed in white jumps onto the goat's back. He rides over the other figures and jumps off the roof.

Ursula Jost's visions tell us more about the religious attitudes of the Strasbourg Prophets than do Hoffman's dogmatic proclamations, which were moulded largely by tradition. They reveal a murderous hatred of existing society and a willingness to resort to violence. "The bright light of God" shines from the Turks because they are prepared to destroy a corrupt society of tyrants and parasites. The conflict between ascetic morality and suppressed sensuality increases the desire to use force against those who "eat and drink" in comfort. Hopes are pinned on a charismatic leader who will lead the people out of servitude into freedom – into a new and spiritual life.

We only possess one extract from Hoffman's collection of the visions of Lienhard Jost – an extract Hoffman submitted to the Strasbourg synodal commission in 1533. But it is sufficient to indicate the way in which Lienhard Jost implemented his wife's visions.[190] Jost no longer drew any distinction between the "Lutheran and the Zwinglian mobs" (i.e. the Strasbourg reformers). They are "the most cruel of Antichrists since the time of the Apostles" because they persecute and murder true Christians. But the tables will soon be turned. He prophesied that Strasbourg had been chosen to be the "spiritual Jerusalem". It was from this city that the 144,000 "apostolic messengers" whose coming had been prophesied in the Book of Revelation would go out to spread true knowledge of Christ throughout the earth to establish the covenant between God and His people by means of believers' baptism. Before this the city will be besieged by the Emperor (the dragon of the Apocalypse), but it will not fall. Only after undergoing this military trial will Strasbourg be able to produce the band of apostles who will "lead the heathen to pasture with a rod of iron." Any innocent blood that has been spilt will be sternly avenged on the "bloodthirsty hordes of Zwinglians and Lutherans."

The Strasbourg Prophets felt their expectations confirmed in the wild prophecies of Venturinus, an Italian who visited Strasbourg in 1530. On the basis of his fantastic biography (modelled on the legend of St. Francis), we can assume that he stemmed from the Franciscan Spiritualists. He told the people of Strasbourg that the Lord was again speaking to his people face to face as in the time of Moses. Strasbourg must repent and call upon Luther to come and complete the work of reformation. God would use the Turks to destroy the unrepentant, particularly the pope, "that prince of Satan", and his "trembling wolves", the priests and the monks. The Mohammedans would also take captive the Emperor Charles V and would slay King Ferdinand. But after this judgment on Germany there would appear a "pastor angelicus" who would convert the whole earth and

[190] *TAE* II No. 444, pp. 184-185.

eventually even baptize the Turks. After revealing the mysteries of Scripture he would burn the Bible.[191] As in the visions of the Josts we see a mixture of ideas in Venturinus' prophecies; belief in direct revelation is linked to fantasies of destruction and expectations of a total transformation of the world to be brought about by a new prophet. Barbara Rebstock's visions were later (after 1533) to refer specifically to the prophecies of Venturinus.[192]

Whereas Bucer did not take the wandering preacher from Italy particularly seriously, he did see Lienhard Jost's writings as a dangerous call to violence and rebellion. No Christian government could tolerate this.[193]

The spiritual outlook of Lienhard and Ursula Jost is in many respects so similar to that of Hans Hut that we must conclude that they had been influenced by him, either through Barbara Rebstock or through the Augsburg refugees. The most important ideas shared by Hut's followers, the Strasbourg Prophets and Hoffman, are the following:

1. The hope that true believers would achieve a political and military victory after a period of misery and persecution and that they would take over control of the earth.
2. The conviction that true Christians would find refuge in a Free Imperial City.
3. The firm belief in a chronology of the apocalypse: the judgment on the world; the persecution of the true church; the victory of the apostolic messengers.
4. The belief that there would be a prophet in the last days who would make a final appeal for the world to repent.
5. The concept of a group of 144,000 elect united in a baptized fraternity.
6. The belief that the Turks would be the instruments of God's judgment.

---

[191] *TAE* I Nos. 205, 206, 206a, pp. 253-256.
[192] Strasbourg, Thomas Archive No. 166, f. 301.
[193] *TAE* I No. 343, p. 561, *TAE* II No. 402, p. 114.

7. A belief in the sinlessness of those who possess the "Pentecostal spirit".[194]

8. Trust in dreams and visions as divine revelations.

Despite these similarities we should, however, not overlook the differences between Hut and the Strasbourg Prophets (including Hoffman).

Unlike Hut, the Strasbourg prophets did not command believers to carry arms and Hoffman forbade his "apostolic messengers" to use the sword. Up until 1530 he believed that the two Christian Kings were the defenders of Christendom, and he also believed that the Strasbourg Council (and all magistrates of the Free Imperial Cities) were the protectors of the true church. As against this, Hut tended to identify all authorities with the godless. Whereas Hoffman (like Müntzer until his "Sermon to the Princes") still believed in a world revolution which would be imposed from above with the aid of a few pious princes, Hut had given up such an idea; he wanted to enforce a change by means of a rebellion by all believers in alliance with the Turks. Finally, Hut venerated the memory of Müntzer and Pfeiffer, but for Hoffman these two leaders of the rebellion at Mühlhausen were false prophets who had been led astray by the devil.[195]

4. Schwenckfeld and Hoffman.

The most bizarre element of the Melchiorite dogma (Hoffman's Monophysite Christology) arose from his exchange of ideas with Caspar Schwenckfeld. Like Hoffman, Schwenckfeld had been banished from his homeland (Silesia) for rejecting the Lutheran doctrine of the Eucharist, and he had arrived at Strasbourg in May, 1529. Hoffman and Schwenckfeld had always entertained a strong personal respect for each other. They declared to their common enemy, the Strasbourg

---

[194] Cf. *TAE* I No. 148, p. 181 and M. Hoffman, *Römerbrief* F3a. Hut himself did not say the elect were sinless but some of his followers in Augsburg do seem to have had this belief.

[195] C. Meyer, *op. cit.*, p. 244, cf. above n. 76.

preachers, that each considered the other to be "pious and honourable."[196]

The two men felt a particular affinity because they had a common concept of the Eucharist. Both believed in a spiritual eating of "Christ's body and blood" by faith, whereby the resurrected Christ is present for them in the World.[197] Like Hoffman, Schwenckfeld considered Luther's "doctrine of impanation" to be a "foul idolatry" because it confused the Creator with the created and delivered up "the body of Christ" to the godless. According to Schwenckfeld such a materialization of salvation prevents a true religious experience of God, which can only come through the Word. It is this experience which brings about the death of the old Adam and the resurrection of a new creature.[198] But Schwenckfeld was not satisfied with Zwingli's early Eucharistic doctrine which stressed the symbolic nature of the Sacrament. To him this ignored the capacity of the Eucharist to impart Christ's glorified, heavenly humanity to the believer and thus to lead to his regeneration.[199]

But Hoffman's and Schwenckfeld's controversy on Christology had its roots in their common Eucharistic doctrine.[200] Schwenckfeld claimed to be the first person to see the consequences of the spiritualistic doctrine of the Eucharist for the doctrine of the Incarnation. Since it was axiomatic for spiritualist views that the divine spirit could never mix with matter (which had been created) the question emerged, "In what way could 'the

---

[196] *TAE* II No. 368, p. 19, *CS* IV: 835.

[197] *CS* III: 627.

[198] *CS* III: 405, 572-575, *CS* IV: 841. On the relationship between Eucharistic doctrine and Christology cf. H. Weigelt, *Spiritualistische Tradition im Protestantismus. Die Geschichte des Schwenckfeldertums in Schlesien* Berlin and New York 1973, pp. 160-167.

[199] *CS* III: 410.

[200] Hans-Joachim Schoeps inverts the process when he says that it was Christology which had an impact on Eucharistic doctrine. For Hoffman and Schwenckfeld Christological speculation emerged from the doctrine of the Eucharist, cf. H.-J. Schoeps, *Vom himmlischen Fleisch Christi* 1951, p. 44.

flesh of Christ' be a carrier of the divine Logos?" The problem was intensified by the fact that in the 16th century there was no general consensus concerning the doctrine of the immaculate conception of Mary.[201] Many regarded the Virgin Mary simply as a "sinful daughter of Adam." The Dominicans and Franciscans had had a bitter dispute in Berne on the issue of the *conceptio immaculata* in 1509, during which the Dominicans had resorted to a number of grotesque tricks (such as simulating visions of the Virgin Mary) in order to support the cause of the non-immaculate conception.[202]

In this debate, which was followed with particular interest on the Upper Rhine, Hoffman sided with the "maculists". He was probably influenced by Karlstadt on this issue; in 1524 Karlstadt had objected to treating Mary as a mediator on the grounds that a human being like her, "born of wretched seed", could not alleviate or propitiate our sins.[203] Hoffman formulated his Monophysite Christology on the basis of this idea. Given that Mary was sinful, Christ could only have been a spotless sacrificial offering if he had brought his body with him from heaven and had passed through Mary like water through a pipe.

Hoffman and Schwenckfeld were constantly aware of each other's positions as they developed their Christologies. For Schwenckfeld, unlike Hoffman, Mary had always been a spotless virgin.[204] Until 1538 he concluded from this that Christ had taken his human, sinless nature from his mother and that in his "state of humility" (up until his Crucifixion) he was a creature of God who experienced hunger, thirst, fear, fatigue and pain like any other man. In his "state of glory" (after the Resurrection)

---

[201] The doctrine did not become dogma until 8th December, 1854 when Pope Pius IX issued the bull *Ineffabilis Deus*.

[202] Cf. S. Franck, *Chronica* 1531, part 2, p. CCXIX – CCXXIIII.

[203] A. Karlstadt, *Ein frag/ ob auch yemand möge selig werden/ on die fürbitt Marie.* 1524 A2b. Michael Sattler also denied Mary's role as a mediator and said that like all sinners she would have to await the Last Judgment cf. H. Fast (ed.), *Der linke Flügel* p. 74.

[204] *CS* III: 657, *CS* V: 522, Schwenckfeld, *Epistolar* Vol. 1, 1566, p. 608.

Christ's flesh "was filled with the whole power of the Word" and exchanged servitude for omnipotence. All creatureliness was then removed from him.[205] Only in this form could "the flesh of Christ" become our spiritual food. Hoffman and Schwenckfeld both believed that the glorified humanity of Christ which men share in the Eucharist is uncreaturely.

After 1538 Schwenckfeld no longer believed in the doctrine of Christ's creatureliness in the "state of humility". Christ had certainly taken his flesh from the "created", sinless Virgin, but he was conceived by the Holy Spirit, not after the manner of creaturely things. Thus even during his earthly life Christ should not be referred to as a "creature". He was "begotten" of the Father, "not made." As uncreaturely substance Christ's flesh was substantially different from the flesh of the children of Adam, even during his state of humility. This meant that Schwenckfeld was not very far from Hoffman's position.[206]

Nevertheless these differences were enough to distance the two men from each other. Schwenckfeld said that Hoffman and Sebastian Franck had "both taken their errors out of our truth, like a spider sucking poison from a beautiful flower."[207] Indeed, Hoffman did not expound his Monophysite Christology until after his encounter with Schwenckfeld: he first wrote about the subject in a passage at the end of his commentary on Revelation, which appeared in April, 1530.[208] This certainly indicates that the impulse to formulate this doctrine had come from Schwenckfeld.

In fact, Hoffman never publicly admitted his dependence on the Silesian reformer; he saw himself as the sole teacher of truth. "Oh God, what a wretched age where I know of not one true evangelist . . . not even a single author within the whole German nation who has given true witness in writing to the true faith and

---

[205] *CS* III: 261, 559, 629, *Epistolar* Vol. 1. pp. 581, 585.

[206] *Epistolar* I: 592, 613; E. Hirsch, "Schwenckfeld und Luther" in W. Hubatsch (ed.), *Weltwirkungen der Reformation* 1967, pp. 229-231; H.-J. Schoeps, *op. cit.*, pp. 34-35; H. Weigelt, *op.cit.*, p. 167.

[207] *CS* V: 522-523.

[208] M. Hoffman, *Auslegung der heimlichen Offenbarung* 1530, Z4b. The passage in question is not related to the text under discussion.

the eternal gospel."[209] He obviously counted Schwenckfeld as one of the heretical teachers: "Some, whom I regard as the most knowledgeable, openly preach and debase Christ Jesus, the eternal Word of God, as a divinised man."[210]

5. Hoffman's Conversion to Adult Baptism.

All of the Strasbourg nonconformists were united in rejecting infant baptism, even if, like Clemens Ziegler and Caspar Schwenckfeld, they were not themselves Anabaptists. They believed that the enforced union of church, state and society which resulted from infant baptism was a form of "evangelical Judaism"; for them the true church was a voluntary society of the reborn. They regarded Zwingli's comparison of Christian baptism with Jewish circumcision as a dangerous error because it ignored the fundamental distinction between the Old and New Testaments. The Old Covenant was established for the granting of earthly goods (such as the land of Canaan) to all members of the people, hence everyone had to be circumcised and had to submit to the Law. But under the New Covenant *individual* men are granted *spiritual* gifts, to which they respond in baptism by promising obedience. Thus nobody should undergo external baptism until he has been purified and renewed by the "inner spiritual water."[211]

We do not know who it was that urged Hoffman eventually to accept the validity of adult baptism, nor do the sources indicate whether he was in fact himself baptised again. Hoffman's declaration that he was the only true preacher of the gospel in Germany shows that he considered himself to be

[209] From a lost work of 1532. The last surviving copy was burnt with the Strasbourg Library in 1870. Part of it is printed in F.O. zur Linden, *Melchior Hofmann*, Haarlem, 1885, p. 432.

[210] M. Hoffman, *Van der waren hochprachtlichen eynigen magestadt gottes* 1532, B4a.

[211] Cf. Ziegler (*TAE* I No. 8, pp. 3-14), Sattler (B. Jenny, *op. cit.* pp. 10-11) Denck (*Schriften* Vol. 2. pp. 80-81), Marbeck (*TAE* I No. 302), Schwenckfeld (*CS* III: 817-818, *CS* IV: 414-443, 750-777, 827-830, 836,839).

independent of any *successio Anabaptistica* (whether authorized by Konrad Grebel or Denck and Hut). Most probably he felt authorized to baptise because he considered himself to be the final prophet of the last days.[212]

Hoffman began a public battle with the official evangelical church of Strasbourg in April, 1530. He was used to disputing with kings and princes, and now urged the Strasbourg Council to give the proscribed Anabaptists a church for their services.[213] The Council reacted to this provocation by ordering his arrest. At the same time an order was issued to imprison Balthasar Beck (who had printed Hoffman's commentary on Revelation) and Christian Egenolf (the engraver who had produced its title-page). Egenolf's engraving had portrayed the Emperor kneeling in prayer before the great whore of Babylon. Hoffman had identified the "head of the Holy Roman Empire" with the dragon of the Apocalypse in the commentary,[214] and the Council thus tried him for "lèse-majesté". In fact, the trial did not take place because Hoffman managed to escape secretly from the city.

As at Flensburg Hoffman again blamed the priests for his expulsion. He thought they had called in the secular arm because they were no match for the "witness of the Most High", i.e. himself. "That is why the bailiff and the hangman must bring the disputation to an end, by banishing and confiscating."[215]

Thus Hoffman's first period in Strasbourg did not turn out as he had expected. The "Zwinglian" theologians of the city, on whom he had set his hopes, rejected him, whereas the "Strasbourg Prophets", who were despised by the world, hailed him as the second Elijah. Under their influence militant-activist

---

[212] There is no evidence for Wiswedel's assertion that Hoffman was baptised by Melchior Rinck in Emden in 1530 (W. Wiswedel, *Bilder und Führergestalten aus dem Täufertum*. Kassel 1928-1952. Vol. 2. p. 64). Rinck was in fact in a prison in Hesse between the beginning of 1529 and May 1531.

[213] *TAE* I No. 211, p. 261.

[214] *TAE* I No. 210, p. 259.

[215] M. Hoffman, *Esau unde Jacob*. 1532, A 2a.

ideas infiltrated his apocalypticism, whereas hitherto he had always urged caution. Schwenckfeld led him to formulate a Monophysite Christology and, in accepting Denck's doctrines of the universality of divine grace and of the freedom of the will, he finally broke with his Lutheran past. Last, but not least, it was from the Strasbourg nonconformists that he derived the idea of a voluntary church which the individual enters by means of believers' baptism.

The reorientation of his theology was completed within a single year. His "Ordinance of God", written in 1530, already contains these new ideas in embryo.

Chapter Six

Hoffman's Theology After His Break with Luther.

It would be tedious to outline the content of each of Hoffman's tracts written after 1530, since the doctrinal points he formulated under the influence of the Strasbourg nonconformists are repeated so often. Despite the contradictions in his theory of history and secular authority, his basic ideas on the nature of God and man have a logical connection. It is not unfair therefore to present his thoughts as a unified system. In all important matters Hoffman was now concerned with constructing a rival position to Luther's; this meant that he returned to the medieval federal theology which Luther had rejected with his discovery of the *Justitia Dei*.

1. The Righteousness of God.

Hoffman proceeds from the premise that God, who is eternally good, can only create something which is an expression of His own nature.[1] Just as no darkness can emerge from the sun, it is impossible for God to be the source of evil. God's "unchangeable and authentic will" is always directed towards the salvation of the whole of creation.[2] If God were the father of sin, death and the devil, we would have to conclude that the divine nature was contradictory and would fill both heaven and hell.[3] How, then did evil enter the world? According to Hoffman, the angels and Adam voluntarily abused the freedom

---

[1] M. Hoffman, *Ordinance* (G. H. Williams and A. M. Mergal (ed.), *Spiritual and Anabaptist writers*, (London, 1957)), p. 198.

[2] M. Hoffman, *Warhafftige erklerung aus heyliger Biblischer schrifft/das der Satan/ Todt/ Hell/ Sund/ und die ewige verdammnuss im ursprung nit auss gott* 1531, A1b-A2a.

[3] *Ibid* A6a, *Römerbrief* O2b.

that had been granted to them in order to impose their own wills upon the divine will. Their fall from the kingdom of God came about when "the creature resorted to its own will."[4] A voluntary decision to oppose God led to their damnation [5]. If, like Luther, anyone says that it was the sovereign will of the Creator to lead creatures into sin and then to condemn them, then he is guilty of the sin against Holy Spirit for he is making God into an unjust tyrant.[6] The righteousness of God and man's accountability for his own fate constitute the two corner-stones of Hoffman's new theology.

But how are these two beliefs to be reconciled with the biblical testimonies on predestination and divine omnipotence, which include passages like Romans 9 in which Paul speaks of "the vessels of wrath made for destruction" (Rom. 9:22)? Despite the original meaning of Paul's text, Hoffman, like Denck, says that God did know who would and who would not live a devout life, and he thus imparts grace or wrath, not by predetermination but by foreknowledge. Hence he used Judas to arrest Christ because he knew from the beginning that he would be a traitor, "and would fall from the kingdom of his own free will, just like the devil and Adam".[7] God's prescience is not a result of predestination, it is the other way round; he intervenes in history because he already knows about the free actions of his creatures. If God uses evil men to test and improve believers as part of his "strange work" it does not mean that he has created the godless for this purpose. Only when a man has fallen from God because of his own free will does he take on a negative role in the plan of salvation.[8]

So as to reconcile the contradictory ideas of "divine omnipotence" and of "human freedom", Hoffman drew a distinction between God's own "eternal" will and his "permissive" will, i.e.

---

[4] *Warhafftige erklerung* A2b.

[5] *Römerbrief* N3b, D5b–D6a.

[6] *Ordinance* p. 198, *Das ware trostliche und freudenreiche Evangelion* 1531 B1a.

[7] *Römerbrief* N7b.

[8] *Esau unde Jacob* A8-b.

between what God desires and what he allows. He derived this
distinction from Karlstadt, Hubmaier and Denck. God's own
will is that all men should come to a knowledge of the truth, do
good and be saved. But his "permissive" will allows men
wantonly to fall away from him, to do evil and to damn
themselves. Yet no one is ever so tempted by God or by other
men that he loses his ability to resist temptation. "God's desire
and his permission should be clearly distinguished so that no one
thinks God desires men to sin".[9]

Hoffman gives a totally new interpretation of Paul's example
of God's groundless preference for Jacob and His damnation of
Esau (Rom. 9:10-13). God's ordinance here does not refer to
salvation or damnation, but to different roles and talents. God
chooses some men to rule and some to serve, paying no
attention to their will or to any *adequate* deserts of those chosen.
The gift of the Holy Spirit is granted to the "Jacob-type" at an
early stage so that he can easily overcome any temptation, but
God condemns the "Esau-type" to a lifetime of hard battles
against the lusts of the flesh. Here again God's decisions are
based on his foreknowledge of the actions of those to whom he
grants or does not grant his grace. Gifts and merits are thus
related by *congruence*. In the strict sense, nobody can "merit"
God's gifts; but the different gifts of God reflect the different
merits of men on a much higher level.[10]

These ideas are clearly related to the popular ideas of late
scholastic Nominalism as expounded by, for example, Gabriel
Biel. They spoke of God's commitment to a particular ordinance

---

[9] *Warhafftige erklerung* A5b-A7b. Erasmus was also influential in
establishing the Anabaptist conviction that God is not the author of sin,
cf. his Paraphrase of Rom. 9:15-16 and his *De libero arbitrio*. On the
connection between Erasmus and the Anabaptists cf. T. Bergsten,
Balthasar Hubmaier 1961, p. 441; T. Hall, "Possibilities of Erasmian
Influence on Denck and Hubmaier" in *MQR* 35 (1961) pp. 149-170; J.B.
Payne, "Erasmus, Interpreter of Romans" in C.S. Meyer (ed.), *Sixteenth
Century Essays and Studies* Vol. 2., 1971, pp. 12-15; K. Davis, "Erasmus
as a Progenitor of Anabaptist Theology and Piety" in *MQR* 47 (1973)
pp. 163-178.

[10] *Een waraftyghe tuchenisse* 1532, A4b-A5a, *Römerbrief* L7a-L8a, M8a,
N4b-O1a.

of law and salvation (*potentia Dei ordinata*) and attempted to reconcile divine predestination with human accountability by interpreting God's predestination in terms of his prescience. In the same way Hoffman repeats the scholastic distinction between *meritum de condigno* and *meritum de congruo*. Like Biel, Hoffman sees the basic relationship between human actions and divine grace as *meritum de congruo*. These ideas may have reached the Anabaptist group in Strasbourg *via* Hubmaier, who had made a close study of Gabriel Biel's writings,[11] though this is by no means certain, since such ideas had a common currency in the late Middle Ages.

2. The "Heavenly" Christ as Liberator from Original Sin.

The function of Hoffman's Monophysite Christology is to develop the traditional doctrine of original sin in such a direction that it becomes compatible with his doctrine of God's righteousness and man's freedom and capacity for self-control.

Hoffman followed the traditional formula in saying that Christ made atonement for Adam's sin on the cross so as to release the whole of humanity, without exception, from the curse of original sin and the threat of eternal damnation. But if we consider its effects on Adam's descendants rather than on Adam himself this action seems more like an act of justice than of divine grace. "When all of Adam's seed was damned under the curse, *through no fault of their own*, Jesus Christ the Son of God made them free once more. He delivered them out of the kingdom of Satan *without their merits*. They became justified and sanctified by the belief in God's promises."[12] There is no question of attributing Adam's guilt to his descendants.

For Hoffman original sin is not, as for Luther, a leaven which affects the whole of human life. He does not believe that the human spirit is totally corrupt or subjected to death; when men

---

[11] Cf. D.C. Steinmetz, "Scholasticism and Radical Reform: Nominalist Motifs in the Theology of Balthasar Hubmaier" in *MQR* 45 (1971), pp. 127-128; H.A. Oberman, "The Shape of Late Medieval Thought: the Birthpangs of the Modern Era" in *ARG* 64(1973), pp. 23-24.

[12] *Römerbrief* D7a.

die the flesh reverts to dust but the spirit returns to God.[13] After
the fall man's nature, implanted in him by God, yearns to return
to its source.[14] Even the heathen are aware of the nature and the
will of God because of the voice of conscience and the starry
firmament.[15] Hoffman quotes Aristotle as an example of a pagan
who recognized that there must be a God who rules the world
because of his observation of the movement of celestial bodies.[16]
There have been "just and God-fearing heathen" in every age
"who have lived in total righteousness according to the will of
God".[17] The Jews were also protected from the worst effects of
original sin by the Mosaic Law. In itself the act of conception is
not sinful, nor is this the means whereby sins are transmitted
from one generation to the next.[18]

The trichotomous medieval anthropology stemming from
Origen is clearly the basis of Hoffman's concept of man. It can
also be found in Erasmus, Gabriel Biel, Hans Denck and
Balthasar Hubmaier. The worst effects of man's fall were on the
flesh; the will suffered a limitation of its freedom because of the
inordinate pressure from lustful desires, but the spirit retained its
inherited righteousness and its freedom of knowledge. The spirit
lives like a prisoner within the body. But despite its weakness
the will is still able to follow the obvious commands of reason.
Thus the essential core of man remains his will, which although
it has been weakened, is still enlightened by reason and is still
free.[19]

God's assessment of men is based solely on the extent to
which they have been true to the will of God, however incapable
they may have been of recognising this, as a result of original

[13] F.O. zur Linden, *Melchior Hofmann* p. 439.
[14] *Römerbrief* M3a
[15] *Ibid.* M3a.
[16] *Ibid.* C7a, E1a.
[17] *Ibid.* E1b.
[18] *Ibid.* G8b.
[19] Cf. B. Hubmaier, *On Free Will* in G.H. Williams and A.M.
Mergal (ed.), Spiritual and Anabaptist Writers, London 1957, pp.
114-135; C. Windhorst, *Täuferisches Taufverständnis* Leiden 1976, pp.
205-208; W. Joest, *Ontologie der Person bei Luther* pp. 154-156 and pp.
196-210, 265-267 (for Luther's rejection of medieval anthropology).

sin. "Thus it is the same for every man, be he Jew, Turk, or Christian; he will be judged as a person for what he has done in the light of the knowledge he has, to the extent that he has seen the truth."[20] "In Adam all men come under the curse of original sin, but not all became sinners or unjust. Even so in Christ all came to salvation by grace, but they do not all reach this same stage of justification because of their selfishness."[21] At all times salvation and damnation depend upon the personal efforts of the individual.

But Hoffman then flatly contradicts this optimistic anthropology which had been so influenced by a simple rationalism and humanism; he returns to the Christian tradition to take up the idea that all men after Adam's fall belong, by right, to Satan. In order to liberate man from the power of evil Christ, the "pure Word", had to offer himself as a sacrifice for them. No man who was stained by original sin could have been offered as a ransom to the devil. The devil would have been deceived if Christ took flesh from Mary, a sinful daughter of Adam, because in that case God would have paid Satan in his own coin, with something which already belonged to him. "For it is certain that the whole of Adam's seed was cursed and damned and belonged to death and Satan. If redemption emerged and took effect from the same seed of Adam it would logically follow that sinners were redeemed by sin... that filthy people were cleansed and purified by filth. . . If redemption had been achieved by Mary's flesh and blood God would have wronged Satan, which never can happen, because God is a just God who gives everybody that which he deserves, no matter whether he is good or wicked." [22] If Christ had shared Mary's nature we would have had to wait for another redeemer. For Hoffman redemption and assurance of salvation depend upon "the heavenly flesh of Christ" and its recognition. [23]

Hoffman takes a passage in Pliny on the origin of pearls as a "symbol" for his Monophysite Christology. "We can under-

---

[20] *Römerbrief* D8a.
[21] *Ibid.* H2a-b.
[22] *Magestadt* B3b-B4a, *Warhafftige erklerung* A8a.
[23] F.O. zur Linden, *Melchior Hofmann* pp. 442-443.

stand it if we consider pearls. Pliny, in his writings on nature, explains how pearls are formed and made up of dew. When a dew-drop enters a shell, it becomes a hard pearl inside. It is born without the addition of any other substance, but simply watery dew and a hard shell."[24] This idea, that Christ was born of the Virgin Mary "like a pearl from heavenly dew in a shell," had already appeared during the 15th century. But the Dutchman Alain de La Roche had used this image as a symbol for Christ's virgin birth ("sine admixtione cuiuscunque seminis propagationis") whereas to Hoffman the comparison served to reject any idea that *Mary* had contributed to Christ's body.[25]

Hoffman's most usual argument in favour of a Monophysite Christology was that this was the only way in which adequate satisfaction could be guaranteed for Adam's sin. Yet a second reason, which he did not mention so often, was that he was concerned with conserving the unity of the divine being. In a book on "the single majesty of God's nature" (possibly written in 1532) Hoffman himself makes explicit the relationships between the dispute about the Eucharist and his Christology. He explains how for many people the Lord's table has become "a snare" because they do not acknowledge Christ's nature.[26] He felt that Luther's "false" doctrine of the Eucharist, whereby Christ is confused with created matter had been able to come about because of the erroneous two-nature doctrine. Hoffman opposed this doctrine by stressing the "venerable *single* majesty of God." He supported this with the help of Ursula Jost's 22nd vision in which she had seen a bright light refracted into a spectrum of three distinct colours. In the middle of the spectrum there appeared a transfigured child and then the three colours merged to form a single light once again. Hoffman gave the following interpretation to this "vision": it means that there has been one single God from the beginning of eternity and in the same way there will be one single and true divine nature for the

---

[24] *Römerbrief* A6b, *Auslegung der heimlichen Offenbarung* Z5a, *TAE* I No. 210, p. 261.
[25] For Alain de la Roche cf. J. Huizinga, *The Waning of the Middle Ages* Penguin 1955, p. 200.
[26] *Van der waren hochprachtlichen eynigen magestadt gottes* A1b.

rest of eternity. *A single unity* will remain for ever."[27] For Hoffman the trinity is simply a transitory mode of appearance of the eternal, single Godhead, whereby God cannot allow himself to be involved in a second nature.

So as to avoid the charge of Gnosticism regarding his doctrine, Hoffman insisted that Christ was the "physical, tangible, visible Word" and "the true flesh", who was capable of suffering and was mortal. He explicitly rejected Clemens Ziegler's doctrine that the historical Jesus "had taken a shell from the flesh and blood of Mary, that this shell had suffered and died on the cross and that it was this same flesh and blood of Mary which was laid in the tomb."[28]

Hoffman used the Fourth Gospel and the Epistle to the Hebrews as the biblical foundations for his Monophysite Christology. On the basis of John 1:14 ("The Word became flesh") he concluded that the eternal Word had simply turned into human flesh. To interpret it to mean "The Word *took* flesh" would imply a misunderstanding of the word "to become."[29] The second crucial text for Hoffman was Hebrews 7:3, which refers to Melchizedek, the type of Christ, who "is without father or mother or descent and has neither beginning of days nor end of life."

To Hoffman acceptance of his Monophysite Christology was decisive for man's salvation; anyone who does not accept this dogma cannot be a true Christian. The false Christians of the Reformation would stumble over this true knowledge of Christ in the way like the Jews over the historical Jesus.[30] Even after retracting some of his doctrines in 1539 Hoffman held on to his Christology. His favourite quotation, "The word became flesh," became the battlecry of the Anabaptists in Münster, who engraved it on their coins and medals.[31] For them Monophysite

---

[27] *Ibid.* A3b–A4a.

[28] *Ibid.* B3b, A5b.

[29] Bucer had already rejected such an interpretation of the word "became", *Handlung inn dem öffentlichen gesprech* B2a-b.

[30] *Römerbrief* P1a.

[31] C.A. Cornelius (ed.), *Berichte der Augenzeugen über das Münsterische Wiedertäuferreich* 2nd ed. 1965, p. 17.

Christology was simply a means of exalting Christ, yet it in fact
meant that the figure of Jesus lost significance because the first and
second persons of the Trinity were fused together. The
Münsterite Anabaptists followed Hoffman's order to pray only
to the Father and not to the Son.[32] Hoffman's Monophysitism in
fact eventually resulted in a return to the God of the Old
Testament. Well after Hoffman's death the doctrine spread to
the Anabaptists in Holland, Northern Germany, and England.
Menno Simons and Dirk Philips preached it and in 1547 Adam
Pastor was actually excluded from an Anabaptist congregation
for denying it.[33] For the modern historian Monophysitism is the
most certain indication of the Melchiorite origin of an Anabaptist group.

To sum up, we can point out the threefold significance of
Hoffman's Monophysite Christology:

1.   It guarantees our assurance in salvation from the power of
evil because Hoffman saw this as the only means by which full
satisfaction could be achieved.[34]
2.   It protects the unity and spirituality of God and, above all,
avoids any confusion of the divine nature with the created order.
3.   Finally it commands the individual to strive for moral
improvement and spiritualization. As Heinold Fast says about
this, "the bridegroom is dressed in heavenly flesh and if the

---

[32] *Römerbrief* B6a, C.A. Cornelius (ed.), *op. cit.* pp. 94-96.
[33] For Simons' attitude to Hoffman's Christology cf. C. Bornhäuser,
Leben und Lehre des Menno Simons' 1973 pp. 63-69. On Hoffman's
monophysitism in England cf. I.B. Horst, *The Radical Brethren.
Anabaptism and the English Reformation to 1558* Nieuwkoop 1972, pp.
172-73. For Adam Pastor's eviction cf. J. ten Doornkaat-Koolman,
Dirk Philips. Vriend en Medewerker van Menno Simons 1504-1568 Haarlem
1964, pp. 36-37.
[34] Gerhard Brendler (in *Das Täuferreich zu Münster* 1966, p. 107) says
that "the Melchiorite Christ, whose flesh comes directly from heaven, is
eschatologically more trustworthy than one born of the Virgin Mary".
But it is not the case, as Brendler argues, that Hoffman's Christology is
an expression of his chiliasm; for Hoffman Christ does not guarantee
salvation at the Last Judgement. The coming Christ is the judge, not the
redeemer.

individual Christian or the community desires to be his bride they must become like him. Giving oneself to the Lord in baptism and becoming united with him in the Eucharist are hence moral acts which call for a heavenly transformation so that he can be presented with a spotless bride."[35]

3. The Way of Salvation.

Hoffman declares that the way of salvation begins with the acceptance by faith of Christ's sacrificial death, which has done away with the curse of damnation. We can only be justified by putting our trust in God's grace which precedes all human acts. Even the Old Testament Patriarchs were justified by faith in the promises of God. This belief in God's faithfulness is necessary in order to calm our nagging consciences which constantly remind us of our guilt.[36] So far this sounds thoroughly Lutheran. As long as he was influenced by Lutheran theology Hoffman regarded faith as a gift of God. On this basis he had argued for religious toleration; in his commentary on Revelation in 1530 he still said that it was meaningless to persecute someone for his faith since faith is not subject to man's will.[37] But after his encounter with Denck's theology (i.e. after the middle of 1530), Hoffman said that although only the Word remained a gift of God, man's acceptance or rejection of faith was a matter of his own free choice. The Gospel speaks of a general disposition of man towards accepting God's salvation, an inclination which had not been totally destroyed by the fall. Everyone could believe if they wanted to do so.[38]

By faith in Christ man, who had fallen to Satan, is reborn to become a "natural man." In this "first birth" man's natural will and his ability to discern good and evil are fully restored to him, as is the freedom of his will which had formerly been limited

---

[35] H. Fast, "Variationen des Kirchenbegriffes bei den Täufern" in *MGB* NF 22 (1970) p. 12.

[36] *Römerbrief* C2b-C3b.

[37] *Offenbarung* A6a, O7a and *Jhesus* in *WA* 18:427.

[38] *Römerbrief* F2b. P. Kawerau (*Melchior Hoffman* p. 58) overlooked the change in Hoffman's position on this issue.

because of fear and delusion.[39] At the same time Christ also frees men from slavery to the letter of the Law. Christ is the "end of the Law" in that he fulfils its purpose by "killing Moses."[40] Christ replaces the justification that comes from the letter with the "justification from the spirit." But the acceptance of faith is not enough to bring salvation; man must respond to God's gift of grace with the obedience which derives from faith.[41] So long as man is not fully in possession of the Holy Spirit, Christ's way must remain a "prophetic word" or a "new law" for him.

Unlike Luther Hoffman drew a distinction between "first and second justifications," i.e. between the first ("literal") and second ("pentecostal, spiritual") regeneration. The first justification is based on God's gift of grace, viz. the forgiveness of original sin brought about by the death of Christ but appropriated by man through faith in the Word (hence "literal" regeneration). The second, spiritual regeneration can only be achieved by the moral strivings of the individual man. Only this second rebirth can lead to eternal salvation; the first justification only provides man with a "foretaste of the kingdom of God."[42] If a man wants to reach the promised land (i.e. to receive the Holy Spirit), he must follow the example of the people of Israel and leave the fleshpots of Egypt to wander through the wilderness.

Baptism is the beginning of this process. Here man responds to God's gift of grace, which has removed from him the curse of original sin, and he establishes a new covenant with God. The believer publicly betrothes himself to Christ the bridegroom in the sacrament of baptism; he promises to mortify his own will, to obey God's will and to "give himself over to God resigned and mortified."[43]

Baptism can only be a pledge of the covenant for adults who have already come to an understanding of the Gospel. Furthermore the practice of the New Testament rules out infant

[39] *Römerbrief* K8a.
[40] *Römerbrief* J4a, 05a.
[41] *Ibid.* B3b-B4a.
[42] BRN V, p. 196.
[43] *Ordinance* p. 187

baptism.[44] The active partner in baptism is the Lord's bride who "has given herself over to the Bridegroom in baptism, which is the sign of the covenant, and has betrothed herself and yielded herself to him of her own free will."[45]

God's response to man's commitment is to be found in the Eucharist: "Thereupon the Bridegroom and exalted Lord Christ Jesus comes and by his hand – the apostolic messengers are the hand – takes bread (just as a bridegroom takes a ring or a piece of gold) and gives himself to his bride with the bread (just as the bridegroom gives himself to his bride with the ring) . . . and together they are thus one body, one flesh, one spirit, and one passion, as bridegroom and bride."[46] Here, in the Eucharist, it is Christ who is the active partner.

Baptism and Eucharist belong together inextricably like the two halves of a single contract. They are the basis on which the two parties contract with each other. In baptism the bride (the believer) promises to be faithful to Christ and the bridegroom responds in the Eucharist by making the same vow.

If the bride becomes "bespotted by whoredom", she is to be expelled from the Lord's house by the "apostolic messengers" should she not heed the three warnings specified in the New Testament (Matt. 18:15-17). Just as a bridegroom takes back his ring from a bride who has been unfaithful, so faithless Christians are forbidden the bread and wine of the Eucharist by imposition of the ban.[47]

Hoffman's concept of baptism and of the Eucharist pays almost no attention to the significance of these two sacraments for the establishment and self-understanding of the Christian community. He is interested simply in the impact of the sacraments on the relationship between God and the individual soul. The congregation takes no active part until it appears (in the person of the "apostolic messengers") to enforce excommunication. This explains why the Dutch Melchiorites limited the idea of "covenant membership" to the contract between the

---

[44] *Ibid* p. 192.
[45] *Ibid* p. 193.
[46] *Ibid* pp.193-194.
[47] *Ibid* pp. 196-197.

individual and God. All Anabaptist leaders rejected the contemporary allegation that the contract was a secret vow made by the
Melchiorites as a pledge of loyalty to one another.

Nor was Hoffman's understanding of baptism in any sense
sacramental. Reception of the Holy Spirit and the forgiveness of
sins are not dependent on the act of baptism. Nor, as Hubmaier
argued, is baptism in the spirit a precondition for baptism in
water. For Hoffman baptism is no more than a public sign of a
subjective acceptance of the "first justification" brought about
by Christ, in which the believer expresses his gratitude by
promising to follow Christ in his life. Since baptism was simply
an external sign of a man's inner commitment, Hoffman was
able to order his followers to dispense with it after the execution
of Jan Volkerts Trijpmaker in 1531. The first point Hoffman
renounced in his partial retraction in 1539 was the doctrine of
adult baptism.

Hoffman saw historical significance in the reintroduction of
believers' baptism, for it created the holy community of the last
days which Christ would soon take to himself when he came to
take up his role on earth.[48] Yet baptism had no magic power in
this apocalyptic context; it was in no sense an *opus operatum* that
could protect the baptised from the messianic holocaust or from
the judgment of God. It was Hoffman's followers, Jan Matthijs
and Bernd Rothmann, who were the first to regard baptism as a
magical *signum Tau* which would put a seal on believers to
protect them from God's wrath during the last judgment (Rev.
7:3).[49]

On the way from the first to the second justification the
baptised are led along by the "fear of God". This drives out
human fear and provides the strength to resist tyrants (as it did
for the three men in the burning furnace and for Daniel in the
lion's den). In particular it liberates man from himself and from
lust for all creaturely things.[50] This fear of God, which is

[48] *Ibid* p. 186.
[49] C.A. Cornelius (ed.), *Berichte der Augenzeugen* p. 405, B.
Rothmann, *Schriften* (ed. R. Stupperich 1970) p. 287.
[50] *Von der reinen Furcht Gottes* A3b-A4a.

enlightened by the divine law, constitutes the mystical power of self-annihilation, which must be achieved before God can enter the human heart, for God desires man's heart to a much greater extent than man is prepared to give it to him.[51] "Thus there is nothing higher than the pure fear of God, which leads man on to perfect love".[52]

On the way to fulfilment man is always tormented by the temptations of the flesh and Satan's wiles.[53] Whenever a man thinks that he can live in his own strength, God removes His hand from him and admits the tempter thus, demonstrating man's dependence. Yet God never subjects man to more than could be endured by his looking up to Christ, man's true physician and helper. Every transgression is severely punished, even if the punishment is of short duration.[54] The progress to perfection involves a co-operation between God's rod of correction and human strivings.

In the course of this development man learns the humility of *Gelassenheit* (self-surrender), which enables him to leave behind all that binds him to the creaturely realm. In *Gelassenheit* man finds inner peace in the assurance that all things are of, from and directed towards God; it is here that the "nagging conscience" comes to rest.[55] Like the medieval mystics Hoffman had said, in his commentary on Daniel, that the highest form of *Gelassenheit* was *resignatio ad infernum*.[56] But he now rejects this idea, partly because he feels it is blasphemous to believe that the Creator desires a single man to be damned, and partly because such a form of self-sacrifice is incompatible with man's nature, whose origin is in God and which yearns to return to him.[57]

If anyone opposes God on the path towards the second justification he must expect to be damned.[58] Any man who

---

[51] *BRN* V p. 195.

[52] *Von der reinen Furcht Gottes* A3b-A4a.

[53] *Römerbrief* J7a, J8b-K1a.

[54] *Ibid* K2b, S5b.

[55] *Ibid* B5a, S4a.

[56] *Daniel* c3a.

[57] *Das ware tröstliche und freudenreiche Evangelion* B1b-B2a, *Römerbrief* M3a.

[58] *Die Epistel des Apostels Sanct Judas*, 1534, A7b.

commits a sin in full knowledge of his error brings about his own eternal damnation. Hoffman regards this as the "sin against the Holy Spirit"[59] Christ's sacrifice is only valid for sins committed before conversion and for those weaknesses of the flesh which continue to trouble believers because of the remaining traces of original sin.[60] Bucer was being unfair when he said that Hoffman taught that any sin committed after baptism could not be forgiven,[61] but Hoffman did insist that there was no grace for those who consciously and deliberately sinned after conversion. Anyone who breaks one commandment breaks them all "because man lives not on one, or a few, of God's words, but on all of them."[62] Every intentional wrong deed breaks the covenant between God and man and sets off a process of self-destruction, because man is thereby setting himself in opposition to the voice of his own conscience.[63]

For Hoffman apostasy was the most usual "sin against the Holy Spirit." "Those who have once been enlightened and have received the taste of the wisdom of God, and who have delivered themselves up and given themselves over to the Lord Christ and who then fall away again and, after having confessed the truth, have departed from the faith and the true betrothal: it is impossible to restore these broken traitors". Just as an oak tree can only be planted once, so faith is granted once only.[64] There was a particular context which gave meaning to Hoffman's doctrine of the "unforgivable sin" after enlightenment: it served as a warning to his followers not to fall away during a time of persecution. By threatening them with what amounted to eternal destruction he hoped to spur on his followers to take a firm stand.

As well as the apostates from his own party, Hoffman regarded also as "sinners against the Holy Spirit" those who

---

[59] *Ordinance* pp. 199-200, *Römerbrief* C8b, F4a, *Von der reinen Furcht Gottes* A4a-A7a. This doctrine also appears in the Schleitheim Confession.
[60] *TAE* II No. 368, p. 19. *Offenbarung* L2a.
[61] *TAE* II No. 617, p. 394.
[62] *Judas* A8b.
[63] *Römerbrief* X1b.
[64] *Ordinance* p. 199.

preached the doctrine of predestination, the "sacramentalist magicians" and those who oppressed the true faith. Above all it was "spiritual" rather then "fleshly" errors which counted as unforgivable sins for Hoffman.[65]

But anyone who does not fall as he wanders through the wilderness will be rewarded by receiving the Holy Spirit. At the point of his deepest abasement, when he is exhausted and thoroughly destroyed, man's "old Adam", who had reigned in him hitherto, is defeated and he becomes a "spiritual, heavenly man" who cannot sin any more. "To the extent that the old man is truly killed and crucified with Christ, it inevitably follows that the mortal body will come to its sabbath rest . . . . leaving behind all its work, just as God rested from His work (Hebr. 4). Man will become a true child of God (Matt. 13). By the death and crucifixion of the flesh he has been delivered from the lusts and passions (Gal. 5) of his own will, which is now dead (Rev. 14); only God's fruitfulness remains alive. These are they who will sin no more". Those who have died to the world with Christ will rise with him spiritually. "True rising with Christ is nothing other than receiving the pentecostal rebirth, and being changed from a child of the moon to a child of the sun. All unnaturally mortal men are born again by the prophetic word as natural men and by the spirit they become spiritual, heavenly men."[66]

Hoffman saw this second justification as the birth of Christ within the human soul. If anyone possesses true faith but resists giving birth to Christ in his soul, he shares the guilt of those who crucified the Son of God. Divinisation is not an exception

---

[65] *Ibid.* p. 199. *Offenbarung* Q4a, *Römerbrief* N8a. Luther and Melanchthon repeatedly alleged that this doctrine of the unforgivable sin originated in Catholicism (cf. e.g. the *Confession of Augsburg*). In fact, it was not a genuinely Catholic doctrine, but it may go back to the Catholic view that baptism only removes original sin and sins committed before baptism, and that any further sins must be atoned for by extra acts of repentance. From this the idea would develop that Christ had only died to remove original sin. cf. G.H. Williams, "Sanctification in the Testimony of Several So-Called Schwärmer" in *MQR* 42 (1968) pp. 5-25.

[66] *Römerbrief* H4b, cf. *Jacobus* B2b-B3a.

expected only of the Saints; it must be the aim of every Christian.[67]

The new "spiritual man" has given up his free will[68]; the law of the Spirit dwells within him and so he has no need of Christ's external Law.[69] Faith and hope too are only transitory stages in the spiritual development of the children of the sun. They attain salvation in the vision of God and in acts of love.[70] And finally Hoffman takes mysticism to its ultimate conclusion: he exalts the perfected man above the law. "Whoever is empowered by the Holy Spirit, the lawgiver, has the law removed from him."[71]

Hoffman refers to the "sins" of the patriarchs, prophets and apostles, in order to give a biblical foundation to this antinomianism. He quotes as examples the action of an old Testament prophet who allowed a harmless wayfarer to be attacked by a lion simply because he refused to strike him (the prophet) (1 Kings 20: 35-36); the Israelites who had God's consent to steal property before they fled from Egypt (Exod. 12:35–36), and the lies of Peter (Gal. 2:11–21) when he denied having had table fellowship with Gentiles in order (so Hoffman thought) to allow Paul to remain the fearless advocate of Gentile Christianity.[72]

Hoffman was aware of the dangers involved in his antinomian ethic. This doctrine was a "strong drink" which only "heavenly men" could take. It should not be given to those young in the faith.[73] Hoffman drew no practical implications for himself from his theoretical antinomianism. Bucer himself admitted that Hoffman led an impeccable life, and Hoffman's wrath always descended on those of his fellow believers who used their Christian freedom as an excuse to indulge in adultery, polygamy

---

[67] *Römerbrief* P7b.
[68] *Ibid.* K2b-K3a, L1a-b.
[69] *Ibid.* F3a.
[70] *Ibid.* L5a.
[71] *Ibid.* H6b.
[72] *Ibid.* H6a-H6b. cf. R.H. Bainton, "The Immoralities of the Patriarchs According to the Exegesis of the Late Middle Ages and of the Reformation" in *Harvard Theological Review* 23(1930) pp. 39-40.
[73] *Römerbrief* N2b.

or personal vindictiveness.[74] But his Dutch and Westphalian followers (including Jan van Batenburg) were able to use this aspect of his ethic to justify their "holy terror".

The process of justification does not only consist in undergoing self-annihilation; it also involves the pursuit of good works. Hoffman refers to the Epistle of James and says that faith without works is dead. "All that is acceptable to God is that true faith which becomes active and fruitful in love." We see in the example of Abraham, who was both faithful and obedient, "that man is justified by works and not by faith alone."[75] At the Last Judgement man will be rewarded according to his works rather than his faith.[76] Hoffman demanded that the "apostolic messengers" literally renounce all their property.[77] He expected all Christians to help their needy brothers to such an extent that their lot would be permanently improved [78].

Like all other Anabaptist leaders, Hoffman was here launching an attack on the Reformation doctrine of justification. The theologians of Wittenberg and Zürich made such a mockery of Christianity with their talk of "justification by faith alone" that the devil himself could happily join them. Dead faith rules throughout the world accompanied by "endless prattling" about God and man, which accomplishes nothing whatsoever. He compares the Lutheran and Zwinglian preachers to "clouds with no rain" or "barren trees which produce nothing but green leaves."[79]

Hoffman may have been justified in complaining about the

---

[74] *TAE* II No. 362, p. 13, No. 368, p. 19, *Offenbarung* E 2b.

[75] *Jakobus* C5a, C6a-b. *Ordinance*, p. 201.

[76] *Römerbrief* D6b.

[77] *TAE* II No. 368, p. 19. On the relationship between mysticism and communism cf. G. H. Williams, "Popularized German Mysticism as a Factor in the Rise of Anabaptist Communism" in *Glaube, Geist, Geschichte. Festschrift für Ernst Benz*. Leiden 1967, part. pp. 293ff.

[78] *Jakobus* C5a.

[79] *Judas* D2a-b. *Jakobus* C5b. For Hoffman as the author of these commentaries on Jude and James cf. K. Deppermann, "Melchior Hoffmans letzte Schriften aus dem Jahre 1534" in *ARG* 63 (1972) pp. 81-82.

meagre fruit of the Reformation in terms of improved individual
and social life, but on a theological level he was unfair to the
reformers when he maintained that they omitted to preach good
works. Luther and Melanchthon insisted that living faith was
an active faith which produced good works.[80] But "good works
are not sufficient to merit us God's grace if He is not already
gracious to us on Christ's behalf".[81] For them good works had
a role in the plan of salvation in terms of the Christian's relationship with his neighbours but not in terms of the relationship between God and man. They do not add to Christ's work
for our redemption, but emerge out of man's gratitude for
his unmerited salvation, and benefit his fellow men. But for
Hoffman good works were essential for man to be able to justify
his existence before God. If faith is to mean anything, justification by faith must lead to justification by works.

Hoffman chose a collection of impressive images from the
Christian tradition to illustrate the growth of the "unnatural
child of Satan" into the "natural" and thence into the "heavenly
spiritual man." The most common image is that of the exodus of
the children of Israel, which he regarded as a historical "symbol"
of the process of salvation which every individual soul under-
goes. The exodus began with the sacrifice of the Passover lamb.
This symbolized the subjective appropriation of Christ's sacrificial death by faith by which man is restored to complete freedom
and wisdom and by which he attains the capacity transcending
the world. On the first day of the journey the soul suffers from
persecution and inner temptations, like the Jews before they
arrived at the Red Sea. The passage of the children of Israel
through the Red Sea corresponds to baptism, the symbol of the
death of the old Adam. But before the believer can enter the Holy
Land, he must wander in the wilderness for 40 days as a
"natural man" in a battle against temptation. On the last of the
42 days of the journey man enters the land of Canaan – i.e. he

---

[80] Cf. Luther's sermon "On Good Works" in *WA* 6:211, 213-216.
[81] Melanchthon, *Apology for the Confession of Augsburg* in *Bekenntnisschriften* p. 210.

receives the Holy Spirit, which liberates him from inner temptation and from the letter of the external law.[82]

In the commentary on Revelation, Hoffman interprets the tabernacle of Moses and Solomon's Temple as images for the path of the soul. By faith in Christ man enters the outer court, where the flesh is killed. The old Adam dies in the Holy Place and man is released from his own lusts. With the reception of the Spirit "he walks into the Holy of Holies" from where he looks into the third and fourth heavens and comes to know Christ in glory."[83]

Hoffman also uses astral symbolism to illustrate the various stages of spiritual growth. So long as man is led by the "external word" and the image of the historical Christ, he is illuminated by "the moon of faith." The "morning star" rises in his heart when he has killed the old Adam within himself but on receiving the Holy Spirit the full light of the sun breaks forth. Here the face of God shines down upon man as spirit answers spirit.[84]

Hoffman also uses erotic imagery to illustrate the relationship between God and the believing soul in his best-known book *The Ordinance of God*. In baptism the bride pledges herself to Christ, her bridegroom; in the Eucharist she receives her wedding-ring, and after victory over her selfishness she "comes completely naked and resigned to enter the bed of the Bridegroom", there to be united with him.[85]

---

[82] Ordinance p. 187. *BRN* V, p. 197, *Römerbrief* B2b, L6a.

[83] *Offenbarung*, G7b. *Ordinance*, pp. 188-189. *Jakobus*, A7b, B2b.

[84] *Römerbrief* P6a. Rollin S. Armour (*Anabaptist Baptism* 1966, p. 98) misinterprets Hoffman's astral symbolism. The "light of the moon" does not refer to the unenlightened understanding before the first birth, but to the spiritual state of man *after* his first regeneration, so long as he serves the letter as a "natural" man. The sunlight only bursts forth when Christ is directly revealed in the soul. Armour is also wrong in saying that this spiritual birth of Christ in the soul could only take place at particular times. This is the aim of all Christians, although there had only been three times in history when a great number of men had attained it; the age of the apostles, of Jan Hus, and the present age.

[85] *Ordinance* p. 191, pp. 193–194. Karlstadt had used such erotic metaphors at Orlamünde to illustrate the relationship between Christ and the soul (*WA* 15:346). Luther also used such symbolism but unlike

Thus in essence Hoffman was repeating the late medieval mystics' doctrine of justification, which also appeared in different forms in Thomas Müntzer and his followers Hans Hut and Jörg Haug von Juchsen.[86] Whereas for Luther the essence of faith consisted in the sinner's trust in God's unmerited mercy, Hoffman saw it in terms of the process of the fulfilment of man's potential in the hard school of God's law. The covenant between God and man should initiate an educational process which ends in man's divinisation. Man's capacity to develop and change derives from his free will and his natural reason and also from God's grace, his law and his correcting rod. By "fear of God" man liberates himself from subjection to his tiny, egotistical self and from his creaturely lusts. He becomes empty and receptive, ready to receive the Holy Spirit. Anyone who becomes more like God has no more need of the literal law. But anyone who deliberately falls away from the steep path towards divinisation will remain fallen. The sum of Hoffman's whole theology is that he wants to call upon everyone to be a perfected, spiritual man. This is in total contrast to Luther's understanding of the Gospel, for Luther said, "God Himself perfects and absolves us without paying attention to our strivings and plans. We are to be men, not God. This is the 'summa'. It cannot be otherwise, or our reward would be endless trouble and suffering of the heart."[87]

---

[86] Cf. H.-J. Goertz, *Innere und äussere Ordnung in der Theologie Thomas Müntzers* Leiden 1967, pp. 114–132. H. Hut, in L. Müller (ed.), *Glaubenszeugnisse oberdeutscher Taufgesinnter*, Vol I, 1938, pp. 12–38, J. Haug von Juchsen in *ibid.* pp. 3–10.

[87] Luther's letter to Spalatin of 30th June, 1530, *WA Br* 5:414.

note 85 continued

Hoffman did not believe that the soul had to be "purified" before it could be unified with Christ. It is rather the "rich and devout" bridegroom who takes a "poor and godless servant" as his wife. "The third incomparable benefit of faith is that it unites the soul with Christ as a bride is united with the bridegroom. By this mystery, as the Apostle teaches, Christ and the soul become one flesh . . . Christ is full of grace, life and salvation. The soul is full of sins, death and damnation . . . Here this rich and divine bridegroom Christ marries this poor, wicked harlot, redeems her from all her evil, and adorns her with all his goodness." *The Freedom of a Christian*, *WA* 7:54–55, *LW* 31:351–352.

4. Hermeneutics and Hoffman's Theology of History.

Hoffman's hermeneutics is inextricably bound up with his theology of history. He sees the plan of salvation as a developing process of spiritualisation, and the role of "the witness of God" is thus to make people aware of this emerging spirituality by his interpretation of history. The "witness of the Most High", by his exposition of past history, becomes the greatest promoter of the whole process of spiritualization; with his typological and allegorical interpretation of history he is able to release the spiritual potential that has always been latent in historical "figures".

a) Typological and allegorical exegesis

The typological exegesis of biblical texts used by Hoffman is based on the idea that the present and the future are "prefigured" in the events and visions of the Old and New Testaments. He took Isaiah 46:9-10 to support this view, using a translation which ran, "I am God and there is none like me; I proclaim from the beginning what is to come, and in advance things which have not yet happened, saying, 'My plan will be accomplished'".[88]

Everything that is of importance for salvation must have been indicated beforehand with a sign. Conversely this means that everything that has been prophesied in dreams or "figures" will one day come to pass.[89] He sees history as a process determined by God's plan of salvation, and thus there can be a possibility of typological interpretation for historical events in different periods (types and antitypes) which have a link beyond normal causality. "Natural" causes and effects become irrelevant.

Hoffman felt that his particular gift was the ability to reveal the "spiritual" meaning hidden behind the "literal" meaning of the sacred texts. Although he did believe in continuing revelation and in direct revelations of God in the present age, he did not himself claim to have received immediate visions or orders from God. He sometimes refused to call himself a

---

[88] *Prophetische Gesicht und Offenbarung* A2a.
[89] *Weissagung* A1b-A2a.

"prophet."[90] But he did feel able to prophesy future events by means of an allegorical and typological interpretation of the Bible or on the basis of the "prophetic visions" granted to his disciples.[91]

The typological method should be distinguished from the allegorical. Typological interpretation brings together actual figures and characters by "figuration", the linking of concrete persons or events to form pairs (e.g. Melchizedek and Christ). But the allegorical method aims at revealing the hidden spiritual meaning of a past external event (e.g. the exodus of the Israelites = the progress of the human soul) or to interpret a hidden "figure" as a reference to an actual character or incident (e.g. the Dragon of Revelation = Emperor Charles V).[92] For Hoffman both typological and allegorical exegesis are involved in "figurative exposition."

b) The "cloven claw" as the structure of the Word of God

Hoffman's frequently used concept of the "cloven claw" has given rise to numerous misunderstandings even in present-day interpretations. Some of his followers in the Netherlands dissociated themselves from his typological interpretation, and such disciples as Obbe Philips and Hans Scheerder of Leeuwarden rejected it, objecting that Scripture was not based on a "cloven claw" and that it had only one interpretation, viz. the literal interpretation. But Jakob van Campen, the Anabaptist bishop of Amsterdam, Dirk Philips and David Joris defended Hoffman's typological/allegorical exegesis and used this method to interpret Old Testament events as indications of New Testament truths.

As Hoffman understood it the "cloven claw" did not relate to the typological structure of Scripture but to its apparent contradictions, in the sense "that all of God's words are ambiguous or seem opposed to one another."[93] In fact, there are

---

[90] *TAE* II No. 364, p. 15.

[91] Kawerau has pointed out Hofman's similarity to Joachim di Fiore in this respect, cf. P. Kawerau, *Melchior Hoffman*, p. 107.

[92] *Offenbarung* O8a.

[93] F.O. zur Linden, *Melchior Hofmann, p. 430, BRN* V p. 189.

no actual contradictions, simply complementary opposites. Hence both of the following verses are true: 1 Tim. 2:4, "God desires all men to be saved and to come to the knowledge of the truth" and 2 Thess. 3:2, "faith is not for everybody."[94] This apparent contradiction is solved if we accept Hoffman's conviction that the universality of divine grace does not override man's free will. If we are to understand the Bible correctly we must "accept both halves of the claw and grasp the centre", i.e. bring together seemingly contradictory passages in a balanced and consistent formula.[95]

Such an exegesis is only possible if we possess "the key of David" (Isaiah 22:22).[96] But this is only given to those who live in the "pure fear of God". "Thus the spirit of fear that dwells within is a noble spirit. It is the beginning of wisdom."[97]

The hermeneutic concepts of the "cloven claw" and of "the key of David" again reveal Hoffman as a disciple of the German mystics. Hans Denck and Sebastian Franck also saw the "contradictions in Scripture" as the central problem of hermeneutics. It was this which revealed whether or not someone possessed the Holy Spirit," for whoever leaves contradictions and cannot unite them is lacking in basic truth."[98] The Bible, "the book sealed with seven seals," can only be opened by someone who follows Christ in his life in the school of the cross. "Impure swine" and "wild dogs" will never be admitted to the "rose-garden of truth."[99]

c) The results of "figurative exposition"
The hermeneutical methods used by Hoffman led to the following results:

---

[94] *BRN* V pp. 188-191.
[95] Römerbrief N2a, V6a, *TAE* II No. 594, p. 370.
[96] *Offenbarung* F7b.
[97] *Von der reinen Furcht Gottes* A4a, *Weissagung* A2b.
[98] H. Denck, *Schriften* Vol. 2, p. 68.
[99] Denck collected forty "contradictions" in one of his pamphlets, Schriften Vol 2, p. 69, of which at least two were discussed by Hoffman. Franck was concerned with contradictions also, and he, too, used the idea of the "cloven claw" and the "key of David". This latter concept can also be found in Erasmus, Müntzer and Hut.

1. They preserved the connection between the Old and New Testament and the relationship between the biblical text and contemporary salvation history. They avoided the Marcionite separation of the Old Covenant from the New, yet did not lead to the opposite heresy of identifying the two. By regarding figures and events of the Old Testament as prototypes of the New Covenant, Hoffman created the impression that a single developing principle unites the two. The Old Testament could remain a sacred text without being absolutely binding.[100]

2. There is a genuine development in the unfolding of the plan of salvation. Appearance gives way to essence, and shadow to reality. God's people are led from a half-blind faith in the letter towards the clarity of an inner conviction. Things do not repeat themselves identically in successive stages of salvation history. Early signs lead on to more developed stages of fulfilment as history progresses. Prefiguration cannot be exchanged with fulfilment; the figure leads beyond itself but fulfilment includes the "figure" within itself.[101]

3. By using the allegorical method and the principle of the "cloven claw", Hoffman was able to make the biblical figures the bearers of his own ideas. If he felt inclined to do so, he could rationalize or spiritualize biblical passages so as to do away with their literal meaning. This is how "Christ's return on the clouds of heaven" could come to mean the revelation of Christ's spirit within the "spiritual clouds", i.e. the "apostolic messengers."[102]

In accordance with the "cloven claw" principle, Hoffman could deal with biblical texts of which he did not approve by citing contradictory passages taken from other contexts so as to transform the meaning of the original text. For example, he uses a text from the Wisdom of Solomon (Wisdom 11:24, "For thou lovest everything that is, and hatest nothing that thou hast

---

[100] Hoffman thus stood in the tradition of medieval biblical exegesis which took Origen's search for the "spiritual meaning" as its prototype. cf H. de Lubac, *Exégèse médiévale. Les quatre sens de l'Ecriture* Paris 1959-1964.

[101] Cf. M. Henschel, "Figuraldeutung und Geschichtlichkeit" in *Kerygma und Dogma* Vol. 5. 1959, pp. 306f.

[102] *Offenbarung* C1b-C2a.

made") in order to shake the unacceptable Pauline doctrine that Esau had been damned even before his birth (Romans 9:1-23).[103]

4. His fascination with the typological/allegorical method served to protect Hoffman from the current contemporary interest in superstitions, astrology and alleged natural miracles. In this he differed from Luther (a man otherwise much more rational), who was intrigued by Lichtenberg's astrological fantasies and who interpreted stories of the birth of horrific monsters as sure signs of the imminence of the Last Judgment.[104]

According to Hoffman there would be no unnatural happenings in heaven or on earth until Christ's second coming. Astrologers and sorcerers could not predict the future; this was the role of God's witnesses alone, who were able to expound the texts of the past and the dreams of the present because of their prophetic gifts. God does not reveal himself in natural miracles, but in the signs of history.[105]

d)   The ages of history

For Hoffman post-lapsarian history is divided into three major periods.[106] The first was the age of the Old Testament, in which man lived under the yoke of an inadequately understood, literal Law and possessed only a "shadowy" righteousness before God. This age was the night of history.[107] With the New Testament came the dawn; Christ removed the effects of

---

[103] *Römerbrief* N2a-N4a.

[104] Cf. e.g. *WA* 10(1, 2): 98-99,103-108.

[105] *Daniel* IIIb, *Prophecy* C4a, *Weissagung* A2a.

[106] The most important sources indicating Hoffman's theology of history are *Weissagung auss heiliger göttlicher geschrifft* (1529), *Prophecey oder weissagung* (1530) (both written for Ulrich von Dornum), the Revelation commentary of 1530 dedicated to King Frederick I of Denmark and, finally, the commentary on Romans. The most important documents testifying to the changes in his views of the final stage of the apocalypse are *Underrichtung von der reiner forchte Gottes* (a tract written in prison in Strasbourg in 1533), the concluding comments of the commentary on Romans concerned with the invulnerability of the "apostolic witnesses" and the minutes recording his interrogations while he was in prison. Since these latter accounts are consistent with Hoffman's own writings and with his editon of the Jost visions, there is no reason to doubt their authenticity.

[107] *Römerbrief* V2b, C2a.

original sin by his sacrificial death and restored to man the freedom of his will.[108] He revealed a higher, spiritual Law which man can accept quite voluntarily. The full light of day has burst forth in the present age. Because of the power of the Holy Spirit God's Law is now planted in the hearts of believers so that man no longer needs guidance from outside.[109]

The three great stages of history, which correspond to the three persons of the trinity, are characterised by covenants. All covenants of the Old Testament point to the New Covenant. This has been corrupted by the Papacy but is now being restored with the restoration of believers' baptism.

God established a covenant with Adam and Eve immediately after the Fall. He made "coats of fur" for them, showing that in time the whole of humanity would be clothed with Christ the lamb. In the same way the covenant with Noah expressed in the rainbow points forward to Christ's appearance in the "spiritual clouds" (the "apostolic messengers") who will raise the standard of God's peace over the whole earth. Similarly the covenant with Abraham was a "figure of the New Covenant" because the circumcision of the foreskin prefigures the circumcision of the heart by Christ.[110]

All of man's justification is based on these covenants. It was through them that Adam, Noah, Abraham and the people of Israel (representing the whole of humanity) entered into a trusting relationship with Yahweh based on God's gift of grace and a corresponding commitment by man. God promised the Jews their land and a future Messiah; the Jews swore to keep the Law. Faith was the *beginning* of justification for the Jews, but *complete* justification could only come from trust in God's promises *and* from living according to the Law.[111] Justification by faith did not make justification by works superfluous, it rather made it possible.[112]

But justification for the Jews was still only a "shadow", because it consisted of external things: circumcision, entry into

---

[108] *Ibid*. H2a-b.
[109] *Offenbarung* Z5b.
[110] *Das ware trostliche und freudenreiche Evangelion* A1b–A3b.
[111] *Römerbrief* C2b.
[112] *Ibid*. D8b, P3a–P4b.

the land of Canaan and observance of dietary, purification and Sabbath rituals. When Christ offered a higher form of grace and of justification the Jews retained the outdated form of the Mosaic Law and rejected the proffered gift. God for his part then rejected them.[113] Hoffman compared what had happened to the Jews to what was happening in the Lutheran Reformation. The Lutherans, he said, had inverted the error of the Jews. The Jews, blinded by the Law of Moses, had rejected a more exalted form of justification in the form of faith in Christ's grace, whereas the learned men of the Reformation were ensnared by a misunderstanding of St. Paul. They derived from his writings the error that only faith can bring salvation, irrespective of the moral standard it calls for. The Jews foundered on Christ's grace, the Reformers foundered on his Law.[114] Hoffman's condemnation of Jewish legalism and of the alleged antinomianism of the reformers was based on his principle of federal theology.

Unlike Karlstadt and Rothmann, Hoffman was free of "Judaism." The ceremonial and penal laws of the Old Testament became invalid when Christ appeared.[115] Because it was necessary to show love for one's neighbour, there was to be a day of rest for servants, maids and cattle.[116]

Through Christ God's covenant has spread to all men. It has spread "to every race on earth and not a single man is excluded from it."[117] Christ has released all the children of Adam from their bondage and has enabled the heathen to share in the new creation.[118] Hoffman did not enter into speculation about whether Christ's sacrificial death had brought about a qualitative change in human nature by reducing original sin to a mere "infirmity" (instead of a fatal disease).[119] Christ's work of

---

[113] *Ibid.* R1b.

[114] *Ibid.* P2a, Y8a-b.

[115] *Ibid.* O5a, *TAE* II No. 594, p. 370, No. 617, p. 393.

[116] *Römerbrief* B8b.

[117] *Das ware trostliche und freudenreiche Evangelion* A3b.

[118] *Römerbrief* B8b.

[119] This was the view of Pilgram Marbeck who concluded that infants had no guilt, *TAE* I No. 302-303, p. 126. R. Armour (*Anabaptist Baptism* p. 98) says that Hoffman shared this opinion, though there is no basis for this. On the whole question cf. G. H. Williams "Popularized German Mysticism", pp. 294-295, 310.

redemption is concerned much more with liberating mankind from the dominion of Satan and with restoring man's free will by enlightening man's understanding by the Word.[120]

There have been "three proclamations of the divine Word" since Christ's resurrection: the mission to the Jews and Gentiles in the age of the Apostles, the Hussite movement and finally the Reformation.[121] Hoffman understands the millennial kingdom as the early period of Church history when the spirit of Christ was still alive. This age was ushered in when Paul preached the Gospel to the Gentiles and this bound the devil for a thousand years (Rev. 20:2). When the papacy eventually triumphed, this golden age of the church came to an end.[122]

The papacy's gradual apostasy from the true faith of Christ began as early as the end of the first century A.D.[123] For Hoffman the church declined for the following reasons:

1. The claim of the Bishop of Rome to control doctrine led to the suppression of the laity and the destruction of the congregational structure of the primitive church.[124]

2. The alliance of the Pope and the Emperor under Constantine made the Popes into secular princes. Instead of fear of God it was fear of men which then took control of the church. It was when the "dragon" (i.e. the Emperor) gave "his power, his throne and his great authority" to the "beast from the sea" (i.e. the pope) that the papacy actually became the Antichrist.[125]

3. The substitution of the idolatrous sacrifice of the Mass for Christ's one true sacrifice.[126]

4. The introduction, despite the apostolic ordinance, of infant baptism under Pope Innocent I (401–417) and Pope Martin I (649–655) destroyed the voluntary character of the church.[127]

5. The introduction of mediators between God and man

---

[120] *Römerbrief* A2b, F2a.
[121] *Offenbarung* X5b.
[122] *Ibid.* X4b–X5a.
[123] *Römerbrief* O8b.
[124] *Offenbarung* I7a.
[125] *Ibid.* P7a–P8b.
[126] *Prophecey* C3b.
[127] *Ordinance* pp. 192-193, *TAE* II No. 444, p. 184.

(so-called "saints"). This went against God's clear commandment. "And you shall not go up by steps to my altar" (Ex.
20:26).[128] Hoffman's particular wrath was directed against the
veneration of St. Francis.

Because of all this Hoffman agreed with Luther that the
Roman Church and all of its institutions belonged to the realm
of Satan. The pope is the Antichrist predicted by Paul (2 Thess.
2:3-4). His exposure is a sign that Christ will soon return.[129]

But Christ's spirit never totally disappeared throughout this
dark age of history. The Russian Orthodox Church was able to
uphold the apostolic ordinance because of its schism from
Rome; it did not allow human glosses to be included in the
preaching of the Word of God, it allowed priests to marry and it
celebrated the Eucharist in the way Christ instituted it. Hoffman
had come to know the Russian Orthodox Church during his
time in Dorpat, and set such high store by it that he even
identified it with the famous church of Philadelphia in the Book
of Revelation.[130]

"The Beast of Rome" experienced its first severe wound at
the hands of Jan Hus "who wielded the sword of the Holy
Spirit against the Pope's kingdom for 39 years".[131] To protect
themselves from the sun of Christ the bishops called on the
secular princes and sheltered under their shields. "The dragon"
lent its power to "the beast from the abyss" and it did away with
Jan Hus ("the witness of God") at the Council of Constance. In
1415 it became apparent that "Western Christendom" was
essentially an unholy alliance of Pope and Emperor, established
to suppress the Gospel. "I think that Constance showed what it
was like. The Gospel was decried, God's witness was burnt and
Sigismund the dragon kissed the Pope's feet."[132]

Hus's call to repentance had no impact on the papal church. It
was the Bohemian Brethren (successors to the Hussites) who

---

[128] *Weissagung* B3a.
[129] *Offenbarung* E7b–E8a.
[130] *Ibid.* F8a.
[131] *Ibid.* K4b.
[132] *Ibid.* P7b–P8a.

first separated from Rome and rejected some false doctrines. But they did not realize "the depths of the devil" and they erred in compromising with the "Woman Jezebel." Hoffman identified the "Unitas Fratrum" with the church of Thyatira, which was pleasing to God although it still tolerated the false prophetess in its midst.[133]

But the Reformation led to the irreversible decline of the papacy. Luther had the honour of being the first to lead the people out of servitude. Yet the reformer of Wittenberg soon became a Judas to the movement of the Spirit which he had himself initiated.[134]

As Lutheranism fell from the truth it repeated the errors first established by the papacy:

1. The reformers (and all scholarly Lutheran or Zwinglian clergymen) claimed sole doctrinal authority and ignored their congregations.[135]

2. Like the Popes before them they called in the secular arm to enforce their doctrines. The use of force in matters of belief can never be justified, not even if it is used to defend pure truth. "We praise ourselves as Christians, but we despise, dishonour and destroy those who cannot come to true knowledge – this is certainly not the wisdom from above, that we are called to destroy instead to improve. Yet there are nowadays new Papists who depend on the fleshly arm, i.e. the secular authority. Where Scripture cannot help, flesh and force must do their bidding, and I myself put a greater blame on those who incite the tyrants than on the tyrants themselves." Hoffman (rightly) felt that the Protestant secular princes and Council members were more tolerant than their spiritual advisors (Tegetmeier, Amsdorf, Weidensee, Bugenhagen, Melanchthon, Bucer, Hedio etc.): "Even if poor Pilate (by which I mean the secular powers) is merciful and says, 'I cannot find any cause to kill this Christ' (i.e.

---

[133] *Ibid.* F4a.
[134] *Ibid.* O2b.
[135] *Ibid.* R4a.

Plate 9: Caspar Hedio

Plate 10: Caspar Schwenckfeld von Ossig

the "heretics") it makes no difference. He must still be put to death."[136]

3. As in the Catholic Mass a piece of bread is idolized in the Lutheran Eucharist. The "eternal Word" is soiled by being used as physical food for believers and unbelievers alike. To demonstrate their mastery these false shepherds claim to their flocks that they "could invoke Christ down from heaven just as black magic could summon Satan into a crystal."[137]

4. Reformed state churches still retained infant baptism, "the first scandal of the Papacy." In rejecting Karlstadt's doctrine of the Eucharist the reformers were consciously setting themselves against the truth, and thus became guilty of the sin against the Holy Spirit for which there is no forgiveness.[138] As "worshippers of the creaturely" in the Eucharist, as "killers of the soul" in their passion to persecute and as "false teachers" despite their better knowledge, they cannot attain the kingdom of God.[139] The main reason for this degeneration of Lutheranism as Hoffman saw it was the spiritual pride of the reformers. If they had become aware of their spiritual poverty, they would not have called on the secular arm to enforce their doctrines, and they would have replaced religious narrow-mindedness with love for their fellow men.[140] Despite significantly reducing the power of the papacy, the Reformation had done nothing to root out the cancer within Christianity. The message to the church of Sardis applies to the Lutherans, "You have the name of being alive, and you are dead."[141]

But the dawn of the third, the "final day of the Spirit" is already breaking over the horizon. "Apostolic messengers" have begun to assemble Christ's flock which had wandered and strayed throughout the earth. The Word of God is being

---

[136] *Weissagung* D3b. *Offenbarung* A6a-A8a, O1b-O2A. For the present age as the high water-mark of evil in history cf. *Römerbrief* E8a, N5b-N6a.

[137] *Weissagung* B3b, *Offenbarung* K7b-K8a, Q3b.

[138] *Offenbarung* Q4a.

[139] *Ibid.* Z4a.

[140] *Weissagung* B1a.

[141] *Offenbarung* F5b.

proclaimed everywhere so that no one at the Last Judgment can claim to have been ignorant.[142] The messengers are not "tainted by women," i.e. they are free from the false doctrines of the "Roman whore". They have nothing to do with such false practices as fasting regulations, indulgences and pilgrimages which all aim at attaining human righteousness. They replace the "old whore song of Rome" with the "new and joyful song of Christ" who has made men righteous before God by his sacrificial death.[143] All of this sounds thoroughly Lutheran, but when we hear of the other functions of the "apostolic messengers" we see that incompatible elements are superimposed on the doctrines of the Reformation.

Hoffman's theology of the covenant demands that the offer of grace be followed by a corresponding commitment. This takes the form of an absolute fulfilment of the divine Law after enlightenment. The "apostolic messengers" are called upon to be spiritual "reapers"; they cut men from the earth with the "scythe of the Law".[144] Believers must crucify their flesh along with all its lusts until they have conquered the works of the old Adam and have attained the inner Sabbath in a state of "true *Gelassenheit*" and can sin no more.[145]

The final aim of the mission of the "apostolic messengers" is to lead men from a "literal" to a "clear" (i.e. self-evident) knowledge of God.

The Lutheran Reformation aimed at renewing the letter of the divine Word. The principle of *sola scriptura* had had the function of destroying the corrupt tradition of the papal church, but "when the literal function has served its purpose *clarity* will be revealed to the children of God."[146] The "clarity" emerges when Christ, the morning star, rises in men's hearts and day dawns within.[147] Only when the believing soul has come to be like Christ can His nature be fully understood. "Anyone who has this

---

[142] *Ibid.* A3a, M5a-b.
[143] *Ibid.* R1b.
[144] *Ibid,* R5b-R6a.
[145] *Ibid.* R5a, R2b (for the "sinlessness" of the "apostolic messengers").
[146] *Ibid.* V6a.
[147] *Ibid.* Z5b.

tree of life within his heart will come to know Christ (outside of himself) by this same Christ (within him)."[148]

But the learned scribes will persecute this higher form of faith. Christendom is divided into three parts: the Catholics still imprisoned in the errors of the papacy, the Lutherans and Zwinglians gathered around "the letter of the Word" and the true Christians assembled round "the office of clarity", whose bearers are directly enlightened by God.[149]

As in the commentary on Daniel, those who receive the highest revelation of the spirit are "primarily the poor, those of a shattered and humble disposition."[150] God will remove the vain-glorious from their thrones and exalt the humble to be kings and priests; the first will be last.[151] Yet in exceptional cases even a prince or a rich man can come to an awareness of his "spiritual poverty" and then he, too, will belong to the people of God.[152]

According to Paul's prophecy in Romans 11:25-32 the Jews will play a special role during the last days. By means of the "apostolic messengers" Christ will become their Messiah, but not in the "fleshly" way, as the Jews imagine. He will not be an earthly king who restores the kingdom of Israel in Palestine, but he will be their spiritual leader. The Jews will then be the "summit of the whole of Mount Zion." They will exercise spiritual dominion over the earth whilst Christian tyrants remain blind and obdurate. Hoffman himself will be a servant of the persecuted Jews "day and night without ceasing." He hoped that they would soon be delivered from oppression and be enabled to live in security.[153] It is a fact that a few Jews in Alsace did join the Melchiorites.[154]

---

[148] *Ibid.* V7b, O6a.
[149] *Ibid.* S7a.
[150] *Ibid.* A3b.
[151] *Ibid.* J1b, *Römerbrief* G3b, O6b-O7a.
[152] *Offenbarung* A4b.
[153] *Römerbrief* R8b-S1b.
[154] Cf. N. Blesdijk (Blesdikius), *Historia Vitae, doctrinae ac rerum gestarum Davidis Georgii Haeresiarchae* Deventer 1642, pp. 73-74. Since Jews were only allowed to enter Strasbourg during the day for trade purposes, these must have been inhabitants of the surrounding villages.

A comparison of the commentary on Daniel of 1526 with Hoffman's apocalyptic writings of 1529-1530 shows that his eschatology had not essentially changed. He merely provided more detail on several points. He clearly expected King Frederick I of Denmark, in whom he had "inspired a great ardour for divine truth and justice", to be one of the two kings who would put up a staunch, but doomed, defence to protect the true Christians during the final stage of persecution. Hoffman now foresees two Councils, not one. At the first Council, in the middle of the seven years, the two witnesses, Elijah and Enoch, will be tried for their faith and eventually crucified.[155] This will bring to an end the age of the successful world mission of the "apostolic messengers." The well-known scenario of the second 3½-year-period will begin to run its course. During these last three and a half years there will be an attempt to destroy the "spiritual Temple" built up by the "apostolic messengers." This will take the form of a counter-attack by the powers of darkness: the Pope (the beast of the Apocalypse), the Emperor (the dragon) and the monks (the false prophets). There will be a second Council of this "infernal trinity" which will prepare plans to wipe out the true church.[156] A band of "kings and God's warriors" will then assemble to protect the "spiritual Jerusalem." But then the Turks will appear as the heathen peoples of Gog and Magog. Those princes who have allied themselves with Antichrist will be destroyed by the Turks and their best warriors will die in battle. "Thus God punishes foe by foe."[157] But believers, too, will experience nothing but "strangling and murder, crucifixion and suffering." The holy people will be scattered to the four winds of heaven. At the climax of the cataclysm "when everything is corrupt" the Last Day will dawn, "beginning with fire."[158] "Heaven and

---

[155] *Offenbarung* O1b-O2a.

[156] *Ibid.* A4a, X3a-X6b. Hoffman defines the "infernal trinity" with pope, Emperor and monks in *Prophecey* B2a and *Offenbarung* S7b. G. List's assertion (in *Chiliastische Utopie* p. 193) that the trinity was made up of Emperor, Lutherans and Turks cannot be supported by the primary documents.

[157] *Weissagung* B2a, *Offenbarung* X6a.

[158] *Prophecey* A4a, *Offenbarung* X6a-b.

earth will be reduced by fire,"[159] i.e. "this transitory world will be destroyed and make way for an eternal world."[160] Christ's reign of peace will eventually be established by a sudden intervention of God.

Hoffman's commentary on Revelation in no sense urged his followers to prepare for another uprising. They should be involved in mission-work and should live holy lives in readiness for a time of trial which might come at any moment. The prospect of the imminent Last Judgment should give them strength to withstand persecution. Human history will end in a frightful débâcle which will necessitate God's direct intervention.

Hoffman used allegorical exegesis in an attempt to reinterpret the meaning of those violent passages in the Book of Revelation which he feared might be used to justify another Peasants' War.

In the Book of Revelation the "two witnesses" have demonic powers; fire issues from their mouths so that their enemies are consumed, they are able to close the sky to prevent rain and they can change water into blood (Rev. 11:5-6). Hoffman interprets the fire as the "fire of the Spirit" which destroys the Law of the devil; the "closing of the heaven" refers to the prohibition of evangelical preaching and the changing of water into blood indicates a change from human folly to divine wisdom.[161] The "power over the nations . . . . with a rod of iron" (Rev. 2:26-27) becomes the "austere feeding with the word of God"[162] He interprets the order given to the vultures – "Come, gather for the great supper of God, to eat the flesh of kings and of captains" (Rev. 19:17-18) – as a command to secular rulers to take over ecclesiastical principalities and to appropriate church property.[163] According to Revelation 19:19-20 the beast (the Pope) and the "false prophet" (the assembly of monks) will be cast alive into the burning lake. According to Hoffman this cannot refer to a physical destruction; it simply means that the

---

[159] *Offenbarung* C1b.
[160] *Prophecey* A4b.
[161] *Offenbarung* N8a.
[162] *Ibid.* X1b.
[163] *Ibid.* X2b.

Pope will be killed by the sword of the spirit and will lose his powers.[164] Hoffman points out that this passage does not contain any reference to a punishment for the dragon (the Emperor). In this way Hoffman hoped to make his commentary acceptable to his former royal patron.

What, then, were the essential elements in Hoffman's apocalyptic writings in his middle period (1529-1530)?

His thinking is grounded on a dualistic world view which sees the spiritual set up in opposition to the "worldly". The world in itself is a "wild desert," a kingdom of greed and violence where nothing good is to be found.[165] Although there have been three outpourings of the Spirit in the course of history, the world has always managed to thwart the Spirit by blind legalism or sacramentalism. It has cheated the laity by means of priestly hierarchies and it has crucified God's true witnesses. Yesterday's true prophets (the Jews, the primitive Catholic church, Luther) become tomorrow's false prophets. The oppressed turn into oppressors.

But there is also a higher development of the Spirit, leading from ceremonialism and sacramentalism through blind faith in the letter to self-evident clarity. History repeats on a larger scale the different stages of the individual believer's spiritual growth, or, vice-versa, it can be said that the inner journey of the soul is the development of humanity in miniature.

But the spirit on its own is incapable of overcoming the world. God himself must intervene to help the saints to victory. Because of this contradiction the world is two things at one and the same time; the Golgotha of the spirit and the site of its resurrection.[166]

---

[164] *Ibid.* X3b.

[165] *Ibid.* P2a.

[166] Sebastian Franck had a similar, though more developed, view of the relationship between the "spirit" and the "world", cf. R. Stadelmann, *Vom Geist des ausgehenden Mittelalters* Halle 1929, pp. 148,249-250, G. Zaepernick, "Welt und Mensch bei Sebastian Franck" in A. Lindt and K. Deppermann (ed.), *Pietismus und Neuzeit* Vol. 1. 1974, pp. 9-24.

e) The transformation of Hoffman's apocalyptic thinking under the impact of Denck and Lienhard Jost

The ideas developed in the commentary on Revelation did not remain Hoffman's last words on eschatology. Under the influence of the writings of Hans Denck and the prophecies of Lienhard Jost some of his ideas changed or became more specific and he eventually became, though unwittingly, a spiritual forbear of the Anabaptist kingdom of Münster.

The change in the heralding of the "apostolic messengers" was relatively harmless. They were to preach not the doctrine of predestination (which Hoffman himself still taught in the commentary on Revelation),[167] but the doctrine of the universality of divine grace. The proclamation of this doctrine throughout the earth was to be their main function, for so long as the dogma of double election was being preached by "Satan's hellish messengers (the Lutherans), there will be no peace with God in the heart, but hell, unbelief, death, strife and an evil conscience will still remain; we will have no idea of our standing before God."[168]

Rather more serious was the conviction Hoffman derived from the enthusiastic veneration accorded to him by the "Strasbourg Prophets". He now felt that "in him they had the true Elijah who is to come before the Last Day"[169] "Enoch" was either Cornelis Poldermann of Middelburg or Caspar Schwenckfeld.[170]

But the most portentous change was Hoffman's acceptance of revolutionary ideas and the concept of a theocratic interregnum which would prepare the way for the second coming of Christ.

Where Hoffman had unspecifically identified the "spiritual

---

[167] *Offenbarung* A6a.

[168] *Das ware trostliche und freudenreiche Evangelion* 1531, B2a.

[169] *TAE* II No. 607, p. 386.

[170] O. Philips, *A Confession* in G. H. Williams and A. M. Mergal (Ed.), *Spiritual and Anabaptist Writers* p. 212. The identification of the two witnesses (Rev. 11:3–12) is based on Malachi 4:5, Ecclesiasticus 44:16, 48:12. The Book of the Secrets of Enoch 3:1 (in R. H. Charles (ed.), *The Apocrypha and Pseudoepigrapha of the Old Testament* Oxford 1913. Vol. 2. p. 432.)

Jerusalem" with "the present Christian community" in his commentary on Revelation,[171] he said after 1530 that it was the actual city of Strasbourg. He repeatedly told the City Council "that he knew this to be the town which God has chosen to glorify him out of all of the towns on earth. And also that the leaders of this town are called upon to establish His total truth, which is the standard of justice as proclaimed by him, the prophet".[172] The final stage of the Messianic holocaust is now to be a time not of suffering but of triumph for the saints. The chosen city will fight a successful defensive battle against the powers of darkness, taking its orders from the saints. Hoffman repeatedly urged Strasbourg's military leaders to build up a store of weapons and provisions so that they could be successful when the "dragon" (the Emperor) besieged them. The Anabaptists would not themselves take up the sword in this battle, but they would support the fighters. Hoffman himself would pray and his followers would dig trenches and do guard duty. In this battle Strasbourg would set a glorious example to all Imperial Cities, who would undergo the same hardships as would the "spiritual Jerusalem."[173]

After their victory over the Emperor the "apostolic messengers" would pour out from the city and proclaim the true Gospel in every corner of the earth. Unlike the martyrs of former times they would be invulnerable. "God will then wake up 144,000 servants, these are all that are called to be apostles. Rev. 14 says they are the summit of Mount Zion and of the spiritual men. Let us see whether they can be slaughtered! But I know for sure: it cannot happen".[174]

The most important precondition for the establishment of the reign of peace on earth is the downfall of the priests. "According to Holy Scriptures there will be uproars and rebellions all over the earth; these have already begun. *All the priests must perish.* The true Jerusalem cannot arise or be built until *Babylon with all*

---

[171] *Offenbarung* P1a,07a-b, X6a-b.
[172] *TAE* II No. 617, p. 393 No. 444, p. 185-186.
[173] *TAE* II No. 654, pp. 444-445.
[174] *Römerbrief* Z1a.

its hordes and followers has been deposed and destroyed".[175] The authorities will have to follow Old Testament precedent and put to death all "the impudent prophets who know that they are telling lies."[176]

In the summer of 1533 Hoffman finally spoke of the establishment of an earthly theocracy which would fill the time between the destruction of Babylon and the return of Christ. The appearance of this kingdom is imminent, for the sixth trumpet (which signals the time of tribulation for the people of God) has already sounded and the time of the seventh trumpet (which introduces the descent of God's wrath on the godless) has arrived. The meanings given to the sixth and seventh trumpets are here quite the reverse of those given them in the commentary on Daniel.[177]

"At the seventh trumpet the angel of wrath will slay all of the firstborn of Egypt. The kingdoms of Babylon and Sodom will be brought low along with all their pomp. Then joyful alleluias will be sung. Samson and Jonah will return in the spirit. Joseph and Solomon will rule with God's power over the whole earth . . . then at the midnight hour (when the darkness is forced to withdraw) the Bridegroom will come and take up those that are His."[178] "For eternal vengeance is at the door. It is such a vengeance that it will last from the rising of the sun until its setting. There will be eternal torment and suffering for those who have gone against the Lord's will on purpose and for those who have knowingly spilt innocent blood and for those who have unjustly rejected and hindered God's truth."[179]

The most important revolutionary ideas which anticipate the Anabaptist kingdom of Münster make their appearance here:

1. The idea that the godless will be rooted out *before* the Last Judgment.
2. The idea of an earthly dominion of saints, taking the form of

---

[175] *TAE* II No. 368, p. 18.
[176] *TAE* II No. 617, p. 393.
[177] *Daniel* g1b-g2a.
[178] *Von der reiner forchte Gottes*, 1533 A2a-b.
[179] *Ibid.* A7b.

an alliance between prophets (Jonah, Samson) and secular kings
(Joseph, Solomon).

3. The expectation that Christ would only return after the
second Solomon had appeared, who would prefigure Christos
Pantocrator and prepare the earth to receive the Son of God.

What brought about this change in Hoffman's apocalyptic
thinking? Did his acceptance of Lienhard Jost's visions upset his
inner development?

This change was certainly related to Hoffman's burning desire
for vengeance. Almost all of his writings contain visions of the
downfall of tyrants. He frequently reminds his readers that God
is just as well as merciful, and that the blood of those who shed
blood must also be shed. "For with the judgment you
pronounce you will be judged" (Matt. 7:2) was one of his
favourite quotations.[180] Obbe Philips said that he had never in
his whole life seen anyone who uttered more attacks, slanders,
curses and damnations than did Melchior Hoffman; "all who did
not say yes and amen were devilish and satanic spirits, godless
heretics and people damned to eternity. This (was done) in such
a frightful way that the hair on a man's head would stand on
end."[181] According to Hoffman those gentle prophets like Hans
Denck who could not imagine an angry God were speaking
"only with the voice of reason" and not with the "spirit of the
Most High."[182]

On the other hand Hoffman always tried to suppress this
desire for vengeance. As late as 1532 he warned his followers not
to "attack the tyrants of the two great packs (the Lutherans and
Zwinglians) lest they suffer God's stern wrath, for the punish-
ment of falsehood belongs solely to the sword of the Holy
Spirit."[183] Anabaptists should follow the example of the gentle
Jacob, who offered nothing but friendship to his hostile brother
Esau.[184]

---

[180] *Offenbarung* Q2b, *Weissagung* B1b.
[181] O. Philips, *A Confession* in G. H. Williams and A. M. Mergal
(ed.), *Spiritual and Anabaptist Writers* p. 209.
[182] *Römerbrief* C5a-b.
[183] *Esau unde Jacob* A2b-A3a.
[184] *Römerbrief* T6b-T7a.

During the years of the siege of Vienna Hoffman expected the Turks to punish religious and secular tyrants.[185] When this did not come about he turned to the idea of a "revolution from above." The "pious authorities" of the Free Imperial Cities would break the spine of the powers of Antichrist in a defensive military action. Hoffman never totally ruled out the use of force in matters of faith, yet in the commentaries on Daniel and Revelation his understanding of the role of the two devout kings was such that he felt that in the end they would only be able to defend the true church for a short while and would then be defeated.

This conflict in Hoffman's own thinking was to lead to the eventual break-up of the Melchiorite movement. Whereas the Strasbourg Melchiorites remained pacifists and Hoffman himself became a defenceless prisoner, many of his followers in the Netherlands and Westphalia took up "God's sword" and Jan Matthijs fell before the gates of Münster as one of "God's warriors".

The idea of an earthly theocracy can also be found in embryonic form in the commentary on Revelation, particularly in the passages where Hoffman allegorized the ideas of "the return of Christ" and the "new heaven and the new earth." Hoffman interpreted the verse "Behold, he is coming in the clouds, and every eye will see him" (Rev. 1:7) to mean both Christ's epiphany in the clouds of the sky and also the "appearance of Christ's spirit" in the "spiritual clouds", viz. the "apostolic messengers."[186] The idea of a new heaven can mean either a totally transformed cosmos brought about by the burning up of the world, or "the chosen band of believers."[187] He sees the verse "the sea is no more" as a "metaphor" for the removal of evil men.[188] On the other hand the general course of history is painted so gloomily in the commentary on Revelation that we cannot assert that Hoffman understood the "Last Judgment" to mean a world revolution or that he interpreted the

---

[185] *Weissagung* B2a, *Prophecey* (Title page), *Offenbarung* X6a.
[186] *Offenbarung* C1b-C2b.
[187] *Prophecey* A4a, *Offenbarung* X8a.
[188] *Offenbarung* X8b.

"kingdom of God" to mean simply an ideal human society of freedom and equality.[189] There was a tendency in this direction, but there was also another opposed to it which expected salvation to be brought by a direct intervention of God, since all human strivings could be expected to fail.

The inclusion of Denck's voluntarism helped to clarify Hoffman's apocalyptic ideas. No longer did it seem to him that human attempts to prepare man for God's reign on earth were doomed to failure. The apocalypse no longer had the character of a strictly predetermined tragedy which could only turn out for the best by the intervention of a *Deus ex machina*.

The main motivation which led Hoffman to proclaim the demise of the godless and a future earthly theocracy was his dream of man in the state of perfection, which he had cherished from the very beginning. Both the tradition of the Hussites and his own experience had taught him that no perfect community could be established without a violent overthrow of the forces of Antichrist. But both the New Testament and his own misgivings also told him that no Christian could with impunity take up the sword, if he had not received an official call to do so. Thus Hoffman came to the same solution as had the Cathari; although *"those who were perfect"* should not be tainted by blood and were thus unable to take up the sword, the "believers" (in this case the devout magistrates of the Free Imperial Cities) could take orders from them to seize the sword of vengeance and annihilate the godless.[190]

---

[189] *pace* F. O. zur Linden, *Melchior Hofmann* p. 201. S. Cramer in *BRN* V:130 and P. Kawerau, *Melchior Hoffman als religiöser Denker* p. 76. cf. e.g. *Prophecey* A4a, where he clearly says that the Last Judgment "will break in when all things are decayed, and after the Temple and the city of Jerusalem have been destroyed by false doctrine, pain and suffering."

[190] A. Borst, *Die Katharer* 1953, p. 187. I agree with James Stayer (*Anabaptists and the Sword* 1973, p. 223) that Hoffman's views led to divergent attitudes, but unlike him I feel that his apocalyptic ideas underwent a profound change under the impact of the Josts, and that he eventually believed in a military theocracy on earth. It is also questionable to say that Obbe Philips and Menno Simons represent the true line of descent from Hoffman whilst Matthijs and Rothmann

5. Hoffman's Doctrines Concerning Secular Authority and Church Ordinance; His Controversy with the Reublin-Marbeck Circle.

a)   The doctrine of the "sword"

The political implications of his apocalyptic theology of history as well as the remnants of his Lutheran past brought Hoffman into sharp conflict with the Reublin-Marbeck circle in Strasbourg, which adhered to the stipulations of the Schleitheim Confession.

Hoffman felt that the followers of Reublin and Marbeck must be blind since they denied that any holder of office could be a Christian. To him this was a threat to the whole divine ordinance of the world.[191] As long as the authorities carry out their commission to protect the good and punish the evil they can enjoy peace with God. Such sins of weakness and ignorance that a Christian ruler will commit in the course of his work cannot threaten his salvation, for Christ atoned for these sins on the cross.[192] Even the executioner is a servant of God if he is using the axe to enforce justice.[193]

Hoffman's Lutheran background also comes to the fore when he speaks of the obligation of the subjects to obey and when he discusses the limits of secular authority.

Although at the present time the use of the sword is often applied wrongly, so that the good live in fear of their rulers whilst the evil enjoy their protection, nevertheless a Christian must always obey even a tyrannical power in all secular matters. The only time when a Christian need not obey is when a prince

---

[191] *Römerbrief* V1a. On this whole question cf J. M. Stayer, "Melchior Hoffman and the Sword" in *MQR* 45(1971) pp. 265-277.

[192] *Römerbrief* T8b.

[193] *Ibid.* O2a.

---

note 190 continued

constituted an illegitimate development. Hoffman's idea of the "revolution from above" is not found in either tradition. The sources refute G. List's assertion (*Chiliastische Utopie* pp. 194-195) that Hoffman had no influence on the apocalypticism of Münster and that he did not believe in a "utopian interregnum".

attempts to impose an erroneous faith on his subjects or when he orders them to disobey an explicit commandment of God.[194] For Hoffman the secular sword has no place in the realm of faith, at least under normal circumstances. The only force that can be used on "Mount Zion" is the "Sword of the Spirit" - the power of teaching and of excommunication.[195] In the New Covenant false prophets, so long as they are not deliberate liars, never need to be stoned.[196] These ideas are obviously based on Luther's theoretical division of spiritual and secular authority.

Yet as soon as Hoffman's doctrine of authority comes within the range of his apocalypticism, God's two modes of governance become confused. This may either mean that the two "devout kings" undertake to protect the persecuted church, or that the Free Imperial Cities will take up the sword in order to enforce divine justice.

This apparent contradiction in Hoffman's thinking is easily solved. In normal circumstances, that is, before the "seventh trumpet" ushered in the apocalyptic crisis, he urged for tolerance in matters of faith in order to create an environment which would favour the spread of Anabaptism. It was not until the apocalypse itself that the sword of the authorities would be used to protect or establish the true faith. His basic objection was not to the use of force in spiritual matters but to the use of the sword in favour of false doctrine. Such a dialectic meant that the Anabaptists' interests (as he understood them) would always be protected.

b) The doctrine of the church

Within the context of the charismatic atmosphere in Strasbourg Hoffman developed the theory of a hierarchical structure of the congregation quite different from the democratic congregationalism of the Anabaptists of southern Germany. He rejected their levelling tendency, saying he considered it to be "the greatest scandal that these clods will not recognize distinctions but want to make everybody apostles."[197] Hoffman replaced their concept with a hierarchy of four groups:

---

[194] *Ibid.* T7b–T8a.
[195] *Ibid.* T1b.
[196] *Ibid.* V7a, *TAE* II No. 594, p. 370, No. 617, p. 393.
[197] *Römerbrief* S7b–T1a.

1. The "throng of apostolic messengers", or "God's Temple", who like the resurrected Christ are fully justified and unable to sin. They have no possessions but travel around the land preaching the Gospel as poor messengers.[198] This concept of the "apostolic messengers" was derived from the Hussite tradition.

2. The band of the "firstborn" who function as "prophets". Their place is in the "Temple porch" and they are subject to the apostles in the way that the tribe of Levi is subject to the tribe of Aaron.

3. "The whole troop of pastors" who lead the congregations and at times represent the "common people". Their relationship to their congregations is that of man and wife.

4. The simple members of the congregation. As a rule these people have no direct contact with the "apostolic messengers". Generally, the apostles give orders only to the pastors.

The subjection of the prophets to control by the "apostolic messengers" is the critical point in this order. Hoffman drew a distinction between those prophets who received their visions in broad daylight and in full consciousness and those to whom the secrets of the future were revealed in dreams. Since dreams could also originate from the devil, prophets had to be subjected to some spiritual authority. Prophets are often not in a position to explain their own visions and dreams or to test them by the norm of the Word of God. Neither were the simple members of the congregation in a position to do this. "It is not up to anybody to discern spirits, it is a particular role given to some by God and His Holy Spirit."[199] Only the "apostolic messengers" are able to tell whether the hidden meanings of the voices and visions conform to the spirit of Christ.[200] The congregations are thus totally dependent on the apostles. If the apostle is wrong he will lead astray everyone who depends upon him.[201]

Hoffman's new theory of the hierarchy left no place of authority for the congregation. They were now dependent on

---

[198] *TAE* II No. 368, p. 19.
[199] *Prophetische Gesicht und Offenbarung* C7a.
[200] *Römerbrief* T1a, A4b-A5b.
[201] *Ibid.* R5a.

"apostolic messengers" instead of on priests and scholars. The role of the leader of each congregation gave him almost royal powers, for he was able to enforce excommunication.[202] Every member of the congregation certainly retained the right to express his own opinion within the assembly, but it was now left to the "apostolic messengers" rather than the to the majority of the congregation to decide which doctrine was true.[203] This hierarchical view, whereby it was God alone and not the will of the majority who ordained individuals to perform particular functions in the light of their natural gifts, was underlined by Hoffman's modified doctrine of predestination.[204]

This ecclesiology determined Melchiorite practice. Hoffman himself and his "apostolic messengers" co-opted new leaders of the movement. Such leaders were considered to be sent by God and they were correspondingly authoritarian and charismatic in their demeanour.[205]

Hoffman's hierarchical views now contradicted his earlier democratic arguments in Livonia, where he had pressed for the rights of the congregations to elect their own pastors, but they were nevertheless a consequence of his personal experience and activity. He had begun his preaching career in Livonia as a divinely appointed lay-missionary with no formal authorization, and his call for electoral rights for the congregations was aimed first and foremost at discrediting the official clergy who had been appointed by the magistrates. But even then his belief in inspired prophecy could hardly be reconciled with a strict form of congregational democracy. Such a practice was absolutely unthinkable in the environment of the "Strasbourg Prophets." The excitable visionaries of Strasbourg came to regard Hoffman as the new Elijah who was able to interpret their mysterious visions for them. They submitted themselves to his authority on a personal level but also claimed a general authority over every Melchiorite community. The result of this process was that

[202] *Ibid.* T2b.
[203] *Prophecey oder weissagung* 1530, C1a, *Prophetische Gesicht und Offenbarung* C7a–b.
[204] *Römerbrief* N1b.
[205] Cf. O. Philips' *Confession* (above in n. 170).

Hoffman saw a distinction between "apostolic messengers," prophets and congregational leaders.

No lasting community could be established on these principles. The movement was dependent on the continuing agreement of all the self-appointed and co-opted "apostolic messengers". As soon as they disagreed with each other the community would be forced to split up since there was no means whereby the conflict could be settled.

Because of these doctrines, Hoffman's relationship with the Reublin-Marbeck circle developed into open enmity. The upshot was that Hoffman and Hans Frisch (the deacon in charge of the poor in Reublin's assembly) betrayed the names of their opposing Anabaptist group to the secular authorities.[206]

---

[206] *TAE* II No. 368, pp. 19-20, No. 533, p. 299.

CHAPTER SEVEN

The Climax and Turning-Point of the Anabaptist Movement in Strasbourg:

Apocalyptic Excitement around 1530, the Synod of 1533 and the End of the City Council's Policy of Tolerance.

1. The Causes of the Intensification of Apocalypticism.

The major catalysts which brought about the growth of Hoffmanite apocalypticism within the population of Strasbourg were the dreadful famines of the years between 1528 and 1534 and the intensified persecution of Anabaptists throughout the Empire after 1528.

An imperial mandate of 4th January, 1528 imposed the death sentence on all Anabaptists for "rebellion".[1] The Second Diet of Speyer in 1529 accepted this decree and ordered the execution of every adult Anabaptist even without prior trial before an ecclesiastical court.[2] Ferdinand I of Austria, the Dutch Court, the Swabian League, Elector Ludwig V of the Palatinate, Margrave Philipp of Baden and the Free Imperial City of Augsburg all implemented this law.[3] This led to a staggering rise in the number of executions; whereas in 1527 "only" 56 Anabaptists gave up their lives for their religious beliefs in Central and Southern Germany, that figure must have risen to

---

[1] P. Wappler, *Die Täuferbewegung in Thüringen (1526-1584)* Jena 1913, pp. 268-269.

[2] *Deutsche Reichstagsakten, Jüngere Reihe (Karl V.)* Vol. 7,2. 2.A. 1962, No. 153, pp. 1325-1327.

[3] M. Krebs (ed.), *Baden und Pfalz. Quellen zur Geschichte der Täufer* Vol. 4. 1951 Nos. 1, 134, 138, 209. But the Palatine judges refused to enforce the policy imposed on them from above. – cf. also F. Roth, *Augsburgs Reformationsgeschichte* Vol. 1. 1881, p. 226.

200 for the same area in 1528. 152 Anabaptists were condemned to death in 1529 and another 80 in 1530. 80% of the Anabaptists who were killed between 1525 and 1618 died within the seven years from 1527 and 1533; 41% perished in the years 1528- 1529 alone.[4]

Strasbourg at this period served as the most popular haven for refugees. Strasbourg granted citizens' rights to 260 people in 1528. This was the second highest figure in the 16th century and represented about three times the number in an average year.[5]

The Strasbourg Council unwittingly fuelled the apocalyptic frenzy amongst the Anabaptist refugees by depriving them of all their moderate leaders. In March, 1529 Wilhelm Reublin was banished from the city (for life) after a short period of imprisonment.[6] Jakob Kautz followed him in November, 1529.[7] In 1532 the same fate befell the most influential Anabaptist leader in Strasbourg, Pilgram Marbeck, after his long controversy with Bucer.[8] His place as leader of the Marbeck Circle was taken by Leopold Scharnschlager.[9]

With Marbeck's banishment the Strasbourg Anabaptists lost their last monumental figure. He was probably the only person who could successfully have opposed Hoffman's apocalyptic

---

[4] C. P. Clasen, *Anabaptism. A Social History. 1525-1618*. Ithaca and London 1972, p. 371 and "Executions of Anabaptists 1527-1618" in *MQR* 47 (1973) pp. 115-152 (esp. p. 119).

[5] C. Wittmer and J. C. Meyer, *Le premier livre de bourgeoisie de la Ville de Strasbourg*. 1954 Vol. 1. p. XLVII Vol. 2. p. 774f.

[6] *TAE* I No. 170, p. 200.

[7] *TAE* I No. 196, p. 250.

[8] For this controversy cf. *TAE* I No. 277, pp. 351-354, Nos. 302-303, pp. 416-528. For Marbeck's expulsion, *TAE* I No. 287, pp. 359-360 and No. 360, p. 362. cf. also W. Klassen, "Pilgram Marbeck's two books of 1531" in *MQR* 33 (1959) p. 18-31. The circle of personal friends around Marbeck was not identical with any existing Anabaptist group. Marbeck's followers were closest to Wilhelm Reublin's Anabaptist community, but Marbeck and the "Swiss Brethren" later disagreed over Marbeck's retention of the Lutheran doctrine of justification and the rigorous legalism of the Brethren. cf. H. Fast, "Pilgram Marbeck und das oberdeutsche Täufertum" in *ARG* 47(1956) p. 225 and J. M. Stayer, "Die Schweizer Brüder" in *MGB* NF 29(1977) pp. 21-22.

[9] M. Krebs (ed.), *Baden und Pfalz* p. 424.

fantasies. Scharnschlager certainly knew the points on which to oppose Hoffman, but he lacked the personal charisma needed to put a stop to the missionary success of the eloquent furrier.[10]

The period of the most intense persecution of the Anabaptists coincided with a series of successive crop failures throughout the whole of Central and Western Europe from 1528 to 1534.[11] Since Strasbourg had made adequate provision for times of need the number of refugees flooding into Strasbourg rose even more. Between 1527 and 1533 wheat and rye prices throughout the Empire (including Northern Italy) and France soared to three times their average in a normal year.[12] Though there were reasonably good harvests in Alsace between 1529 and 1535, external demand pushed the prices up even here. Wheat doubled and rye almost trebled in price in Strasbourg between 1527 and 1531.[13] Contemporaries attributed the rises to human malice, and in fact speculators from elsewhere often appeared in villages and bought corn that had not yet been harvested, keeping it back until well after the harvest, so aggravating the crisis, and only selling it (at a great profit) at the worst point in the famine. In 1531 and 1533 the Bishop of Strasbourg persuaded the nobles and landlords of Alsace to unite to outlaw pre-emption and to fix an upper limit for the price of corn. Those who disobeyed these crisis measures were to be fined.[14] But although basic food prices doubled, there was no increase in wages in Strasbourg. The accounts of the Cathedral building-workers indicate that there were only slight fluctuations in the weekly wages of stonemasons and unskilled labourers between 1513 and 1539.[15]

---

[10] *TAE* II No. 368, pp. 19–20.

[11] Cf. W. Abel, *Massenarmut und Hungerkrisen im vorindustriellen Europa* 1974, pp. 47–54.

[12] Cf. M. J. Elsas, *Umriss einer Geschichte der Preise und Löhne in Deutschland vom ausgehenden Mittelalter bis zum Beginn des 19. Jahrhunderts.* Vol. 1. Leiden 1936, pp. 594 and 634–635.

[13] A. Hanauer. *Etudes économiques sur l'Alsace ancienne et moderne.* Vol. 2: *Denrées et salaires* Strasbourg 1878, p. 94.

[14] Cf. W. Abel, *Massenarmut* p. 51.

[15] The archives show that a mason's weekly wages varied from 9s. 5d. to 8s. 4d. between 1513 and 1539. Porters and unskilled labourers were always paid either 5s. or 4s.

Yet the inhabitants of Strasbourg were protected from the worst effects of the famine. In 1529 the city granaries contained about 60,000 quarts (= 4,000 tons) of corn. In 1529, 1530 and 1531 the Council sold corn and meal to the poorest inhabitants at well under the market price. On 1st May, 1531 alone 380 hundred-weights of corn were distributed to the needy: there was so much jostling in the crowd that one girl died in the crush.[16]

Despite the increasing famine in the city the Council nevertheless took steps to lighten the load of the refugees who were seeking help. In November, 1528 they removed the stipulations which had governed the control of alms-distribution since 1523. They had previously said that only long-established residents were eligible for support, not newcomers or beggars from outside the town. "But since God has been merciful to us in giving us more food than others", all foreign refugees were to be supported by public funds, "be they young or old, healthy or sick," all except the "young, healthy and strong Walloons (= Frenchmen) who are mainly a wicked, wild and proud people."[17]

Since the stipulations of 1523 had forbidden private begging in Strasbourg under pain of banishment, all able-bodied refugees were offered "food and lodgings" in return for working on the defences along the town wall. Women, children, the elderly and infirm were taken to the Franciscan priory where they were looked after free of charge. In the winter of 1529-1530 there were 1,600 people, the following winter as many as 2,500, who were accommodated here for a full three months.[18] The services rendered at the paupers' hostel were equally remarkable. Here beggars were usually lodged and cared for for a single night and then given a travelling allowance. 18,000 people passed through it between June, 1529 and June, 1530; 23,548 (*sic*) between June, 1530 and June, 1531 and 8,879 between June, 1531 and June, 1532.[19] Compared to a normal average of 120, 400 patients were

[16] L. Schneegans, *Strassburgische Geschichten, Sagen, Denkmäler* Strasbourg 1855, pp. 135-136.

[17] O. Winckelmann, *Das Fürsorgewesen der Stadt Strassburg* Vol. 2. 1922, No. 85, p. 125, No. 43, p. 97.

[18] *Ibid.* Vol. 2. No. 87, pp 127-128, No. 118, p. 168.

[19] *Ibid.* Vol. 2. p. 168, Vol. 1, p. 150.

cared for in 1531 in the city hospitals and hospice for victims of smallpox; of these 400, 250 were suffering from syphilis.[20]

When the Strasbourg granaries were almost empty and the Council felt obliged to raise the property tax in order to be able to fulfil its social commitments,[21] strong protests were lodged against the extent of public support for the refugees. The city treasury was criticised "because its coffers seem to be bottomless . . . It is benefices, churches and priories that are being consumed . . . What we are caring for are simply well-fed clods and whores. It is cursing, swearing, scoffing, drinking, lying, deception, lasciviousness and fornication that are gaining the victory."[22]

Even if we regard much of this as the usual stereotyped view of foreigners, the refugees clearly did increase the city's moral problems. In August, 1529 the Council increased the penalties for blasphemy, cursing, gambling, drunkenness, adultery and whore-mongering. Fathers or husbands who sold the services of their wives or daughters faced the death penalty, and in March, 1533 a hitherto unknown paragraph in the legal code was implemented which penalised all public assemblies aimed at encouraging fornication.

The feelings of resentment about the support given the refugees was exacerbated because Lucas Hackfurt, the controller of the alms-fund and Alexander Berner, the deacon for the poor (and Hackfurt's immediate subordinate),were in the habit of giving aid to foreign Anabaptists before other needy people. Hackfurt had dissociated himself from the offical evangelical movement in 1525 and he expressed public sympathy for the Anabaptists until July, 1531.[23] Alexander Berner was a disciple of Schwenckfeld's and was forced to leave Strasbourg in 1535.[24] In effect, the distributers of the municipal funds had worked hand-in-glove with the welfare-workers of the Anabaptist

---

[20] *Ibid.* Vol. 1. p. 109, Vol. 2. pp. 150.

[21] L. Schneegans, *Strassburgische Geschichten* p. 136.

[22] O. Winckelmann, *op. cit.* Vol. 2. No. 113, pp. 160, 162.

[23] *TAE* I No. 130, p. 155, No. 252, p. 334.

[24] *TAE* I No. 257, p. 338, O. Winckelmann, *op. cit.*, Vol. 2, No. 660, p. 449.

community in looking after the needy foreign Anabaptists.[25]

In view of the city's seriously dwindling resources and the growing hostility towards the refugees the Council decided in March, 1533 to change its social policy. Articles 26 and 32 of the alms-distribution stipulations of 1523, which had been suspended in November, 1529, were now reinstated. This meant that any townsman who became a burden to public welfare within five years of attaining citizen's rights would no longer be eligible for municipal support. People unable to support themselves within five years of attaining minor rights ("Schultheissenbürger") were to be expelled immediately.[26] This crisis in Strasbourg's support for its poor and refugees coincided with the climax of the apocalyptic movement and with the arrest of Melchior Hoffman.

The apocalyptic unrest in Strasbourg was not based on an unstable economic or social situation within the city: it was introduced from outside by the refugees. Naturally religious persecution and famine alone do not fully account for the growth of apocalyptic expectations. Other factors leading to the crisis were Hoffman's own personality and the widespread belief shared by many ever since the beginning of the Reformation that there was soon to be a cataclysm that would bring about the destruction of the old world. A comparison of the economic crisis of 1540-1541 with that of 1528-1534 makes a telling point.[27] Once more the price of basic foodstuffs had trebled within a short space of time throughout Alsace, yet did not this time produce here (or anywhere else in the Empire) anything that can be compared with the collective disturbances which took place between 1529 and 1533. It was probably the disillusionary experience of the Anabaptist Kingdom of Münster which prevented a social-economic crisis from giving rise to wishful religious fantasies.

[25] *TAE* I No. 153, p .185, No. 234, p. 289.
[26] O. Winckelmann, *op. cit.* Vol. 2. No. 122.
[27] W. Abel, *Massenarmut* p. 54; A. Hanauer, *Etudes économiques* Vol. 2. p. 94.

2. The Social Components and Strength of the Anabaptist Movement in Strasbourg.

We cannot give any precise description of the extent of the Anabaptist movement in Strasbourg since most of the recorded figures are based on rough estimates or frequently simply on hearsay. But the minutes of the trials do mean that we can assume a certain degree of probability regarding the rise and decline of the movement, the members' occupations and the relationship between the local and the foreign members.

The number of Anabaptists living in Strasbourg in April, 1528 was estimated at 250,[28] but after the influx of refugees from Augsburg it was reckoned that the figure rose to 500 in August, 1528.[29] At the height of the Anabaptist movement in October, 1530 Andreas Panner, an opponent of the Anabaptists, declared that he had "heard it said" that there were 2,000 of them within the city.[30] According to this at least 20% of the *adults* in a total population of 20,000 must have been Anabaptists. But the number declined sharply as a result of the repressive measures introduced in 1534 and 1535 after the tragedy at Münster. In August, 1537 Adam Slegel (an Anabaptist from Nuremberg) declared that about 200 "brethren" possessed a general support fund. After the collapse of the Hoffmanites in 1538 and 1539 Ruprecht Schwarz, the "herald" of the Anabaptists, estimated the number of "Swiss Brethren" in 1546 at 100; at that point there were only five Melchiorites still in the city. Thus the remarkable rise in the Anabaptist movement between 1528 and 1533 was followed by an equally rapid fall after 1535.

We must also take into account the great fluctuation that existed between the seven distinct groupings of Strasbourg nonconformity, namely the "Gardeners" around Clemens Ziegler; the Anabaptists around Wilhelm Reublin and Michael Sattler (who were later called "Swiss Brethren"); the Marbeck-Scharnschlager circle; the followers of Denck and Kautz; the

---

[28] *TAE* I No. 130, p. 155.
[29] *TAE* I No. 148, p. 181 n. 7.
[30] *TAE* I No. 224, p. 277.

Augsburg refugees (of whom the greater part had been won over by Hans Hut); the Melchiorites and Schwenckfeldians. Reublin's followers were close doctrinally to those of Marbeck, though Marbeck was never admitted to be a genuine "Swiss Brother" because of his Lutheran doctrine of justification and because he criticized the rigidity of congregations in the excommunication of sinners. The Denck-Kautz circle seems to have disbanded by 1532.[31] Those refugees from Augsburg who had been under the influence of Hut seem to have joined forces with the Melchiorites after 1529. It was the "Swiss Brethren" who profited in the main from the collapse of the Hoffmanites in 1538 and 1539,[32] since they were able to become the natural rallying point of nonconformity after the dashing of all chiliastic hopes. The spiritualist and apocalyptic groups (the Denck-Kautz circle, Hut's followers and the Melchiorites) were much less stable than the other congregations, who recruited new members as the Messianic movements collapsed. It seems as if Clemens Ziegler's circle and the Schwenckfeldians were the two groups least affected by fluctuations.

The social constitution of the individual Anabaptist groups cannot be established because only in exceptional cases did the interrogators ask for the membership of a particular group. The minutes list the jobs of 129 Strasbourg Anabaptists between 1526 and 1540 as: 16 intellectuals (including seven former priests and former teachers); 40 members of the textile guild (13 weavers, 10 tailors, 9 furriers, 6 drapers); 15 members of the metal-working guilds (including 10 smiths and 3 goldsmiths); 9 cobblers; 4 publicans and pedlars; 4 gardeners; 6 bakers, millers and butchers; 18 general artisans and 17 "beggars" (unemployed).

The relatively high number of intellectuals is typical of the early stage of the Anabaptist movement.[33] The textile workers were also over-represented in comparison to the total Stras-

---

[31] Cf. *TAE* I No. 340-342.
[32] N. Blesdijk, *Historia* pp. 108-109.
[33] Cf. C. P. Clasen, "Schwenckfeld's Friends" in *MQR* 46 (1972) pp. 58-67.

bourg population, but this industry had been a hotbed of heresy since the high Middle Ages. In contrast, the gardeners were under-represented, since they made up 20% of the burghers of Strasbourg and constituted by far the largest guild in the city. Those gardeners who did not fully support the course of the Strasbourg Reformation sided with Clemens Ziegler. Those members of the middle and higher classes who wanted to protest against the official Reformation took up the cause of either Denck or Schwenckfeld,[34] whereas the lesser townsfolk seem to have preferred to find their spiritual home with either Hoffman or Clemens Ziegler. Although the writings of Hoffman and Hut repeatedly exalted the poor as God's particular tools the Anabaptists had no "class-consciousness." Solidarity with one's "neighbour" depended exclusively upon his membership of one's own religious group. They were denounced for this exclusivity by Clemens Ziegler and Eckhard zum Drübel, both of whom had theological affinities with the Anabaptists of Strasbourg. Eckhard zum Drübel made the following comment on their behaviour: "The Anabaptists aim to show their holiness to the world by giving no greeting or thanks to anyone else. They live like troublesome and stubborn oxen in their unfriendly dealings with all other human creatures."[35]

The most striking factor in the sociology of the Anabaptist movement in Strasbourg is the enormous disproportion of refugees in relation to the permanent population of the city. About 80% of the Anabaptists who feature in the records were refugees.[36] This situation naturally complicated any collective political activity particularly in the crucial year of 1533 when Hoffman, the "charismatic" leader, lost control. The high proportion of refugees also explains the strong fluctuations and the rapid decline of the whole movement. Anabaptism had few roots in the local population. The variety of occupations of the Strasbourg Anabaptists means that we cannot account for the

[34] Cf. C. P. Clasen, *Anabaptism* p. 310.
[35] *TAE* II No. 604, p. 384 (for Ziegler's comments, *TAE* I No. 346, p. 573).
[36] Cf. above all *TAE* I Nos. 67, 218, 224, 234, 235.

phenomenon in terms of the particular problems encountered within a single profession.

Another element in the Anabaptist movement in Strasbourg was the circle of "sympathizers" who encouraged its growth by publicly urging toleration for the nonconformists. The most significant group in this respect were the "Epicureans", who counted the following amongst their numbers: the humanists Jakob Ziegler and Johannes Sapidus, Otto Brunfels, the doctor and botanist, Anton Engelbrecht and Wolfgang Schultheiss, both preachers.[37] The Anabaptists also received support, at least for a while, from Wolfgang Capito and Hugo Volz, the former abbot, and from the stewards of the municipal welfare funds, Lucas Hackfurt and Alexander Berner.

The spread of Hoffman's influence can also be attributed to the readiness of Alsatian printers to publish his tracts; Balthasar Beck printed seven works either written or edited by Hoffman within a nine-month period between 1529 and 1530. Beck had a personal involvement with the left-wing movement within the Reformation. His step-daughter, Margarethe, became the second wife of Sebastian Franck (whose *Chronicle* Beck had published with tremendous financial losses in 1531[38]), and in November, 1533 he extended hospitality to Cornelis Poldermann, Hoffman's close friend from Holland.[39] During his second stay in Strasbourg, at the end of 1531, Hoffman was able to persuade Jakob Cammerlander to print two more of his tracts. After Beck had fallen out of favour with the Council because of the heretical writings he had published, it was Cammerlander and Valentin Kobian (Beck's business colleague in Hagenau) who printed Hoffman's final tracts after they had been smuggled out of prison.

The Strasbourg Preachers were fully aware of the extent to which the printers were encouraging the heretics. In May, 1534 Capito (who had in the meanwhile reverted to orthodoxy) complained to Ambrosius Blaurer that the Strasbourg printers

---

[37] *TAE* I No. 236a.
[38] *TAE* I Nos. 262 and 286.
[39] *TAE* II No. 462, p. 214.

were motivated "by profit" to take more interest in selling heretical pamphlets than in publishing sound literature. But in view of the financial risk involved in publishing heretical books, Capito's view of the motives of the Alsatian printers would seem to be somewhat one-sided.[40]

3. Strasbourg's Move Towards Lutheranism, 1530-1532.

There were two decisive causes for the termination of Strasbourg's policy of toleration: firstly, the continued growth of increasingly radical sectarian movements within the city, and secondly, the inclination of all those Southern German cities which had come under Zwinglian influence towards Lutheranism as a reaction against the threatened alliance between the Elector of Saxony and the Emperor Charles V.

After the Second Diet of Speyer in 1529, Elector John of Saxony was determined to make his peace with the Emperor. To this end he hoped to underline the essential conservatism of Lutheranism by taking a firm stand against the Zwinglians.[41] This meant that the Colloquy of Marburg in the autumn of 1529 was doomed to failure. The Schwabach Articles, which were intended to serve as the doctrinal basis for the League of Schmalkalden, were formulated in such uncompromisingly anti-Zwinglian terms that the Southern German cities felt unable to join the projected defensive alliance at the Assembly of Schmalkalden in December, 1529. The Strasbourg Council was afraid that the Lutherans would ally with the Emperor in order to annihilate the "sacramentarians" within the Empire.[42] Stras-

---

[40] *TAE* II No. 55, p. 314 cf. also F. Ritter, "Elsässische Drucker im Dienst der Strassburger Sektenbewegungen zur Zeit der Reformation" in *Gutenberg – Jahrbuch* 1962, pp. 225-333, 1963, pp. 97-108.

[41] Cf. T. A. Brady, "Jacob Sturm of Strasbourg and the Lutherans at the Diet of Augsburg, 1530" in *Church History* 42 (1973) pp. 183–202, Hans Baron, "Religion and Politics in the German Imperial Cities during the Reformation" in *English Historical Review* 52, 1937, pp. 405–427; 614–633; O. Winckelmann, *Der Schmalkaldische Bund* 1892.

[42] Cf. M. Lenz (ed.), *Briefwechsel Philipps des Grossmütigen mit Bucer* p. 14.

bourg consequently signed a treaty with Zürich, Basel and Berne in January, 1530 in which each city promised mutual aid in defence.

But after February, 1530, in the light of the hopeless inferiority of the Zwinglians in the event of a conflict with the combined forces of Lutherans and Catholics, Jacob Sturm began to press for Strasbourg to move closer towards Lutheranism. He had become so tired of the interminable Eucharistic controversy that for years he refrained from taking the sacrament.[43] Strasbourg's policy remained fundamentally anti-Catholic, but it was motivated first and foremost by defensive considerations.

The Strasbourgers began to distance themselves from Zwinglianism during the Diet of Augsburg of 1530. The *Tetrapolitana*, the Confession prepared for this Diet, spoke of the Eucharist as a sign of Christ's real presence and not, as in Zwinglian theology, as a memorial of the bodily absent Lord; Article 18 reads, "In this sacrament the Lord actually gives His *true body and true blood* to his disciples and to believers to eat and drink, as *food for their souls* and eternal life."[44] But the idea that the Eucharist is a food for the *soul* and for *believers* only conformed to what Bucer had been teaching up to this point. As a further gesture of compromise the Strasbourg Council ordered Karlstadt's banishment in May, 1530, since it was felt that the presence of the Wittenberg theologians' arch-enemy within the city threatened Strasbourg's relationship with the Elector of Saxony.[45]

Melanchthon's desperate attempt to achieve toleratión for the Wittenberg Reformation by stressing the Catholic elements within Lutheranism in his formulation of the Confession of Augsburg turned out to be unsuccessful. The Emperor insisted that all religious innovations be withdrawn until such time as a General Council could meet to settle the issue. The Elector, deeply disappointed, thus urged the Lutheran theologians to come to terms with those South German cities that were

---

[43] J. Sturm, *Antipappi quarti . . . pars tertia* Neustadt. 1580, p. 166.
[44] R. Stupperich (ed.), *Bucers Werke*. Reihe 1. Vol. 3. 1969, pp. 123-124.
[45] *TAE* I No. 214, p. 263.

prepared to compromise. He would then be able to lead them in a defensive alliance. At the end of August, 1530 Melanchthon and Bucer agreed on a compromise formula to settle the Eucharistic controversy, and they then informed Luther by letter of their arrangement.[46]

Bucer was prepared to make far-reaching compromises with the Lutherans if this would help the cause of the evangelical faith and the security of the Protestant cities of Southern Germany. In his *Book of Concord* written at the end of 1530 for Duke Ernst of Lüneburg he stated that "the believer's *soul* physically (*sic*) receives . . . . Christ's body in sacramental union with the bread".[47] Zwingli rightly regarded this logical contradiction as a "confusion" of truth and error. He was convinced that "this mixing of truth with error was serving the cause of darkness not of light."[48] The Lutheran princes responded to Strasbourg's submission over the Eucharistic question by admitting the city to the League of Schmalkalden on February 3rd, 1531. It was after this that Bucer examined his conscience for a final time and eventually admitted that Christ's body "is eaten by the *physical mouth* also, as a result of the sacramental union" – an idea which hitherto he had always condemned.[49]

Strasbourg's peace with Wittenberg brought about a breach with Zürich. Zwingli wrote an indignant letter accusing his friend Bucer of betraying evangelical truth for political ends.[50] Since the evangelical cities of Southern Germany followed Strasbourg's example, Zürich was left dangerously isolated; in the second battle of Kappel in October, 1531 the town had to fight all the Swiss Catholic Cantons single-handed. It was in this decisive battle that Zwingli lost his life.

With the rejection of the "sacramentarian" doctrine of the Eucharist one of the last unifying factors which linked the Strasbourg Reformers to the town's radical nonconformists had

---

[46] Cf. *CR* 2 No. 798, p. 224; *WA Br* 5 No. 1969, pp. 566–572; *WA* 12, No. 4243a, p. 126.

[47] *CR* 98 No. 1134.

[48] *CR* 98 No. 1136.

[49] *WABr* 6 No. 1779.

[50] *CR* 98 No. 1168 (Letter dated 12th February, 1531)

been abandoned. The Strasbourg Council also expected that the city's membership of the League of Schmalkalden should have implications for their policy towards the sects, and so in December, 1530 its ambassador was ordered to ask the Lutheran princes "how the Anabaptists are to be dealt with in future".[51]

The Strasbourgers were forced to give up all their autonomy in religious matters in 1532 as a result of moves which formed part of the Emperor's policy of dividing the League of Schmalkalden. The Electors of Mainz and of the Palatinate acted as agents for the Emperor at the Assembly at Schweinfurt in April, 1532, where they proposed a religious settlement between the Catholics and supporters of the Confession of Augsburg.[52] The Southern German cities who had proposed the *Tetrapolitana* in 1530 were thus faced with the prospect of being isolated from the Lutheran princes and serving as a scapegoat to be offered to the Emperor. In view of this the Strasbourg Council instructed its representatives never to allow themselves, whatever the circumstances, to be cut off from the Lutheran princes, even if this meant they had to accept the Saxon confession.[53] This command was obeyed; Strasbourg accepted the Confession of Augsburg with the words, "in order that we shall not be divided".[54] Yet the *Tetrapolitana* lost none of its validity. The Strasbourg preachers were willing to give assurances that according to Melanchthon's *Apologia* the articles on the Eucharist (Art. 10 of the Confession of Augsburg and Art. 18 of the *Confessio Tetrapolitana*) were "in conformity and equal". They pretended to feel that the two evangelical confessions were in agreement on all matters.[55] This religious self-denial did produce political results. The evangelical cities of Southern Germany established a provisional religious peace in the "Nuremberg Truce" of 1532.

Surprisingly, Wolfgang Capito accepted the Strasbourg

---

[51] *Politische Korrespondenz der Stadt Strassburg.* Vol. 1 p. 561. Vol. 2, p. 2.
[52] *Ibid.* Vol. 2, pp. 120-121.
[53] *Ibid.* Vol. 2, pp. 106-107.
[54] *Ibid.* Vol. 2, p. 110.
[55] *Ibid.* Vol. 2, pp. 107-109.

church's inclination towards Lutheranism. Personal reasons must have played a considerable part in this. The deaths of his two friends Zwingli and Oecolampadius, as well as that of his wife, within the span of two months (October–November 1531), and coming on top of a mountain of debts, plunged this sensitive man into deep melancholy. In his despair he expressed his desire to marry Sabina Bader, the widow of Augustin Bader, the executed Anabaptist leader; in doing so he would have ruined all his reputation with the Protestant reformers. [56] But Bucer's psychological insight showed him that he had a chance of winning Capito back to the Strasbourg church by showing him practical friendship during his depression. He thus arranged Capito's next engagement – to Wibrandis Rosenblatt, Oecolampadius's widow. He then sent him on a journey to mutual friends in Basel, Berne, Zürich, Memmingen and Augsburg. Before he set off Bucer managed to win him over to his new understanding of the Eucharist. On arriving in Berne in January, 1532 Capito was asked to formulate a new Ecclesiastical Ordinance for the divided local church. He then expounded a "simultaneous parallelism" of what happens spiritually and physically in the reception of the Eucharist whereas earlier, in his Commentary on Hosea and in his Children's Catechism, he had insisted that there was a temporal separation of the symbol (i.e. the Sacrament) from the gift (belief in forgiveness). [57] Now in the *Berner Synodus* Capito wrote, "this sacrament of the altar is not made up of signs only but of signs *and* God's mysterious power, both working *together*, just as in holy baptism, where the minister baptises with water, and at the same time Christ with his spirit." [58] Thus in receiving the sacrament the external breaking of the bread is simultaneous with the "inner feeding of the soul." He does not agree with Luther that the bread and wine are the actual bearers of God's power, because "the mouth

---

[56] Cf. T. Schiess (ed.), *Briefwechsel der Brüder Thomas und Ambrosius Blaurer* Vol. 1. 1908, pp. 307, 317, 320.

[57] Cf. O. E. Strasser, *Capitos Beziehungen zu Bern* 1928, p. 107 and W. Köhler, *Zwingli und Luther* Vol. 2. 1953, p. 308.

[58] *Acta Synodi Bernensis. Simone Sulzero Interprete* 1532. Ch. 20 p. 32.

Plate 11: Otto Brunfels

GOTTES
MACHT IST
MYN
CRACHT

Plate 12: Jan van Leiden

receives only perishable bread," but in view of the temporal convergence of the physical and the spiritual the sacrament does again take on the character of a supernatural mystery.[59] This led Capito back to the idea of a sacramental mediation of salvation by means of an official and ordered church.

The battle against the Strasbourg Anabaptists was thus launched with united forces.

4. The Preliminary Strasbourg Synod, 3 June – 6 June, 1533.

In 1532 Bucer began to step up his complaints about the Anabaptist movement, which he felt was being encouraged by the inaction of the Council and the sympathy of the "Epicureans". He anticipated that Strasbourg's evangelical church would be doomed unless action was taken to check the Anabaptists.[60] After Basel, Berne, Ulm, Constance and Memmingen had all revised their ecclesiastical structures in the years between 1530 and 1532, Bucer was afraid that Strasbourg, regarded as a sectarians' paradise, would lose its leading role in the religious life of Southern Germany. In the course of 1533 his disquiet turned into a fear that there might be a far-reaching social upheaval.[61]

To avoid such an upheaval Bucer began to place more emphasis on a plan he had already been considering for a long time; he proposed to refute the sectarians in a public disputation and to enforce a rigorous ecclesiastical and moral code. In August and November, 1532 the preacher wrote letters (which, incidentally, were also signed by Capito) appealing to the Council to proclaim a moral code and to hold a public disputation with the sectarian leaders. They reminded the Council of the duty of Christian authorities to follow the example of the Christian Emperors in protecting the Church

---

[59] *Ibid.* Ch. 22, p. 36.
[60] *TAE* I Nos. 300, 321, 344, *TAE* II No. 353.
[61] *TAE* II No. 470.

from heretics and "disruptive elements" and in assuming responsibility for the establishment of moral rules.[62]

The Council decided that four of its most respected members (namely Jakob Sturm, Martin Herlin, Andreas Mieg and Sebastian Erb) would lead the public disputation between the evangelical preachers and the nonconformists.[63]

With this support behind him Bucer expanded on his demands for a fundamentally new ecclesiastical ordinance for Strasbourg, making the following requests:

1. There should be a new confession of faith which would distance the church of Strasbourg from the "left-wing of the Reformation" as the *Confessio Tetrapolitana* had distanced itself from Catholicism.

2. The authorities should be obliged to enforce pure doctrine and Christian morality.

3. There should be unity in religious matters between the city and its dependent surrounding territory.

4. There should be supervision of the preachers' personal lives.[64]

The projected synod was to be constituted as follows: four councillors as chairmen, all of the preachers and vicars of Strasbourg and the surrounding area, the city's 21 church-wardens, two representatives of each rural congregation (one appointed by the Council and one delegated by the congregation), the school teachers (including the humanist Jakob Ziegler who held a municipal appointment), representatives of the Cathedral Chapter, four jurors from each guild (as well as free access for all other jurors) and the leaders of the nonconformists within Strasbourg, including Clemens Ziegler, Melchior Hoffman and Caspar Schwenckfeld.[65] The Council refused access to any other townsmen so as to prevent inaccurate "rumours

---

[62] *TAE* I Nos. 332a and 348.
[63] *TAE* I No. 349, *TAE* II No. 357.
[64] *TAE* II No. 358.
[65] *TAE* II Nos. 370, 376.

giving a false impression of the city", and to stop the disputation from "falling into disarray."[66]

At the same time they formulated a strategy for achieving conformity. A preliminary synod was to be held which would exclude all of the sectarians, the guild members and the representatives of the rural congregations. This would decide on a confession of faith and a liturgical structure and it would investigate the private lives of the preachers. The role and the morality of the rural clergy was to be investigated during the main synod, in the presence of the guilds and the representatives of the rural congregations. The heretics would not be admitted until the end of the proceedings after doctrinal unity had been imposed on the whole Strasbourg church, and they would thus find themselves facing a united front. In this way the crucial decision which would determine the course the Strasbourg church was to take would be reached during the preliminary synod.

The *Sixteen Articles* which were drawn up by an editorial board consisting of Bucer, Capito, and the two church administrators, Conrat and Lindenfels, and then presented to the Synod, were a revised version of the 22 Articles Bucer had put forward in April, 1533 in a private letter to his colleagues.[67]

Article 1 rejects Servetus' denial of the Trinity.

Article 2 rejects Clemens Ziegler's doctrine of universal forgiveness and his denial of the existence of the devil and demons.

Article 3 deals with the Anabaptist doctrine that Christ has expunged the consequences of original sin and that man after conversion is capable of doing good by his own strength. As against this it asserts man's total corruption brought about by original sin.

[66] *TAE* II No. 370, p. 24. No. 375, p. 64, No. 380.

[67] *TAE* II Nos. 358 and 371. We know that there was an editorial board on the basis of *TAE* II No. 373, p. 45 and No. 441, p. 179 cf. F. Wendel, *L'Eglise de Strasbourg. Sa constitution et son organisation.* Paris 1942, p. 62 n. 23.

Article 4 condemns Hoffman's Monophysite Christology as a "most serious blasphemy."

Article 5 again denies the freedom of the will by asserting that the knowledge of God is the highest good and the consequent ability to do good is solely dependent on divine grace.

Article 6 stresses the need for preaching and the sacraments as mediators of faith. But it draws a distinction between the "external word" and the inner activity of the Holy Spirit, which gives power to preaching and the sacraments. It thus opposed both the doctrines of Hoffman and Denck, who argued for the possibility of direct revelations, and of Bernhard Wacker (the vicar of Old St. Peter's, who was a conservative Lutheran), who believed that preaching and the sacraments naturally possessed spiritual power in themselves.[68]

Article 7 calls the sacraments "Visible Gospels"; they portray the redemption brought about by Christ. Since they are seen as signs of God's grace preceding human action, infant baptism is justified. The Anabaptists' rejection of it goes against God's ordinance.

Article 8 rejects the Anabaptists' doctrine that baptism is primarily a verbal commitment on the part of the believer to keep God's commandments. It is defined rather as God's offer of forgiveness for sins, which must be brought about by the Holy Spirit, "but the servant (i.e. the priest) collaborates in this by bringing together the word and the sign."

Article 9 asserts simultaneous parallelism in the sacraments. The believer receives communion with Christ *together with* the bread and the wine; in the same way purification from sin comes about when we are sprinkled with water.

Article 10 attacks Schwenckfeld's practice of denying access to the Lord's Table to those who live an "openly unrepentant life" -

[68] *TAE* II No. 373, p. 41, No. 379, p. 445.

i.e. everyone who hopes to attain salvation should be allowed to share in the Eucharist.

Article 11 condemns the establishment of exclusive communities in which sincere Christians subject themselves to particularly harsh moral demands. There should be "complete love and unity" between all Christians.

Article 12 limits excommunication to those sinners who have refused to give up their "foul vices" after repeated warnings.

Article 13 rejects all anathemas which are based on human precepts – a reference not only to papist regulations but also to the rigorous demands of the Anabaptists.

Article 14 calls on the secular authorities "to ensure to the best of their abilities that God's name be hallowed, His kingdom come and His will be done among their subjects." The "Epicureans" and the Swiss Brethren who wanted to limit the role of secular authorities to secular tasks are called "destroyers of all that is good."

Article 15 lists the religious duties of the authorities as the protection and proclamation of pure doctrine, the suppression of "error and blasphemy", and the punishment of those sinners who cause scandal by their disgusting activities. Anyone who opposes the right of the authorities to enforce punishment over religious issues opens the door to anarchy and destruction.

Article 16 attacks those who defend the freedom of the will (for the third time!). Although faith is mediated by the clergy and by secular authorities, man's salvation is dependent solely on God's election. The exertions of the church will only make those men whom God has chosen as "vessels of wrath" (Romans 9:22) more obdurate and violent.

The two major concerns of the *Sixteen Articles* are clear: to defend the unity of church, state and society and to justify the official church as an institution which mediates salvation. Every individual point derives from these two principles (the rejection of adult baptism, the rejection of the idea of a voluntary church independent of the state, the unwillingness to enforce excommunication rigorously, the assertion of the necessity for preaching and the sacraments even if they are not prerequisites for attaining salvation).

The Article on baptism (No. 8) aroused something of a controversy at the preliminary synod because a few of the preachers (Altbiesser, Schultheiss, Schweblin, Hechtlin) wanted to leave it to the parents, or whoever was to be baptized, to decide on when baptism should be administered since Scripture does not decree baptism of infants. The objection was overcome by saying that it is the "inner purification", not the baptism by water, that is to be regarded as the activity of God, though they did not at this point of the discussion reject the theory of simultaneous parallelism.[69]

The major conflict arose over the question of the rights of secular authorities in matters of faith (Articles 14 and 15). The "Epicureans" (Engelbrecht, Schultheiss, Sapidus) were afraid that a new evangelical papacy was being established. According to them the power of the authorities should be limited to secular matters, which could all be controlled by unaided reason. Except in cases of serious public blasphemy, magistrates had no mandate to punish erroneous doctrine or unbelief.[70] Yet Engelbrecht, who acted as chief-spokesman for the "Epicureans", was more afraid of the usurpation of the worldly sword by the clergy than of Caesaropapism on the part of the secular authorities. He wanted the *city* to take decisions about the liturgy.[71] Bucer dealt with the objections of the "Epicureans" by writing an explanation of Articles 14, 15 and 16, in which he stated that the authorities were not called upon to force any particular belief on people or to take over the church's role in laying out specific doctrines. The secular arm should not obey

---

[69] *TAE* II No. 373, pp. 37, 41.
[70] *TAE* II No. 373, pp. 39, 43, 45, No. 374.
[71] *TAE* II No. 373, p. 47, No. 374, pp. 56, 57-58, No. 453, pp. 204–206.

the church's orders if it is not itself convinced of the justice of the cause. No preacher should appeal to the authorities for personal protection.[72] But this clarification was not sufficient for Engelbrecht and Schultheiss, and Engelbrecht eventually declared that he would never approve of the Articles because the acceptance of secular power would doom any church, making it into a "false church". For him there could only be one, free, universal church ruled by its only king, Christ.[73] Only Sapidus (the teacher in the Latin school) finally accepted Bucer's exposition of the doctrine of secular authority, yet he accepted it reluctantly, believing that it would come to be abused.[74]

Jakob Sturm vainly urged the preachers to come to an agreement by pointing out the dire consequences of their dispute on the credibility of their doctrine and on the prospects for the city. But not even he was able to cause the "Epicureans" to change their minds. The Sixteen Articles had to be returned to the small committee of the organizers of the synod to be reconsidered.[75]

The "Epicureans", as "liberal and tolerant humanists, open-minded in their beliefs",[76] wanted to protect the nonconformists of Strasbourg from the persecution that was being threatened. Bucer said that Engelbrecht was a staunch supporter of the sectarians even though he was not one of them.[77] Schultheiss's policy of toleration was based on the idea of a new outpouring of the Holy Spirit, a belief shared by the Anabaptists and spiritualists. Like them he also believed in the primitive church's structure of the congregation (1 Cor. 14) whereby everyone had the right to prophesy.[78]

The "Epicureans" had to pay a heavy price for their opposition to the *Sixteen Articles*. Jakob Ziegler (the humanist)

---

[72] *TAE* II No. 371, pp. 29-31.
[73] Cf. W. Bellardi, "Anton Engelbrecht (1485-1558)" in *ARG* 64 (1973) p. 197.
[74] *TAE* II No.392, p. 95, No. 453, p. 205.
[75] *TAE* II No. 373, p. 45.
[76] W. Bellardi, *op. cit.* p. 191.
[77] T. Schiess (ed.), *op. cit.* I p. 467.
[78] *TAE* II No. 236a, p. 291, p. 293.

left Strasbourg even before the Synod began because he found
the atmosphere there unbearable. In Baden-Baden he proceeded
to publish a tract directed against the Strasbourg reformers.[79] In
the autumn of 1533 Brunfels gave up his position in the town
and went to Berne. Schultheiss was threatened with dismissal in
March, 1534 since he had "no respect for the authorities."[80] But
he was not removed from office until after 1538 (possibly not
until 1542).[81] In December, 1533 the Council took the "paupers'
hospice" out of Engelbrecht's control, and they followed this in
January, 1534 by closing his church (St. Stephen's). Thus they
removed his livelihood without formally deposing him as
pastor.[82] After these experiences with evangelical church
government, Engelbrecht and Schultheiss finally reverted to
Catholicism.

With the suppression of the "Epicureans", the Anabaptist
movement in Strasbourg lost its support amongst the wealthier
townsfolk within the city.

5. Hoffman's Arrest and the Main Strasbourg Synod, 10-14 June, 1533.

Hoffman returned from Eastern Frisia to Strasbourg for the
third time in March, 1533.[83] An old Frisian had prophesied that
he would spend six months suffering in a prison at Strasbourg
but that after that his doctrine would spread over the earth.[84] His

[79] *TAE* II No. 478, No. 504.

[80] *TAE* II No. 524.

[81] I am grateful to M. Rott for indicating the sources in the
Strasbourg archives. cf. W. Bellardi, *Wolfgang Schultheiss* Frankfurt
1976.

[82] *TAE* II Nos. 476, 501 and 514.

[83] There were definitely three periods when Hoffman was in
Strasbourg: the first from the end of June 1529 to April 1530 (*TAE* I
Nos. 188 and 211) the second in December 1531 (*TAE* I Nos. 279, 280,
298) and the third from March 1533 to his death at the end of 1543
(*TAE* II No. 364, Schwenckfeld, *Epistolar* I p. 594).

[84] O. Philips, *A Confession* in G. H. Williams and A. M. Mergal
(ed.), *op. cit.* p. 209.

own calculations also pointed to 1533 as the year in which the world was to be transformed. He had said in 1526 in his commentary on Daniel that the apocalyptic cataclysm was then beginning; it was to last for seven years and be followed in 1533 by the return of Christ. After the execution of his followers in Amsterdam in 1531 he ordered that no more baptisms be carried out for two years until the time of persecution had come to an end. All of these calculations pointed to 1533 as the year that was to bring a decisive breakthrough.

Hoffman and Johannes Eisenburg spent nine weeks as guests of the goldsmith Valentin Dufft, a well-to-do supporter of Hoffman's ideas.[85] Hoffman then drew attention to himself and to the role he envisaged for the Strasbourg Council by ordering Lienhard Jost to take his book "Concerning the Sword" to the town hall. [86] But the Council took no action which would have fulfilled the prophecies.

Events were brought to a head when Claus Frey, a furrier and former fellow-believer of Hoffman's, denounced him to the Council, accusing him of plotting a rebellion.

Frey had been baptised in Windsheim (in the Margraviate of Ansbach-Bayreuth) by the Zürich Anabaptist Julius Loher (Leuber).[87] The Council there had imprisoned him and then ordered him to make a public confession. Since he was too proud to undergo the shame of the public confession he managed to leave the area with the connivance of his wife. But she then refused to join him in his exile. Frey separated from her, giving her half of his possessions.[88] Because of his fortitude the Franconian Anabaptists made him their leader. It was at this time that Frey seems to have come into contact with a sect of visionaries who were in the habit of sharing their wives with each other as well as their visions and revelations.[89] Frey was

---

[85] *TAE* II No. 326, p. 13. Krebs and Rott are mistaken in identifying the man "from Cologne" as Poldermann.

[86] *TAE* I No. 364.

[87] *TAE* I No. 246 n.l.

[88] *TAE* I Nos. 369 and 388.

[89] K. Schornbaum (ed.), *Quellen zur Geschichte der Wiedertäufer* Vol. II. Markgraftum Brandenburg (Bayern I) 193 Nos. 253 and 298 et al.

finally given hospitality by Georg Gross (Pfersfelder), an Anabaptist nobleman and friend of Schwenckfeld's.[90] It was at his castle at Weilersbach in Upper Franconia that Frey got to know Pfersfelder's widowed sister Elisabeth, who was so taken with him that one night she decided she would give herself to him "along with my goods, my honour and my body so that he can do what he likes with me."[91]

The lady's submission excited Frey so much that he exalted her as the "mother of all believers" and the "eternal virgin". He himself became "Christ according to the Word" and the "head of the church". His unfaithful wife became "the old Satanic serpent" whose head must be crushed.[92] When Georg Pfersfelder had thrown this silly couple out of his castle, Frey and Elisabeth (his "spiritual bride and sister") sought refuge amongst the Anabaptists of Strasbourg.

Melchior Hoffman, Valentin Dufft and Barbara Rebstock were not impressed by Frey's fantasies and ordered him to terminate his relationship with Elisabeth Pfersfelder and return to his wife. When Frey refused, Hoffman ejected him from the Anabaptist congregation, delivering him to the devil as a "robber of God's honour and a Satanic whoremonger". Frey's romance soon led to a public scandal. The couple were jeered at in the street and both eventually had to be arrested as disturbers of the peace.[93]

Frey decided to take his revenge on Hoffman by informing the Council of his address and accusing him of having urged "almost all the Anabaptists" to rise in a rebellion by means of his prophecies. But he said that he (Frey) was quite prepared to pledge his life to the "pious noblemen" and to the Council.[94] He said that many of the Anabaptists were disruptive and had required him to reject the authority of the Strasbourg Council.[95] He had clearly confused the Hoffmanites with the 'Swiss Brethren' in this respect.

[90] *CS* 4:778–779.
[91] *TAE* II No. 564, p. 324.
[92] *TAE* II No. 564, pp.327-328.
[93] *TAE* II No. 361, p. 12.
[94] *TAE* II No. 362, pp. 13-14, No. 564, p. 329.
[95] *TAE* II No. 361, pp. 12, No. 362, p. 14.

As a consequence of Frey's accusation Hoffman was arrested on 20 May, 1533. As the police entered his house Hoffman took on the role of the "witness of the Most High": "When Melchior saw that he was going to prison, he thanked God that the hour had come and threw his hat from his head and took a knife and cut off his hose at the ankles, threw his shoes away, and extended the fingers of his hand to heaven and swore by the living God who lives there from eternity to eternity that he would take no food and enjoy no drink other than bread and water until the time that he could point out with his hand and outstretched fingers the One who had sent him. And with this he went willingly, cheerfully and well-comforted to prison."[96]

In the course of the subsequent trial Hoffman rejected Frey's accusations. He said that he had always called on his brothers and sisters to obey the authorities; yet he admitted that there were "a lot of scoundrels" amongst the Anabaptists. He then accused the Strasbourg preachers of not upholding the truth and of abusing their positions for personal gain. All that he himself had actually earned were beatings, shame and poverty. He himself was not a prophet but the "witness of the Most High." But the sun, the "real Gospel" of the true apostles, would still rise in Strasbourg."[97]

On 28 May, 1533 the Council decided to try Hoffman at the coming Synod. Hoffman saw this as yet another fulfilment of one of his prophecies, for ever since 1526 he had predicted a great council at which the two apocalyptic witnesses would be brought to trial. The local Strasbourg Synod thus took on the dimensions of a World Council. He came to regard himself as standing at the turning-point in the history of the world – to such an extent that the Strasboug Council eventually doubted his sanity.[98] These strange ideas gave him the strength to put up with any form of attack, with imprisonment and with the interrogations even though he was living only on bread and water. Nor did he allow any interruption in his production of

[96] O .Philips, *A Confession* in G. H. Williams and A. M. Mergal (ed.), *op. cit.* pp. 209-210.
[97] *TAE* II No. 364.
[98] *TAE* II No. 471, p. 224.

books. Even Bucer expressed astonishment at the incredible "Satanic energy" which motivated Hoffman.[99]

One day later Hoffman was asked to specify who were the "scoundrels" that he had said existed amongst the Anabaptists. He tried to pacify the Council by saying that he had been thinking of such criminals who had killed their wives or brothers.[100] There were lots of tramps calling themselves Anabaptists, who only wanted to fill their stomachs and indulge in mischief. But these vagabonds did not constitute a threat to the city. He himself wished Strasbourg nothing but good. If it were God's will he would be prepared to give up his life to spare the city from disgrace. But he then changed his tone: "According to Holy Scripture there will be uproars and rebellions all over the earth; these have already begun. All the priests must perish. The true Jerusalem cannot arise or be built until Babylon, with all its hordes and followers, has been deposed and destroyed."[101] The removal of the "priests" (of whatever denomination) was thus the *sine qua non* of the appearance of the new Jerusalem. But he did not say who it was who was to slay the servants of Baal.

In the next session Frey withdrew his accusations against Hoffman, saying he had "never claimed a lot of people here are disruptive, but there *are* a lot of contentious sects and beliefs. If people are not careful there will in time be a growth in evil and rebelliousness." But he was unable to provide any evidence showing that the Melchiorites had plotted an uprising.[102]

At the Main Synod (10-14 June, 1533) the charge that Hoffman had aimed to incite rebellion by the spreading of his apocalyptic visions was dropped. But this did not mean that the charge had no further part in deciding Hoffman's fate. Bucer and Capito remained convinced that the Melchiorites were envisag-

---

[99] *TAE* II No. 417, p. 124.

[100] Thomas Schugger of St. Gallen killed his brother, and an Anabaptist in Esslingen (whose name is not known) killed his wife in a religious frenzy (cf. *TAE* II No. 472 n.l).

[101] *TAE* II No. 368, p. 18.

[102] *TAE* II No. 369, p. 20, No. 564, p. 329. But in November 1533 Frey did repeat his former charge, cf. *TAE* II No. 456, p. 209.

ing an uprising aimed against the whole of the existing structure
and that they were simply waiting for an opportunity to trigger
it off.[103]

On two afternoons during the Synod, Hoffman expounded
the five major points of his doctrine, viz. his Monophysite
Christology, his doctrine of the universality of divine grace, the
freedom of the human will after enlightenment, the invalidity of
infant baptism and the impossibility of forgiveness for mortal
sins committed after conversion. Bucer was responsible for the
refutation. Hoffman also took the opportunity of putting
forward his doctrine that prayer should never be addressed to
the Son or to the Holy Spirit.[104] The scanty and inaccurate
minutes give us no reliable account of the course of the debate.
Schwenckfeld, who had also been summoned to explain his
major doctrines to the Synod, took the opportunity of distancing himself from Hoffman. There had originally been two
natures in Christ and both had been united, yet the essence of
God's Word contains all that it needs to make them conformable, i.e. to suffuse and to deify the human nature of Christ.[105]

It was clear at the ensuing Synod on 20 June that the
arguments of the sectarians had made no impression on the
preachers. None of the clergy changed their views.[106] Although, with the one exception of Sapidus, Bucer had been
unable to win over any of his opponents, the Synod had been a
great personal success for him. It was he who had led the
disputation against the "Epicureans" and the sectarians, and the
Sixteen Articles, to which the majority of the Strasbourg
preachers subscribed, were essentially his work.

Theobald Schwarz, one of Bucer's supporters, speaking of the
effects of the Synod on the population of Strasbourg, said that
many who could not previously stand Bucer's name now began
to revere him in their hearts. Several papists who had hitherto
found the new faith unacceptable also began to change their

---

[103] Cf. Bucer, *TAE* II No. 402, pp. 113-114, Capito, *TAE* II No.
564, pp. 341-342.
[104] *TAE* II No. 384, p. 83, cf. p. 79.
[105] *TAE* II No. 384, p. 89.
[106] *TAE* II No. 392.

opinions.[107] Hence the battle against religious radicalism and the return to sacramentalism led a group of Catholics to join forces with Strasbourg's evangelical state church.

6. The End of Strasbourg's Policy of Toleration and the Suppression of Nonconformity, 1533-1535.

The Strasbourg Synod and the arrest of Hoffman eventually brought about a break between Schwenckfeld and the Strasbourg reformers. Schwenckfeld felt that a new "Judaism" was emerging in Strasbourg; the secular sword was being used to enforce uniformity of belief within their territory. This could only appear as cruel and foolish to anyone who had become aware of the essence of Christian freedom.

This was why Schwenckfeld objected to Hoffman's arrest. Neither Hoffman nor any other Anabaptists constituted a danger and there was thus no need for anyone to call on the authorities to deal with them. Hoffman's Christology should not be regarded as blasphemous, for his monophysitism, although erroneous, was aimed at glorifying Christ. If he was being tried for denying Christ's true humanity, then Bucer and Luther would have to be given the same treatment. Bucer had called Luther's doctrine of ubiquity a denial of Christ's incarnation, and Luther had regarded the original Eucharistic doctrine of the Strasbourg theologians as an attack on the text, "The Word became flesh." "Scholars fight each other with pens. But a poor fellow has to pay for his error dearly. Why? The poor have no-one to protect them. They cannot get revenge."[108]

But Schwenckfeld's attempt to clarify his position before the Council only deepened the rift. On 22 July, 1534 the Council politely but firmly requested him to "remove himself and leave their lordships undisturbed."[109] Barely a year later Alexander Berner (the administrator of poor-relief) was dismissed for propagating Schwenckfeld's doctrines.[110]

[107] *TAE* II No. 405, p. 118.
[108] *CS* 4 : 836.
[109] *TAE* II No. 588, p. 368.
[110] *TAE* II No. 660.

Neither Hoffman nor his followers allowed themselves to be intimidated by the Synod. Anabaptists turned up daily at the Schiessrain Tower where he was imprisoned in order to hear the sermons he gave from the window. A rumour spread that the Hoffmanites had assembled in the forest at Benfeld with a view to plotting an uprising in Strasbourg. As a result Hoffman was transferred to another prison. Jakob Kron, his warder, was ordered to refuse access to him unless visitors had the prior consent of the Council. But when even here forty people appeared at his window the Council decided that Hoffman would have to be caged like a wild animal.[111]

Yet Hoffman was undaunted. He continued to write pamphlets expounding his doctrines for his followers and the Synodal committee. Cornelis Poldermann managed to bribe his way in to see Hoffman and smuggle his books out. The most important of these tracts was one on the "pure fear of God", in which Hoffman urged his followers not to allow fear of men to separate them from God's truth, lest they fall into damnation. At the same time he comforted them with the hope of imminent vengeance on their persecutors and of the establishment of a theocratic interregnum which would usher in the Last Judgment.[112]

As a result of these events and as news spread of Anabaptists meeting together in assemblies, the Council decided to take further measures to suppress the Melchiorites. Hoffman was ordered to stop writing, Schwenckfeld was no longer to be allowed to visit him, Lienhard Jost was to be tried and everyone who had housed an Anabaptist assembly was to be arrested.[113] Nevertheless a Hoffmanite view of the Synod was published despite the Council. The work's stylistic elegance (so different from Hoffman's awkward sentence construction), and its factual precision, indicate that it was written by a scholarly Melchiorite, probably Johannes Eisenburg.[114]

[111] *TAE* II Nos. 390, 395.
[112] Hoffman, *Underrichtung von der reiner forchte Gottes* A2b.
[113] *TAE* II No. 400.
[114] *Eyn sendbrieff an alle gottsförchtigen liebhaber der ewigen warheyt/ inn welchem angezeyget seind die artickel des Melchior Hoffmans TAE* II No. 399.

Bucer (despite the objections of the Strasbourg Council) replied with his own account of the Synod.[115] He dedicated this work to the Protestants in the Netherlands, since Hoffman had claimed at the Synod that he had a lot of followers there. Dutch Christians should be on their guard against the "obstinate and pompous agitator" because the inner temptations he promotes are more dangerous than any external threat in the form of violent persecution. Bucer regarded Hoffman as a heretic the like of whom had been all too common in the history of the church. He dresses as an angel of light and impresses the world with his asceticism. But he uses his wiles to divide groups of allegedly perfect saints from the rest of the Christian community. After a short period of exaggerated asceticism everyone then falls into moral lassitude, because some believe that to the "pure" everything is pure and the others are disappointed and give up religion altogether, thinking nothing of falling into Epicureanism. Bucer sees an example of this transformation of asceticism into chaos in the "blood-thirsty and rebellious visions" spread about by Jost and his wife, with Hoffman's help.[116] But Bucer ignored the apocalyptic prophecies, which he felt spoke for themselves, and concentrated on Hoffman's special dogmatic teachings, which he reduced to four major doctrines: Monophysite Christology, the universality of grace and the doctrine of the freedom of the will (both seen as a single doctrine), the impossibility of forgiveness for sins committed after conversion, and the rejection of infant baptism.

According to Bucer Hoffman's appeal to John 1:14 ("The Word became flesh") as the biblical foundation for his Christology, derives from a false interpretation of the verb "to become". Hoffman used it to mean "to change into." But no such meaning can apply here, otherwise we would have to say that Christ's divine nature was subject to change. "To become" means, rather, "to take on" in the sense that we say "Charles became Emperor", meaning that he remained the same person

---

[115] *Handlung inn dem offentlichen gesprech zu Strassburg iüngst im Synodo gehalten/gegen Melchior Hoffman, 1533. Excerpt in TAE* II No. 402.
[116] Bucer, *Handlung* A4b-B1a.

but took on a new quality. Thus "the Word became flesh" means that the "eternal Word" took on human nature as well, taking it from the flesh of Mary. It was only on the basis of his descent from Mary that Christ was a true man, that he could be a brother, a prototype for men, that he could be subjected to suffering and to death and that he could act as a sacrificial offering to bring about our redemption.[117]

Bucer rejects Hoffman's argument that Christ would not have been able to serve as an atoning sacrifice for man if he had taken over "Adam's accursed flesh" from Mary. He stresses Christ's supernatural conception by the Holy Spirit which washed away original sin and which meant that Christ embodied man's prelapsarian nature.[118] In short, Hoffman denies both the divinity and the humanity of Christ: the divinity, because he allows change in the inalterable divine substance and the humanity, because he removes Christ from the line of the descendants of Adam.

Bucer's reply to Hoffman's doctrines of the freedom of the will and of the universality of grace takes the form of a detailed exposition of his anthropology. He admits that all men possess "free will" as regards their own understanding and their own desires. Men cannot be treated by external pressure as if they were lifeless matter. Thus all men are convinced that by their own consciences they can act "freely" in their own strength. Man is free to do or not to do whatever he wills, but he cannot will as he wills. His will is dependent on his ability to understand, and his understanding has been adversely affected by the Fall. Bucer thus reduced the problem of the freedom of the will to the problem of the freedom of the understanding.

Fallen man "loves the creation but despises the Creator." Even when his reason leads him to conclude that God exists he still lacks the "true, all-embracing and active understanding of God". Hence he cannot but choose false values as his highest aims: the life, honour and lusts of the body. It is because of this that he acts wrongly. Divine revelation, which restores man's "free will",

[117] *Ibid.* B2a-B3b.
[118] *Ibid.* C1a-D2a.

does not consist, as Hoffman believes, of a single act of inner enlightenment which then makes possible a free choice between good and evil. Rather "God gives and brings about devotion in the same way that the sun creates daylight in the world. Just as the sun must continue to shine, so must the children of God be continuously led and encouraged by the Spirit of God." The believer does not co-operate with God in the process of salvation. Christ lives in him and his ego dies. Whenever there is a living understanding of God, good works will follow.[119]

God has reserved true understanding of Christ solely for the elect. Bucer deals with the host of biblical texts Hoffman had used in defence of his universalism of grace (Gen. 12:3, 1 Tim. 2:4, 1 John 2:2) by saying that these are examples of the use of an inexact idiom whereby "all" means "many" or "all peoples" but not "all men". Bucer feels that Hoffman's idea that God's condemnation of some men is based on divine prescience is foolish. He asks, "How could God be sure that certain men will be evil if they are free to act differently?" Logically God's omniscience is based on his omnipotence. The third error discussed by Bucer is Hoffman's doctrine that there is no forgiveness for sins committed after conversion in full awareness of one's culpability. According to Bucer any sin, even if committed deliberately, can be forgiven if the sinner truly repents (all sins, that is, except the sin against the Holy Spirit). He takes Peter's denial as an example. Bucer's concept of the "sin against the Holy Spirit" is much narrower than Hoffman's: it is not the breaking of a commandment in full consciousness of error but a major rebellion against the spirit of God when one is fully aware of the gravity of the offence – a revolt of the evil will against one's better knowledge. How this is possible remains Bucer's mystery (as he previously maintained that our will is dependent on our understanding).[120]

Finally Bucer turns to Hoffman's attacks on infant baptism. He feels that Hoffman's erroneous doctrine of believers' baptism is based on a false understanding of the sacraments. The

---

[119] *Ibid.* G2a.
[120] *Ibid.* J2a-J4a.

sacraments were not instituted "for us to be able to swear how we intend to behave before God", rather they are "meaningful promises and gifts that God has given us in His goodness through Christ our Lord". Baptism and the Eucharist are celebrated "so that we can remember all His grace and goodness and so that we can receive that same grace and goodness in and with such offers".[121] The sacraments should not be seen as separate from the mediating work of the Holy Spirit and it is through them that the forgiveness of sins is "offered and established."[122]

Since God has included children in his covenant of grace there is no reason to exclude them from baptism.

In conclusion Bucer declares that Hoffman is a tool of Satan because:

1. he denies the humanity and the divinity of Christ,
2. he ascribes redemption to the "inadequate and empty capacity of human nature",
3. he denies the solace of the Gospel to repentant sinners,
4. he destroys the unity of the church by rejecting infant baptism.[123]

He sees in him a reincarnation of all the most dangerous heretics of the early church: Valentinus the Gnostic, with his Monophysite Christology, Pelagius with the doctrine of the freedom of the will, and Novatian the Donatist, with his error concerning the impossibility of forgiveness for sins committed after believers' baptism.

Bucer's polemical work made it clear that, apart from Christology, the most fundamental difference between the theology of the Strasbourg reformers and that of Hoffman centred on their divergent views of man. In Hoffman's theology man becomes a responsible active partner of God after his enlightenment; he collaborates in his own salvation by means of

---

[121] *Ibid.* K2a-b
[122] *Ibid.* K2b-K3a.
[123] *Ibid.* L5b.

his liberated will. He is fully accountable for everything he does after making his contract with God in baptism. As against this Bucer feels that man is always a child in terms of his relationship with God; he receives justification and sanctification as an unmerited gift of God.

Bucer sent copies of his book to various friends with a view to restoring Strasbourg's good name. Copies were sent to, amongst others, Ambrosius Blaurer and Johannes Zwick in Constance, to the Zürich theologians, Bullinger, Jud, Pellikan and Bibliander and to Landgrave Philipp of Hesse (who had once heard Hoffman preach).[124] So as to win over Hoffman's supporters in the Netherlands the work was translated into Dutch.[125] But at the same time a rumour was spreading in Münster that Hoffman had been victorious at the Strasbourg Synod and had won over the whole city to his cause. Johann van der Wieck, Bailiff of Münster, therefore requested Jakob Sturm to provide an official attestation from the Council and the Strasbourg preachers of the inaccuracy of the rumour "otherwise there might be great unrest in Münster."[126] Jakob Sturm denied the truth of the rumour and the Council of Münster had Bucer's polemical book translated into Low German by Brixius ten Norden, a preacher and the brother-in-law of Bernd Rothmann. But this was not enough to stop the growth of the Melchiorite movement within Münster. The events in Strasbourg had also aroused the attention of Wittenberg and Zürich. Bullinger in Zürich warned the Constance reformers to avoid following Strasbourg's example in giving hospitality to exiled Anabaptists. It would be preferable to expel them beforehand rather than execute them later.[127] In Wittenberg Melanchthon spoke approvingly of Hoffman's imprisonment, since he had "filled Belgium and the whole Baltic with his wild ideas".[128]

To the disappointment of the preachers the Council still refused to take quick, harsh measures to reconstitute the

---

[124] *TAE* II Nos. 404, 407, 408.
[125] The Dutch version is printed in *BRN* V pp. 199–314.
[126] *TAE* II No. 452.
[127] T. Schiess (ed.), *op. cit.* I No. 347.
[128] *TAE* II No. 430.

religious life of Strasbourg. The Council rejected a proposal of the Chairman of the Synod to establish a commission made up of preachers and church-wardens that would subject all nonconformists to interrogation. They decided that the commission should be made up solely of the four Chairmen of the Synod and of the church-wardens.[129] The Autumn Synod of 23 to 29 October, 1533 (which was not public) ended in failure for the preachers. The Synod made two proposals. The following elements were included in an outline of a new ecclesiastical ordinance:

1. Warnings should be issued to the townspeople when erroneous doctrines appeared;
2. the church-wardens should ensure orthodoxy;
3. a commission, consisting of two councillors, three church-wardens and two preachers, should be set up to examine dissidents;
4. all unlicensed preaching should be banned;
5. infant baptism should be enforced within a given length of time after every child's birth.

The Autumn Synod actually began with discord. The Council accused the preachers of being divided on the issue of the relationship of the "inner" to the "outer Word" and of the rights of secular authorities in religious matters. They condemned the trials of individual heretics held by the Synodal commission even though the accused had sworn to remain silent about their diverging views. "It is not a Council's job to enforce particular beliefs on anyone, but simply to root out or discipline elements which threaten the common good."[130] This was at least a move in the right direction towards a policy of toleration which was founded on a secularized concept of the state (although the theoretical foundation was shaky). But, on the other hand, the Council rejected the ideas of the "Epicureans", who wanted to separate the Church from the state. They wanted to retain a general supervisory role over the church in order to be able to

---

[129] Cf. *TAE* II No. 384, p. 90 with No. 387, pp. 91-92.
[130] *TAE* II No.441, p. 178.

channel and smooth over religious disputes and avoid destruction of church-unity.

When it turned out that the preachers were unable to agree on
these matters or on the new question of compulsory baptism,
the Council urged that things be left as they were. Bucer,
convinced that the proposal was impractical, became deeply
despondent. On the day the Autumn Synod opened, he wrote to
Ambrosius Blaurer, saying that such dangerous and godless
lassitude in the face of the sectarians would be the end of both
the church and the state in Strasbourg.[131] A second commission
met to study the books Hoffman and Schwenckfeld had
submitted to the Autumn Synod to explain their doctrines. In
the case of Schwenckfeld the commission simply said that the
Strasbourg preachers and the Silesian nobleman were "far apart
from each other". The verdict on Hoffman was damning and
unequivocal – this "blasphemer" was leading the "simple mass
of people" away from God's Word and posed a threat to the
city's reputation.[132] But no further consequences were drawn
from this statement.

Meanwhile Hoffman had fallen ill with dysentery. He wrote
numerous tracts in which he complained that the Council was
treating him like "poor Lazarus". Mathis Pfarrer, the burgomaster, denied the accusation and said that the illness was due to
Hoffman's decision to live on bread and water. He could have a
hot meal at any time he wished.[133] So as not to create a martyr
the Council ordered his cell to be heated and asked Katharina
Zell to look after him. Cornelis Poldermann and Hoffman's
congregation in Emden tried in vain to get him released on
bail.[134] Poldermann foolishly accompanied his request with a
crude joke about Bucer. Bucer, he said, is well-named "because
he has covered up (*ausgebutzt*) the light in Strasbourg. He has
removed its inhabitants from the realm of eternal salvation and
blessedness and they grope along the wall like blind men at

---

[131] *TAE* II No. 442.
[132] *TAE* II No. 444, pp. 192-193.
[133] *TAE* II No. 467.
[134] *TAE* II Nos. 428 and 461.

midday". Poldermann was consequently arrested and banished from the city for the rest of his life.[135] Nevertheless, he remained secretly in Strasbourg until the summer of 1534, involved with the printing of Hoffman's writings.[136]

Hedio and Zell visited the great heretic in his cell on 5 January, 1534. They discovered that, despite his illness, Hoffman's spirit remained undaunted and that he was expecting the year 1534 to see the triumph of his cause. After their visit they told the Council that Hoffman, because of his "grave errors", could no longer be regarded as a "Christian brother". Since he had not been condemned to death, and since it looked from the outside as if he were being allowed to die as a result of the appalling conditions under which he was being held, they asked that he be moved somewhere else, where he could be kept alive more easily. Meanwhile the Council must take steps to ensure that he does not escape, to stop him "bringing about pain, suffering, death and damnation of souls by his stupidity".[137] The Council responded by moving him to a new room, which could be heated. They requested that he be washed and shaved more frequently, but always in the presence of two members of the Council.[138] It was probably considered opportune, because of the large numbers of his supporters, neither to kill him nor to release him. But probably also the fact that no concrete evidence could be found to show that he had plotted a rebellion left the Council with no cause to put him to death. But, on the other hand, they were convinced that his doctrines would eventually lead to bloodshed and murder. Thus he was to spend the rest of his life in prison without ever being formally sentenced.

The apocalyptic fervour within Strasbourg reached fever pitch at the turn of 1533–1534. Hoffman believed he would be in prison for only six months and then the new epoch would be ushered in with his release. The Melchiorites exploited the Council's passivity after the June Synod to increase their

---

[135] Cf. *TAE* II Nos. 462, 466, 468. Quotation from No. 461, p. 213.
[136] *TAE* II Nos. 491 and 610.
[137] *TAE* II No. 484.
[138] *TAE* II No. 485.

missionary activity. On 18 December, 1533 Bucer wrote the following to Ambrosius Blaurer: "The heretics are almost destroying us. We are now paying for our great laxity. The Council now realises that Hoffman's fanaticism affected so many people that there might be a revolt and they want to do something about it. But it is too late."[139] But the Council did take action. Mathis Pfarrer, the burgomaster, issued a mandate against the Melchiorites on 26 December, 1533. He informed the Council that the leadership of the Melchiorites had been taken over by Johannes Eisenburg, a Dutchman from Cologne, who was even more adept at spreading Hoffman's ideas than Hoffman himself. Unfortunately they had not been able to arrest him. He urged his fellow Council members to adopt stringent measures against the Melchiorites. Although the Council had still not decided whether to accept the Synod commission's recommendation that they establish conformity of belief, they agreed to a preliminary measure whereby all Melchiorites who did not recant their errors would have to leave the city, regardless of their rights as citizens. A special commission was set up to supervise the enforcement of this order.[140]

On 14 January, 1534, the day on which the townsmen annually swore their allegiance to the Council, Hedio preached the "Council sermon", in which he harangued the authorities and the people, complaining about the desperate state of the church in Strasbourg: "The preachers are being destroyed and torn apart by the thankless and unspiritual world, like an ass by a lion." The Council must protect the Gospel and its preachers against those "violent, saturnine, melancholic and fanatic men who are going about." The citizens should support the Council and the preachers in "putting the church in good order, and especially in taking care of the poor". The "disruptive elements" would then disappear automatically.[141] Capito, Bucer, Hedio and Zell all appeared in the Council Chamber on 28 January, 1534 intending to issue an ultimatum in order to force the Council to take action. Things had become so bad in Stras-

---

[139] *TAE* II No. 470.
[140] *TAE* II No. 475.
[141] *TAE* II No. 492.

bourg, they said, that the town had "become a great scandal throughout all of Germany; it has become a blasphemy against the Gospel." Since the Council exerts authority for the glory of God, it should accept the Synod's decision and take charge of the establishment of divine truth. It should not allow preachers to be slandered. It should enforce attendance at sermons and take charge of Christian discipline and education. If necessary the Council must use its power to ensure that the Sabbath is hallowed, that sermons are attended and that heresy is uprooted. Council-members should set a good example and always appear at church on Sundays. But obviously the Council seemed to think that all its other duties were more important than the supervision of the church. This would provoke a harsh punishment from God. Although innocent themselves, the preachers declared that they were prepared to resign collectively and make way for other preachers who would be more richly blessed for their troubles. This was a threat. If they were to stay in office and the Council remained inactive, they would inform the people of the miserable situation from the pulpits. Their concrete demand was for the *Sixteen Articles* and the *Confessio Tetrapolitana* to be declared as the city's official confession. These demands were signed by all the preachers except Schultheiss and Engelbrecht.[142]

Eight days later the Chairmen of the Synod, speaking for the Council, promised that soon a decision would be taken concerning the *Tetrapolitana*, the *Sixteen Articles*, and the new church ordinance. The preachers should be patient, and under no circumstances should they inform the "common people" of their grievances.[143]

It was at this point that the catastrophe in Münster came to the aid of the Strasbourg preachers. In February, 1534 the Melchiorites deposed the Lutheran authorities in Münster. The warnings of the Strasbourg preachers now carried real weight; the Strasbourg Council was so frightened by the events in

[142] *TAE* II Nos. 498 and 499. The threatened resignation is in the archives, but not printed in *TAE*.
[143] *TAE* II No. 503.

Münster,[144] that it promulgated a series of measures against the nonconformists:

1. The *Tetrapolitana* and the *Sixteen Articles* were declared to be the norms of orthodoxy for the inhabitants of Strasbourg on 4th March, 1534.[145]

2. A mandate followed on 13th April, 1534 proclaiming that any Anabaptist who was not prepared to make peace with the Strasbourg church should leave the city within eight days, along with his family.[146]

3. In the course of four sittings in rapid succession (on 19th, 24th, 26th and 27th June, 1534) the Council undertook to pay special attention to the reputation and honour of its preachers. It explicitly condemned the doctrines of Clemens Ziegler, Hoffman and other Anabaptists. All Anabaptists were called upon to swear an oath in which they promised to serve in the militia and not to hold or visit any special assemblies. Anyone refusing to take the oath would have to leave the city within fourteen days along with his wife and children.

So as to prevent the growth of sects right from the start, all children were ordered to be baptised within six weeks after birth. Children not yet baptised must be christened immediately. Anyone who did not voluntarily agree to the baptism of his children would lose his rights as a townsman. In such cases the Council would give orders for the children to be forcibly baptised.

This looked like a complete victory for the preachers, but appearances were deceptive. At the same time the Council passed a series of measures which prevented the *preachers* from dictating faith and morals:

a) Supervision of matters of faith was put in the hands of the church-wardens.

b) In the event of anyone in future raising an objection to the city's official confession of faith he would have to appear before a Commission made up of two Council members and three church-wardens. Two preachers could sit on the

---

[144] *TAE* II No. 611.
[145] *TAE* II No. 518.
[146] *TAE* II No. 535.

commission, but only as observers. It was for the Council as a whole to make the final judgments.

c) "Church discipline" was placed exclusively in the hands of the wardens. They should use "all gentleness" to correct those who avoid attending worship or receiving the sacrament or who lead a grossly immoral life. Those who do not improve even after these warnings should be left by the church-wardens "to the judgment of God." This was not to take the form of expulsion from the community; indeed the word "excommunication" was avoided in the relevant article (par. 4). The practical significance of this was that the Council renounced effective control of morality. The preachers' request that everyone should be forced to attend at least one sermon a week was explicitly rejected.

d) In future the private and public lives of the ministers were to be placed under the supervision of the church-wardens. The presence of three wardens at the "Convocation" (a fortnightly assembly of the clergy) was made mandatory. Here they had the right to intervene in any disputes between clergymen and to submit issues to the Council.[147] This prevented the preachers from closing ranks against the Council.

So in 1533 and 1534 the orthodox clergy, aided by the secular authorities, had triumphed over the heretics, but eventually they had to pay for this victory by accepting the control of the Council over the evangelical church.

Since many of the Anabaptists decided to flee to the surrounding villages, the Council issued a decree on 28th March, 1535 extending the city's legislation against them to cover the rural regions, too.[148]

The fact that it was the laity who had enforced the repressive measures against religious nonconformity worked to the advan-

---

[147] *TAE* II No. 577. On these decisions cf. M. U. Chrisman, *Strasbourg and the Reform* pp. 223-224, F. Wendel, *L'Eglise de Strasbourg* pp. 108-135, 172-187. On the rights of the church wardens cf. T. W. Röhrich, *Mitteilungen aus der Geschichte der evangelischen Kirche des Elsasses*. Vol. 1 1855, pp. 225-227.

[148] *TAE* II No. 657.

tage of the Anabaptists in the following years. Although many of them were banished from the city in 1534 and 1535, there could be no question of the determined expulsion of every single Anabaptist. The Council issued a revised code as early as March, 1535 ensuring a more liberal application of the mandate of June, 1534. The oath sworn by Anabaptists wanting to remain in the city was framed in such a way that they only had to commit themselves to their duties as townsmen and to refrain from inveighing against the official faith of the city in public. It did not require acceptance of the *Sixteen Articles* or of the *Confessio Tetapolitana*. No one was to be forced to accept a creed if it conflicted with the voice of his own conscience.[149] In May, 1535, in the wake of the catastrophe at Münster, the evangelical preachers pressed for more severe punishments for the Anabaptists. Anabaptists leaders who encouraged rebellion should be dealt with according to the Imperial laws of 1529, i.e. they should be executed. Ordinary members of Anabaptist congregations should no longer simply be banished; they should be sentenced to hard labour. Care should be taken that by making them into refugees they were not given the opportunity to spread their ideas further.[150] The Council did not respond to this appeal. It also rejected demands from King Ferdinand and the Bishop of Strasbourg to deal more firmly with the Anabaptists.[151] Ferdinand had established a special court at Ensisheim in May, 1535 for the specific purpose of sentencing Anabaptists to death. He sent bands of mercenaries to scout around Western Austria looking for Anabaptist refugees.[152] At the two Diets of Molsheim in May and June, 1535 the Bishop of Strasbourg wanted to unite the whole of Alsace in a concerted campaign against the Anabaptists. But Strasbourg was not prepared to carry out Ferdinand's harsh policy, and the assemblies thus produced no decisive result.[153]

---

[149] *TAE* II Nos. 647 and 672.
[150] *TAE* II No. 673.
[151] *TAE* II Nos. 667, 668, 674.
[152] M. Krebs (ed.), *Täuferakten Baden-Pfalz* 1951, Nos. 389 and 391.
[153] *TAE* II No. 676.

Despite this, the June Mandate of 1534 remained the pivotal point in the history of Anabaptism in Strasbourg. The movement went downhill after this. When David Joris came to Strasbourg as a refugee from the Netherlands in 1535, Lienhard Jost greeted him with the words "Brother, what are you doing coming to this godless town?"[154]

---

[154] *TAE* II No. 665.

CHAPTER EIGHT

Hoffman's Return to Eastern Frisia (May-November 1530).

It was after he had joined the Anabaptists, in May, 1530, that Hoffman sought asylum for a second time in Eastern Frisia, in order to avoid arrest in Strasbourg. Here he finally succeeded in establishing a long-lasting influence. The Anabaptism he advocated took such root in Emden and the surrounding area that it could not be uprooted there. His ideas spread like wildfire through the Netherlands and Flanders within the space of three years.

This chapter will describe the environment in which radical Anabaptism was able to develop. It was mainly the disastrous policies of Enno II which brought about this situation. His foreign and ecclesiastical policies led first to local unrest and eventually to a devastating military defeat.

The dispute between the Count and the Zwinglians had already become acute during Hoffman's first visit to Strasbourg (June, 1529-April, 1530). At the Second Diet of Speyer (March-April, 1529) Enno II joined the Catholic estates for fear of an attack by Charles V or Duke Karl von Geldern. He also signed the Diet's final decree, which ordered that the Catholic Mass be celebrated everywhere and that every Zwinglian and Anabaptist be rooted out of the Empire.[1] In autumn, 1529 Enno requested the Bremen preachers to draw up an Ecclesiastical Ordinance for Eastern Frisia based on this Imperial decree and on the Marburg Articles of 1529. But this was impossible. The Colloquy of Marburg had not come to any agreement on the question of the Eucharist, and

---

[1] Cf. C. A. Cornelius, *Der Antheil Ostfrieslands an der Reformation* p. 57, E. Kochs, "Die Anfänge der ostfriesischen Reformation" in *Jahrbuch für Altertümer*. Emden 20 (1920) p. 64, G. Ohling, *Junker Ulrich von Dornum*. Aurich 1955, p. 107.

in any event the other 14 articles issued at Marburg were irreconcilable with the decree of Speyer.

Tiemann and Pelt, the Bremen preachers, attempted to solve the problem by omitting the controversial articles on the Eucharist and otherwise used a phraseology which was in keeping with orthodox Lutheranism.[2]

In future a superintendent was to make sure that there was conformity of belief in Eastern Frisia. Where before it had been argued that the "external Word" was superfluous, the eighth article of Marburg was now applied, which stated that no one could come to faith without hearing the preaching of the Word. The Eucharist was to be celebrated "according to the Saxon rite" – i.e. the priest was to wear a white surplice, he was to use Latin chant and was to distribute unleavened bread and wine to all the communicants. Infant baptism was made compulsory, as was the keeping of Sundays and Saints' days. The authorities gave special protection to all images of saints and to the Franciscan cloister in Emden.[3]

Enno II, urged by the Saxon reformers and by Elector John of Saxony, commanded all of his preachers to assemble at Emden on 13 January, 1530 in order to sign this so-called "Church Ordinance of Bremen". He expected them to sign without exact knowledge of the text and without having a chance to discuss or alter it, though the new articles contradicted all of the preachers' previous doctrines. The clergy protested at being treated in such a way and explained that they would only be prepared to support the new Ecclesiastical Ordinance if none of them felt that it opposed the Word of God in any respect. The only capitulation they made was on the question of the "external Word"; they admitted that God could not work in men without the mediation of the "external Word".

Soon after this a public controversy flared up. Johann Stevens, the leader of the Lutherans, went to the diet at Emden to accuse

---

[2] Cf. J. Weerda, "Das ostfriesische Experiment" in *Zeitschrift für evangelisches Kirchenrecht* 1956, pp. 159-196.

[3] E. Sehling (ed.), *Die Evangelischen Kirchenordnungen des 16. Jahrhunderts* Vol. VII, 2. 1963, pp. 360-372.

Rode and Rese of teaching false doctrine. Both were removed from their office. Oldeguil and two other Zwinglian preachers suffered the same fate.[4] Because of an edict against the Anabaptists, issued on 19th January, 1530, Karlstadt also had to leave the country, supposedly for having doubted the validity of infant baptism.[5] Some of the nobles took up the cause of the persecuted ministers. The chieftain Hicco Howerda found a position for Hinne Rode in Wolthusen. The congregation of Norden had the Bailiff of Berum depose their own minister Stevens, because he was a Lutheran. The Wittenberg theologians responded to this by urging the Count to use all his power to enforce the new Ecclesiastical Ordinance and to execute all those "blasphemers" who dared to disturb the Lutheran form of worship.[6] But the Sacramentarians, under the leadership of Ulrich von Dornum, mobilized their friends to urge Enno to put an end to the persecution. Philip of Hesse, Zwingli and the Strasbourg reformers all united to call on the Count to treat his opponents with clemency.[7]

Enno eventually gave in to this pressure. He refrained from using coercion to impose the new ordinance. In January, 1531 Luther complained about his party's defeat and of the "victorious trickery of the Sacramentarians." The will of the Count (who had offered strong resistance hitherto) had been broken and he was now allowing people in Eastern Frisia to teach whatever they liked.[8] The "Church Ordinance of Bremen" was never formally revoked, but only the Lutherans continued to adhere to it.

[4] E. Beninga, *Cronica der Fresen* (ed. 1961) p. 611, E. Meiners, *Oostvrieschlandts kerkelyke geschiedenisse*. 173$_9$, vol. 1. p. 68, E. Kochs, *op. cit.* p. 58, C. A. Cornelius, *op. cit.* pp. 33, 36, 58.

[5] H. Hamelmann, *Opera Genealogica* 1711, p. 828.

[6] *WABr* 5, Nos. 1577 and 1578.

[7] E. Meiners, *op. cit.* Vol. 1. p. 98, U. Emmius, *Rerum Frisicarum Historia* 1616, p. 845, *CR* 97:498f (Zwingli's letter to Philip of Hesse). Philip's letter to Enno is lost, but can be reconstructed from Enno's reply (C. A. Cornelius, *op. cit.* p. 57). cf. also H. Barge, *Karlstadt* Vol. 2, p. 588.

[8] *WABr* 6, No. 1772, p. 16.

In many places the Eucharist was again celebrated as was customary with radical Zwinglians and Anabaptists. The communicants sat around a simple table in front of the altar. The preacher, who spoke the Words of Institution in German, wore everyday clothes. It was the local white bread which was broken and the communicant put it in his mouth with his own hands.[9]

Enno avenged this defeat with a ruthless secularisation of church property. He used the riches of the Catholic church, not, as he had promised, to employ preachers or to care for the poor, but to hire mercenaries and to increase his own personal wealth. The congregations were forced to make substantial contributions so as to be able to support the evangelical preachers. There was no money to continue the work of the abbeys in caring for the needy and the sick. Anonymous poems and inscriptions expressed the indignation aroused by Enno's appropriation of Church property.[10]

Enno, having built up an army with the aid of the stolen church treasures, invaded the Harlingerland in June, 1530, in order to subjugate Balthasar von Esen, an independent-minded East Frisian nobleman. He also wanted to appropriate the land of his bride forsaken by him, Maria von Jever. But this invasion brought about what Enno had been trying to avoid with his conservative ecclesiastical policy. Balthasar von Esen became a vassal of Duke Karl von Geldern and Maria von Jever took her land in fief from the Court of Burgundy in Brussels. Thus Enno's invasion gave the Catholic powers a legitimate cause for intervening in Eastern Frisia. Thanks to Karl von Geldern, Balthasar von Esen was able to stand his ground against Enno. What was planned as a simple foray became a devastating three-year-long war in which most of the country's castles and many of its towns and villages went up in flames. The knock-out blow Enno received at the battle of Jemgum on 12 October, 1533 sealed his fate and forced him to give up his plans of conquest.

[9] A. Sprengler-Ruppenthal, "Zur reformatorischen Kirchenrechtsbildung in Ostfriesland" in *Zeitschrift für evangelisches Kirchenrecht* 10 (1963-1964) p. 320, E. Sehling (ed.), *op. cit.* Vol. VII, 2, 1. p. 340.
[10] E. Beninga, *op. cit.* p. 601.

These were the circumstances which encouraged the spread of Melchiorism in Eastern Frisia: the implausibility and the failure of the Count's pro-Lutheran ecclesiastical policies; the devastation of the land and the misery of its inhabitants brought about by the ill-fated war against Balthasar von Esen; the existence of a spiritualist "sacramentarian movement" supported by the nobility and, finally, the unbroken Germanic tradition of liberty, which meant that nobles, townsmen and peasants all united in opposition to the religious decrees issued by the Count.

There had already been individual sympathizers with the Anabaptists in Eastern Frisia before Hoffman's arrival. They were probably insurgent peasants from Central Germany who had fled to Eastern Frisia as refugees. In a letter of 25 March, 1530 Enno II informed Philipp of Hesse that some of his subjects were not having their children baptised, even though some children had reached the age of five.[11] According to Beninga Anabaptists had already "swarmed in" to Eastern Frisia by 1528.[12] But it is not clear from this chronicle, or from the first East Frisian mandate against the Anabaptists (19 January, 1530), whether they had actually practised adult baptism at this time. More probably it was simply a question of parents refusing to have their children baptised.[13] The Anabaptist movement in Switzerland had begun in the same way – by the rejection of infant baptism.[14]

Despite the mandate against the Anabaptists, Hoffman, on his return to Eastern Frisia in May, 1530, did find it possible to baptise adults in public. This must indicate that he had influential patrons. The first mass baptism took place in the sacristy of the Great Church at Emden which the elders had made available to Hoffman.[15] Obbe Philips states that Hoffman baptised members of every class, "both burgher and peasant, lord and servant".[16]

[11] In C. A. Cornelius, *op. cit.* p. 57.

[12] E. Beninga, *op. cit.* p. 602.

[13] *Ibid.* p. 611.

[14] L. von Muralt and W. Schmid (ed.), *Quellen zur Geschichte der Täufer in der Schweiz I. Zürich.* 2nd ed. 1974 No. 11, p. 10.

[15] E. Beninga, *op. cit.* p. 602.

[16] O. Philips, *A Confession* in G. H. Williams and A. M. Mergal (ed.), *op. cit.* p. 208.

He put the number of Hoffman's followers in Emden at about 300. Hoffman also seems to have had a following amongst the nobility. Ulrich von Dornum's daughter, Margarete, married Christoffer von Ewsum, the Lord of Jennelt, who was a sympathizer with the Anabaptists. Alba referred to this nobleman as a "principal Mennonite."[17] Ubbo Emmius says that Ulrich von Dornum's second daughter, Essa, "was seduced by an Anabaptist tailor" and she then married him. The man was, in fact, Johann Gerdsma, a refugee from Holland who was actually not a tailor but an "eminent, honest and well-to-do cloth merchant."[18] Ulrich von Dornum's youngest daughter, Imele, is said to have married a son of the Anabaptist robber-leader, Johann van Batenburg.[19]

The friendship Hoffman had enjoyed with the sacramentarians of Eastern Frisia came to an end when he began baptising adults. Johann Oldeguil appealed to the municipal authorities of Emden, urging them to expel Hoffman since he posed a threat to public order.[20] Luther also heard news of Hoffman's missionary successes in Eastern Frisia. In a letter to Johann Zelst of Bremen (dated 1 June, 1530) he warned his followers in Northern Germany against this dangerous furrier "who has long been an instrument of Satan." He must be avoided since his fantastic speculations leave no room for Christ.[21] In fact, Hoffman was forced to leave Eastern Frisia in the late autumn of 1530. Yet he had already managed to write his most important book, *The Ordinance of God*, in the East Frisian dialect. Except for a few comments by Obbe Philips, nothing is known about Hoffman's third visit to Eastern Frisia, from the end of 1532 to early in 1533.

The spreading of Anabaptism in East Frisia took place in conditions similar to those from which it had arisen. The peace-treaty of Logum concluded with the Catholic Karl von

---

[17] G. Ohling, *Ulrich von Dornum* p. 24.
[18] U. Emmius, *Rerum Frisicarum Historia* 1616, p. 885, G. Ohling, *Op. cit.* pp. 25-26.
[19] G. Ohling, *op. cit.* p. 28.
[20] U. Emmius, *op. cit.* p. 861, E. Meiners, *op. cit.* Vol. 1. p. 47.
[21] *WABr* 5, No. 1578 p. 343.

Geldern (1534), committed Enno II to the enforcement of a strongly conservative and Lutheran Church Ordinance within his domains.[22] Thus there was almost a repetition of the events which had led to the "Church Ordinance of Bremen" in 1529.

Enno II called on two foreign theologians, Martin Undermarck and Matthaus Ginderich from the Duchy of Lüneburg, to set up his new ordinance. But the "imported" authorities refused to collaborate with the East Frisian preachers in their reforming activities.[23] In comparison with the "Bremen Ordinance" the conservative elements in the new system were even more marked. It explicitly rejected the Zwinglian doctrine of the Eucharist and urged that the Catholic liturgy be retained as far as possible. Exorcism should again be included in the baptism service. The Lüneburg theologians proposed that the patronage rights of the nobles and of the rural congregations should be drastically reduced in favour of the Consistory appointed by the Count. This body was to be headed by a "superintendent" who was given extensive powers. The Lüneburg theologians insisted that the East Frisian pastors clearly distance themselves from the peasants. Ministers were to be better paid in future so that they would no longer have to work in the fields or be involved in trade. The intention of this directive was presumably to remove all traces of Karlstadt and his ideas from the area.[24] A specifically ecclesiastical court of justice was to be re-established. All civil and criminal cases in which clergymen were involved should be taken from the hands of village juries and put before the Consistory.

In fact, the mandate known as the "Twenty Articles", which established the "Church Ordinance of Lüneburg", did not totally abolish the patronage rights of the nobles and the congregations, but it did make the appointment of clergy dependent on the approval of the Count's superintendent. Sentences of imprisonment were to be imposed on people who refused to baptise their infants or who were rebaptised. It was

---

[22] The text of the treaty is in U. Emmius, *op. cit.* pp. 880-881.
[23] E. Beninga, *op.cit.* p. 638, E. Meiners, *op. cit.* Vol. 1. p. 137.
[24] M. Smid, *Ostfriesische Kirchengeschichte* pp. 147-148.

also an offence to dispute the sanctity of the Eucharistic elements, to deny Christ's divinity or humanity, and to disturb the Lutheran form of worship. To repeat the offence would be punishable with death. Priests had to be distinguished from peasants (who usually wore short fur coats), so they were made to wear long garments.[25]

The local reaction was similar to that in 1529-1531. The ministers who were inclined toward Zwinglianism either refused to sign the new Ordinance or signed it, but did not keep to it. Many of them were therefore banished, including Johann Oldeguil and Reiner Dagma (and possibly also Lubbert Canz of Leer). A group of noblemen (again led by Ulrich von Dornum) and many congregations supported the sacramentarians.[26] In spite of all his threats the Count could not overcome the stubborn resistance.[27] Since he was financially dependent on the Estates, he had to end the persecution of Zwinglians in 1538 when he needed to raise new taxes. But at the same time Enno II was toying with the idea of restoring Catholicism to Eastern Frisia.[28]

Thus the established church government of Eastern Frisia had seized every opportunity to discredit itself. Enno II had begun his reign as a disciple of Aportanus and as a Zwinglian. He supported the Catholic party at Speyer in 1529, but this did not prevent him from plundering church property. He was then converted to Lutheranism before making plans to reintroduce Catholicism to his domains. The bitter dispute between the Lutherans and Zwinglians was bound up with a dispute between the ruler and the nobility (as well as the congregations) over patronage rights. This conflict between members of the ruling class left room for the growth of Anabaptism. They had no difficulty in taking control of those congregations whose pastors

---

[25] E. Sehling (ed.), *op. cit.* Vol. VII ,2, 1, pp. 373-382. cf. pp. 383-397.

[26] H. Hamelmann, *Op. cit.* p. 828.

[27] T. D. Wiarda, *Ostfriesische Geschichte* Vol.12, 1792, pp. 415-417.

[28] Cf. F. Ritter, "Ein Gegenreformationsversuch Graf Ennos II." in *Jahrbuch der Gesellschaft für bildende Kunst und vaterländische Altertümer zu Emden.* 21 (1915) pp. 197-215, M. Smid, *op. cit.* pp. 153-155.

had been banished because of their Zwinglianism. Enno's wavering ecclesiastical policies, the arrogance of his Lutheran advisers and, last but not least, the effects of the war, all created a situation which made many people ready to accept the radical preaching of an Anabaptist apostle.

CHAPTER NINE

Hoffman's Relationship With Anabaptism in the Netherlands and Westphalia, 1530-1535.

1. The Religious and Social Causes of Hoffman's Success in the Netherlands.

Nowhere was Hoffman more successful than in the Netherlands. It was there that the ideas of the Strasbourg enthusiasts which were propagated by him found the mass support necessary to bring about a revolution. Without the Dutch Melchiorites there would have been no Anabaptist kingdom in Münster; this Westphalian Zion was simply the place where the upheaval which affected the whole region from Groningen to Maastricht had its strongest impact. What then were the religious and social factors which favoured the spread of Hoffman's apocalyptic ideas in the Netherlands?

Influential Dutch and American historians have given the impression that there was an unbroken and direct line of pietism from the "Devotio Moderna", through Wessel Gansfort, Erasmus and the "Sacramentarians" (Cornelis Hoen, Hinne Rode) to culminate in Anabaptism.[1]

Certainly there were similarities in the pietistic concepts of the "Devotio Moderna" and later Mennonites; both shared the ideal of a simple and secluded life within a voluntary community devoted to the practical imitation of Christ. Undoubtedly Erasmus also had great significance for Grebel, Hubmaier, Denck

---

[1] Cf. W.J. Kühler, *Geschiedenis der Nederlandsche Doopsgezinden in de Zestiende Eeuw*, Haarlem 1932, pp. 23f.; J. Huizinga, *Erasmus of Rotterdam* ET, London 1952, pp. 188ff.; G.H. Williams, *The Radical Reformation*, Philadelphia, 1962, pp. 31-33, 360.; C. Krahn, *Dutch Anabaptism. Origin, Spread, Life and Thought. 1450-1600* The Hague, 1968, p. 47;K.R. Davis, *Anabaptism and Asceticism: a Study in Intellectual Origins* Scottdale, Pa. 1974.

and Menno Simons.[2] But none of this is enough to account for the mass support Hoffman attracted or for the beginning of the Anabaptist movement in the Netherlands.

The discrepancy between the quiet world of the communities of the "Devotio Moderna" and the revolutionary impact of the Dutch Melchiorites is much greater than the similarities. Well after the Reformation had become a popular movement, the communities of the "Devotio Moderna" remained loyal to the Papacy and to the Catholic sacramental system; indeed, the Windsheim congregation (part of the regulated branch of the "Devotio Moderna") was one of the staunchest supporters of the old faith.[3] Not one community, not even a single rector, ever joined the Anabaptists, let alone the Melchiorites.

The same objection can be raised against any attempt to portray Erasmus as the founder of Dutch Anabaptism.[4] There are certainly a few peripheral areas of agreement between Erasmus and Hoffman, e.g. the belief in the universality of divine grace, in the freedom of man's will after conversion and in a continual process of justification and sanctification which comes about by co-operation between divine grace and human striving.[5] It is quite possible that in the last analysis Hoffman did take these ideas from Erasmus, though they came *via* Denck and Hubmaier. But the differences here again are much greater than the similarities.

---

[2] Cf. H. Fast, "The Dependence of the First Anabaptists on Luther, Erasmus and Zwingli:" in *MQR* 30(1956), pp. 104–119.

[3] Cf. R. R. Post, *The Modern Devotion. Confrontation with Reformation and Humanism* Leiden 1968, pp. 86, 477–486, 573–592. Post rejects the idea of Albert Hyma (*The Christian Renaissance, a History of the Devotio Moderna* 1924) that both Christian humanism north of the Alps and the Reformation derived from the "Brethren of the Common Life." K. R. Davis' writings are strongly influenced by Hyma. Unlike Hyma and Davis, Post says that neither Wessel Gansfort, nor Erasmus, nor the Sacramentarians were typical representatives of the piety of the "Devotio Moderna". S. Axters also stresses the orthodox, conservative character of the "Devotio Moderna" in *Geschiedenis van de Vroomheid in de Nederlanden. III: De moderne Devotio* Antwerp 1956, pp. 396, 414–415.

[4] W. Köhler in *Historische Zeitschrift* 121 (1920) p. 322; J. Huizinga, *Erasmus* pp. 188 ff; W. J. Kühler, *op. cit.* pp. 40–41.

[5] Cf. L. W. Spitz, *The Religious Renaissance of the German Humanists.* Cambridge, Mass. 1963, pp. 221, 226, 232, 235.

Erasmus was working for reform within the Catholic Church, which he always regarded as the mystical body of Christ, whereas for Hoffman and the Anabaptists it was "the whore of Babylon." Erasmus had such a low estimation of the Book of Revelation that he never wrote a single "Paraphrase" on it, but this book was central to the Melchiorites' thought and work. Erasmus's love of peace is totally irreconcilable with Hoffman's demand for the eradication of all "godless priests." Erasmus could only regard the Melchiorite movement in the Netherlands and Westphalia as a "mortal sickness, which practises open robbery under the mask of piety."[6]

Yet "sacramentarianism" must certainly count as a precursor of the Dutch Anabaptist movement. Like Hoffman, Jan Matthijs and David Joris were first separated from the official church because they objected to the doctrine of Christ's physical presence in the bread and wine. In 1528 both Matthijs and Joris were found guilty of blasphemy against the body of Christ and sentenced to have their tongues pierced.[7] The minutes of an inquisition of a group of Anabaptists arrested in Amsterdam in 1534 and 1535 reveal that some of them had not received communion for ten, or even fifteen years.[8] In rejecting the doctrine of transubstantiation the Dutch Anabaptist leaders had made an inner break with the Catholic Church many years before being rebaptised.

The spirituality of the Dutch Sacramentarians was set out by Cornelis Hoen in his *Epistula Christiana* of 1525. This was of central importance for Hoffman. In it Hoen had elaborated the logical implications of Wessel Gansfort's doctrine and had rejected the tenet of transubstantiation as priestly humbug which enforced the dominion of the Catholic Church over the common

---

[6] H. M. Allen and H. W. Garrod, *Opus Epistolarum Des. Erasmi Roterodami* Vol. 11 Oxford 1947, Nos. 2956, 2961, 2965.

[7] Cf. A. F. Mellink, *De Wederdopers in de Noordelijke Nederlanden 1531–1544* Groningen 1953, pp. 339–343.

[8] G. Grosheide, "Verhooren en Vonnissen der Wederdopers, betrokken bij de anslaagen op Amsterdam in 1534 en 1535" in *Bijdragen en Mededeelingen van het Historisch Genootschap* 41 (1920) pp. 35, 40, 86, 94, 165.

people. Small conventicles of sacramentarians began to grow up in Delft, the Hague, Haarlem, Amsterdam, Groningen and Leeuwarden. Scholarly laymen and recreant clergymen (including Cornelis Hoen, a lawyer; Gnapheus, the rector of the Latin school in the Hague; and Hondebeeke, Rode, Geldenhauer and Gellius Faber, who were all former monks) met together in these groups to expound the Bible and to press for church reforms. They wanted to do away with the Pope, bishops, priests, monks and the whole sacramental system of transmitting grace.

But the sacramentarian movement was soon deprived of its leaders. Cornelis Hoen had died by 1524 (even before his famous letter had been published), Hondebeeke left the Netherlands in 1525, Hinne Rode and Geldenhauer followed in 1526 and Gnapheus in 1530. The conventicles had been led by former priests or scholars originally, but they now came under the control of simple artisans who at least in part prepared the way for radical (i.e. social revolutionary) ideas. The Melchiorite movement was to find its firmest foothold in these lay-conventicles of Bible students.

Naturally the main impetus which led to the Netherlands' break with Rome came from Luther, but the sacramentarian movement interpreted him in its own way. Luther's greatest influence on the Dutch Reformation was established by his early tracts, written up to 1520, in which he appeared as a critic of the old church and as the proponent of a new morality. His early books, *On the Lord's Prayer* (1519), *The Ten Commandments, On Good Works* and *On the Freedom of the Christian Man* (all written in 1520), ran to three or four editions in the Netherlands. Yet there was no demand for the books in which he protested against the "sacramentarians", the Christian humanists and the insurgent peasants. *De Servo Arbitrio, Against the Heavenly Prophets* and the other works of 1525 written against the peasants, which were all books dealing with the core of Luther's theology, were not printed in the Netherlands. Nor did Dutch Bibles carry his negative comments on the Epistle of James.[9] It is clear from this selective attitude to Luther that there was a climate which

[9] Cf. C. Ch.G. Visser, *Luthers Geschriften in de Nederlanden tot 1546* Assen 1969, pp. 130-132; W. J. Kühler, *op. cit.* p. 38.

indicated that the Reformation here would not necessarily develop along the same lines as in Wittenberg.

Sacramentarianism was based, socially and economically, on - the urban population in Holland, whose growing wealth favoured their spiritual emancipation from the clergy. Although the Dutch Anabaptist movement had its ideological roots in sacramentarianism, far different factors, of a sociological nature, furthered its development. The great attraction of Hoffman's apocalyptic prophecies for the simple people is best explained by the economic depression which had a great impact on the urban middle and lower classes between 1531 and 1537.[10] As soon as the social-revolutionary implications of the Melchiorite movement became apparent early in 1534, many sacramentarians began to distance themselves from the Anabaptists.

The economic situation worsened every year after 1531 because of the conflict between the Emperor Charles V and the Danish Kings Frederick I and Christian III. The Emperor, who wanted to restore his brother-in-law, Christian II, to power in Denmark, assembled ships and soldiers in Holland, intending to launch the invasion from there. The Danes responded to these military preparations by closing the Sound to all Dutch ships. They were supported by Lübeck, which began a pirate war against all Dutch fishing and cargo vessels. The Dutch could thus only fish in the Zuider Sea or in their own coastal waters. But Dutch trade at this time was carried on almost exclusively with Northern and Eastern Europe. They bought cheap corn from Livonia and Poland and caught cheap herring in the Baltic. These basic foodstuffs quickly escalated in price. In 1532 the price of rye was three times that of a normal year (before 1529). It was not until 1537 that Dutchmen could again sail unmolested in the Baltic. As the price of corn fell, social unrest came to an end.[11]

At the same time England was posing a serious threat to Holland's highly developed cloth trade. Since the end of the fifteenth century the English government had limited wool exports to the Continent so as to speed up the development of a

---

[10] K. Vos, "Revolutionnaire Hervorming" in *De Gids* (Amsterdam) 1920, pp. 433-450; A. F. Mellink, *op. cit.* pp. 1-17.

[11] W. J. Kühler, *op. cit.* pp. 96f.

strong domestic textile industry. In 1527 Cardinal Wolsey forbade all direct trade in wool between England and the Netherlands. England's continental wool-market was moved to Calais, but even this was closed in 1533.[12]

After 1529 unemployment grew amongst Dutch dockers and textile-workers, whilst food was becoming increasingly expensive. Famine led to the increased incidence of the "English sweat" or "hot sickness" (probably tuberculosis). The Burgomaster of Leiden gave the following account of the situation in his town in 1530: "Now that it is hard to come by food in the town, there is great poverty and terrible hunger. The wretched people are suffering all the time and every day someone says, 'Oh dear God, do not pass over us with our 'hot sickness' but give us quick release, for we would rather die than go on living.' Because of their poverty many become thieves, and much is stolen in our towns every day, and many of the spinners and weavers leave . . ."[13] Faced with such bleak prospects many people left home, going from place to place in search of work and food.

Almost all of the early Melchiorites who appear in the minutes of the inquisition before 1536 were artisans (except for a few priests and one or two members of the ruling class). Not one seems to have been a peasant. The most commonly mentioned vocations are those of sailors, weavers, blacksmiths, glass-makers and book-keepers.[14] A mandate from the Dutch Court dated 4th March, 1535 forbade boat owners from hiring crew members who belonged to the "new sects". Sailors had to obtain references

---

[12] O. Rammstedt, *Sekte und soziale Bewegung.* Cologne and Opladen 1966, pp. 20-22.

[13] Quoted in A. F. Mellink, *op. cit.* p. 11. cf. H. v. d. Wee, "La Réforme Protestante dans l'optique de la conjoncture économique et sociale des Pays-Bas meridionaux au XVI^c siècle" in *Sources de l'histoire religieuse de la Belgique. Moyen Age et Temps Moderne.* Louvain 1968, pp. 303-315.

[14] G. Grosheide (ed.), "Verhooren en Vonnissen der Wederdopers" in *Bijdragen en Mededeelingen van het Historisch Genootschap.* 41 (1920) pp. 48, 49, 64, 75, 122, 131 and G. Grosheide, *Bijdrage tot de Geschiedenis der Anabaptisten in Amsterdam* Hilversum 1938 pp. 71-72.

from priests showing that they had received communion.[15] In their accounts of the "Great Exodus" of the Melchiorites in March, 1534, both the Court of Holland and Reynier Brunt, the General Procurator, state that all the heretics were "poor folk, all of them badly off", "for there is not a single nobleman or anyone of name or repute involved in this affair". Brunt wrote of the Anabaptists in Amsterdam that "many are starving and all are poor".[16] The property confiscated from the heretics was not even enough to support the twenty-five soldiers who were employed in northern Holland to track down sect members.[17] This poverty probably explains the generally low level of education amongst the Anabaptists. Most of the simple people obviously did not realise the danger they faced by being rebaptised at the time of the "Great Exodus" of 1534. They believed that rebaptism would safeguard them, and they began to "rage like madmen" when they were arrested. The Court of Holland, in its report to the regent, Maria of Hungary, said that they were "simple, rough people, of limited understanding."[18]

This interpretation of the Dutch Melchiorite movement has been questioned. The names of nobles and patricians who took up this cause have been marshalled to show that it was not made up solely of the poor and oppressed. Such figures are, in Amsterdam: Cornelis de Vlaming, a corn merchant and son of a Burgomaster, Aefgen Listincx, a rich merchant's widow, and about sixty members of the wealthy riflemen's association; in Deventer: the Burgomaster, Jacob van Wynssem and the patricians, Lubbe van Wynssem, Alidt ter Porten and Hylle van Ressem; in Frisia: Christoffer van Ewsum, a nobleman who owned most of Groningen, and also Elsa van Lostadt, Drostin von Benscop and Joachim van Berchem (David Joris' "patron").[19]

The irrefutable fact that a few members of the patriciate and of

---

[15] C. A. Cornelius, *Die niederländischen Wiedertäufer während der Belagerung Münsters 1534-1535* Munich 1869, p. 90.

[16] *Ibid.* pp. 77,93.

[17] G. Grosheide (ed.), "Verhooren" p. 24.

[18] C. A. Cornelius, *Geschichte des Münsterschen Aufruhrs* Vol. 2 1860, pp. 388-389.

[19] W. J. Kühler, *op. cit.* pp. 397-401; G. Grosheide, *Bijdrage* pp. 75-81.

the lesser nobility joined the apocalyptic movement does not invalidate the argument that the movement was caused by a grave economic depression. In almost all times of crisis some members of the ruling class have come to doubt the validity of their traditional values and have worked against their own "class interest". Also the idea that man is simply *homo oeconomicus*, quite rationally concerned with his material interests, cannot be applied to the men of the sixteenth century for whom fear of God and the Last Judgment constituted spiritual realities of enormous power. The apparently endless poverty being suffered by a large part of the population and also the equally insoluble conflict between the pro-Catholic policy of the Habsburgs and the urgent need for radical church reforms created a sense of despair and uncertainty amongst members of the middle and upper classes. They were thus prepared to accept the idea of a radical transformation of the world, even though they were not themselves the immediate sufferers from the economic misery.[20]

2. The Beginnings of the Melchiorite Movement in the Netherlands.

Dutch Anabaptism began in Eastern Frisia. It was Count Enno II who provided the impetus for missionary activity by issuing his repressive measures.

Hoffman had to leave Emden in June, 1530 after the great success of his mission. He nominated Jan Volkerts Trijpmaker as his successor, but he in turn was banished by the Emden municipal authorities in December, 1530.[21] Shortly before this Jan Volkerts had baptised Sikke Freerks Snijder in Emden. Jan Volkerts fled to Amsterdam and Sikke Snijder fled to Leeuwarden where he won over a small Bible conventicle to Hoffman's ideas. Obbe and Dirk Philips were probably also members of this group. Sikke Freerks Snijder was executed

---

[20] Cf. C.-P. Clasen, *Die Wiedertäufer im Herzogtum Württemberg und in benachbarten Herrschaften. Ausbreitung, Geisteswelt, Soziologie.* Stuttgart 1965, pp. 147-151.

[21] O. Philips, *A Confession* in G. H. Williams and A. M. Mergal (ed.), *op. cit.* p. 209-210.

before the governor's chancellery on 20th March, 1531 because he had been baptised a second time.[22] Apparently he had not been involved in baptising others, for this was not mentioned in the charge. Obbe and Dirk Philips were not baptised until January, 1534.

But Jan Volkerts was already dispensing rebaptism in Amsterdam in 1531, acting as the representative of Hoffman. His first candidates for baptism were Bartholomeus Boekbinder and Pieter de Houtzager.[23] Hoffman himself appeared in Amsterdam in the summer of 1531. The tolerant attitude of the Amsterdam Magistrate meant that Hoffman and Jan Volkerts were able to baptise about fifty people and "converse with them publicly."[24] When the Court of Holland heard of this, orders were sent to the Mayor of Amsterdam (Jan Hubrechts) for Volkerts to be arrested. But the police could not find him. Then the incredible thing happened: Volkerts went voluntarily to the Mayor's house to give himself up. But Hubrechts wanted to give him the opportunity to escape and sent him off saying, "Go to the prison and get arrested!". Though unaccompanied by a guard, Volkerts did the mayor's bidding. He wanted to earn a martyr's crown and marched direct to his prison. The Court ordered him to be sent to the Hague and here the apostle who was so anxious for martyrdom revealed the names of all those who had been baptised by him or Hoffman. Reynier Brunt, the General Procurator, then ordered the Mayor of Amsterdam to imprison every Anabaptist in the city. But the Mayor's young wife sent out a warning to all she could reach; the police only managed to arrest nine out of a suspected number of fifty Anabaptists.[25] Of the people arrested only one, Jan Hermans, had drawn attention to himself. He had once prevented a dying woman from receiving extreme unction, and in order to show his disgust with Catholic ceremonies had buried her corpse underneath the gallows

---

[22] *Documenta Anabaptistica Neerlandica* I. No. III p. 4.

[23] G. Grosheide, *Bijdrage* p. 36; C. A. Cornelius, *Geschichte des Münsterschen Aufruhrs*. Vol. 2. p. 407.

[24] C. A. Cornelius, *Geschichte des Münsterschen Aufruhrs* Vol. 2. p. 404.

[25] *Ibid.* Vol. 2. p. 404. G. Grosheide, *Bijdrage* p. 302.

without holding official rites, but singing Lutheran hymns. Despite this blasphemous provocation the Burgomasters of Amsterdam did not punish Hermans. Instead they censured the chaplain who had refused to transfer the corpse Hermans had buried into "holy ground."[26]

Jan Volkerts and those who had been apprehended along with him were taken to the Hague on 5th December, 1531 after having recanted their faith. Cornelis Benninck and Pieter Colijn, the Burgomasters of Amsterdam, had to be present to witness the executions. As the heads rolled into the sand Benninck turned to Colijn (despite the presence of the Emperor's delegate) and said "In future we shall not deliver them up to the butchers again!"[27] The heads of the victims were sent to Amsterdam to be impaled at Volewijk as a warning. But the Mayor (Hubrechts) refused to obey an explicit order to be present at this grim ceremony. Ruysch Jans, the Burgomaster, told the General Procurator's representatives that it would have been better to leave the heads with the lifeless bodies. When the Court's emissary explained that the ten heretics had renounced their errors before being put to death and that they had died as orthodox Christians, the Burgomaster asked the disconcerting question, "Have they forsaken God after all?"[28] All of those who died were so poor that they did not leave behind anything that could be confiscated.[29]

Hoffman was shocked by the news of the execution of his ten followers. He ordered that there should be no baptisms for two years (until the end of 1533). He saw a precedent for this move in Ezra 4:24, when there was an interruption in the building of the second Temple.[30]

In his commentary on Romans, written in 1533, Hoffman condemned those who sought a martyr's death, as had Volkerts. If anyone throws a fellow-believer onto the butcher's bench (and

---

[26] C. A. Cornelius, *Geschichte des Münsterschen Aufruhrs* Vol. 2. p. 405.

[27] *Ibid.* Vol. 2. p. 409.

[28] *Ibid.* Vol. 2. p. 405.

[29] G. Grosheide, *Bijdrage* p. 73.

[30] O. Philips, *A Confession* in G. H. Williams and A. M. Mergal (ed.), *op. cit.* p. 211.

the latter becomes a "blood-witness of the Gospel"), then he is as guilty of his death as is the hangman who dispatches him. He rejects as a total misunderstanding the idea that a martyr's death is the most forceful way of proclaiming the truth; he considers this to be totally senseless.[31]

With the prohibition of believers' baptism, Hoffman's followers seemed to develop into a radical grouping within the sacramentarian movement. Since the sacramentarians enjoyed the protection of most of the local Councils in the Dutch towns, the Melchiorites were able to recruit new members without trouble. Up to December, 1533 (i.e. during the whole period when there was a ban on adult baptism), only one Melchiorite was executed – Philip Wijntgen of Westbrouck, who was put to death on 10th March, 1532. Another Hoffmanite, Martyn Alberts, was tried but acquitted.[32]

Because there were no baptisms it is difficult to trace the growth of the Melchiorites up to the end of 1533. Cornelis Poldermann of Middelburg told the Strasbourg Council in November, 1533 that Hoffman's doctrines "were publicly proclaimed as the truth in many places in the Netherlands."[33] It appears that the movement had spread from Frisia to Zeeland within two years. It is not clear to what extent Hoffman was involved in this growth. Since all of his tracts written in 1532 and early 1533 were written in Dutch and printed in Holland, we can conclude that he had remained in the Netherlands during 1532.[34] Later, in 1537, Hoffman himself said that he "had travelled through the Netherlands" before his last visit to Strasbourg.

---

[31] *Römerbrief* Y 3a.

[32] G. Grosheide, *Bijdrage* p. 302. The facts do not support the frequently propounded theory (most recently put forward by R. van Dülmen in *Das Täuferreich in Münster* 1974, pp. 14 and 25) that it was in response to the cruel persecution by the authorities that the Dutch Anabaptists developed an apocalyptic, vengeful fury.

[33] *TAE* II No. 461, p. 213.

[34] Hoffman presumably spoke Low German whilst he was in Holland. Since all of his books in Dutch are on a much higher linguistic level than his German texts, a scholarly Dutchman must have translated his tracts from German (possibly this was Johannes Eisenburg, who came from an area – Cologne – where High German, Low German and Dutch were all spoken).

The remarkable growth of the Melchiorites was only possible because of the conflicts between the Imperial administration (the Great Council in Brussels, the Court of Holland in the Hague and the Regent's Chancellors in each individual province) and the local Magistrates who refused to implement the Edict of Worms and the mandates against the Anabaptists of 1528-1529. Reynier Brunt, the General Procurator, complained to Count Hoogstraten, of the County of Holland, that "all these problems are due principally to error and negligence on the part of the officers." Above all, he accused the Mayors of Amsterdam and Haarlem and the Bailiff of Waterland of total apathy regarding the heretics.[35] The Magistrates of Amsterdam were particularly firm in their opposition to the Court's ecclesiastical policy. They refused to suppress the sacramentarians because "if we were to enforce justice on all those who blaspheme against the sacrament we would be able to do nothing else." In March, 1534, the authorities in Amsterdam refrained from taking action as they watched the Anabaptists amassing arms and hiring boats in which to sail for Münster. They interceded only at the last moment on the orders of the Court. The Melchiorite "streakers" (who had run through the streets of Amsterdam on 10th February, 1535 calling everyone to repentance) declared after their arrest that they considered the Burgomasters – Colijn, Heymann and Reecalf – to be their brothers.[36] The Hoffmanites also had a high regard for Karl von Geldern the younger, the city governor of Groningen. He was an illegitimate son of Duke Karl von Geldern, who had desperately defended Groningen against the expansionist plans of Charles V, after he had already taken control of Frisia in 1524 and Utrecht and Overijssel in 1528.[37] Jakob van Wynssem, the Burgomaster of Deventer (in Overijssel), was in fact a Melchiorite.

Persecuting heretics had an important political impact on local authorities, for it posed a threat to the local autonomy of each

---

[35] C. A. Cornelius, *Die niederländischen Wiedertäufer* p. 70.

[36] C. A. Cornelius, *Geschichte des Münsterischen Aufruhrs* Vol. 2. 1860, pp. 406-412.

[37] Cf. J. ten Doornkaat-Koolman, *Dirk Philips* 1964 p. 8; *BRN* VII: 361-370.

town. By setting up heresy courts Charles V was flouting two civic privileges: the *ius de non evocando* (a privilege granted to the Counties of Holland and Western Frisia in 1452), and the "Hundred Pound Privilege" (a prerogative of the towns within the Counties of Holland and Zeeland since 1404). The first privilege gave the towns the right to try criminal cases by a local jury (except cases of High Treason). The second privilege set a limit of a hundred pounds of property that could be legally confiscated. Charles V regarded "heresy" as High Treason, and justification enough to ignore such privileges. He demanded that everyone who was tainted with heresy be handed over to the Court of Holland or to the Great Council in Brussels. The towns found that the simplest way to protect their local autonomy was simply not to disclose cases of heresy. They thus did not need to hand people over and obviated the inevitable legal wrangles with the Imperial authorities over the confiscation of property.[38]

In fact, those who chose to protect the Anabaptists sometimes lost their jobs and possessions as a result. Count Hoogstraten dismissed Jan Hubrechts, the Mayor of Amsterdam, in March, 1534. Similarly his successor, Heymann Jacobs, was deposed in September, 1535 for being too lenient towards the Anabaptists. Later in 1535 the Duke of Geldern removed his son Karl from his post as Governor of Groningen because of his sympathies with the sacramentarians and his leniency to the Anabaptists.[39]

3. The Usurpation of the Leadership of the Dutch Melchiorites by Jan Matthijs, 1533–1534.

The small Melchiorite groups in the Netherlands took a strong interest in the apocalyptic visions of the Josts and of Barbara Rebstock. The visions were seen to refer to identifiable people, places and future events.[40] Hoffman himself said that "all the prophecies, both old and new, which relate to this town (Strasbourg) have been revealed to the brethren in the

---

[38] G. Grosheide, *Bijdrage* pp. 259, 265, 272-274, 290.
[39] *Ibid.* pp. 92-93.
[40] *TAE* II No. 461, p. 213, No. 466, pp. 218-219.

Netherlands but have been hidden from this city".[41] The
spirituality of the Dutch Melchiorites was in essence identical
with that of the Strasbourg "Enthusiasts", but it was more
dangerous because it tended to interpret signs more and more
literally. As expectations became more precise, the more
unbearable did the Melchiorites find the ban on baptism. They
considered believers' baptism to be the magical "Tau sign";
anyone with this seal on his forehead would be protected from
the terrors of the apocalypse and from the punishment of God at
the Last Judgment (according to Revelation 7:3). Those with
"pure and simple hearts" decided to reinstitute baptism in the
autumn of 1533 because all of their calculations had led them to
the conclusion that the old world would give way to the new age
at the end of that year.[42]

Without seeking Hoffman's permission, Jan Matthijs lifted the
ban on baptism on All Saints Day, 1533, about one and a half
months before the expiry of the date fixed by Hoffman. On the
same day he met Jan Beukels, a bankrupt merchant and formerly
a tailor. Matthijs claimed to have experienced the outpouring of
the Holy Spirit and the revelation from God that Hoffman had
prophesied. He claimed to be Enoch, the second witness of the
Apocalypse. He said that Hoffman was wrong in maintaining
that because persecution against the Anabaptists was too
dangerous this was not yet the time to administer adult baptism.
On the contrary, the time was now ripe for adult baptism so that
God's chosen people could be assembled for the apocalypse.
"God wants to raise up a chosen people. If anyone is not signed
with the Signum Tau he will be subjected to the Father's wrath
and punishment." Jan Beukels had himself baptised by Matthijs
and he was sent as an "apostolic messenger" along with Gerrit
Boekbinder (alias Gerrit thom Kloster) to Den Briel and
Rotterdam where they baptised between eight and ten further
people.[43] From there they went on to Amsterdam, Leiden, Horn,

---

[41] *TAE* II No. 617, p. 393.
[42] O. Philips *A Confession* in G. H. Williams and A. M. Mergal (ed.),
op. cit. p. 212.
[43] J. Niesert (ed.), *Münstersche Urkundensammlung* Vol. 1. Coesfeld
1826, p.. 175; C. A. Cornelius(ed.), *Berichte der Augenzeugen über das
Münstersche Wiedertäuferreich* (1853) Reprint 1965, p. 370 cf. p. 405.

Enckhuizen and Alckmaar.

From Leiden Ian Matthijs returned immediately to Amsterdam where he had hidden his beautiful mistress Diewer (a brewer's daughter, later "Queen Divara"), so that her parents could not find her. This was the second instance of Matthijs' emancipation from Hoffman. Like Claus Frey before him he repudiated his first "shrewish" wife and (solely on his own authority) committed himself to a "spiritual sister and bride." Hoffman could only condemn such an act as whoredom.

Matthijs then encountered opposition amongst the Melchiorites in Amsterdam. Hoffman's ban on baptism was still valid there. Furthermore this group had until then identified "Enoch" with Cornelis Poldermann, of Middelburg.[44] Matthijs reacted to their objections with fearful cursings, and he condemned all those who opposed him to eternal damnation. His opponents lost their composure in the face of such words, spoken "with all the power of the Holy Ghost", by this bear of a man with his sombre face and black beard. The threat of hell struck them to the core; they felt they were about to be thrown into the everlasting bonfire. Then, soon after, Matthijs sent a twelve-year old boy as messenger and offered them peace. This sudden alternation between terror and love had the desired effect. Doubters were converted into convinced and obedient disciples.[45] The same technique of suddenly alternating proclamations of mercy with devastating messages of doom ensured similar obedience to Matthijs during his later and short-lived reign in the city of Münster. People were fascinated by this lone and sombre prophet, so far removed from them because he was possessed by the Holy Spirit yet capable of suddenly encompassing them with boundless love.[46]

Matthijs's success in Amsterdam must have been decisive in respect of his ability to establish a new spiritual authority amongst

[44] O. Philips, *A Confession* in G. H. Williams and A. M. Mergal (ed.), *op. cit.* p. 212.
[45] *Ibid.* p. 214; C.A. Cornelius, *Berichte der Augenzeugen* p. 40.
[46] C. A. Cornelius *Berichte der Augenzeugen* pp. 21, 39, 408.

most of the Dutch Melchiorites, since Amsterdam was the home of men who had supported Hoffman for longer than any others – Bartholomeus Boekbinder, Pieter Houtzager and Willem de Kuyper. If these men could accept Matthijs as their new leader all the rest would follow them.

The first of Jan Matthijs's missionaries to appear in Frisia was Pieter Houtzager who arrived at the end of 1533. He proclaimed the imminence of the Last Judgment and urged everyone to repent. To attain salvation it was necessary to be baptised as an adult, since baptism without faith (i.e. infant baptism) was invalid. Anyone who did not accept his invitation to be baptised would be damned for eternity. It was now the time to assemble the 144,000 who, according to Revelation 7:4 and 14:1, would oppose the Antichrist. Many people were baptised and swore to take no more part in the worship or sacraments of the Catholic Church.[47] Matthijs also sent off Bartholomeus Boekbinder and Willem de Kuyper to convert the Melchiorites of Leeuwarden. They arrived there claiming to be empowered by the Holy Spirit in the same way the apostles had been on the day of Pentecost. They urged any Melchiorite who had not yet been baptised to submit to baptism at their hands. They calmed those amongst the fifteen members of the congregation who were afraid of the consequences by saying that the time of persecution had come to an end. No more Christian blood was to be shed. God would shortly wipe every tyrant off the face of the earth.[48] The prophecy of the irresistible world-mission of the "apostolic messengers" derived from Hoffman himself. At the end of his commentary on Romans he had said that they would appear quite openly and that no tyrant would be able to destroy them.[49] After such a comforting assurance no-one dared raise any more objections. Everyone was baptised.

---

[47] *Documenta Anabaptistica Neerlandica* I. No. IV pp. 5-6.
[48] O. Philips, *A Confession* in G. H. Williams and A. M. Mergal (ed.), *op. cit.* p. 216 (Philips says that de Kuyper's Christian name was "Dirk", but it was in fact "Willem").
[49] *Römerbrief* Z1a.

From Leeuwarden Boekbinder and de Kuyper went on to Münster, arriving there on 5th January, 1534. Here they baptised Bernd Rothmann and Roll, Klopriss, Vinne and Stralen, the preachers of Wassenberg, as well as a rich merchant, Bernd Knipperdolling. Both Rothmann and Knipperdolling declared that at the moment of baptism they had still assumed that they would be put to death by godless men. They had had no thought of rebellion or revenge.[50] Eight days later Matthijs' second pair of apostles, Jan Beukels and Gerrit Boekbinder, arrived in Münster.[51] They declared that the Second Enoch taught that Christians were allowed to take up the sword against a godless secular authority.[52] This set the scene for the events to come.

Both Hoffman and Matthijs were convinced that two things were necessary before the world could be transformed: the "apostolic messengers" had to go on a mission to the whole world and the godless had to be destroyed. These two events were to usher in the Second Coming of Christ. Hoffman felt that before this process could begin his followers would have to receive a new outpouring of the Holy Spirit, so as to become invulnerable, and the established authorities in the Free Imperial cities would have to be prepared to do battle with the forces of Antichrist. Hoffman understood the "godless" to be first and foremost the "priests of Baal", whatever confession they belonged to.

Jan Matthijs, however, regarded all religious and secular tyrants as enemies of the new kingdom of God. All had to be destroyed, without exception. He probably considered the collaboration of established authorities in the work of dispensing vengeance to be desirable but not essential. If necessary the holy congregation of the last days should itself take up the sword – an idea which Hoffman rejected until the very end. Matthijs believed that he was already experiencing the new Pentecost whereas Hoffman believed it was yet to come. But Jan Matthijs

---

[50] Cf. R. Stupperich (ed.), *Die Schriften Bernhard Rothmanns* p. 280; J. Niesert (ed.), *Münstersche Urkundensammlung* Vol. 1. p. 186.

[51] R. Stupperich (ed.), *Die Schriften Bernhard Rothmanns* p. 279; C. A. Cornelius, *Berichte der Augenzeugen* p. 403.

[52] C. A. Cornelius, *Berichte der Augenzeugen* p. 398.

was only drawing the logical conclusions from Hoffman's visions of the future. Was it not reasonable that, after expectations had been raised and the established authorities had refused to play the role appointed to them in the apocalypse, the elect should take the sword into their own hands?

There were other less important differences, such as Matthijs seeing himself as Enoch, a role Hoffman had attributed to his friend Poldermann, and Matthijs' acceptance of polygamy (in spite of already being married, he consorted with the young and beautiful Diewer, his "spiritual sister and bride").

Hoffman's attitude to the Anabaptist kingdom of Münster remained ambivalent and vacillating. After the Anabaptists of Münster had been successful in defending themselves against the mercenary-armies who attacked them in 1534, Hoffman seems to have identified himself with the New Zion in Westphalia and considered that it was undefeatable. In November, 1534 he made the following remark, recorded in the minutes of the city: "In Münster there is a prophet, Jan Matthijs by name, who says he is God's witness. Münster shall not be overcome."[53] Yet he was not distressed in 1536 when he was informed of the fall of Münster and the execution of Jan van Leiden, Bernd Knipperdolling and Bernd Krechting. "He said he did not care. What is not of God is bound to fall." Blesdijk's comments on Hoffman's relationship to Jan Matthijs made about 1550 are probably accurate. "He did neither order nor approve of Jan Matthijs' rebaptising, nor did he extol any of the popular uprisings. He frequently expressed his sorrow because of these events, both orally and also in his letters. Finally he predicted that Jan Matthijs and Jan van Leiden would end in the same dreadful way as Korah, Dathan and Abiram (Num 16:1-30). He also decided that no renewal should be undertaken unless the apostolic messengers had been confirmed by a new heavenly spirit, as it had once come down on the Apostles, i.e. at the day of Pentecost. And he considered it legitimate, if – to achieve this end (a new order) – the magistracy should wield its sword,

[53] *TAE* II No. 617, p. 395.

which was given to it according to the Old as well as the New Testament."[54]

The different attitudes of both the Dutch and Westphalian Melchiorites to the use of force played no part in the dispute between the Anabaptist communities of Strasbourg and Münster. The conflict centred much more on Münster's claim to be the new Jerusalem and on the issue of polygamy. The Strasbourgers predicted that Münster, despite its claim to leadership, would suffer the same fate as Troy. Jan Matthijs responded to the charges of the Strasbourg "Enthusiasts" by saying, "the Strasbourgers are gluttons and topers. They are like bloodhounds sitting in a temple of idolatry". The Strasbourgers rejected polygamy as practised by Jan Matthijs and Jan van Leiden, as well as Jan van Batenburg's teaching that a believer should divorce an unbelieving or a barren wife.

4. Pacifist and Militant Melchiorites in the Netherlands.

The question as to whether the majority of the Dutch Melchiorites was "pacifist" or "revolutionary" has still not been resolved. Whereas A. F. Mellink tends to play down the significance of Anabaptist pacifism and Karel Vos even argues that almost none of the Anabaptists were pacifists, Kühler and van der Zijpp (both Mennonites) claim that the pacifist Melchiorites remained in the majority before, during and after the appearance of the revolutionary groups.[55]

There are no exact percentages on the relation of the two groups since we do not know the total number of Melchiorites in individual towns. The estimates given by contemporaries

[54] N. Blesdikius, *Historia Vitae Davidis Georgii* p. 5.

[55] A. F. Mellink, *De Wederdopers* pp. 362-365; K. Vos, "Revolutionnaire Hervorming" in *De Gids* 1920, pp. 435, 437, 441-442; W. J. Kühler, *Geschiedenis* pp. 151-152; N. van der Zijpp, *Geschiedenis der Doopsgezinden in Nederland* Arnheim 1952, p. 37.

vary so widely that any attempt to fix a specific figure is quite arbitrary.[56]

Any speculation about the ratio of revolutionary to pacifist Anabaptists must presuppose a constant regarding human behaviour which cannot be assumed in times of crisis. No one can say how many "pacifist" Anabaptists would have taken up arms if an uprising in one of the Dutch towns had had anything like the success of that in Münster. Followers are attracted by success but deterred by defeat.

Nor is there any sharp distinction between the militant and the pacifist attitudes. When Jan van Geelen appealed to the Melchiorites of Amsterdam to arm themselves, Jacob van Campen, the Anabaptist bishop, supported him, but with the following reservations: weapons should only be used in self-defence or when God gave a clear signal to mount an attack (as, for example, in Münster, where three suns are said to have appeared in the sky).[57] But Jan Paeuw, the Anabaptist deacon in Amsterdam with responsibility for the poor, refused even to use a knife in self-defence.[58] These differing attitudes to the use of force appeared in all Anabaptist circles: some were prepared to indulge in direct revolutionary activity (e.g. Jan Matthijs), some would support a rebellion, if God gave a clear sign (e.g. Hans Hut), some justified the use of arms in self-defence (e.g. Balthasar Hubmaier), and some (e.g. Michael Sattler) absolutely refused to use force in any form. The boundaries between the first three stands were obviously quite fluid.

---

[56] For example in Amsterdam the following figures are mentioned: When two Anabaptists, Jan van Scellingwoude and Jan Claes, were sent to the Dutch Court in October 1534, they told the Council of Amsterdam that they had 1,500 townsmen who would protect them. In January 1535, another Anabaptist, Meinaert von Emden, said that there were 3,500 Melchiorites in Amsterdam. But Reynier Brunt, the General Procurator, said in March 1535 that at most there were only one hundred Anabaptists in Amsterdam. Although the authorities had an interest in keeping the figures low it seems that the Anabaptists greatly exaggerated their own strength.

[57] G. Grosheide, "Verhooren en Vonnissen" p. 96.

[58] Ibid. pp. 46–47.

It ought to be pointed out, too, that there is no strict correlation, either positive or negative, between apocalyptic expectations and revolutionary activity.

Up to 1535 all Dutch Anabaptists were looking forward to a radical transformation of the world and they were thus quite prepared to break with the established patterns of society. Yet at the same time these fantastic and revolutionary apocalyptic expectations hindered the strategic planning of armed resistance and were responsible for the failure of the large-scale uprising in the Netherlands.

The most impressive example for this was the history of the "Great Exodus". In March, 1534 Jan van Leiden called on his brethren in Holland to set off for Münster "for here there are sufficient good things for the saints." They were all to assemble in the cloister at Hasselt (in Overijssel), taking with them nothing but money, clothing and arms.[59] Between 14,000 and 16,000 believers from Spaarndam, Amsterdam, Edam, Monnickendam, and Enckuizen gathered together for the exodus from "Egypt". 27 ships, with about 3,000 people on board, left Monnickendam and arrived at Swarte Water, near Genemuiden. Here they were captured and disarmed by a tiny band of soldiers (less than a hundred men). No one resisted, for they were expecting Jeremiah, the heavenly prophet who was in charge of them, to come and lead them into the land of Canaan. The exiles in the cloister at Hasselt were also hoping to receive the Holy Spirit. When the "seventh trumpet" did not sound and Jeremiah did not appear in the clouds of heaven, no one unsheathed "the sword of Gideon". The whole episode was a disastrous failure. It was the same story in Amsterdam. There the Anabaptists had commissioned six ships and bought a great pile of weapons. After much hesitation the Magistracy impounded the weapons and the ships at the last moment. But the Anabaptists did not react violently; the only form of protest was that of Willem de Kuyper, Bartholomeus Boekbinder and Pieter de Houtzager who ran through the streets brandishing their swords, shouting

---

[59] R. van Dülmen, *Das Täuferreich zu Münster* 1974, pp. 78-79.

"Woe, woe". They were then arrested and executed three days later.[60]

Finally it appears that the simple members of the congregations had a different attitude to the use of force from that of their leaders. Most of the leaders of the congregations in the Northern Netherlands turned against the use of force after the catastrophe of the "Great Exodus" (as, for example, Obbe and Dirk Philips, Jacob van Campen, David Joris and most of the 32 leaders who had assembled at Spaarndam in December, 1534). But David Joris and Obbe Philips were unable to win over their congregations to their pacifist views.[61]

5. Hoffman's Impact on Bernhard Rothmann's Theology.

The influence of Melchior Hoffman on the Anabaptist kingdom of Münster can be seen most clearly in the late tracts of Bernhard Rothmann, which he wrote after 1533 to justify the Anabaptists' "holy war". We shall restrict ourselves here to a sketch of the final phase of Rothmann's spiritual development.

The predominant idea in Rothmann's thought is that of the "restitution" of God's dominion on earth. There must be a radical conquest of sin both in the individual and in society. The belief in individual perfectibility has its political equivalent in the concept of a militant theocracy. Rothmann derived this basic idea from Hoffman, but took it to its logical conclusion in the special circumstances of Münster.

---

[60] For the "Great Exodus" cf. A. F. Mellink, *De Wederdopers* pp. 31-37, 356-358 and "The Mutual Relations between the Münster Anabaptists and the Netherlands" in *ARG* 50 (1959) p. 19; K. Vos, "Revolutionnaire Hervorming" pp. 440-441; C.A. Cornelius, *Die niederländischen Wiedertäufer* pp. 52-55, 76-78.

[61] Cf. G. Grosheide, "Verhooren en Vonnissen" pp. 182-183; O. Philips, *A Confession* in G. H. Williams and A. M. Mergal (ed.), *op. cit.* p. 223; G. Arnold, *Unpartheyische Kirchen-und Ketzerhistorie* 3rd ed. Schaffhausen 1740-1742, Vol. I, 2. p. 1319; W. J. Kühler, *Geschiedenis* p. 141; K.-H. Kirchhoff, "Gab es eine friedliche Täufergemeinde in Münster 1534?" in *Jahrbuch des Vereins für Westfälische Kirchengeschichte* 55-56 (1962-1963) pp. 7-21.

Hoffman plays a particularly important role in Rothmann's history of salvation. After Christ and his unlearned apostles had established the true doctrine on earth and the scholars had obscured the truth again, God now works the opposite way and has begun the "restitution" of His reign on earth with such scholars as Erasmus, Luther and Zwingli, but "then it was continued by Melchior (Hoffman) and Jan Matthijs, and finally our brother Jan van Leiden, who is quite unlearned in the eyes of the world, yet did triumphantly introduce God's truth."[62]

Rothmann took over Hoffman's most important doctrinal principles. Very often his theological arguments were more incisive than Hoffman's, but they added nothing substantially new. The following doctrines in particular derived from Hoffman:

1. the universality of divine grace;[63]
2. the freedom of man's will after enlightenment;[64]
3. the idea that man must be justified twice by means of a "first justifica-tion" based on grace alone and a "second justification" based on human strivings;[65]
4. the concept of human life as a process leading through three stages until man reaches fulfilment as he eventually shares in the divine nature;[66]
5. the impossibility of forgiveness for sins committed in full awareness of one's error;[67]
6. Monophysite Christology.[68]

[62] R. Stupperich (ed.), *Die Schriften Bernhard Rothmanns* 1970, p. 219.
[63] *Ibid*. pp. 232-235, 331.
[64] *Ibid*. pp. 247, 249-252.
[65] *Ibid*. pp. 234-235, 321.
[66] *Ibid*. pp. 309-312, 323-325, 342. A half-blind, literal faith constitutes the *Way* into the outer court of the Temple. Within the Temple a clear knowledge of the *Truth* takes over. In the Holy of Holies man is united with God and all creation in selfless love. This union of perfect love is *Life* in God. According to Rothmann, Christ's words: "I am the way, the truth and the life" (John 14:6) refer to this threefold progress of the Christian.
[67] *Ibid*. pp. 233, 254.
[68] *Ibid*. pp. 199, 130, 317-318. The importance of this doctrine in Münster can be seen from their coins which bore four letters, DWWF, which stood for "Dat wort wurde fleisch' (The Word became flesh). C. A. Cornelius, *Berichte der Augenzeugen* pp. 27-28.

Hoffman's basic hermeneutical ideas also occur in Rothmann's theology, e.g. the "figure", the "key of David" ("pure
fear of God") and the "cloven claw".[69] Rothmann uses the idea
of the "cloven claw" (i.e. the unity and eternal truth of the Bible
despite apparent contradictions) to explain why God's Word
changes at different times. All contradictions in the Bible can be
explained when it is realized that God's commandments are
bound up with the ages in which they are issued. Different laws
are valid in the period of "restitution" from those in the age of
suffering.[70]

Rothmann is more precise than Hoffman in his account of the
"canon within the canon." The Pentateuch and the Old
Testament prophets make up "the principal and incontrovertible
Scriptures, against which all other Scriptures must be judged."[71]
But this does not mean that we should return to the religion of
the Jews, because Rothmann says that Christ has done away
with the ceremonies and sacrifices of the Old Testament. It is
not the letter but the spirit which contains the true meaning and
which retains its permanent veracity.[72] Rothmann was fascinated not by individual features of the Old Testament but by the
general idea of a theocracy on earth which is prepared to use
force to establish its laws if the need arises. This was related to
Hoffman's theology of the last days and to the visions of the
Strasbourg prophets.

Rothman's theology of history resumes the ideas propounded
in Hoffman's late tract, *On the Pure Fear of God*. When the
"seventh angel of wrath" gave the sign (so Hoffman declared in
the summer of 1533), the "first-born of Egypt" would be slain
and the "kingdom of Babylon and Sodom" would be destroyed.
Its place would be taken by a new kingdom of Joseph and
Solomon, which would be advised by prophets in the spirit of
Jonah and Samson, and this theocracy would spread all over the

---

[69] B. Rothmann, *Schriften* pp. 237, 258, 274, 301-305.
[70] *Ibid.* pp. 254, 274, 332, 353.
[71] *Ibid.* p. 302.
[72] *Ibid.* pp. 224, 309, 334. One can hardly accept G. List's statement
(*Chiliastische Utopie* 1973, p. 203) that "Rothmann did not question the
priority of the New Testament."

world. Only after the darkness had been vanquished on earth would Christ, the bridegroom, appear to celebrate a Great Supper with his people.[73]

Rothmann, under the influence of Jan Matthijs, took these ideas of Hoffman to their logical conclusion and carried them even further with a radical reflection on the nature of earthly lordship. His resulting concept of the role of secular authorities and of the people of God in the last days diverged, however, considerably from Hoffman's.

According to Rothmann the history of the world so far has been marked by man's incessant rejection of the will of God and the repeated "restitution" of divine order. At the beginning of the "second age of the world" (which began with the Flood and has lasted until the present) Nimrod, who founded the first empire on earth and who is the first in the line of Kings, disobeyed God's will. Full of wickedness and lust for power he took unto himself the exercise of earthly power which had become necessary as a result of Adam's fall.[74] Ever since then worldly authority has essentially been a usurpation of God's power.[75] The fact that Nimrod's power can also be used (in God's sense) to punish evil and establish a certain degree of human justice and equity makes no difference; the secular state is still a "Babylonian authority."

At the same time God had chosen the Jews as a special people over whom he intended to rule directly. The law of the Jewish state was to be God's Law. Hence there was a divergence between the history of salvation and the history of the secular world.[76] But the Jews also transgressed against God's Law. Even the "restitution" brought about by Christ had no long-lasting effect; under the Papacy the so-called Christians fell even further away from God.[77]

Like Müntzer before him, Rothmann read the course of world history in the "figures" of Daniel, Chapter 2. The succession of

---

[73] Hoffman, *Von der reinen Furcht Gottes* A2b.
[74] Rothmann, *Schriften* pp. 381, 383-384, 400.
[75] *Ibid.* p. 389.
[76] *Ibid.* p. 388 cf. J. M. Stayer, *Anabaptists and the Sword* p. 242.
[77] *Ibid.* p. 215.

gold, silver, bronze and a mixture of iron and clay (which together make up the statue of history) symbolizes the increasing corruption in the chronological sequence of the empires of Assyria, Persia, Greece and Rome. All the evil within sacred and secular history culminates in the German Empire, which is the successor to the fourth empire, that of the Romans. Whereas the world empires of the past were ruled by stable monarchies, there is now an unstable "polyarchy" made up of an unnatural blend of spiritual and worldly power. This reveals new and ever-increasing processes of disintegration because realms and institutions have been built on the incompatible elements of iron and clay. The spiritual and temporal powers are similarly incompatible, and spiritual certainty has not been built on the solid foundation's of God's will. The prelates call themselves "shepherds of souls", but they rule like heathen kings. The "little horn" (Dan. 7:8) which knocks off and then assimilates three of the ten horns of the fourth monarchy is a symbol of the Pope (his triple-crowned tiara shows his similarity to the horn). After the Pope had subjected the Emperor, he used his newly-usurped worldly power in order to impose his own law in the place of God's ordinance.[78] Thus, until shortly before it comes to an end, this second age is one of suffering for the few who are true Christians. During this period the saints are not permitted to use force in their fight against evil. Although the apostles bought swords, they kept them in their sheaths.[79]

Towards the end of the world's second age the papist Antichrist will be unmasked and deposed.[80] The "Babylonian government" will also soon be overthrown.[81] Then Jan van Leiden will establish the militant "Kingdom of David." All of Christ's foes will then be condemned "to lick the earth."[82] The "restitution" of God's ordinance on earth must now be brought about by the sword as well as by spiritual weapons. It is God's servants on earth, not heavenly angels, who will wreak

[78] *Ibid.* pp. 396, 402–404.
[79] *Ibid.* p. 420.
[80] *Ibid.* pp. 350-351.
[81] *Ibid.* p. 420.
[82] *Ibid.* pp. 281, 352-356, 358, 362.

Dis ist die græs vnd gestalt der guldenn vff beyden seiten/ die der nawe Konig zu Munster schlagenn lest/ das stuck x gulden ist gut golot/ synd bey den Propheten zu Saust vnd Wardendorff gefunden die worffenn sie von sich/ da sie angriffen wurden Vnd wurdenn alle gericht/ kamen dem konige nicht wider dan sie auffgehaben:

Dieses Konigs Tyttel.

Johann vonn Gottis gnaden, Konig In dem Newe Tempel Gottes ein warhafftiger dyner der gerechtigkeit/ aus krafft d ftadt Munster.

Der Konig mit seinen Rethen vnd hoffgesinde vnd wie vil Ehewei ber ein Jtzlicher hatt/

Der konig Johann schneyder hat	5	}
Sein stadthalder Bernd kreppердelig	3	} Eheweyber.
Der Hoffmeister Herman Tybercke	3	}
Seynn Cantzler Bernd Radtman	4	}

Nach seindt alda xIIII. Propheten aus des konigs hoffgesinde/ die seine nechsten Rethe sein/ haben auch an weibern keine gebruch.

M. D. XXXV.

Plate 13: Coins of the Anabaptists: the ten-guilder piece

Een seer goede Reden berst my ter herten wt. Psalm.45.

Plate 14: David Joris: The breaking-forth of the Holy Spirit

vengeance on the godless.[83] Rothmann explicitly tells his followers that "at this point Christians are allowed to take up the sword against godless governments." They are "permitted to punish all who do evil and who practise injustice throughout the whole earth, which He will renew so that only justice remains in it; and in the cup which she [Babylon] mingled mingle her double!" (Revelation 18:6).[84] Only when the "second David", the warrior, has achieved all this, will Christ, the "peace-loving Solomon," take the earth for his own. His dominion will then usher in a third, invincible world, which will lead eventually to the "Kingdom of the Father," in which God is all in all.[85]

The most significant differences between Hoffman and Rothmann are quite apparent. Whereas until the very last Hoffman regarded any secular authority that did not actively support the cause of the papacy as a servant of God, for Rothmann they were all heathen successors to Nimrod. Hoffman looked for "restitution" to be implemented by legally appointed and pious kings or councillors, and unlike Rothmann, he did not justify rebellion on the part of the believers. Hoffman felt that the saints should carry no weapons during their apocalyptic battle against the forces of evil; they should have nothing whatsoever to do with the bloody handiwork of their secular patrons. But Rothmann believed that "God's servants" were expected to use the sword themselves in their campaign of revenge against the godless.

It would be false to construe a complete break between Hoffman and Rothmann out of these differences. All that Jan Matthijs did in practical terms, and that Rothmann did on a theoretical level, was to change the means whereby according to Hoffman vengeance was to be carried out and an earthly theocracy was to be established. If the kings and oligarchies refused to implement the apocalyptic programme, and if no angels descended with scythes to cut down the godless, then it was left to the Anabaptists themselves to bring about the "restitution" of God's rule.

[83] *Ibid.* pp. 365-366.
[84] *Ibid.* p. 282.
[85] *Ibid.* pp. 297, 346, 364.

People in Münster took the predictions of Hoffman and Rothmann very seriously. Gresbeck reports that the Anabaptists planned to extend the town as far as the blockhouses occupied by the besieging army in order to accommodate the 144,000 "apostolic messengers". Eight families were to be billetted in each house. When God gave the sign everyone would go out from the city in order to establish justice over the whole earth.[86] In Warendorf, Klopriss and Stralen (two of Jan van Leiden's "twelve apostles") said that after the siege the 144,000 would go out to sit in apocalyptic judgment over the rest of the world. Any noblemen or clergy who refused to accept their faith would have to be destroyed.[87]

Jan van Leiden's emblem of dominion was a globe surmounted by a golden cross. Two golden swords, the sword of vengeance and the sword of the spirit, transfixed the globe to symbolize the restored unity of spiritual and worldly power. As the "second David" Jan van Leiden clearly saw himself as "a king over the whole earth."[88]

[86] C. A. Cornelius, *Berichte der Augenzeugen* p. 97.

[87] Cf. J. Niesert, *Urkundensammlung* Vol. 1. pp. 58, 63, 116, 123.

[88] Cf. C. A. Cornelius, *Berichte der Augenzeugen* p. 378 and G. Brendler, Das Täuferreich zu Münster 1966, p. 146. The above account goes somewhat against the thesis of Richard van Dülmen (*Das Täuferreich zu Münster 1534-1535* 1974 p. 25) who plays down the military tendencies of the Melchiorites. I also disagree with Günther List (*Chiliastiche Utopie* 1973, pp. 201–202), who feels that utopian and chiliastic ideas did not affect the Münsterites until they were faced with defeat.

CHAPTER TEN

The Decline of the Melchiorite Movement.

1. Hoffman's Behaviour Towards the Strasbourg Melchiorites up to 1538.

1533 came and went without Hoffman's prophecies being fulfilled. Once more the now familiar old Melchiorite spectacle repeated itself: their faith was not to be shaken even when it had been based on events once predicted but which did not take place.[1] The Hoffmanites lived with the discrepancy between prophecy and reality for a long time (around five years), since this was easier than giving up all the hopes on which they had based their exaggerated self-confidence. Hoffman and his followers attempted to overcome their disappointment by revising their chronological calculations and by indulging in new activities.

Hoffman first of all postponed Christ's return for only a few months, to the end of 1534. But then it was put off to 1535, then to 1537 and finally to 1539.[2] In order to remove any doubts he explained that everything else had been running according to plan.[3] Early in May, 1534 he decided to invoke God's intervention by an act of self-imposed suffering: he asked to be thrown into a dungeon "where he could see neither the sun nor the moon till God have mercy on him and bring matters to an end."[4]

In his commentaries on the Epistles of James and Jude he compensated for the non-appearance of the Parousia by recommending self-purification to his disciples.[5]

[1] L. Festinger, H. Riecken and S. Schlachter, *When Prophecy Fails* New York. 2nd ed. 1964, p. 3.
[2] *TAE* II No. 484. p. 255, No. 594. p. 371.
[3] *TAE* II No. 617. p. 393.
[4] *TAE* II No. 551.
[5] Cf. K. Deppermann, "Melchior Hoffmans letzte Schriften" in *ARG* 63 (1972) pp. 72-93.

The first deadline he had set for his liberation was December, 1533, but when this passed Hoffman broke his oath, stating that he would live on bread and water until Christ's appearance.[6] His health improved with this return to a normal diet. On 28th April, 1534 Jakob Kron, the prison warder, reported that Hoffman had been singing in a loud voice in his cell and that he had shouted out of the window three times, "Woe on you godless scribes of Strasbourg!" The whole neighbourhood had run to his window to hear him.[7] Barely two months later Hoffman risked his last major assault on the city's preachers.

After Claus Frey had been drowned for blasphemy and bigamy (on 22nd May, 1534), Capito had written a book about his life and death, in which he linked Frey's name with that of Hoffman. The pamphlet concluded with the insinuation that Hoffman had taught that before the Last Judgment the "144,000 apostolic messengers would slay any priest, monk, nobleman, townsman or peasant who inclined toward popery, Lutheranism or Zwinglianism."[8]

Hoffman felt that he had been unjustly accused since he had expelled Frey from the Anabaptist congregation and because Frey had withdrawn his claim that the Melchiorites had been plotting a rebellion. Capito was aware of all this.[9] In his trial on 29th May, 1533 Hoffman had indeed said that "the whole priesthood" must perish, but he had not said that the "apostolic messengers" would be the instruments of vengeance. He had certainly never threatened that anyone who was not an Anabaptist would be wiped off the face of the earth.

This unjust attack aroused Hoffman's violent anger, which he expressed in a pseudonymous tract, attributed to a certain Caspar Beck.[10]

Here Hoffman speaks of himself as an innocent servant of

---

[6] *TAE* II No. 516.
[7] *TAE* II No. 546.
[8] *TAE* II No. 564, p. 342.
[9] *TAE* II No. 564, p. 329.
[10] *Sendbrieff an den achtbaren Michel Wachter.* This tract was first discovered in a library in Laubach and printed by E. W. Kohls in *Theologische Zeitschrift* 17 (1961)pp. 356-361.

God, who has been imprisoned in Jerusalem, which is in reality "a spiritual Egypt." It was in this place that Christ, the eternal Word, had been condemned and murdered publicly in 1533 (an allusion to the rejection of Hoffman's Christology). The evangelical preachers ("those lying Pharisees") had "established a covenant with everlasting death and hell". Like the whore of Babylon they had a thirst for the blood of anyone who witnessed to God's truth. The religious leaders had shown themselves to be "bloodhounds", "raging wolves in sheepskins", "blind, murdering spirits who are shameless liars", and "bloodsuckers, frothing at the mouth with their own shame." Hoffman justified his rage because that one bloodhound (Capito) had written that the Lord's guiltless witness was in fact a "rebel and a murderer" and that it was because of this, not because of his faith, that he had been imprisoned. Caspar Beck, the supposed author, then urged "dear Michael Wachter" to read the witness's interpretation of the Apocalypse and compare it to these accusations. He would then see who it was that was guilty of planning to murder – viz. he who, despite his better knowledge, accused an innocent man.

But such an expression of indignation was not totally candid, for since writing his commentary of Revelation, Hoffman had considerably altered his apocalyptic ideas, and there is no question that the slaying of the priests before the Last Judgment formed part of his programme.

So that everyone should know who was meant, a handwritten note was added to the text (which was pinned up in various places throughout the town), which read, "The innocent imprisoned witness is Melchior Hoffman. Jerusalem is Strasbourg. The bloodhounds are Hedio, Butzer, Capito. Capito has written lies in his book on Claus Kurtzener (Frey)."

The Council was furious when this abusive pamphlet appeared. The Strasbourg printers were ordered to the town hall on 22nd August, 1534 and asked whether they had printed the "shameful book". All protested their innocence and suggested that Valentin Kobian of Hagenau was the most likely culprit, since he was the only printer in Alsace apart from Balthasar Beck who used this particular typesetting.[11] At the trial on 21st

[11] *TAE* II No. 597.

September, 1534, Hoffman confessed to having written the book
but would not give the name of the printer. Since an
incriminating letter had been discovered in Poldermann's hiding-
place, he did concede that Poldermann had been involved in the
printing. He himself had not agreed to the indiscriminate
circulation of the pamphlet; it had been intended solely for the
"brethren" in order to refute the lies of the preachers. Finally he
admitted that he had given a bribe of one gulden to the wife of
Jakob Kron, his warder. Her maid Margret had handed over the
manuscript to Hoffman's disciples in Strasbourg. He defended the
use of the pseudonyms Wachter and Beck rather eccentrically by
claiming that Christ had also given new names to his apostles, and
that the Most High had prompted the name Casper Beck, which
he had already used once before in the summer of 1533. He
claimed also that he had retracted his original intention of having
the book printed and that he had begged Poldermann to "leave it
alone".[12]

Indeed, the appearance of the pamphlet on or around 20th
August, 1534 was highly inopportune. A few days earlier, on
15th August, he had attempted a reconciliation with Hedio,
Bucer and Zell, who visited him in prison. In the presence of the
two councillors in charge of the Anabaptists, Mathis Pfarrer and
Georg Pfitzer, he explained that his position was not so far
removed from that of the preachers. All the Strasbourg
theologians needed to do to be "totally at one" with him was to
"recognise the cloven claw." Hoffman saw no possibility of
compromise on the question as to whether the authorities had the
right to persecute anyone for their faith. He rejected the
preachers' recourse to Mosaic Law, which ordered false prophets
to be stoned (Deut. 13:5), for this only gave grounds to the
"bloodthirsty" to do away with him. He felt that all his followers
would return to the Strasbourg church if he could come to an
agreement with the preachers. But Hedio, on behalf of his
colleagues, rejected any reconciliation as long as Hoffman held to
his five basic errors.[13]

---

[12] *TAE* II No. 610. The preface to the anonymous *Eyn sendbrieff an
alle gottsförchtigen liebhaber der ewigen warheyt* (1553) was signed by
Caspar *Becker (sic.)*.
[13] *TAE* II No. 594.

But despite his imprisonment, his false prophecies and his alienation from the preachers, Hoffman's self-confidence did not waver. He informed the Council on 9th September, 1534 that "people should realise that they have amongst them the true Elijah who is to come before Christ's day of judgment. God has sent him to us, but we refused to acknowledge him. He is the last one; God will send us no more after him."[14]

After the failure of his attempted reconciliation with the preachers Hoffman tried to win over the Council. He told the Council members on 23rd November, 1534 that Strasbourg was the chosen city and that the leaders of this city would impose the Truth throughout the world. His prophecies were not false, because Barbara Rebstock had predicted all the persecutions and even the divisions within the Council. He would not retract his five central doctrines. The preachers had misunderstood and falsely represented him. If he were released he would refrain from preaching in the city until the Council members had perceived the veracity of his message. Since these discussions were also aimed at saving his own neck, Hoffman explained to the Council that he believed that no false prophet, who spoke on his own authority and not under the inspiration of the Holy Spirit, should be killed. But "arrogant prophets, who are convinced in their hearts that they are proclaiming lies" (this did not include him, even if he had erred, but did include Capito, Bucer and Hedio) were worthy of death.[15] Thus in 1534 Hoffman exhausted every method short of violence to gain his release from prison.

The events in Münster had an adverse effect on Hoffman's position. After the defeat of the Anabaptist kingdom in Westphalia, it was decided to move him to a deep dungeon.[16] At the end of September, 1535 the Council sent a patrician, Bernhard Wurmser, to Westphalia to find out from the imprisoned Anabaptist leaders Jan van Leiden and Bernd Knipperdolling whether they had had any personal connections with Hoffman. The Council wanted to find solid evidence which would enable them to have Hoffman executed whilst leaving

[14] *TAE* II No. 607.
[15] *TAE* II No. 617.
[16] *TAE* II Nos. 684, 685.

them with a clear conscience.[17] But Jan van Leiden and
Knipperdolling both agreed that they had only read Hoffman's
books – they did not know him personally.[18]

Then came months of silence. The hard terms of his
imprisonment remained. In April, 1536 he complained of his
new warder, "Schneider Jörgen", who gave him stale bread, foul ·
water and often a whipping. The Council ordered Hoffman to be
treated more gently and that he should be given hot meals. At an
opportune moment he was also informed of the fall of Münster
and of the execution of Jan van Leiden, Knipperdolling and
Krechting. Hoffman said he did not care. "He listened to this
without showing any emotion. What is not of God is bound to
fall." Because of the three years of imprisonment his eyesight had
failed to the extent that he could not even read the broadsheet
about the end of the Anabaptist kingdom in Westphalia.

Twenty-four handwritten pieces of cloth were found in
Hoffman's cell in December, 1537. As he had been denied
writing paper since the summer of 1533, he had used pieces of
cloth to write down the biblical texts which formed the basis of
his doctrines and prophecies – chapters from Revelation and
Ezekiel, part of the Gospel according to St John and the Epistle to
the Hebrews, texts against whoredom, and finally the names of
sixteen prophets. Since we only know what was written on the
evidence of a copy by a Strasbourg archivist (Jakob Wencker II,
1668–1743), we probably have neither the original order nor the
full list of the names, but the following did appear:

Elijah	Abel
Ananias	John the Baptist
Jeremiah	Schnepfer Hans
	(Hans Rebstock?)
Daniel	Hans Fuht
Daniel (*sic*)	Jörg Jubele

---

[17] *TAE* II No. 699.
[18] *TAE* II No. 700, p. 482 C. A. Cornelius *Berichte der Augenzeugen*
p. 399.

Michael	Bärbel (Rebstock)
Caspar (Schwenckfeld)[19]	Ursel (Jost)
Johannes Eyhsenburg	(Gertrud) Lorenz
	(Wilhelm) Blum

This fragmentary table is probably based on two lists of twelve prophets, in which every prophet of the past is seen as "prefiguring" present-day prophets. With this writing on the pieces of cloth, Hoffman created clearly perceptible evidence which, in circumstances of utter desolation, would strengthen his faith.

On the 22nd and 23rd pieces of cloth, Hoffman had written letters to the Council and to the Strasbourg preachers. In the letter to the Council he affirmed his love for the city, the future Jerusalem against which he had never felt any malice, and he apologized for the harsh words he had used in his pseudonymous pamphlet, arguing that Capito had tempted him too sorely. In his letter to the preachers he complained of their unwillingness to talk to him. He warned them against shedding his innocent blood by reminding them of Zwingli's miserable end. In his opinion the Reformer of Zürich had perished because he was responsible for the drowning of the innocent Anabaptist Felix Mantz. Neither the Council nor the preachers took any notice of these letters, which he claimed came from "the heart of a dove."

Hoffman's health continued to deteriorate. Pfitzer and Gerfalk, the councillors in charge of the Anabaptists, said in March, 1539 that Hoffman's legs and face were swollen (probably symptoms of dropsy caused by lack of protein). Then, after spending three years in a dark dungeon, Hoffman asked to be allowed to see the sunlight again; after a month he would willingly return to darkness.

Despite his weakness and the deterioration in his health, Hoffman held fast to his convictions. Nor were there any signs of a falling-off of the Melchiorite movement in the years up to 1539. Persecution of the Melchiorites had begun at the end of

---

[19] Obbe Philips says that the Melchiorites disagreed as to whether Schwenckfeld or Poldermann was "Enoch". Cf. *A Confession* in G. H. Williams and A. M. Mergal (ed.), *op. cit.* p. 212.

December, 1533. Hoffman's hosts, Valentin Dufft, the goldsmith, and Katharina Seid, were amongst the first to be banished.[20] Wilhelm Blum the younger also had to leave the town even though he possessed burgher's rights.[21] But most of these expelled were refugees, who had no civic rights.[22] We do not know the total number of Hoffmanites who were forced to leave Strasbourg, since the orders of banishment make no distinction between them and other Anabaptists. The persecution was most intense in March and April, 1535 (during the final stages of the conflict at Münster).[23]

Many Anabaptists seem to have fled to the countryside, for we hear of enlarged Anabaptist congregations in the neighbouring villages of Schiltigheim, Mundolsheim and Ottrott. The "brethren" held assemblies outside the city-walls, particularly in the wood at Eckboldsheim and around Krutenau. But some well-known Melchiorites like Lienhard Jost and Barbara Rebstock were able to remain in the city without recanting their faith.[24]

The fourteen Anabaptist tracts from Speyer, which came into the hands of the Strasbourg Council in December, 1537, gave the magistrates information about the fears and the expectations of the Melchiorites after Hoffman's arrest. They contained miraculous stories concerning Hoffman, his imminent release, the vengeance in store for Strasbourg and much more the conflict between the Melchiorites of Strasbourg and Münster.

They clearly believed Hoffman was invulnerable. Four attempts had already been made to cut off his head, but only a couple of hairs could be removed. "A red flag" would soon come to Strasbourg from the Netherlands and "put all things right." Disappointed love for the city turned into a deadly hatred. Strasbourg, "the new Sodom and Gomorrah", would soon be totally burnt down. Barbara Rebstock, referring to Venturinus, predicted that the city would revert to a village if it did not better

---

[20] *TAE* II Nos. 520 and 547.

[21] *TAE* II Nos. 539, 664. His father had bought burgher's-rights in 1508, cf. C. Wittmer and J. C. Meyer (ed.), *Le Livre de Bourgeoisie de la Ville de Strasbourg 1440-1530* Vol. 2. Strasbourg 1954 No. 5782.

[22] *TAE* II No. 533.

[23] *TAE* II Nos. 637, 639, 644, 645, 649, 653, 660.

[24] *TAE* II No. 540.

itself. Lienhard Jost saw a vision in which Strasbourg was besieged by the Emperor. The lower classes then arose against the Council and much blood was shed. Before this happened the townsfolk would secure Hoffman's release at a time when the city's leaders and soldiers were all drunk. Another Melchiorite saw "that the princes and lords would be deprived of all power and that there would be great bloodshed. Above all, the city of Strasbourg would lose all its power."

The major targets of the Melchiorites' wrath were the evangelical preachers. Ursula Jost saw a vision in which Hedio fell from the Cathedral pulpit. She also saw people wading up to their knees in blood. Her husband Lienhard saw death strike the clock of the town hall and heard a noise coming from it crying, "The time is come! All your deceit will now be uncovered!" Valentin Dufft claimed that Bucer had used a false Bible during the disputation with Hoffman at the Synod. Capito had become their prophet's Judas; Barbara Rebstock explained that he had first kissed Hoffman in the printing-shop but had then betrayed him.[25]

This abstruse mixture of dread visions and predictions of the future forced the Council to issue an even harsher anti-Anabaptist mandate on 23rd March, 1538. They probably did not realise that the fourteen tracts from Speyer reflected much more the attitudes of the Melchiorites between 1533 and 1535 than their state of mind at the beginning of 1538. They were certainly more moderate at this stage, as the disputation with David Joris (cf. below) indicates. The mandate of March, 1538 was aimed at preventing expelled Anabaptists from secretly returning to the city after a few months. The Anabaptists did not feel that their sentences of banishment were binding, since they were imposed by force under violation of divine justice. Furthermore, they said, "the earth is the Lord's, and no one has the power to remove anyone from a particular place." Members of Hoffman's most immediate circle, such as Katharina Seid and Wilhelm Blum the younger, did return home secretly despite having been banished.[26] But severe punishments were now imposed on

---

[25] There are excerpts from the 14 tracts in the Strasbourg archives. Some of them date from as early as 1533 cf. *TAE* II No. 444, p. 186.

[26] *TAE* II Nos. 664, 547, p. 310.

anyone attempting to return illegally. Anyone banished who set foot in the town without authorization would, on a first offence, be imprisoned for four weeks and put on a diet of bread and water. A second attempt would be punished by cutting off the index finger or by burning a hole through the cheek. A third attempt would bring capital punishment – death by drowning, "because of an outrageous offence, and not because of their faith". These measures were aimed at avoiding a repetition in Strasbourg of the events at Münster. In fact the new mandate against the Anabaptists served more as a means of intimidation than as an effective instrument of persecution. No Anabaptists within Strasbourg were executed or seriously disfigured during the following years.

2. The Splintering of the Melchiorite Movement throughout the Empire into rival groups.

The Melchiorite movement splintered into four groups after the disaster at Münster:

1. The Obbenites (the followers of Obbe Philips, in the Netherlands and Eastern Frisia).

2. The original Melchiorites (in Strasbourg, Hesse, Eastern Frisia, the Netherlands and England).

3. The remaining Münsterite Anabaptists (in Westphalia and Oldenburg).

4. The followers of Jan van Batenburg (in Westphalia and along the Lower Rhine).

Unlike the Münsterite Anabaptists, the Obbenites and Melchiorites rejected polygamy and any attempt to establish the kingdom of God on earth by force. But they differed amongst themselves over the question of direct revelation, and in their expectations for the future. The Obbenites looked for no kingdom of Christ on this earth other than the present-day suffering community of those who were truly baptised. In the same way they rejected any concept of a progressive divine revelation in their own age. Thus they had set forth on the path toward Puritan congregationalism. Preachers were to be elected by the congregations and their teaching was to conform to

Scripture. They refused to structure the church as a hierarchy of charismatic leaders.

In contrast to this the Melchiorites, led now by Jan Matthijs (of Middelburg), Jan van Tricht and Jan van Schoonhoven, still anticipated that world-history would be completed in the near future. They felt that they were in the period between Good Friday (Hoffman's imprisonment) and Pentecost (when there was to be a new outpouring of the Holy Spirit). Nothing was to be done until then. The world was to be renewed by the future spiritual men who would work alongside pious kings in deposing ecclesiastical princes and destroying the dominion of the priests.

Jan van Batenburg regarded the Obbenites and the Melchiorites as cowardly defeatists. The time for grace, forgiveness and baptism had passed; the moment for vengeance had arrived. God's enemies should be punished as harshly as they had abused the children of God previously. Anyone joining the Batenburgers after 1536 would not be baptized; he would be accepted as a servant, not as an equal. The proviso for entry into Batenburg's community was a willingness to participate in group marriage. Bands of Batenburgers plundered their way through Westphalia and the Netherlands, looting churches and attacking farms whose inhabitants were either beaten to death or burned alive.

The Münsterite Anabaptists (led by Tjaard van Sneek, Matthijs van Balk, Jan van Gulik, Christoffel and Hendrik van Zutphen) who had now dispersed to Oldenburg, rejected Batenburg's terrorist banditry. They saw no point in it. But they still believed that the kingdom of God would be established by military power. They also believed polygamy to be legitimate. They also regarded the Obbenites and Melchiorites as "Antichrists".[27]

About 20 or 25 leaders of the various Melchiorite groups assembled at Bocholt in August, 1536 with the intention of

---

[27] On these different groups cf. N. Blesdikius, *Davidis Georgii* 1642 pp. 6-10, 13f.; G. Arnold, *Unpartheyische Kirchen – und Ketzerhistorie* 3rd ed. 1740-1742, Vol. I, 2. pp. 1332f.; F. Nippold, "David Joris van Delft" in *Zeitschrift für historische Theologie* 33 (1863) pp. 48-49; J. ten Doornkaat-Koolman, *Dirk Philips* Haarlem 1964, pp. 12-14; J. M. Stayer, *Anabaptists and the Sword* 1972, pp. 283-305.

restoring unity to the movement. From the very beginning it appeared that there was only a minimal chance that a durable settlement could be reached, since the most important leaders had decided not to attend. Obbe Philips felt that his life would be in danger, Batenburg expected that his practices would be condemned, and the Strasbourg Melchiorites had been warned against travelling to Bocholt in a dream. The major disputes at Bocholt involved the Melchiorites and the Münsterite Anabaptists. Jan Matthijs of Middelburg believed that the views of the Münsterites were irreconcilable with Hoffman's doctrine and he denounced the experiment in Münster. The Münsterites threatened to kill any brethren that opposed them. David Joris intervened at this difficult point to stress Hoffman's basic doctrines – points on which both disputing parties could come to an agreement; Monophysite Christology, the doctrine of the freedom of the will, the perfectibility of the saints and believers' baptism. On the question of the use of force he proposed the following compromise: the godless must be punished "by God and His saints". Referring to the parable of the tares and the wheat (Matt. 13:24–30), he explained that the wheat symbolized the true Christians and the reapers who cut down the tares were God's angels; the elect could not be both "the reapers" and "the good seed" at the same time. He rejected any further speculation as to who "the reapers" might be. Having smoothed over the disruptive issue as to whether the saints had the right to stir up a revolution, he attempted to postpone a discussion of polygamy to a later date. He himself did not mind if his followers had one wife or more, "so long as they obey God and His truth".[28] Hence David Joris was able to unite the participants of the Bocholt Conference on a minimum programme: rejection of vengeance and violence for the time being; resumption of missionary activity (consisting of preaching and baptism), and retention of Hoffman's major dogmas. Only Jan van Batenburg objected. He saw Joris as a new "Absalom", and declared that he would kill

---

[28] R. H. Bainton, *David Joris* Leipzig 1937, p. 67.

him with his own hands.[29] When Batenburg was arrested in 1537, he betrayed the names of all his major opponents to the authorities. David Joris, "the leader", was first on his list, then Heinrich Krechting, the Münsterite Chancellor, Obbe and Dirk Philips and also Jan Matthijs of Middelburg.[30]

3. David Joris and the Strasbourg Melchiorites.

After his personal success at the Bocholt Conference, Joris received a letter in November, 1536 from one Anneken Jans, a young woman Anabaptist, who urged him to take up the role of the apocalyptic prophet and "to prepare a people acceptable to the Lord so that He will hasten to come to His Temple." He was so delighted to receive this expression of support that "the glory of the Lord" shone around him for eight days, and he did not know where he was. This experience of being overpowered by an inner light came to an end with a vision which threw him to the ground. He saw himself amongst the children of God who were skipping and dancing like a band of joyful children. An otherworldly glow emanated from them. Then the godless rulers of the world stepped onto the scene, but they fell to the ground in terror. They made despairing gestures as they saw the transfigured "new men". When Joris returned to a state of full consciousness, while drawing a deep breath, he had a second vision: he saw himself surrounded by "naked persons" – clearly both men and women. This sight gave him a feeling of total liberation, and he cried out, "Lord, now I may see everything!" He was convinced that he was in total control of his faculties during the vision. He saw the figures quite bodily and tangibly in front of him.

He then wrote down this experience, but the words came "four times faster to the lips than to the pen." He finished by singing a song explaining the significance of the vision:

---

[29] N. Blesdikius, *op. cit.* p. 62.; G. Arnold, *op. cit.* I. 2. p. 1327. On the Bocholt Conference cf. N. Blesdikius, *op. cit.* pp. 14-17, F. Nippold, "David Joris" pp. 53-54; A. F. Mellink, *De Wederdopers* pp. 389f; G. H. Williams, *The Radical Reformation* 1962. pp. 381-383.

[30] Cf. C. A. Cornelius, *Die niederländischen Wiedertäufer während der Belagerung Münsters.* 1869 pp. 108–111.

"My ears have heard from above,
My eyes have seen from afar
– Innocence. Understand this word!
Fleetingly I looked on the
          sheep of Christ –

Although they skip, they
          are travelling straight,
Quite straight.
Undefiled by evil,
Children unwrinkled,
Without shame or hypocrisy,
Like Adam and Eve at the start
Are they at the end."[31]

Joris has thus given his own explanation of the visions: the new man will live in paradisaical innocence like a joyful child without feelings of sexual shame. Despite the evil in the world he will be spiritually pure and undefiled.

This vision, as well as Anneken Jans' letter, strengthened Joris in his conviction that he should try to unite the divergent Melchiorite groups even more closely under his leadership. He wrote two letters to his fellow-believers in Strasbourg and sent them several of his tracts, including one on marriage as an answer to "a little book of Hans Eisenburch produced by Melchior Hoffman."[32] Eisenburg's work is probably one of the fourteen

---

[31] The vision is recounted in a manuscript report of the disputation between Joris and the Strasbourg Melchiorites, *Twistreden tot Straetsburch* 30a–31a (Basel, Universitätsbibliothek). This account agrees with that of an anonymous follower on whom Gottfried Arnold was dependent for his information (*op. cit.*) Vol. I, 2. p. 1322. Blesdijk's account of the vision (pp. 18–19) speaks simply of "naked women" who then turned into doves with whom David Joris as a cock-dove copulated. Bainton's attempt (*David Joris* p. 28) to see the naked figures as a protest against immorality is mistaken. There is no "call to repentance" here; nakedness is simply a symbol of purity. The vision can only be seen in terms of a promised return to the state of Adam.

[32] This, and following quotations are taken from the manuscript, *Twistreden*, referred to in n. 31.

books sent to the Strasboug Council from Speyer.[33] In his answer to Eisenburg Joris explains that sexual shame is a punishment for Adam's fall and that it will be conquered by the "new man", as will "marital lust." A radical public confession followed by a period of abstinence is necessary for the birth of the "new man". Only after this will coitus again be permitted, when the partners are so much inflamed by heavenly things that their desire is to conceive "holy offspring" who will be already sanctified in the womb. Sex with pregnant or barren women is simply "a higher form of fornication." But those of the saints who take more than one wife are not to be condemned; this means that their seed will not be wasted in wet-dreams or on barren women.[34] This is a repetition of the arguments Rothmann used to defend the practice of polygamy in Münster,[35] but it flatly contradicted all of Hoffman's teachings. The "great prophetess", Barbara Rebstock, condemned all of Joris's views as "devilish and false."

Meanwhile Joris was making successful moves towards unification of the Melchiorites in the North. After Batenburg was executed early in 1538, many of his former followers went over to Joris. At the same time Joris also succeeded in winning over, at least temporarily, most of the remaining Münsterites now in Oldenburg. But since he aimed to be Melchior Hoffman's sole successor, he also needed the support of the Melchiorites in Strasbourg, for they were revered as the "elders of Israel" in Holland, in Hesse, along the Rhine and in England. Joris met the Melchiorite leaders (who included Johannes Eisenburg, Peter Tasch, Barbara Rebstock and Lienhard Jost) at Strasbourg in the summer of 1538.[36] He told them to use the "power of the Spirit" to decide whether or not his doctrines were "misleading and impure." But at the same time he said that they were incapable of making a valid judgment because they had not yet attained a

---

[33] *Ein Kurze erclerung von der waren götlichen Ordnung des eelichen Standes* cf. M. Krebs (ed.), *Quellen zur Geschichte der Täufer, Baden und Pfalz.* Vol. 4. 1951 No. 411, p. 426.

[34] N. Blesdikius, *op. cit.* pp. 20-25.

[35] Cf. R. Stupperich (ed.), *Die Schriften Bernhard Rothmanns* 1970, p. 264.

[36] G. Arnold, *op. cit.* Vol. I, 2. p. 1330.

proper understanding of themselves and a "true fear of the Lord."
He asked such provocative questions as, "Have you ever soaked
your bed in tears over your utter corruption? Have you ever
sought the Lord with such contrite hearts that your blood has
turned to water?" Man must be turned to ashes before the "fear of
the Lord" becomes a source of spiritual power. He said that they
(the Strasbourg Melchiorites) were proud, obdurate and
worldly-wise. He demanded that they acknowledge him
immediately as "an obedient servant of the Lord", for without
faith on their part he could proclaim nothing to them. They
should not think him arrogant because of these two demands, for
he considered himself to be nothing but "filthy soil through
which a clear fountain bursts forth." Joris, this "fighter for
toleration" with regard to doctrinal questions, was thoroughly
intolerant as far as his own person was concerned. He could never
tolerate anyone doubting his own prophetic role.

The Strasbourg Melchiorites had a surfeit of people claiming
prophetic powers, and they were not easily intimidated. They
thus refused to bow the knee immediately. Eisenburg was not at
all impressed, and on the following morning, he explained that
they could not acknowledge him as "God's servant" before he
had expounded and justified his doctrines. He also said that they
were not prepared to accept anything which contradicted
Hoffman's doctrines.

Joris thereupon attempted to split the united front against
him. He took Lienhard Jost aside and explained that they were
very close to each other in spiritual matters; they both saw God
as active not in the letter but in action and in simplicity. The
leaders of the Melchiorites in Strasbourg had wanted to exclude
him (Jost) from the discussion, since they felt he was a fool.
Eisenburg had defended the attempted exclusion of Jost on the
grounds that although he possessed the gift of prophecy he did
not possess the capacity to discern the spirits. Neither did he
understand any Dutch. When Joris began to accuse the
Strasbourgers of a lack of Christian virtue, Barbara Rebstock
interrupted him and demanded an end to the discussion. She said
that it was he who wanted to cut the fruit off the tree before it
was ripe. Joris became wildly excited and said that it was the
devil who was speaking through her. People in Strasbourg

should beware of women; men would not deceive them.

This dispute seemed to signal the final break-down of the discussion. Eisenburg supported Barbara Rebstock and said that Joris, because of his ignorance of High German, had condemned her too hastily. Joris said nothing and both he and his attendant refused to take a meal with the Hoffmanites.

After the meal Eisenburg and Tasch spoke in friendly terms to Joris and with seemingly open minds discussed his doctrine of the "third David" and his doctrine of the divine name.

In his theology of history Joris had followed some of Hoffman's ideas through to their logical conclusion. Just as the human spirit develops from childhood through youth to maturity so, too, he felt, does the "shadowy Gospel", the Law of the Old Testament, make way for the "Gospel according to the flesh", which is embodied in Christ, "the second David". This in its turn will lead on to the age of the "Gospel according to the Spirit" in which spirit-filled men will have no need of sacraments or of ceremonies. At the end of time the world will not be consumed and changed materially, but only spiritually. The clouds on which Christ will return are the "spiritual clouds of the apostolic messengers." The saints will enter into beatitude on earth before entering heaven, and the "third David" will reign as an earthly king. The sin against the Holy Spirit consists in clinging to an outdated stage of revelation.[37]

Later, after these discussions in Strasbourg, Joris added trinitarian speculation to his theology of history. The Hoffmanites consulted him, asking for advice on how to deal with the difficulties in understanding the Trinity that had been encountered by the Alsatian Jews who had been converted to their cause. They found it difficult to explain to them how the three persons were both distinct and united. Joris responded by saying that the three persons of the Godhead were simply three chronological stages in the manifestation of a single and indivisible divine essence. These three stages corresponded to the three epochs of world history. But the Strasbourgers felt that

---

[37] N. Blesdikius, *op. cit.* pp. 34–46, R. H. Bainton, *David Joris* p. 36; P. Burckhardt "David Joris und seine Gemeinde in Basel": in *Basler Zeitschrift für Geschichte und Altertumskunde* 48 (1949) pp. 14–17.

such speculation was too daring. They wanted to send the letter
Joris had written to the Jews to Hoffman for his approval. In the
end they decided against doing so and they refrained from
publishing or translating Joris's letter, without even referring the
issue to Hoffman for his advice.[38]

Because of Eisenburg's and Tasch's demonstration of goodwill Joris finally agreed to reveal his special message, even
though his audience had still not acknowledged him as a "divine
prophet."

He had seen with his inner eye the dire straits of Israel and the
rest of the world. He was sent to tell the world that "no one will
be saved in spirit, soul or body until he has confessed his sins and
has thus been purified." He then told the Strasbourgers of his
two great visions in 1536. The controversial question was not
Joris's doctrine of the conquest of sexual shame (they did not get
to this point in the discussion), but his demand for a frank and
public confession of sin as a *sine qua non* of the birth of the new
man. "We must not be ashamed to reveal our sins and to
acknowledge our guilt or to face up to our transgression,
otherwise, as I tell you, you will remain *old* men, united with
your sin. I urge you, no, not I, but the Lord, to do battle with the
devil and to conquer your shame. Nothing prevents you other
than your unbelief, which is due simply to the fact that it is not
written that you are to repent publicly of all the sins committed
since your youth."

Eisenburg complained that there was nothing about this in the
books of the Prophets or the Apostles. Joris responded by asking
where in the Bible could be found the prophecies of Melchior
Hoffman, Lienhard Jost and Barbara Rebstock. Did the patriarchs and prophets of the Old Testament have scriptural
authority for their prophecies? Eisenburg's reply was that
Hoffman had clearly founded his doctrine on the witness of
Scripture. The prophets and apostles had proved the veracity of
their revelations by additional signs and wonders. Christ's
doctrine was complete and would remain forever. According to
Joris the truth of his doctrine could only be experienced in

---

[38] G. Arnold, *op. cit.* p. 1331; N. Blesdikius, *op. cit.* pp. 73-74.

practice – i.e. in a miraculous experience of merciful forgiveness, granted to every sinner who confessed his sins in public. Peter Tasch said, "We have encountered spirits with even grander words and a more holy outward appearance who claimed to be the angels of the Apocalypse or Enoch, e.g. Hans von Rothenburg, Heinrich Schuhmacher, Melchior Rinck and Jan van Batenburg.[39] Should we have believed all of them simply because they claimed to speak through the Spirit? If I came along and said, 'I am speaking through the Spirit' would you believe me? All of them encouraged us to be perfect, to deny our own wills and to become purified, but they were deceivers who left behind nothing but confusion." Joris regarded these objections as "fleshly selfishness" and an obstinate clinging to an earlier stage of revelation.

When Joris's attempt to win them over on the grounds of direct revelation failed he looked for scriptural support for his doctrines. He referred to Ezekiel 36 and 37, Jeremiah 7:19, Psalms 25 and 38, the parable of the Pharisee and the tax collector in the Temple (Luke 18:9-14), James 5:6 and above all the story of David. He wanted to show how this latter story illustrates the way in which the "sins of youth" make a man sick in the soul. This was supported by Psalm 25:7, "Remember not the sins of my youth, or my transgressions," Psalm 38:9-10, "Lord, all my longing is known to Thee, my sighing is not hidden from Thee. My heart throbs, my strength fails me" and Psalm 90:8, "Thou has set our iniquities before Thee, O Lord, and the sins committed in our youth that we have hidden are clearer than day in the light of Thy countenance" (based on a mistranslation by Johannes Campanus). For Joris "sin" was primarily latent guilt about sexuality, which taints the soul. He regarded this as the main source of anxiety and weakness. He felt that a public confession of secret sexual faults was the furthest one could go in self-denial. This would reduce the old Adam to ashes, and the new man could then be reborn, freed from sexual shame or servitude to "fleshly lusts".

---

[39] Batenburg had travelled to Strasbourg with his henchman Gerdt Eickelmann in search of new "confederates" cf. A. F. Mellink, *Wederdopers* p. 92.

Eisenburg was not convinced that any of these arguments proved the necessity of the public confession of these intimate matters. David had only confessed his adultery with Bathsheba to God and to Nathan – there was no public confession in front of the populace. Public sins ought certainly to be acknowledged before the whole congregation, but private sins need only be confessed to those sinned against.

Joris's final attempt to argue the necessity of public confession was based on the imminence of the Last Judgment, which would bring all sins to light anyway. They were living in the time of the "seventh trumpet", the age in which secrecy would cease. Eisenburg had learnt his knowledge from books and there was no point in debating with him. He, Joris, the "apostolic messenger", was not bound to the letter, for even the books of the Bible were contradictory and not without error. Man in the age of the Spirit was subject to a new law; he must neither be ashamed nor dissemble in front of his fellow believers, but had to be prepared to reveal his life unsparingly. Joris ended the discussion with the following request: "Since you rely on Melchior Hoffman, I ask that you inform him of everything that has happened and that has been written (in the minutes)."

The disputation indicates how much the Strasbourg Melchiorites had sobered. They returned to Scripture as their normative authority, justifying Hoffman's leadership on the grounds that his doctrines agreed with the Bible. Strange prophets' claims to direct revelation were regarded as damnable human fabrications; their own leading "enthusiast", Lienhard Jost, was outmanoeuvred. Two intellectuals ("Latinists"), Eisenburg and Tasch, had now taken over the role formerly played by the inspired prophets. The new leaders oriented the movement towards the traditional norms of Christian life, which recommended not to trust even a friend unless he had proved reliable in times of distress (Ecclesiasticus 6:7).

They were probably not aware of David Joris's ultimate aims. Barbara Rebstock rightly suspected him of encouraging sexual libertinism and said that he was threatening the institution of marriage. All of the Strasbourg Melchiorites condemned Joris's attempt to overcome his disappointment at the non-appearance of the universal revolution by establishing a paradisaical garden where "brothers and sisters" need have neither secrets nor shame.

4. The Attempts of Eisenburg and Tasch to Bring About the Dissolution of the Melchiorite Movement in Hesse and Strasbourg.

A few months after the great disputation Joris's main opponents, Eisenburg and Tasch, began to disband the remaining Melchiorite communities in Hesse and Strasbourg. Lienhard Jost and his second wife Agnes renounced Anabaptism in April, 1539 after having been arrested twice and having lost all prestige within the movement.

Meanwhile the Melchiorites of Hesse were already in decline because of the collaboration of Bucer and Tasch. They had suffered a severe blow early in 1536 when the Landgrave had burst into an assembly of thirty Anabaptists in an abandoned church at Gemünden an der Wohrd. Some of the congregation's leading figures were present: Hermann Bastian of Marburg, Leonhard Fälber of Maastricht (a follower of Heinrich Roll, the Wassenberg preacher who had been burnt in Maastricht), Peter Lose and Georg Schnabel of Allendorf (the "keeper of the common coffer"). All but Bastian, who was imprisoned at Marburg, were incarcerated at Wolkersdorf.[40] This prison must have been particularly lax; the prisoners had no trouble in getting past their warders and went off preaching in the surrounding villages. Philip of Hesse could not decide what to do with the Anabaptists. He consulted theologians in Wittenberg, Strasbourg, Ulm, Lüneburg and Tübingen, and in 1537 he issued an anti-Anabaptist Ordinance. But his deputies and governors did not enforce this decree.[41]

A few weeks after the discussions with David Joris, Peter Tasch went off to Hesse on a pastoral visit to his fellow believers

---

[40] G. Franz (ed.), *Urkundliche Quellen zur hessischen Reformationsgeschichte. Vol. 4. Wiedertäuferakten* 1951, p. 91.

[41] *Ibid.* pp. 138-146.

who were imprisoned at Wolkersdorf.[42] He informed them of
the success of the Melchiorite movement in England (where a
book on the Incarnation had been published) and urged them to
stand firm in their faith.[43] The Landgrave ordered a priest
(Fabritius) and a theologian (Professor Noviomagus) to try to
convert them, but they were unsuccessful.[44]

Thereupon the Landgrave called in Bucer in October, 1538.
He wanted him to hold a public disputation in which he would
win over the Anabaptist leaders and bring them back into the
fold of the evangelical state-church. The prisoners were brought to
Marburg for this purpose. In the course of the disputation (which
lasted for three days, from 30th October to 1st November,
1538), Bucer managed to create a high degree of uncertainty
amongst the Anabaptist leaders. He combined a firm stand on
the basic doctrines of the Reformation with compromise on
questions of social ethics, in particular on the issues of
opposition to usury and demands for stricter enforcement of
excommunication. They asked for time to consider Bucer's
proposals indicating that they might be won over.[45] Peter Tasch
was hidden amongst the audience. The day after the disputation
he went to Bucer and said he believed that the separation of the
Anabaptists from the Protestants produced nothing but scandal.
He would ensure that the Melchiorites returned to the state
church on the following conditions:

1. No leader prepared to take his followers back into the
   evangelical church should be asked to make a public
   recantation, for this would deprive him of influence
   amongst his former friends.
2. No ecclesiastical or civil actions were to be brought against
   any Anabaptists who agreed to return to the official church.
3. Those who joined the state church were not to be requested
   to take part in the Eucharist immediately.

[42] *Ibid.* pp. 159f.
[43] Cf. I. B. Horst, *The Radical Brethren* Nieuwkoop 1972, pp. 59f.;
G. Franz (ed.), *Wiedertäuferakten* pp. 162-165.
[44] M. Lenz (ed.), *Briefwechsel Landgraf Philipps des Grossmütigen von
Hessen mit Bucer.* Vol. 1. Leipzig 1880, pp. 317-326.
[45] G. Franz (ed.), *Wiedertäuferakten* pp. 213-239.

Bucer knew from his own experience of nonconformity how difficult it was for an official evangelical preacher to shake the convictions of the Anabaptists. Therefore he urged the Landgrave to accept Tasch's proposal and to appoint him as "missionary" to the Anabaptists of Hesse, but without his former "brethren" being able to recognize him as an apostate. Bucer was already in a position to assure the Landgrave of Tasch's sincerity. Bastian and Lose had declared after a conversation with Tasch that they were prepared to return to the evangelical state church.[46] Philip of Hesse thus accepted Bucer's advice. Tasch had a second success, which he was able to report to Bucer on 11th December, 1538. Georg Schnabel, Leonhard Fälber and six other Melchiorites had joined Tasch in signing a declaration of faith which was based on the Confession of Augsburg. In it they rejected both the militant revolt advocated by the Anabaptists of Münster and the pacifism of the Swiss Brethren. They repudiated Hoffman's doctrine of the freedom of the will and said that the issue of baptism did not provide sufficient grounds for a separation (though they did still regard adult baptism as the form of baptism advocated by Scripture.[47]) In view of this declaration the Landgrave released the imprisoned Anabaptists.

Johannes Eisenburg also told Bucer that he was prepared to return to the Strasbourg church when he met him at the Frankfurt autumn fair in 1538. But he did ask to be excused from taking the oath against Anabaptism which was required by the Council. He said that this would prevent him from visiting Anabaptist assemblies and urging his fellow believers to reject their errors.

Throughout the winter of 1538-1539 Tasch and Eisenburg travelled throughout Hesse hoping to win back Melchiorites and other Anabaptists to the evangelical state church. The Landgrave informed Bucer of their remarkable success on 1st March, 1539; were it not for them, he said, there would still be many sects in

---

[46] *Ibid.* pp. 239-241.
[47] *Ibid.* pp. 247-257.

Hesse.[48] Bucer estimated that Tasch had converted about 200 Melchiorites in Hesse.

In April, 1539 Eisenburg and Tasch requested the Strasbourg Council to allow them to see Hoffman so that they could convince him of his errors. The aim of this mission was to make Hoffman sign a written recantation which would guarantee the break-up of his congregation in Strasbourg. They also hoped for similar results in the Netherlands.[49] The Council agreed after an intervention by Bucer and Capito, but Pfitzer and Gerfalk, the councillors in charge of Anabaptist affairs, were to supervise the discussion. Bucer feared that the presence of Council-members would counteract the persuasive powers of Tasch and Eisenburg. He asked that the two councillors sit in the next room unseen, listening to the conversation, but the Council felt that this would be unworthy and insisted on the original arrangement.

Since Eisenburg and Tasch were regarded as his true followers, their first six-hour conversation with Hoffman was very friendly. But the prisoner refused to return to the official church of Strasbourg on the grounds that it allowed people, both good and bad, to partake indiscriminately of the sacrament. After four further discussions of five hours, both supervising councillors told the Council that Eisenburg and Tasch "could not get any satisfaction out of him." His two former supporters reproached him with being responsible for everything that had been done in his name: people had attacked townhalls, officials had been murdered and one of his followers (Batenburg?) at his execution had even expressed regret at not having killed more people. Hoffman denounced these excesses but would not withdraw his apocalyptic speculations. He clung to his Christology with the same conviction. Only on the question of infant baptism was he prepared to come to a compromise. But as such a recantation would not have been enough to win over the masses, Eisenburg and Tasch asked the Council to allow one of them to spend two days and a night in Hoffman's cell without the presence of the

---

[48] M. Krebs (ed.), *Baden und Pfalz. Quellen zur Geschichte der Täufer.* Vol. 4. 1951 No. 412, pp. 426-427.

[49] *Ibid.* No. 412, pp. 426-427.

Council members. The Council was still wary but agreed on condition that the visitor change his clothes before and after his time in the cell, and that while there he should wear clothing provided by the Council.

One of the two "missionaries" was then able to convince Hoffman by the evidence of Origen and Irenaeus that infant baptism had been practised in the early church, and that Paul had even allowed a Christian to be baptised on behalf of a dead person (1 Cor. 15:29). Hoffman replied that it was no longer worthwhile to argue about infant baptism. "I am quite happy for them to be baptised, as I say, and if I had children myself I should certainly want them baptised".

Hoffman also modified his doctrine of the "unforgivable sin". Earlier he had written that any deliberate sin against the Holy Spirit was unforgivable, but because of the example of the Corinthian "whoremonger" (1 Cor. 5:1-5) who had lived with his step-mother, he had come to realize that forgiveness *was* possible even for serious sins committed after conversation. But this was only a minimal concession, since Hoffman had always taught that a Christian could always obtain forgiveness for sins he had committed after coming to a recognition of the truth "if they are not mortal sins" and if the sinner repented of them.[50] "Mortal sin" was a fluid concept, which for Hoffman centred on a conscious act of apostasy from a truth clearly recognized (as in Hebrews 6:4 and 10:26).

On the doctrine of the freedom of the will Hoffman simply repeated his earlier argument that a man's will cannot be free unless he has first been enlightened by the divine Word.[51]

Thus Hoffman's so-called "recantation" consisted simply of a renunciation of adult baptism (which he had, at least, already made in 1531 under the impact of the execution of his friends in

---

[50] Cf. *TAE* II No. 368, p. 19, No. 617, p. 194.

[51] The text of Hoffman's "recantation" (of which there is a copy in the Strasbourg archives) is printed in A. Hulshof, *Geschiedenis van de Doopsgezinden to Straatsburg van 1525 tot 1557*. Amsterdam 1905, pp. 180-181 cf. *TAE* II No. 617, p. 394. A comparison of the 1539 "recantation" with his confession of 23d November 1534 shows how little his position had changed.

Amsterdam) and of a qualification of the idea of "unforgivable sin". Hoffman firmly upheld his Christology, his doctrines of the universality of God's grace and the freedom of man's will after enlightenment, and his apocalyptic expectations. The declaration extorted from him after five long discussions in two days of intensive debate was in the end so meagre that the Council refused to publish it. Hoffman was not even the author of the text of the so-called "recantation"; he simply put his signature to it.

Capito, Bucer, Hedio and Zell visited Hoffman on 7th June, 1539 at the Council's request in order to see if he had changed his mind. They said that "his certainty had gone" and that he did not hold to his doctrines as firmly as before, but no one could tell what he really felt. They thought it was doubtful whether he would be prepared to urge his followers to renounce the doctrines he himself had taught them. They therefore did not propose that Hoffman should be released. Rather should he be taken to the hospice where he could be given further instruction and admonition so that he would make a "firm" recantation. In this eventuality many who still followed him could then be won back to the church of Strasbourg. Furthermore, "the terms of his imprisonment should not be aggravated, even if he should recover his health, which they did not expect". In short, they considered the "recantation" to be nothing but the temporary weakness of a mortally sick man. They were right to doubt the value of such a document.

The preachers also urged the Council to allow Eisenburg and Tasch secretly to do away with any remaining Melchiorite congregations in Strasbourg. There need be no public recantation in the church or before the Council; it would be sufficient to take the "Anabaptist oath" in front of the two councillors in charge of Anabaptist affairs. Anyone who renounced Anabaptism in public would lose his influence on his colleagues. In addition to this everyone who made a voluntary recantation should be guaranteed immunity from punishment. The Council was prepared to grant such an amnesty, but not to dispense with the oath taken before the plenary session of the Council.

Eisenburg and Tasch let it be known throughout the city that Hoffman had made a full recantation. Ironically this false information had the effect which neither persecution nor discredited prophecies had managed to achieve. Within a year the great community of Melchiorites had been dissolved, to leave only a tiny band of stalwarts in Strasbourg. In 1540 even Valentin Dufft the goldsmith, who had been one of Hoffman's closest friends, begged forgiveness of the evangelical preachers and asked to be allowed to return to the city.

But Eisenburg and Tasch only partially attained their goal. Many Melchiorites joined the "Swiss Brethren" on hearing the disappointing news of the apostasy of their prophet.[52] They excluded Hoffman from the Anabaptist community, labelling him "heathen". After 1539 the "Swiss Brethren", who had played no part in the Synod of 1533, took on a new lease of life. They became particularly numerous in the rural areas around Strasbourg. Eisenburg and Tasch found that they had no control over the "Swiss Brethren", be they original or new members. Their leaders were so determined in their refusal to enter into discussions with the two damnable "traitors" that Tasch and Eisenburg gave up any further attempts at converting them.

In 1540 Ruprecht Schwarz, a friend of the Anabaptists whom many suspected of being their "bailiff" (i.e. convener and treasurer), put the number of "Swiss Brethren" in Strasbourg at about 100 as against "no more than five" Hoffmanites.

Without doubt moral objections can be raised against the methods Tasch and Eisenburg used to eliminate the Melchiorites. But their actions were quite realistic in the light of their reasonable assessment of the hopelessness of the movement. In any event, they helped to prevent much needless suffering on the part of the many Melchiorites in Hesse and Strasbourg. When Eisenburg died of the plague in 1541, Bucer praised him highly in the following words, "Johannes Isenburg has died (of the plague). He was a man unequalled in prudence, zeal and wisdom in ecclesiastical affairs, though he had been a leader of the Anabaptists some years ago. With him our church has suffered an irreparable loss."[53]

---

[52] Cf. N. Blesdikius, *op. cit.* pp. 108-109.
[53] Cf. T. Schiess (ed.), *Briefwechsel* Vol. 2. No. 914, p. 88.

5. Calvin and the French Melchiorites in Strasbourg.

At the same time (1538-1540) Calvin was successfully winning over the French Melchiorites in Strasbourg to the "true faith".

Calvin had already joined battle with Anabaptists in Geneva in 1537. Hermann van Gerbihan (from Gerbehaye near Liege) and Andry Benoit (a barber from Engelen in the Brabant) had arrived in Geneva at the beginning of March, 1537. They were quickly followed by Johannes Bomeromenus (a printer) and Jean Stordeur (a wealthy man from Liege). All four were banished after two discussions with Calvin. Whereas Benoit went to Metz (where he was probably drowned in the Moselle along with other Anabaptists in August, 1538[54]), Stordeur, Hermann van Gerbihan and Bomeromenus went to Strasbourg, where they hoped "to be able to lead a Christian life". But they soon found that Bucer's teachings had changed in many respects, and that he had "revoked many things he taught formerly, notably on the question of the sacraments." Bomeromenus, "a quick and agile man, expert in three languages", wanted to hold a disputation with Bucer. Capito complained that these Anabaptist "Frenchmen" were creating new dissensions amongst the congregations of Strasbourg.

After he was expelled from Geneva in April, 1538, Calvin took up the post of preacher to the French Protestant congregation in Strasbourg (which numbered about 400, and included many who sympathized with the Melchiorites). Here he once more came across his old acquaintances Hermann van Gerbihan and Jean Stordeur, who had joined the Hoffmanites. As soon as he had received burgher's rights in 1539, Calvin registered with the tailors' guild (to which many Anabaptists belonged) in the hope that this would facilitate discussion with the sectarians.[55]

Calvin's main charge against the Strasbourg Anabaptists was that they separated the Holy Spirit from the Word of the Bible:

---

[54] W. Balke, *Calvijn en de Doperse Radikalen* Amsterdam 1973, p. 130.

[55] *Ibid.* p. 133 n. 37.

"For when they boast extravagantly of the Spirit, their tendency certainly is to sink and bury the Word of God, that they may make room for their own falsehoods."[56] But on the other hand, Calvin and the Anabaptists shared conviction that faith and practice should agree with one another. No other Reformer came so close to the Anabaptist idea of the "church of the visible saints", and Calvin, like the Anabaptists, was determined to enforce excommunication quite rigorously in order to create a "community without spot or blemish." In his doctrine of the Eucharist he envisaged a spiritual presence of Christ in the Holy Supper, but refused "to chain down His (glorified) body to earthly elements."[57] This was a similar view to that of the Melchiorites. Thus there was a whole area of shared convictions which formed a basis for a debate over controversial points such as Christology, the doctrines of free will and the universality of grace, the problem of baptism and the relationship between Word and Spirit.

In two letters to Farel written in February, 1540[58] Calvin says that he had succeeded in persuading Jean Stordeur and Hermann van Gerbihan to renounce all of their Anabaptist doctrines except that on the freedom of the will. As a sign of his change of heart Jean Stordeur agreed to the baptism of his son. Calvin, on the other hand, did not insist that Hermann van Gerbihan acknowledge his own doctrine of predestination before accepting him back into the church. After Stordeur's death at the beginning of 1540, Calvin decided to marry his widow Idelette van Büren. She was both learned and pretty and Calvin praised her as a "singularis exempli femina". Their happy marriage lasted for six years.[59]

---

[56] Calvin, *Reply to Sadoleto*. English translation in J. C. Olin (ed.), *A Reformation Debate. Sadoleto's Letter to the Genevans and Calvin's Reply*. New York 1966 p. 61 (Calvin's letter to Sadoleto was written in Strasbourg in the summer of 1539).

[57] *Ibid.* p. 70.

[58] Dated 6th February and 26th February 1540 cf. R. Schwarz (ed.), *Johann Calvins Lebenswerk in seinen Briefen*. Vol. I Tübingen 1909, pp. 87f and 90.

[59] Cf. W. Balke, *Calvijn* pp. 134–139.

6. The Death of Hoffman.

Yet there were still a few diehard Melchiorites in Strasbourg after 1540. Three Hoffmanites were arrested in the city in 1541: Conrad von Bühl, Diebolt Bangarten of Dürrenbach and Maria van Delft. The Council minutes refer to a certain Jörg Norlinger as the leader of the Melchiorites; he was banished (for a second time) on 26th July, 1546. Up to the end of 1541 both the Council and the preachers still hoped to be able to obtain a recantation from Hoffman. But the "witness of the Most High" was not prepared to admit that his prophecies had been a devilish deceit. In November, 1539 Hoffman wrote another warning to the burgomaster of Strasbourg calling on him to lay in provisions and weapons in preparation for the siege, which was now not far off (he wrote his message on tiny scraps of paper torn out of books that had been lent to him). On 6th December, 1539 Tasch and Eisenburg asked the Council to allow them to go to Hoffman with German translations of Ignatius, Gregory and Dionysius Areopagita, which should convince him that his Christology was wrong. On 13th August, 1540 Capito, Bucer and Hedio asked the Council to admit Tasch and Eisenburg to Hoffman again so that they could persuade him of the error of his prophecies. Hoffman finally received a visit from Jakob Wetzel, a Council-member, on 1st April, 1541. He presented him with a book on the incarnation,[60] but his attempt at converting him was no more successful than any of the others.

In December, 1542 a few Melchiorites managed to visit Hoffman by bribing the wife and the maid of the prison warder, Adolf Winter. Wilhelm Blum the younger, Konrad von Bühl and four women all paid a visit to their imprisoned prophet. They had no trouble getting in, for the door to his cell was always left open at this stage. But Hoffman refused to take this

---

[60] Cf. F. O. zur Linden, *Melchior Hofmann* Haarlem 1885, pp. 475-476. The book was probably Schwenckfeld's *Von der menschwerdung Christi*, CS 7 No. 320.

Neemt waer: Die rechte wederbrenginghe of Restitution / dat

Voorbeeldt / Beeldt oft Letterlijcke Figuer des Bruyts Christi.

Plate 15: David Joris: The restoration of the true Church, or the Bride
of Christ

Die eerste Mensch is in een natuerlijck/ die leste in een Gheestlijck leuen ghemaeckt.

Plate 16: David Joris: The figure of the new man

opportunity to escape. He was still expecting to be released by divine intervention. When the Council heard of this incident they again had Hoffman locked up and they decided to keep the key in the Council Chamber. The cell could only be opened in the presence of a member of the Council. He was to get his food from a basket lowered through a hole in the ceiling. Hoffman's illegal visitors were to be imprisoned should they be apprehended.

Konrad von Bühl spoke in detail at the trial about Hoffman's views. He had "asked Melchior whether he still held to the faith he had confessed eight years previously. It was said that he had joined with the preachers like Johannes (Eisenburg) and that he had recanted like Peter Tasch. He replied to this that he had not recanted, but held to the truth as before". When questioned specifically about his Christology Hoffman replied that he held to the doctrine he had put before the Synod. "He had asked him further how much longer they had to wait for the Last Judgment? He replied to this that he knew of no Last Judgment. There would be peace, joy and righteousness." Faced with the non-appearance of the Parousia, Hoffman had finally come to believe that the eternal kingdom of peace could become a reality within history. He had hinted at such a development in his theology of history when he gave an allegorical interpretation of the return of Christ in his commentary on Revelation.

He now totally rejected the revolutionary implications that his followers in Westphalia had drawn out of his doctrines. Hoffman commanded Konrad von Bühl to tell the brethren that they should stop meeting in forests or assembling as militant bands. There was enough evidence (the Peasants' War, Zwingli and the Anabaptists in Münster) to show how dire were the consequences of using force without true justification. Secular authorities, and particularly the pious government of the city of Strasbourg, must be shown respect.

Marriage should also be held in honour. "Not every people respected marriage: many wallow in lasciviousness and the lusts of the flesh." The core of his advice was: live a quiet life, obey the authorities and aim towards an inner perfection, within an unblemished marriage. Thus all that remained of Hoffmanite theology after the failure of his apocalyptic expectations was a conformist, ascetic and bourgeois moralism, similar to that found in Menno Simons.[61]

But the Council did not trust these reports. So that Hoffman would have no chance to escape, the dilapidated walls of his cell were repaired early in 1543. On 2nd June, 1543 the burgomaster reported that the work was finished and that Hoffman could be returned to his former cell. But the prisoner asked to be left in the tower as he was suffering from severe headaches. His request was granted for the duration of his illness, but he was then put back into the dungeon. The burgomaster reported on 7th November, 1543 that Hoffman was so ill that he could no longer eat and that he had been returned to his room in the tower. The Council approved this move, on condition that he was kept in solitary confinement. The last news of Hoffman is an entry in the Council minutes on 19th November, 1543 which reads that Hoffman is "so ill, he needs to be looked after." Since he was having to lie on the bare floor, the Council agreed that he should be given sheets and blankets. It was probably the sudden spell of cold which led to Hoffman's death in 1543. Nothing more is known about how he died.

In the course of ten disillusioning years this "second Elijah", who had once inspired deep fears and glowing hopes in the hearts of kings, noblemen, preachers and the common people, had been reduced to a helpless creature, dying in total isolation.

---

[61] Konrad von Bühl's account of Hoffman's beliefs survives in the Strasbourg archives. Some inadequate excerpts are printed in T.W. Röhrich, "Zur Geschichte der Strassburgischen Wiedertäufer" in *Zeitschrift für die historische Theologie* 30 (1860) pp. 114f.

CHAPTER ELEVEN

Conclusion.

Except for Strasbourg, the places where Melchior Hoffman chose to work were places where the Reformation had already been introduced, but had not achieved a breakthrough: Livonia, Stockholm, Lübeck, Schleswig-Holstein, Eastern Frisia and the Netherlands. These were areas where the Catholic church still had strong support, where neither the Wittenberg nor the Zürich Reformation had prevailed, and yet where there were already radical undercurrents which had created a desire for much wider changes both in the church and in society than Luther or Zwingli would have approved of. Hoffman's apocalypticism had credibility in such an instable environment, where many people were longing for a better future and were yet afraid that they were on the brink of chaos.

The atmosphere of confusion was worse in the Baltic countries because of the political conflict between, on the one hand, the Protestant cities who wanted to set up a united and secularised state in the region to counter the threat from Russia and, on the other, the Catholic prelates who wanted to maintain the region's medieval structure. In Stockholm, the opposition of the German merchants to the conservative, only superficially Protestant, ecclesiastical policy of Gustavus I Wasa of Sweden was part of the struggle of the German minority to achieve political and economic autonomy within the city. Hoffman achieved his success in Eastern Frisia in a situation where the nobility (who were on the whole Zwinglian by inclination) were locked in a dispute with the Lutheran Prince about who had control of the church. In the Netherlands the spread of the Melchiorite movement was encouraged by the local magistrates who were sympathetic to the evangelical cause and opposed the absolutist, Catholic policies of Charles V, since he wanted to deprive them of local autonomy and their political privileges. The divisions within the governing class, in particular the conflict between the estates (town magistrates and noblemen) and the princely rulers, left a gap in which Hoffman's religious radicalism could take root and develop.

Hoffman's following was made up mainly of artisans. Only in Livonia and in Schleswig-Holstein did peasants play a marginal rôle. It was characteristic for his following that many Melchiorites came from groups not fully integrated into society or threatened with disintegration – and there were even members who came from upper class groups threatened with such change.

In Livonia the Hoffmanites had the support of the distinguished "Black-Headed Guild", an organization of German tradesmen. They did not have civic rights in the Livonian cities and were not integrated into the social stucture of the region. Hoffman also had the support of "non-Germans" in Livonia, i.e. members of the oppressed lower class who possessed only minimal rights. In Stockholm he was supported by the rich German merchants who were fighting to defend their interests against the pro-Swedish and anti-Hanseatic nationalistic policies of Gustavus I Wasa. In Kiel Hoffman's allies were those members of the population who opposed the city's patrician government. He attempted here also to gain the support of the peasants of Eastern Holstein who found themselves increasingly being reduced to a state of vassalage because of the new privileges granted to the nobility in 1524. In the Netherlands it was mainly the hungry and the unemployed artisans who joined the Melchiorites. In Strasbourg, too, refugees constituted the majority of the Hoffmanites. The astounding growth of the movement was due mainly to the famine between 1527 and 1535.

For a short while Hoffman managed to win over some high holders of office such as the magistracy of Dorpat, King Frederick I of Denmark and Ulrich von Dornum, the former Chancellor of Eastern Frisia. These patrons wanted to use Hoffman's movement for their own limited political aims. In Livonia and Schleswig-Holstein their aim was to destroy the Catholic church and bring about a secularisation of the state: this also involved the confiscation of church property. In Eastern Frisia the nobility considered the Melchiorite movement to be its ally against the Lutheran state church, which Count Enno II wanted to establish. But as soon as the political leaders realized that the Hoffmanites showed revolutionary tendencies they withdrew their support. In such isolation the Melchiorite movement was doomed to failure everywhere.

Hoffman sought the protection of legal authorities right up to the end of his life. The shock of the Peasants' War, as well as Luther's doctrine of obedience, had a lasting impact on him. In fairly rapid succession he tried to win over the magistracies of the Livonian cities, King Frederick I of Denmark, Ulrich von Dornum of Eastern Frisia and finally the Council of Strasbourg, urging them all to implement his apocalyptic programme. He eventually came to regard the Free Imperial cities as the apocalyptic power that would break the backbone of the forces of Antichrist during the final slaughter that would bring world history to an end. He laid the blame for all his misfortunes on the "priests", who had blinded the secular rulers. Throughout his life he retained the illusion of a "pious government", which he thought would help to bring about the final victory of his ideas. This false hope prevented him from seeing that for the 16th century "dreamers of perfection" there was no middle way between the positions of Thomas Müntzer and Michael Sattler.

We can thus conclude that in most cases Hoffman's message was accepted for a reason other than the one intended. His followers in Livonia, Stockholm, Eastern Holstein, Holland and Westphalia, in so far as they belonged to the lower classes, saw his message as a beacon lighting the way to a total transformation of the world by promising vengeance on religious and secular tyrants. Those who wielded political power saw Hoffman's prophecies in the light of his assurances of loyalty, and they felt that they could use him as a powerful force to help attain their own limited political goals.

On the whole the Melchiorite movement had a negative effect on the course of the Reformation. In Livonia the iconoclastic outburst in Dorpat, which Hoffman had encouraged, however unwittingly, was one of the reasons why the provincial nobles repealed the agreement they had made with the towns in the spring of 1524 approving the introduction of the Reformation; they thus reverted to Catholicism. A very conservative brand of Lutheranism was imposed on the congregations in Livonia and

Schleswig-Holstein in reaction to the anti-sacramentalism propounded by Hoffman and his adherents. Growing apocalyptic
enthusiasm forced the Council of Strasbourg to issue a confession of faith and to introduce a general persecution of nonconformists. The consequences of the events in Münster were
catastrophic for the cause of the Reformation in the city; there
was a total reversion to Catholicism here. Only in Holland did
the popular Melchiorite movement contribute to the victory of
the Reformation, though it survived here not as Anabaptism,
but as Calvinism.

Hoffman began his missionary work in Livonia as a Lutheran.
He explicitly supported the Wittenberg reformers' central
doctrines of justification by faith alone, predestination and the
duty to obey the authorities. But it was not by preaching these
doctrines that Hoffman won over his own particular following.
The secret of his fascination lies in other ideas, such as his
merciless attack on the church as the "whore of Babylon", his
anticlericalism, his prophecies of the imminent end of the world
and the consequent establishment of the Kingdom of God and,
in particular, his promise that it was those who are poor in spirit
and those who suffer, not the mighty or the learned, who would
attain salvation.

At the same time he criticized the shortcomings of the
Reformation, particularly in respect of the Reformation principle of the priesthood of all believers. Like Luther before 1525,
he argued that the congregations rather than the bishops or princes
should elect their ministers. On the lines of the practice of the
early church, where any member of the congregation was
allowed to interpret the Bible (1 Cor. 14), he attacked the
monopoly enjoyed by the learned clergy in expounding
Scripture. He no longer counted confession as a sacrament; it became a voluntary act which brings comfort and forgiveness. By
being directed towards the improvement of the sinner and restitution of the wrong done to the person sinned against, it removed the
laity from the undue influence of the preachers. Hoffman argued
that church property should be administered by the congregations. He denounced the way in which nobles and patricians had
taken control of ecclesiastical property in the course of the
Reformation; he quite rightly saw this as nothing but stealing

from the poor. To him the church was a community of the free and equal in which even the "common man" could find a social and a spiritual home.

But it would be wrong to see Hoffman's early doctrine as primarily a critical revision of a deformed Lutheranism which held firm to Reformation principles. The traditions of late medieval apocalypticism and spiritualism are already apparent in his earliest writings, producing elements that cannot be fully reconciled with genuine Reformation ideas. This medieval heritage can be seen, for example, in his apocalyptic calculations where he foresees two 3½-year-periods as constituting the messianic cataclysm and predicts that the Last Judgment will take place in 1533; in his exaltation of the "inner" above the "outer Word", in his wild "figurative" exegesis of Scripture and in his preference for charismatic prophets over "learned servants of the belly." He fused apocalypticism and spiritualism in his concept of divinisation that comes by suffering. The elect will be tested during the age of wrath and darkness. If they stand firm and enter into true *Gelassenheit* they will be divinised within the present age. But if they fall away from the true faith after their enlightenment they will be lost forever. During the coming age of suffering (i.e. the last 3½-year-period of apocalyptic cataclysm) the "external Word" will be wiped off the face of the earth and its place will be taken by the "inner Word" which will arise within the hearts of believers. God will only be encountered within the soul and faith will be man's last remaining possession. Faith will provide him with an inner freedom and protect him from external assaults. Despite the protection of "two devout kings", the true church of the Reformation will be destroyed and it will appear that the powers of Satan (the Emperor, the Pope and the false teachers) have triumphed. As the chaos reaches its climax Christ will appear on the clouds of heaven to judge the world according to Matthew 25:40, "Whatever you do to one of the least of these my brethren, you do it to me."

The conflict which was to culminate in Hoffman's ejection from the Lutheran church began during his time in Livonia. His spiritualism led him to reject the Lutheran doctrine of Christ's real presence in the Eucharistic elements. For him the Lord's Supper was a spiritual communion of the believing soul with

Christ. The Lord is truly present in the words of forgiveness, and the earthly elements of bread and wine are simply signs of a spiritual nourishment. Hoffman had three basic objections to the Lutheran doctrine of the Eucharist: as a spiritualist he regarded the mixture of the spiritual and the material as a blasphemous misunderstanding of God's nature; as a lay-preacher he feared that the Lutheran concept was a cover for the ambitions of a new power-hungry caste of evangelical pastors who wanted to use "sacramental magic" to assert their authority over the congregation; as a moralist he was afraid that this new form of guaranteed grace would revive the delusion that an external act rather than true faith could reconcile man to God.

At this early stage there were inconsistencies in Hoffman's theology brought about by the tension between his Lutheran background and his spiritualist apocalypticism. The idea of divinisation is irreconcilable with his concept of the Christian man as *simul justus et peccator*. His concept of trial by suffering contradicts the doctrine of predestination, and the dogma of the non-forgiveness of sins committed after enlightenment can hardly be squared with the idea of justification by faith alone or with the doctrine of election.

Hoffman's missionary activity in Schleswig-Holstein, where he enjoyed the personal protection of Frederick I of Denmark, came to an end with his expulsion from the Lutheran church and his banishment from the country. The Flensburg Disputation of 1529, when he was condemned by Bugenhagen, was a turning point in his career. In the course of this dispute with the Lutheran clergy, accentuations shifted. The debate switched from the issues of apocalyptic prophecies and allegorical exegesis of Scripture (in the controversy with Amsdorf) to his spiritualist view of the Eucharist (in the disputes with Schuldorp and Bugenhagen).

The four ideas central to Hoffman's thought (his conviction that the earth would soon be transformed into the Kingdom of God; his belief that revelation is still continuing either in "figurative" scriptural exegesis or in the "inner Word" within the believing soul; his idea of man's divinisation and his concept of the impossibility of forgiveness for any sins committed after enlightenment) made him concentrate on expectations for the future and seemed to cry out for action. Yet until 1530 other ideas seemed to check these calls to action; he was convinced that man was a passive recipient of salvation, partly because of Luther's doctrines of predestination and justification and partly because of the apocalypse of the New Testament which speaks of God saving the "holy remnant" from the final holocaust.

When Hoffman arrived in Strasbourg in June, 1529 after a short stay in Eastern Frisia, he linked these four basic ideas to the belief that human co-operation in God's Work of redemption was necessary. This was more in keeping with a state of expectancy which often needed very little to trigger off concrete action. From Hans Denck he derived the ideas of the universality of divine grace and of the freedom of the will. He built a new doctrine of justification on this basis. A first justification (which comes about by pure grace) liberates man from the curse of original sin by means of the sacrificial death of Christ. But to reach his second justification and attain eternal salvation, man must go through a process of collaboration with God in which the divine Word enlightens the "natural man" and he becomes the "heavenly man". At the highest stage of his development the perfected saint is bound neither to the letter of the external Word nor to the Law. After faith has produced "clarity" and inner conviction within the believer, and after he has come into full possession of the Holy Spirit, the enlightened man will stand above the Law, for he possesses the Spirit who gave the Law.

This idea of co-operation led Hoffman to formulate a federal theory which he expressed in his doctrine of baptism. He saw baptism as a contract between God and man in which both parties commit themselves to be faithful to each other, and in which man promises to deny the world. Hoffman consequently believed that believers' or adult baptism was the valid form of the rite.

Hoffman formulated his Monophysite Christology in the course of a controversy with Schwenckfeld. He denied that Christ had taken flesh and blood from Mary. Although he defended this doctrine on the grounds that Christ could only have atoned for men's sins if he were free of the blemish which even Mary shared as a descendant of Adam, it is more probable that his Christological speculation was rooted in his spiritualistic convictions, which meant that he could not envisage any union of the divine spirit with earthly creatures (an attitude which had already found expression in his Eucharistic doctrine).

Having accepted Denck's doctrine of the freedom of the will, Hoffman was no longer inclined to see the future course of the apocalypse as following a rigidly predetermined programme. His apocalyptic ideas underwent a disastrous change under the influence of the Strasbourg Prophets, particularly as a result of the visions of Ursula and Lienhard Jost. He took over from them the idea that Christ's Parousia would be prepared by a successful military campaign, in which the "Spiritual Jerusalem" would defeat the "hellish trinity" (the Emperor, the Pope and the false prophets), and the "bloodthirsty" band of priests (including the Lutherans and Zwinglians because of their persecution of the Anabaptists) would be slaughtered. Only when this defensive war had been won would the 144,000 "apostolic messengers" go out to fill the world with the light of the true Gospel (i.e. to teach the doctrines of the universality of God's grace and the freedom of man's will). A new theocracy, like those of Joseph and Solomon, would be established and would spread over the whole of the earth. Only then would Christ return and rule as king of this world. Central to this belief was his idea that "the banner of God's justice" would be carried all over the world by the magistracies of the Free Imperial cities under the leadership of Strasbourg.

But this change in his apocalyptic thinking did not constitute a total break in Hoffman's development. In his commentary on Revelation written in 1530 (which shows no trace of the influence of the Strasbourg Prophets), he had interpreted Christ's Parousia both literally (a physical appearance of Christ on the clouds of heaven) and allegorically (as the epiphany of Christ's spirit in the "spiritual clouds", i.e. the "apostolic messengers"). The tendency towards inner-worldliness was already apparent here.

But alongside this militant apocalypticism Hoffman still upheld Luther's doctrine of obedience to secular authority. He would hear of no rebellion against legally established power except against that of the Emperor, whom he regarded as an instrument of Antichrist. Unlike the Swiss Brethren, he believed that people holding official positions could be Christians. Like the early Luther, he urged that force should not be applied to questions of faith (though this was to change during the apocalyptic cataclysm). Torn between condemning the use of force by believers and needing to exact vengeance on the "false teachers", Hoffman settled on the following solution: he and his followers themselves renounced the use of force, but they did call on "pious authorities" to arm themselves in preparation for a final battle against the forces of evil. With its bizarre mixture of Hoffman's earlier apocalypticism, Denck's voluntarism, the revolutionary ideas of the Strasbourg Prophets, traces of the Lutheran doctrine of obedience and the pacifism of the Swiss Brethren, Melchiorite Anabaptism finally became something markedly different from any other movements. Since Hoffman felt that only he possessed the truth, he placed himself outside the *successio Anabaptistica* and dispensed baptism on his own authority as *Elijah redivivus* and as the first apocalyptic witness of the last days. We can thus claim that Melchior Hoffman should be regarded as the founder of a third type of European Anabaptism alongside the Swiss Brethren in Zürich and Hans Hut in Central Germany.

Hoffman also differed from the Swiss Brethren in his rejection of a democratic congregational structure. He rejected his earlier views on this issue (which he had formulated in Livonia) under the influence of the charismatic environment created by the Strasbourg Prophets. He now felt that the Christian church should be structured as a hierarchy of spiritual men, foremost amongst whom were the infallible "apostolic messengers" who could never be deposed.

There were contradictions within Hoffman's thinking in this second stage, although they were not so apparent as during his earlier period. The Lutheran concept of authority could not be reconciled with ideas about the "massacre of the godless" or military struggles of the "Spiritual Jerusalem". Nor could the idea that the "apostolic messengers" should not use force be easily fitted into the picture. There could be no practicable synthesis of Wittenberg, Allstedt and Schleitheim. It was these inner contradictions which eventually broke up the Melchiorite movement. The following three ideas, which were taken up by

Jan Matthijs, show that Hoffman was a precursor of the
Anabaptist kingdom of Münster:

1. The godless must be destroyed *before* the Last Judgment.
2. Christ's Parousia will be ushered in by a theocracy which
   extends over the whole earth. As in the Jewish theocracy a
   new Solomon will be the ruler, taking advice from his
   prophet, a new Jonah.
3. The "apostolic messengers" will be invulnerable and
   invincible.

Hoffman himself gave the signal for the final battle in 1533.
But unlike Matthijs, who considered himself to be the second
apostolic witness, Hoffman attributed this role to Cornelis
Poldermann. He condemned Matthijs's practice of polygamy as
"whoremongering". And finally he disapproved of the uprising
by his followers, for he was waiting for a "revolution from
above." The Anabaptists of Münster claimed to be a "rightful
authority" because they had come to power "legally" as a result
of the election of the town council on 23rd February, 1534. But
this election was only held after the Anabaptists had rebelled
against the Lutheran Council between 9th and 11th February,
and after the uncontrolled influx of Westphalian and Dutch
Melchiorites which had begun at the beginning of the same
month. Thus the election of 23rd February, 1534 took place in an
atmosphere of fear and intimidation. Hardly had the Anabaptists
been "legally" established before they began to dismantle the
whole of the city's constitutional structure. People opposed to the
Melchiorites were driven out by force and the two elected
Burgomasters were stripped of their power. Jan Matthijs relied
on his own charisma; he had never been legitimised by an
election. He did not embody any legal authority in Hoffman's
sense of the word.

But Jan Matthijs drew only one obvious consequence from
Hoffman's theology of history, which became imperative if the
"pious authorities" hesitated to play their apocalyptic role. In
such a case – Jan Matthijs thought – it was the duty of the
"apostolic messengers" to take the sword into their own hands.

The difference between the deaths of Hoffman, as a defenceless prisoner in a Strasbourg jail, and of Jan Matthijs, as a warrior of God before the gates of Münster, symbolizes the inner contradictions within the spiritual world of a single man who balanced an infernal hatred of an imperfect reality with an equally strong yearning for perfection.

Bibliography

1. Unpublished Sources

University of Basel: Ms. Collection.
The David Joris papers: I "Twistreden tot Straetsburch", 1538. "Was David Georg zu Straßburg mitt Melcher Hoffman und anderen gehandelt." (Minutes of the Disputation between David Joris and the Strasbourg Melchiorites).

Municipal Archives of Flensburg:
Lütge Namann: Egenwillion – Evangelion Martini Luthers. (The report by Lütge Namann, a monk and founder of the Flensburg Grammar School, concerning the beginnings of the Reformation in Schleswig-Holstein, written about 1540).

Municipal Archives of Kiel:
Akten Nr. 1025: Parish Register of the Nikolaikirche.
Akten Nr. 1041: Complaints about the misappropriation of ecclesiastical property.

Archives of the Province of Schleswig:
Urkunden der Stadt Kiel Nr. 422 und 423.

Municipal Archives of Straßburg:
Thomas-Archiv (reference numbers are given as they arise in the text).
Minutes of the Council and XXI 1539–1546. (Of the three secret 'Chambers' which determined the political course of medieval Strasbourg — the 'Chamber of the XIII', the 'Chamber of the XV', and the 'Chamber of the XXI' — the latter is named in German 'Rät und XXI', i.e. 'Council and XXI'; it was, however, like the other two, itself a committee of the Council.)
Accounts of the Cathedral's Association of Builders (wages and salaries) 1508–1540, vol. 43m.
Decrees and Fiscal-regulations Serie R 18 and AA.
    My thanks are due to Dr. Rott for allowing me to see the still unpublished collection of documents relating to the Anabaptists in Alsace vol. III, collected by John Adam.

2. Catalogue of the Writings of Melchior Hoffman

1. Jhesus. Der Christlichen gemeyn zu Der = pten ynn Liefflandt wunschet Melcher Hoffman/ Gnad vnd fride/ sterckung des glawbens von Gott dem vater vnd dem hern Jhesu Christo Amen. In: Luther, Martin: Eyne Christliche vormanung von eusserlichem Gottis dienst vnde eyntracht/

an die yn lieffland/ durch D Martinum Luther vnde andere (Johannes Bugenhagen und Melchior Hoffman). Wittenberg, (Michael Lotter), 1525. B4a–C4a (last page blank).
Original: Zentralbibliothek Zürich, Rp. 475,5; Staats- und Stadtbibliothek Augsburg; Bibliothek des Germanischen Nationalmuseums $\frac{8°Rl.2116}{(Post-Inc.)}$; UB Münster, Coll. Erh. 173; Württembergische Landesbibliothek Theol. gt. k982.
Reprint published in Luther WA 18, 426–430.

2. An de gelöfighen vorsambling inn Liflandt ein korte formaninghe, van Melcher Hoffman sich tho wachten vor falscher lere de sich nw ertzeighen vnde inrithen, vnder der sthemme götliker worde. (Stockholm, The Royal Press), 1526. A1a–A8b (A6b–A8b blank).
Original (recently discovered): Zürich, Zentralbibliothek.
An original copy, in the library of the Livonian Knights in Riga, has vanished. A reprint was edited by August Buchholtz, in the *Festschrift für Martin Daniel Taube*, Riga, 1856.

3. Das XII Capitel des propheten Danielis außgelegt/ vnd das evangelion des andern sondages/ gefallendt im Aduent/ vnd von den zeychenn des iün = gsten gerichtes/ auch vom sacrament/ beicht vnd absolucion/ eyn schöne vnterweisung an die in Lieflandt/ vnd eym yden christen nutzlich zu wissen. (Stockholm, The Royal Press), 1526. Ia–IVb (Vorrede) + a1a–o4b (last page blank).
Original: Staats- und Universitätsbibliothek Hamburg, Inc. App. $\frac{A}{126;}$ Royal Library, Copenhagen, 23,–274, 4to. Herzog-August-Bibliothek Wolfenbüttel, Sig.: C 116; Torún (Poland), Biblioteka Glowna Uniwersyetu Kopernika.

4. Dat Nikolaus Amsdorff der Meydeborger Pastor/ nicht weth/ wat he setten/ schriuen edder swetzen schal/ darmede he syne lögen bestedigen möge/ vnde synen gruweliken anlop. Melchior Hoffman Koninckliker Maiestat tho Dennemarcken gesetter Prediger thom Kyll/ ym lande tho Holsten. (Kiel, Melchior-Hoffman Press), 1528. A1a–A4b (last page blank).
Original: the only copy is in the Zentralbibliothek Zürich, XVIII, 418, 12.
Facsimile-reprint edited by Gerhard Ficker under the title "Melchior Hoffman gegen Nikolaus Amsdorff", Preetz 1928 = Schriften des Vereins für Schleswig-Holsteinische Kirchengeschichte, Sonderheft 5.

5. Das Niclas Amsdorff der Magdeburger Pastor ein lugenhafftiger falscher nasen geist sey/ offentlich bewiesen durch Melchior Hoffman/ Königlicher wirden gesetzter prediger zum Kyll/ ym landt zu Holstein. (Kiel, Melchior Hoffman-Press), 1528. A1a–14b, B1a–B2b, C1a–C4b.
Original: the only copy is in the Royal Library, Copenhagen, Hj 490, 4°.
Facsimile-reprint edited by Gerhard Ficker, Preetz 1926 = Schriften des Vereins für Schleswig-Holsteinische Kirchengeschichte, Sonderheft 4.

6. (Das) Erste Capitel des Evangelisten St. Mattheus. (1528). Vorrede.

Original: vanished.

Reprint in: Johannes Melchior Krafft: Ein Zweyfaches Zwey-Hundert-Jähriges Jubel-Gedächtnis. Hamburg 1723, pp. 440–445. UB Hamburg, Ka A $\frac{1946.}{1610}$

7. Dat Boeck Cantica Canticorum odder dat hoge leedt Salomonis uthgelecht dorch Melchior Hoffman koninckliker maiestat tho Dennemarcken gesetter prediger thom Kyll: ym lande tho Holsten. Kiel, (Hoffman's own printing-press), 1529. 4°. 1a–4b B1. + A1a–Q4b; in the only copy, A4b and Q4a–b are blank (numbered from 2–Q II) (available in Prague: Statni knihovna ĈSR).

8. Anonymus [i.e. Hoffman, Melchior and Karlstadt, Andreas Bodenstein von]:

Dialogus vnd gründtliche berichtung gehaltner disputation im land zů Holstein vnderm Künig von Denmarck vom hochwirdigen Sacrament oder Nachtmal des Herren. In gegenwertigkeit Kü. Ma. Sun Hertzog Kerstens sampt Kü. Raten/ vilen vom Adel/ vnd grosser versamlung der Priesterschafft. Yetzt kurtzlich geschehen den andern Donderstag nach Ostern/ im jar Christi. Als man zalt MDXXIX. Straßburg, Balthasar Beck, o.J. (1529). A1a–A8b, B1a–B4b (the two last pages are blank). *Original:* Zentralbibliothek Zürich, D 324. 1.

Copy, likewise anonymous, with the same title up to the word "Priesterschaft". (Augsburg, Philipp Ulhart, 1529). A1a–C4b (the two last pages are blank). Available at: Königliche Bibliothek Kopenhagen, 40^{II},–172, 4 to; Bayrische Staatsbibliothek München 4 to, H. ref. 250; UB Utrecht Rariora F. qu. 104⁴; UB Basel F. NX. 17. Nr. 9.4. und Ki. Ar. J, X. 30. Nr. 7; Edinburgh, National Library of Scotland.

9. Weissagung usz heiliger götlicher geschrifft. Von den trůbsalen diser letsten zeit. Von der schweren hand vnd straff gottes über alles gottloß wesen. Von der zukunfft des Türckischen Thirannen/ vnd seines gantzen anhangs. Wie er sein reiß thůn/ vnnd volbringen wirt/ vns zu einer straff/ vnnd růtten. Wie er durch Gottes gwalt sein niderlegung vnnd straff entpfahen wirt. (No place). (Straßburg, Balthasar Beck), 1529. A1a–D4b (last page blank).

Original: UB Freiburg, F 1011, f; Deutsche Staatsbibliothek (Ost)Berlin, Na 7486; Herzog August Bibliothek Wolfenbüttel 96.21 Theol; British Museum, 1315, c.4/12; Bibliothek der Vereenigde Doopsgezinde Gemeente Amsterdam, II 204, now UB Amsterdam.

10. PRophezey oder weissagung vß warer heiliger götlicher schrifft. Von allen wundern vnd zeichen/ biß zů der zůkunfft Christi Jesu vnsers heillands/ an dem Jüngsten tag/ vnd der welt end. Dise Prophecey wirt sich anfahen am end der weissagung (kürtzlich von mir außgangen/ in ein anderen buchlin) Von der schweren straff gotes/ über alles gotloß wesen/ durch den Türckischen tirannen/ auch wie er regieren vnd ein end nemmen wirt. (No place). (Straßburg, Balthasar Beck), 1530. A1a–C4b (last page blank).

Original: UB Basel, Theol. Conf. 19.8. Nr. 1; Deutsche Staatsbibliothek (Ost)Berlin, Na 7488; British Museum, 1315 c.4/13; Württembergische Landesbibliothek Stuttgart, theol.qᵗ 7895.

11. Außlegung der heimlichen Offenbarung Joannis des heyligen Apostels vnnd Euangelisten. Straßburg, Balthasar Beck, 1530 (the place and printer are given on p. Z7b). A1a–Z8b (the last two pages are blank). *Original:* Zentralbibliothek Zürich, XXVIII. 419; UB Utrecht, Rariora E. oct. 511; UB Basel, f b 1351 Nr. 1; Deutsche Staatsbibliothek (Ost)Berlin, Bt 16 110; Sächsische Landesbibliothek Dresden, Exeges. C 1060; UB Leipzig 2885 f; UB Straßburg R 100 466; Staats- und Stadtbibliothek Augsburg; Bayrische Staatsbibliothek Exeg. 503; Württembergische Landesbibliothek Stuttgart, Theol. 8°8382. Herzog August Bibliothek Wolfenbüttel, Sig. C 515.
Excerpt in: Heinold Fast (ed.): Der linke Flügel der Reformation. 1962, pp. 308–318.

12. Hoffman, Melchior (ed.):
Prophetische gesicht vnd Offenbarung/ der götlichen würckung zů diser letsten zeit/ die vom XXIIIj. jar biß in dz XXX. einer gottes liebhaberin [Ursula Jost] durch den heiligen geist geoffenbart seind/ welcher hie in disem büchlin. LXXVII. verzeichnet seindt. (Straßburg. Balthasar Beck). 1530. A1a–C8b (last page blank).
Original: Bayrische Staatsbibliothek München $\dfrac{6}{\text{polem. }1515^{m}}$
Excerpt in: Heinold Fast (ed.): Der linke Flügel der Reformation. 1962. pp. 298–308.

13. Der leuchter des alten Testaments vß gelegt/ welcher im heylige(n) stund der hütten Mose/ mit seinen siben lampen/ blůmen/ knöpffen/ liechtschneützen vnd Leschnepff. Vnd alles das sich reicht vff die siben versamlung des neüwen Testaments. (Straßburg, Balthasar Beck, 1530?). A1a–A8b.
Original: UB Bern Sig. m 124; UB Straßburg R 100462; Königliche Bibliothek Kopenhagen Sig. 87,–223; UB Freiburg L 8327.

14. Die Ordonnantie Godts/ De welcke hy/ door zijnen Soone Christum Jesum/ inghestelt ende bevesticht heeft/ op die waerachtighe Discipulen des eeuwigen woort Godts. Ten eersten Ghedruckt Anno 1530. Ende nu door een liefhebber der gerechticheydt/ wt het Oostersche/ in Nederduytsche ghetrouwelijcken overgeset. Amsterdam, Claes Gerretsz, 1611. A1a–A8b, B1a–B8b, C1a–C4b.
Original: Bibliothek der Vereenigde Doopsgezinde Gemeente Amsterdam, jetzt UB Amsterdam, II 206.
Reprint: BRN V, pp. 125–170 (with an introduction by S. Cramer). English translation in: Spiritual and Anabaptist Writers. Documents Illustrative of the Radical Reformation. Ed. by George Huntston Williams. London, SCM Press, 1957, pp. 182–203 = The Library of Christian Classics vol. XXV.

15. M.H. [id est: Melchior Hoffman]:

WArhafftige erklerung aus heyliger Biblischer schrifft/ das der Satan/
Todt/ Hell/ Sünd/ und dy ewige verdamnuß im vrsprung nit auß gott/
sundern alleyn auß eygenem will erwachsen sei. (Straßburg, Jakob
Cammerlander), 1531. A1a–A8b.
Original: UB Utrecht, Rariora. E. oct. 511; Dublin, Trinity College.

16. M.H. [id est: Melchior Hoffman]:
    DAs ware trostliche vnnd freudenreiche Euangelion/ welchs zu dieser
    letsten zeit aller welt sol offenbart vnd fürgetragen werden/ durch die
    waren Apostolischen geyster/ vnd knecht deß Herrn Jesu Christi.
    (Straßburg, Jakob Cammerlander), 1531. A1a–A8b, B1a–B4b.
    Original: Dublin, Trinity College, C. pp. 32 no 6.

17. Das freudenreiche zeucknus vam worren friderichen ewigen evangelion,
    Apoc. 14, welchs da ist ein kraft gottes, die da sallig macht alle die daran
    glauben, Rom. 1., welchem worren und ewigen evangelion itzt zu disser
    letzten zeit so vil dausend sathanischer geister mit falscher ketzerischer
    irriger lugenhaftiger zeucknus gegenstandt. 1532.
    Original destroyed by fire in Strasbourg in 1870, comprised seven sheets
    in quarto.
    Reprint: F. O. zur Linden, Hofmann, pp. 429–432 (Excerpt).

18. Anonymus [id est: Melchior Hoffman]:
    Verclaringe van den geuangenen ende vrien wil des menschen/ wat ook
    die waerachtige gehoorsaemheyt des gheloofs/ ende warachtighen
    eewighen Euangelions sy. No place, no date. Title-page missing.
    A2a–A8b, B1a–B4b (the last two pages are blank). Published before
    1533–probably in 1532–in the Netherlands, since Hoffman in his 1533
    Commentary on Romans refers to this tract (J3a).
    Original: UB Utrecht, Rariora, E. oct. 511.
    Reprint: BRN Bd. 5, pp. 173–198 (with an introduction by S. Cramer).

19. Van der waren hochprachtlichen eynigen magestadt gottes/ vnnd vann
    der worhaftigen menschwerdung des ewigen wortzs vnd Suns des
    allerhochsten/ eyn kurtze zeucknus vnd anweissung allen liebhabern der
    ewigen worheit. (Deventer, Albert Paffraet, 1532?). A1a–B8b (last page
    blank).
    Original: in the private collection of Helmuth Domizlaff (München).
    Partial reprint of an incomplete copy by Barthold Nicolaus Krohn,
    appears in Friedrich Otto zur Linden, Hoffman, pp. 433–437; W. J.
    Leendertz, Hoffman, pp. 382–385.

20. M.H. [id est: Melchior Hoffman]:
    Een waraftyghe tuchenisse vnde gruntlyke verclarynge wo die worden
    tho den Ro. IX. Ca. van dem Esau vnd Jacob soldeen verstaen worden/
    teghen   den   falschen/   ketterschen/   dwalenden/   lugenaftygen/
    sathanysschen/ ingevorten verstant/ des Luterschen vnde zuyngelschen
    hupen. (Deventer, Albert Paffraet), 1532, A1a–A8b.
    Original: in the private collection of Helmuth Domizlaff (München).

21. Anonymus [id est: Melchior Hoffman]:
    Die eedele hoghe ende troostlike sendebrief/ den die heylige Apostel
    Paulus to den Romeren gescreuen heeft/ verclaert ende gans vlitich mit

ernste van woort to woorde wtgelecht Tot eener costeliker nutticheyt ende troost allen godtvruchtigen liefhebbers der eewighen onentliken waerheyt. (No place), 1533. A1a–Z8b (Z3a–Z8b blank). *Original:* Bibliothek der Vereenigde Doopsgezinde Gemeente Amsterdam, II 205, now UB Amsterdam.

22. Caspar Becker [Pseudonym, perhaps for Johannes Eisenburg, with the possible collaboration of Melchior Hoffman]:
Eyn sendbrieff an alle gottsförchtigen liebhaber der ewigen warheyt/ inn welchem angezeyget seind die artickel des Melchior Hofmans (sic!)/ derhalben yhn die lerer zu Straßburg als eyn ketzer verdampt/ vnd inn gefencknüß mit trübsal/ qual/ spott vnnd schand gekrönet haben. (Hagenau, Valentin Kobian), 1533. A1a–B8b (B7a to B8b blank). *Original:* UB Utrecht, Rariora E. oct. 511; Zentralbibliothek Zürich. This work comprises the five main doctrines of Hoffman, which he presented at the Strasbourg Synod. The stylistic qualities suggest Johannes Eisenburg as the editor.
Reprint: TAE II Nr. 399, pp. 101–110.

23. Ein rechte warhafftige hohe vnd götliche gruntliche vnderrichtung von der reiner forchte Gottes ann alle liebhaber der ewiger vnentlicher warheit/ auß Götlicher Schrifft angezeygt zům preiß Gottes vnnd heyll seines volcks in ewigkeyt. Mit einer Nachrede von Cornelis Poldermann. (No place), 1533. A1a–A8b (last page blank). *Original:* UB Utrecht, Rariora E. oct. 511; Bayrische Staatsbibliothek München, Asc. $\frac{2}{4367}$

24. Worhafftige zeucknus gegen die nachtwechter vnd sternen/ Das Der Dott mensch Jhesus Christus am kreuz vnd im grab nit ein angenommen fleisch vnd blut aus maria sey/ sundern allein Das pawre vnd ewige wortt vnd Der vnendliche sun Des allerhochsten. (1533). The only original manuscript which still exists. Straßburg, Thomas-Archiv, Sig. 76, Nr. 39, (Hofmanniana Nr. 2).
Reprints: Friedrich Otto zur Linden, Hofmann, pp. 438–444 (defective), W. I. Leendertz, Hofmann, pp. 386–392.

25. [Poldermann, Cornelius] [i.e. composed by Hoffman, published by von Poldermann]:
Die Epistel des Apostell Sanct Judas erklert vnnd gantzs fleissig von wort zů worten/ außgelegt zů eyner ernsten warnungen ia auch zů eynem köstlichen nutz vnd trost/ allen Gotts forchtigen liebhabern der ewigen vnendlichen warheyt. (Hagenau, Valentin Kobian), 1534. A1a–D8b, last page blank. *Original:* UB Basel, fb 1351, Nr. 2 *Reprint:* TAE II Nr. 479, pp. 241–245 (Excerpt).

26. Eisenburgk, Johannes [presumably together with Melchior Hoffman]:
Die Epistel deß Apostels S. Jacobs erklärt/ vnd gantz fleissig von Wort zů wort außgelegt/ zů eyner ernsten warnung/ auch zů eynem kostlichen nůtz vnd trost/ allen gotsförchtigen liebhabern der ewigen warheyt. (Straßburg, Jakob Cammerlander), 1534. A1a–C8b.

Original: UB Basel, fb 1351, Nr. 2.
Reprint: TAE II Nr. 480, pp. 245–248 (Excerpt).

27. Caspar Beck [Pseudonym, id est: Melchior Hoffman]:
Eyn sendbrieff an den achtbaren Michel wachter/ in welchem eroffnet
würt/ die vberauß greuwliche mißhandlung/ die in vergangnen zeyten
zů Jerusalem wider dye ewige worheit vnd der selbigen zeugen gehandlet
ist/ vnd auch noch teglich verbrocht wurt/ ohn alle forcht Gottis.
(Hagenau, Valentin Kobian, 1534). A1a–A8b (A7b–A8b blank).
Original: Gräflich Solmsche Bibliothek in Laubach, Oberhessen.
Reprint: "Ein Sendbrief Melchior Hofmanns aus dem Jahre 1534", ed. by
E. W. Kohls, in: Theol. Zeitschrift 17, 1961, pp. 356–365.

3. Published Sources

Achelis, Th. O. (ed.): Die Haderslebener Artikel von 1528. In: Schriften des
Vereins f. Schleswig-Holsteinische Kirchengeschichte. 1. Reihe, H. 18,
1934.

Acta der Disputation zu Flensburg/ die sache des Hochwirdigen Sacraments
betreffend/ im 1529. Jar/ des Donnerstags nach Quasimodo geniti
geschehen. Hg. von Johannes Bugenhagen. Wittenberg 1529 (= Acta).

Acta Synodi Bernensis. Simone Sulzero Interprete. 1532.

Amsdorf, Nikolaus v.: Grundt und orsake/ worup Marquardus Schuldorp
hefft syner suster dochter thor ehe genamen, boweret dorch Ern
Nicolaum Amßtorp Licentiaten, und Ern Martinum Luther, Doctor yn
der hylligen schrifft. 1526.
Reprint: Luther WA Br. IV, pp. 9f.

——: Eine Vermanung an die von Magdeburg, das sie sich fur falsch
propheten zu hüten wissen. Magdeburg 1527.

——: Das Melchior Hoffman ein falscher Prophet und sein leer vom jüngsten
Tag unrecht, falsch und wider Gott ist; an alle Heilige und Gläubige an J.
Chr. zu Kiel und in ganzen Holstein. 1528.

——: Das Melchior Hoffman/ nicht ein wort auff mein Büchlein geantwort
hat. (No place). 1528. 4°, A–B1b (the only copy is in the Research
Library at Gotha, under the ref. no. Theol. 4,185,7).

Anonymus: Gründtlicker warhafftiger Bericht: Von der Evangelischen
Reformation/ der Christlicken Kercken tho Emden und in Ostfrießland/
van 1520 beth up den hüdigen Dag. Bremen 1594.

Arbusov, Leonid (junior) compiler: Akten und Rezesse der livländischen
Ständetage. Ed. by the Gesellschaft für Geschichte und Alterthumskunde
der Ostseeprovinzen Rußlands. Vol. III. 1494–1535. Riga 1910 (= AR
III).

Arndt, Johann Gottfried (translator and editor): Der Liefländischen Chronik
1. Teil oder die Origines Livoniae Sacrae et Civiles von Johann Daniel
Gruber aus einem alten Manuskript (Henricus Lettus). Halle 1747.

——: Der Liefländischen Chronik andrer Teil. Halle 1753.

Arnold, Gottfried: Unpartheyische Kirchen- und Ketzerhistorie. 3rd edn.,
vol. 1. Schaffhausen 1740.

Die Bekenntnisschriften der evangelisch-lutherischen Kirche. 6th edn., Göttingen 1967.

Beninga, Eggeric: Cronica der Fresen. Bearbeitetvon Louis Hahn. Aus dem Nachlaß herausgegeben von Heinz Ramm. Aurich 1961 = Quellen zur Geschichte Ostfrieslands vol. IV.

Blesdikius (Blesdijk), Nikolaus: Historia Vitae, doctrinae ac rerum gestarum Davidis Georgii, Haeresiarchae. Deventer 1642.

Bredenbach. Tilmann: Belli Livonici nova et memorabilis historia. Köln 1564.

Bremer, Asmus: Chronicon Kiliense tragicum-curiosum. 1432–1717. Ed. by Moritz Stern. Kiel 1916 = Mitteilungen der Gesellschaft für Kieler Stadtgeschichte H.18.

Brenneysen, Enno Rudolph: Ostfriesische Historie und Landesverfassung. 2 vols. Aurich 1720.

Brunfels, Otto: Von dem Pfaffen zehenden/ hundert und zwen fyertzig Schlußreden. 1524.

Bucer, Martin: Deutsche Schriften. Vol. 1. Ed. by Robert Stupperich. 1960.

——: Enarrationum in evangelia Matthaei, Marci et Lucae libri duo. Straßburg 1527.

——: Enarratio in Evangelion Johannis. Straßburg 1528.

——: Sacrorum Psalmorum libri quinque. 1532.

——: Handlung inn dem offentlichen gesprech zu Straßburg iüngst im Synodo gehalten/ gegen Melchior Hoffman/ durch die Prediger daselbst. Straßburg 1533.

Capito, Wolfgang Fabricius: Wasz man halten und antwurten soll, von der spaltung zwischen Martin Luther and Andres Carolstadt. Straßburg 1524.

——: In Hoseam prophetam V.F. Capitonis Commentarius. Straßburg 1528.

——: Kinderbericht und Fragstück vom Glauben. (No place). 1529.

Cellarius, Martinus (Borrhaus, Martin): De operibus Dei electionis et reprobationis. Mit einer Vorrede von Wolfgang Capito. Straßburg 1527.

Cornelius, C. A. (ed.): Berichte der Augenzeugen über das Münstersche Wiedertäuferreich. Neudruck der Ausgabe von 1853. Münster 1965 = Die Geschichtsquellen des Bistums Münster vol. 2.

Corvinus, Antonius: Acta: Handlungen: Legation und schriffte ... Gespreche und disputation Antoni Corvini und Joannis Kymei mit dem Münsterschen König, mit Knipperdolling und Krechting. 1536.

Cramer, S. (ed.): Nederlandsche Anabaptistica. Geschriften van Henrick Roll, Melchior Hoffman, Adam Pastor et al. Den Haag 1909 = BRN V.

Cypraeus, Johann Adolf: Annales Episcoporum Slesvicensium. Köln 1634.

Documenta Anabaptistisca Neerlandica. Eerste Deel: Friesland en Groningen (1530–1550). Ed. by A. F. Mellink. Leiden 1975 = Kerkhistorische Bijdragen Deel VI/I.

Dülmen, Richard van (ed.): Das Täuferreich zu Münster 1534–1535. Dokumente. München 1974 = dtv WR 4150.

Ebel, Wilhelm: Ostfriesische Bauernrechte. 1964 = Quellen zur Geschichte Ostfrieslands vol. 5.

Eekhof, A. (ed.): De avondmaalsbrief von Cornelis Hoen. 1525. s'Gravenhage 1917.

Emmius, Ubbo: Rerum Frisicarum Historia ... distincta in Decades sex, quarum postrema nunc primum prodit. Leiden 1616.

——: Rerum Frisicarum Historiae Decas Septima et Ultima. Emden 1616.

Erasmus, Desiderius: Opus Epistolarum Des. Erasmi Roterodami. Vol. XI. Ed. by H. M. Allen and H. W. Garrod. Oxford 1947.

——: Opera Omnia. Vol. 5. Ed. by Johannes Clericus. Reprint. Hildesheim (Georgs Olms), 1962 (includes: De magnitudine misericordiarum Domini. Sp. 558–588).

Fabricius, Dionysius: Livonicae Historiae compendiosa series. 1795. Neudruck: Ed. by Bergmann. Riga and Leipzig 1884 = Scriptores Rerum Livonicarum vol. 2.

Fast, Heinold (ed.): Der linke Flügel der Reformation. 1962. = Klassiker des Protestantismus IV.

Franck, Sebastian: Chronica, zeitbuch unnd Geschichtsbibell. 1st edn., Straßburg 1531; 2nd edn., Ulm, 1536; 3rd edn., 1543.

——: Germaniae Chronicon. Augsburg 1538.

——: Das verbütschiert mit siben Sigeln verschlossen Buch. 1539.

——: Weltbuch. 1542.

Grefenthal, Bartholomäus: Livländische Chronik. Ed. by F. G. v. Bunge. Riga and Leipzig 1887 = Monumenta Livoniae Antiquae vol. 5.

Grosheide, G. (ed.): Verhooren en Vonnissen der Wederdoopers, betrokken bij de aanslagen op Amsterdam in 1534 en 1535. In: Bijdragen en Mededeelingen van het Historisch Genootschap XLI (1920), 1–197.

Hamelmann, Hermann: Opera Genealogico – Historica de Westphalia et Saxonia Inferiori. Congesta ab Ernesto C. Wasserbach. Lemgo 1711.

Hedio, Caspar: Von dem zehenden zwo treﬄicher predig. 1524.

Hubmaier, Balthasar: Schriften. Ed. by Gunnar Westin and Torsten Bergsten. Gütersloh 1962 = QFR XXIX = Quellen zur Geschichte der Täufer vol. IX.

Jenny, Beatrice (ed.): Das Schleitheimer Täuferbekenntnis 1527. 1951 = Schaffhauser Beiträge zur vaterländischen Geschichte 28.

Jensen, J. C. und Hegewisch, D. H.: Die Privilegien der schleswig-holsteinischen Ritterschaft. Kiel 1797.

Karlstadt, Andreas Bodenstein von: Missive von der allerhöchsten Tugend gelassenheit. 1520 (Barge-Frey Nr. 40).

——: Welche bücher heilig und biblisch seind. 1521 (Barge-Frey Nr. 46).

——: Von abtuhung der Bilder, und das keyn Betdler unter den Christen seyn sollen. 1522. Reprinted: Bonn 1911 = Kleine Texte für theologische und philologische Vorlesungen und Übungen. vol. 74.

——: Predig oder homilien über den propheten Malachiam genannt. Wittenberg 1522 (Barge-Frey Nr. 93).

——: Von manigfeltigkeit des eynfeltigen eynigen willen gottes. Was sundt sey. 1523 (Barge-Frey Nr. 103).

——: Ob man gemach faren/ und des ergernüssen der schwachen verschonen soll/ in sachen so gottis willen angehen. 1524 (Barge-Frey Nr. 138).

——: Ob man mit heyliger geschrifft erweysen möge/ das Christus mit leyb/ blut/ und sele im sacrament sey. 1524 (Barge-Frey Nr. 124).

——: Wie sich der gelaub und unglaub gegen dem liecht und finsternus, gegen wahrheit und luegen, gegen Gott und dem teufel halten. 1524 (Barge-Frey Nr. 139).

——: Was gesagt ist/ "sich gelassen"/ und was das Wort "Gelassenheit" bedeut/ und wo es in hailiger geschrifft begriffen. 1523 (Barge-Frey Nr. 104).

——: Ain Sermon, ob die Ohrenbeicht oder der Glaub allein oder was den Menschen zu wirdiger Empfahung des Hl. Sakraments geschickt mach. 1524 (Barge-Frey Nr. 80).

——: Ap Got ein ursach sey des Teufflischen Falls. 1524 (Barge-Frey Nr. 114).

——: Eyn frage/ ob auch yemant möge selig wer = den/ on die für = bitt Marie. Wittenberg 1524 (Barge-Frey Nr. 107).

——: Wider die alte und neue papistische Messen. 1524 (Barge-Frey Nr. 131).

——: Karlstadts Schriften aus den Jahren 1523–1525. Ed. by Erich Hertzsch. 2 vols. Halle 1956.

Kelch, Christian: Liefländische Historia oder Kurtze Beschreibung der Denkwürdigsten Kriegs- und Friedensgeschichte Esth-, Lief- und Lettlands ... in fünff Büchern abgefaßt. Part III. Reval 1695.

Koch, E. A. (ed.): Teutsche Reichsabschiede. Frankfurt 1747.

Köhler, Walther (ed.): Das Marburger Religionsgespräch 1529. Versuch einer Rekonstruktion. 1929 = Schriften des Vereins für Reformationsgeschichte 148.

Lenz, Max (ed.): Briefwechsel Landgraf Philipps des Großmütigen mit Bucer. Vol. 1. Leipzig 1880.

Lohmüller, Johannes: Das Bapst, Bischove und geistlicher Stand kein Land und Leute besitzen, vorstehn und regieren mugen, auß der heiligen Schrift verfasset. 1525. In: ARG 36, 1939, 59–67.

Meijer, Johann und Dankwerth, Caspar: Newe Landesbeschreibung der zwey Hertzogthümer Schleswich und Holstein. 1652.

Meiners, Eduard: Oostvrieschlandts kerkelyke geschiedenisse. 2 vols. Groningen 1739.

Mettig, Constantin: Materialien zu einer Geschichte der reformatorischen Bewegung in Riga. In: Sitzungsberichte d. Gesellschaft für Geschichte und Alterthumskunde der Ostseeprovinzen Rußlands aus dem Jahre 1890. Riga 1891, 65–71.

——: Die ältesten Bücher der Losträgergilde in Riga. In: Sitzungsberichte d. Gesellschaft für Geschichte und Alterthumskunde der Ostseeprovinzen Rußlands aus dem Jahr 1900. Riga 1901, 120–135.

Mollerus, Johannes: Cimbria Literata. Vol. 2. 1744.

Müntzer, Thomas: Schriften und Briefe. Kritische Gesamtausgabe ed. by Günther Franz (in collaboration with Paul Kirn). Gütersloh 1967 = QFR XXXIII.

Napiersky, C. E.: Rigas ältere Geschichte in Übersicht, Urkunden und alten Aufzeichnungen dargestellt. Riga und Leipzig 1844 = Monumenta Livoniae Antiquae 4.

Niesert, Joseph (ed.): Münstersche Urkundensammlung I. Coesfeld 1826.

Nyenstädt, Franz: Livländische Chronik, ed. by G. Tielemann. Riga 1839 = Monumenta Livoniae Antiquae, vol. 2.

Packull, Werner O.: Melchior Hoffman's Experience in the Livonian Reformation: The Dynamics of Sect Formation. In: MQR LIX, 1985, 130–146.

[Parper, Johannes]: Bericht Johannes Parpers über die Landtage zur Rendsburg und Kiel, 1525 und 1526. In: Archiv für Staats- und Kirchengeschichte der Herzogtümer Schleswig-Holstein-Lauenburg. Vol. 4, Altona 1840, pp. 479–480.

Pater, Calvin Augustine: Karlstadt as the Father of the Baptist Movements: The Emergence of Lay Protestantism. Toronto-Buffalo-London 1984.

Philips, Obbe: Bekenntnisse. In: BRN VII. Den Haag 1910.

Pontoppidan, Erich: Annales Ecclesiae Danicae. Vol. 2. Kopenhagen 1744.

Quellen zur Geschichte der (Wieder)-Täufer = Täuferakten (= TA), vol. 2: Bayern. Part 1: Markgraftum Brandenburg. Ed. by K. Schornbaum. Leipzig 1934 = QFR XVI.

Vol. 3: Glaubenszeugnisse oberdeutscher Taufgesinnter. Vol. I, ed. by Lydia Müller. Leipzig 1938 = QFR XX.

Vol. 4: Baden und Pfalz. Ed. by Manfred Krebs. Gütersloh 1951 = QFR XXII.

Vol. 7: Elsaß I. Stadt Straßburg 1522–1532. Ed. by Manfred Krebs and Hans Georg Rott. Gütersloh 1959 = QFR XXVI (= TAE I).

Vol. 8: Elsaß II. Stadt Straßburg 1533–1535. Ed. by Manfred Krebs and Hans Georg Rott. Gütersloh 1960 = QFR XXVII (= TAE II).

Quellen zur Geschichte der Täufer in der Schweiz. Vol. I: Zürich. Ed. by Leonhard v. Muralt and Walter Schmid. Zürich 1952.

Vol. II: Ostschweiz. Ed. by Heinold Fast, Zürich 1973.

Urkundliche Quellen zur hessischen Reformationsgeschichte. Vol. IV: Wiedertäuferakten 1527–1536. Ed. by Günther Franz. Marburg 1951 (= Wiedertäuferakten Hessen).

Reinhard, Martin (Ed.): Anzaygung wie die gefallene/ Christenhait widerbracht müg werden/ in jenen ersten standt in wölchem sie von/ Christo und seinen Aposteln erstlich/ gepflanzt und auff gebawet ist./ Vor hundert jaren, beschriben/ und yetzt allererst pfunden/ und durch den druck an/ tag geben/ Das concilium zů Basel/ und die Böhmen be/ treffende. 1524.

Ritter, F. (Ed.): Henricus Ubbius' Beschreibung von Ostfriesland vom Jahre 1530. In: Jahrbuch der Gesellschaft für bildende Kunst und vaterländische Altertümer zu Emden. Vol. 18. 1913, 53–141.

Röhrich, Timotheus Wilhelm: Zur Geschichte der Straßburgischen Wiedertäufer in den Jahren 1527–1543. In: Zeitschrift für historische Theologie 30, 1860, 3–121.

Rothmann, Bernhard: Die Schriften. Bearbeitet von Robert Stupperich. Münster 1970 = Veröffentlichungen der Historischen Kommission Westfalens, vol. 32 = Die Schriften der münster. Täufer und ihrer Gegner, vol. 1.

Russow, Balthasar: Chronica der Provintz Lyfflandt. 1584. Nachdruck Riga und Leipzig 1848 = Scriptores Rerum Livonicarum 2.

Schieß, Traugott (Ed.): Briefwechsel der Brüder Thomas und Ambrosius Blaurer. Vol. 1. Freiburg 1908.

Schütz, C.: Historia Rerum Prussicarum. Continuatio: Chyträus, David: Saxonia ab Anno Christi 1500 usque ad MDXCIX. Eisleben/Leipzig 1599.

Schuldorp, Marquard: Breef an de Glövigen der Stadt Kyll. 1529 B1a–C4b, D1–D8b (D6–D8 blank). The title is conjectured, because the title-page and A–A4b are missing. The text begins at B1a: Marquardus Schuldorp gheeschet vnd geordenth tho Schleßwick tho predighen dat wort Gades/ van Jhesu Christo ... wunsche allen gelöuyghen der Stadt Kyle Gnade vnd frede. The only copy is at the Royal Library, Copenhagen, Sign. Hj. 490.

Schwarze, Nikolaus Hermann: Desselb. Nicol. Hermann Schwarze gesammelte Nachrichten von der Stadt Kiel im Holsteinischen. Ed. by M. Joh. Heinrich Fehse. Flensburg 1775.

Schwenckfeld v. Ossig, Caspar: Corpus Schwenckfeldianorum. Ed. by Ch. D. Hartranft et al. Vols. 3, 4, 5. Leipzig 1913, 1914, 1916.

——: Epistular. Part 1, 1566; Part II/ 1 + 2, 1570.

Sehling, Emil (Ed.): Die evangelischen Kirchenordnungen des 16. Jahrhunderts. Vol. V: Livland. 1913.

——: Die evangelischen Kirchenordnungen des 16. Jahrhunderts. Vol. VII/II. First half. Halband: Ostfriesland. Ed. by Annemarie Sprengler-Ruppenthal. 1963.

Stieden, W. and Mettig, C.: Schragen der Gilden und Ämter der Stadt Riga bis 1621. Riga 1896.

Sturm, Johann: Antipappi quarti ... pars tertia. Neustadt a.d. Hardt 1580.

Tegetmeier, Sylvester: Tagebuch. Mitgeteilt von F. Bienemann. In: Mitteilungen aus dem Gebiet der Geschichte Liv-, Est- und Kurlands. Vol. 12. Riga 1880.

Virck, Hans and Winckelmann, Otto (ed.): Politische Korrespondenz der Stadt Straßburg. 5 vols. 1882–1933.

Williams, George Huntston (ed.): Spiritual and Anabaptist Writers. Documents Illustrative of the Radical Reformation. London 1957 = Library of Christian Classics XXV.

Westphalen, Ernestus Joachim de: Monumenta Inedita Rerum Germanicarum, praecipue Cimbricarum. Vols. 3 and 4. Leipzig 1743–1745.

Wittmer, Ch. and Meyer, J. C. (ed.): Le Livre de Bourgeoisie de la Ville de Strasbourg. Vol. 1. Strasbourg 1954.

Wydenszehe, Eberhardt (i.e. Weidensee, Eberhard): Eyn vnderricht uth der hillighen schryfft/ Dem Dorchlůchtygen Hochgebarnen Forsten und Herrn/ Herrn Christarnn/ Erffgenomen tho Norwegenn/Herzoghenn tho Schleßwigh Holsten etc. Melchior Hoffmans sendebreff/ darynne hee schryfft/ dat he nycht bekennen kōne dat eyn stucke lijflikes brodes syn Godt sy/ belangende. 1529. The only copy is at the Royal Library, Copenhagen, Sign. Pal 61.

4. General Bibliography

Abel, Wilhelm: Massenarmut und Hungerkrisen im vorindustriellen Europa. Göttingen 1974.

Adam, Jean: Inventaire des Archives du chapitre de St. Thomas de Strasbourg. 1937.

Adam, Johann: Evangelsiche Kirchengeschichte der Stadt Straßburg. 1922.

Althaus, Paul: Die Theologie Martin Luthers. Gütersloh 1962.

Amelung, F.: Melchior Hoffman in Livland und die Einführung der Reformation in den Kirchspielen Dorpat und Nüggen im Jahre 1525. In: Sb. der Gelehrten Estnischen Gesellschaft. Dorpat 1901–1902, 196–222.

Andreas, Willy: Straßburg an der Wende vom Mittelalter zur Neuzeit. Leipzig 1940.

Anonymus (i.e. Schneegans, Ludwig): Straßburgische Geschichten, Sagen, Denkmäler, Inschriften, Künstler, Kunstgegenstände und Allerlei. Straßburg 1855.

Arbusov, Leonid (junior): Die Aktion der Rigaischen Franziskaner gegen das Vordringen des Luthertums und ihre Folgen. In: Sb. d. Gesellschaft für Geschichte und Alterthumskunde der Osteeprovinzen Rußlands aus dem Jahre 1913. Riga 1914, 21–70.

———: Die Einführung der Reformation in Liv-, Est- und Kurland. Leipzig 1921, Reprinted Aalen 1964 = Quellen und Forschungen zur Reformationsgeschichte, vol. 3.

Arbusov, Leonid (senior): Grundriß der Geschichte Liv-, Est- und Kurlands. Riga 1908.

Armour, Rollin S.: Anabaptist Baptism: A Representative Study. Scottdale, Pa., 1966.

Asendorf, Ulrich: Eschatologie bei Luther. Göttingen 1967.

Axters, Stephanus: Geschiedenis van de Vroomheid in de Nederlanden. Vol. 3: De moderne Devotio. Antwerpen 1956.

Bainton, Roland H.: David Joris. Leipzig 1937 = ARG Ergänzungsband 6.

——: The Immoralities of the Patriarchs according to the Exegesis of the Late Middle Ages and of the Reformation. In: Harvard Theological Review XXIII, 1930, 39–49.

Balke, W.: Calvijn en de Doperse Radikalen. Amsterdam 1973.

Barge, Hermann: Andreas Bodenstein von Carlstadt. 2 vols., Leipzig 1905.

——: and Ernst Frey: Verzeichnis der gedruckten Schriften des Andreas Bodenstein von Karlstadt. In: Zentralblatt für Bibliothekswesen XXI, 1904, 153–179; 209–243; 305–323.

Baring, Georg: Neues von der Theologia Deutsch und ihrer weltweiten Bedeutung. In: ARG 48, 1957, 1–10.

Baron, Hans: Religion and Politics in the German Imperial Cities during the Reformation. In: English Historical Review 52, 1937, 405–427; 614–633.

Baum, Johann Wilhelm: Capito und Butzer. Straßburgs Reformatoren. 1st edn. 1860, reprinted Nieuwkoop 1967.

Bauman, Clarence: Gewaltlosigkeit im Täufertum. Eine Untersuchung zur theologischen Ethik des oberdeutschen Täufertums der Reformationszeit. Leiden 1968 = Studies in the History of Christian Thought 3.

Beachy, Alvin J.: The Grace of God in Christ as Understood by Five Major Anabaptist Writers. In: MQR 37, 1963, 5–33; 52.

Bellardi, Werner: Anton Engelbrecht (1485–1558). In: ARG 64, 1973, 183–206.

——: Wolfgang Schultheiß. Wege und Wandlungen des Straßburger Spiritualisten und Zeitgenossen Martin Bucers. Frankfurt 1975 = Schriften der Erwin-von-Steinbach-Stiftung 5.

Bender, Harold S.: Conrad Grebel, c. 1498–1526: The Founder of the Swiss Brethren. Goshen, Indiana, 1950.

——: Die Zwickauer Propheten, Thomas Müntzer und die Täufer. In: Theologische Zeitschrift VIII, 1952, 262–278.

——: The Anabaptists and Religious Liberty in the Sixteenth Century. In: ARG 44, 1953, 32–51.

Benz, Ernst: Die Vision. Erfahrungsformen und Bilderwelt. Stuttgart 1969.

Benzing, Josef: Die Buchdrucker des 16. und 17. Jahrhunderts im deutschen Sprachgebiet. Wiesbaden 1963 = Beiträge zum Buch- und Bibliotheskwesen 12.

Bergsten, Torsten: Balthasar Hubmaier: Seine Stellung zu Reformation und Täufertum 1521–1528. Kassel 1961.

Bienemann, Fr.: Aus Livlands Luthertagen. Reval 1883.

Bizer, Ernst: Studien zur Geschichte des Abendmahlsstreites im 16. Jahrhundert. Gütersloh 1940.

Blanke, Fritz: Brüder in Christo. Die Geschichte der ältesten Täufergemeinde. Zürich 1955 = Zwingli-Bücherei, vol. 71.

Bloch, Ernst: Thomas Münzer als Theologe der Revolution. 2nd edn., Frankfurt a. M. 1963 = Bibliothek Suhrkamp, vol. 77.

Böthführ, H. J.: Einige Bemerkungen zu Sylvester Tegetmeiers Tagebuch. In: Mitteilungen aus der Geschichte Liv-, Est- und Kurlands. Vol. 13, 1886, 66f.

Bornhäuser, Christoph: Leben und Lehre Menno Simons'. Ein Kampf um das Fundament des Glaubens (c. 1496–1561). Neukirchen-Vluyn 1973 = Beiträge zur Geschichte und Lehre der Reformierten Kirche, vol. XXXV.

Borst, Arno: Die Katharer. Stuttgart 1953 = Schriften der Monumenta Germaniae Historica 12.

Bosse, Heinrich: Der livländische Bauer am Ausgang der Ordenszeit. In: Mitteilungen aus der livländischen Geschichte 24, 1933, 181–511.

Brady, Thomas A. (Jr.): Jacob Sturm of Strasbourg and the Lutherans at the Diet of Augsburg, 1530. In: Church History 42, 1973, 183–247.

——: Ruling Class, Regime and Reformation at Strasbourg. Leiden 1978 = Studies in Medieval and Reformation Thought, vol. XXII.

Brandsma, J. A.: Anabaptistica Frisica. In: Beaken (Assen), 21, 1959, 242–247.

Brendler, Gerhard: Das Täuferreich zu Münste 1534/35. (Ost-)Berlin 1966.

Burckhardt, Paul: David Joris und seine Gemeinde in Basel. In: Basler Zeitschrift für Geschichte und Altertumskunde 48, 1949, 5–106.

Campenhausen, Hans von: Die Bilderfrage in der Reformation. In: ZKG 68, 1957, 69–128.

Chrisman, Miriam Usher: Strasbourg and the Reform. New Haven and London 1967.

Clasen, Claus-Peter: Medieval Heresies in the Reformation. In: Church History 32, 1963, 392–414.

——: Die Wiedertäufer im Herzogtum Württemberg und in benachbarten Herrschaften: Ausbreitung, Geisteswelt und Soziologie. Stuttgart 1966.

——: Anabaptism. A Social History, 1525–1618. Ithaca and London 1972.

——: Schwenckfeld's Friends. A Social Study. In: MQR 46, 1972, 58–67.

——: Executions of Anabaptists 1527–1618. In: MQR 47, 1973, 115–152.

Cohn, Norman: The Pursuit of the Millenium. Revolutionary Messianism in Medieval and Reformation Europe and Its Bearing on Modern Totalitarian Movements. 2nd edn., New York 1961.

Cornelius, Carl Adolf: Geschichte des Münsterischen Aufruhrs. 2 vols., Leipzig 1855/60.

——: Der Antheil Ostfrieslands an der Reformation bis zum Jahre 1535. Münster 1852.

——: Die niederländischen Wiedertäufer während der Belagerung Münsters 1534–1535. München 1869 = Abhandlungen d. historischen Klasse der bayrischen Akademie der Wissenschaften XLI.

Crämer, Ulrich: Die Verfassung und Verwaltung Straßburgs von der Reformationszeit bis zum Fall der Reichsstadt. Frankfurt a. M. 1931.

Czaplinski, Wladylaw: Le problème baltique au XVIe et XVIIe siècles. In: Congrès International des Sciences Historiques. Stockholm 1960. Rapports, vol. 4, Uppsala 1960, 25–47.

Dankbaar, W. F.: Martin Bucers Beziehungen zu den Niederlanden. s'Gravenhage 1961.

Davis, Kenneth R.: Erasmus as a Progenitor of Anabaptist Theology and Piety. In: MQR 47, 1973, 163–178.

——: Anabaptism and Asceticism. Scottdale, Pa., 1974.

Deijl, Willem Simon: Het Chiliasme ten tijde der Hervorming. Academisch Proefschrift an de Hoogeschool te Utrecht. Amsterdam 1872.

Deppermann, Klaus: Die Straßburger Reformatoren und die Krise des oberdeutschen Täufertums im Jahre 1527. In: MGB N.F. 25, 1973, 24–52.

——: Melchior Hoffmans letzte Schrifen aus dem Jahre 1534. In: ARG 63, 1972, 72–93.

——: Melchior Hoffmans Weg von Luther zu den Täufern. In: Umstrittenes Täufertum 1525–1575. Ed. by Hans-Jürgen Goertz. 2nd edn., Göttingen 1977, 173–205.

Dollinger, Philippe (ed.): Histoire d'Alsace. 1970.

Doornkaat-Koolman, J. ten: Dirk Philips. Vriend en Medewerker van Menno Simons 1504–1568. Haarlem 1964.

Ebert, Klaus: Theologie und politisches Handeln. Thomas Müntzer als Modell. Stuttgart 1973 = Urban Taschenbücher 602.

Eckardt, H.: Alt-Kiel in Wort und Bild. Kiel 1899.

Ecke, Karl: Kaspar Schwenckfeld. Ungelöste Geistesfragen der Reformationszeit. 1952.

Eheberg, K. Th.: Verfassungs-, Verwaltungs- und Wirtschaftsgeschichte der Stadt Straßburg bis 1681. Vol. 1, Straßburg 1899.

Elsas, M. J.: Umriß einer Geschichte der Preise und Löhne in Deutschland vom ausgehenden Mittelalter bis zum Beginn des 19. Jahrhunderts. Vol. 1, Leiden 1936.

Fast, Heinold: The Dependence of the First Anabaptists on Luther, Erasmus and Zwingli. In: MQR 30, 1956, 104–119.

——: Pilgram Marbeck und das oberdeutsche Täufertum. In: ARG 47, 1956, 212–242.

——: (ed.): Der linke Flügel der Reformation. Glaubenszeugnisse der Täufer, Spiritualisten, Schwärmer und Antitrinitarier. Bremen 1962 = Klassiker des Protestantismus, vol. IV.

——: Variationen des Kirchenbegriffs bei den Täufern. In: MGB NF 22, 1970, 5–18.

Faust, Georg: Einige Bemerkungen zu Melchior Hoffmans "Dialogus". In: Schriften des Vereins für schleswig-holsteinische Kirchengeschichte II/3, 1903/05, 96–86.

Feddersen, Ernst: Kirchengeschichte Schleswig-Holsteins. Vol. II, 1517–1721. Kiel 1938.

Festinger, Leon – Riecken, Henry – Schlachter, Stanley: When Prophecy Fails. New York, 2nd edn., 1964.

Friedmann, Robert: Das täuferische Glaubensgut. In: ARG 55, 1964, 145–161.

——: The Theology of Anabaptism. Scottdale, Pa., 1973.

Friesen, Abraham: Social Revolution or Religious Reform? Some Salient

Aspects of Anabaptist Historiography. In: Umstrittenes Täufertum 1525–1575. Neue Forschungen. Ed. by Hans-Jürgen Goertz. 2nd edn., Göttingen 1977, pp. 223–243.

——: The Marxist Interpretation of Anabaptism. In: Carl S. Meyer (ed.): Sixteenth Century Essays and Studies. Vol. 1, Saint Louis, Missouri, 1970, 17–34.

Garrelts, Heinrich: Die Reformation Ostfrieslands nach der Darstellung der Lutheraner vom Jahre 1593. Aurich 1925 = Abhandlungen und Vorträge zur Geschichte Ostfrieslands. H. 22 and 23. Contains: Warhafftiger Gegenbericht/ der rechtgläubigen Predicanten in Ostfrießlant/ auff des D. Petzels Vorrede über das Embdische Buch/ Vom handel des Abentmals: Anno 1590/ zu Bremen ausgegangen. Emden 1593.

Goertz, Hans-Jürgen: Innere und äußere Ordnung in der Theologie Thomas Müntzers. Leiden 1967 = Studies in the History of Christian Thought, vol. 2.

——: (ed.): Umstrittenes Täufertum 1525–1575. Neue Forschungen. Göttingen 1975; 2nd edn. 1977.

Goeters, J. F. G.: Die Vorgeschichte des Täufertums in Zürich. In: Studien zur Geschichte und Theologie der Reformation. Festschrift für Ernst Bizer. Ed. by L. Abramowski and J. F. G. Goeters. Neukirchen 1969, 239–281.

Gollwitzer, Heinz: Zur Auslegung von Johannes 6 bei Luther und Zwingli. In: In Memoriam E. Lohmeyer. 1951, 143–168.

Greschat, Martin: Luthers Haltung in Bauernkrieg. In: ARG 56, 1965, 31–47.

Grosheide, Greta: Bijdrage tot de Geschiedenis der Anabaptisten in Amsterdam. Hilversum 1938.

Haas, Martin: Täufertum und Revolution. In: Festgabe für Leonhard v. Muralt. Zürich 1970, 286–295.

——: Täufertum und Volkskirche – Faktoren der Trennung. In: Zwingliana XIII, (1970–72), 261–278.

——: Die Täuferkirchen des 16. Jahrhunderts in der Schweiz und in Münster – ein Vergleich. In: Zwingliana XIII (1970–1972), 434–462.

——: Der Weg der Täufer in die Absonderung. In: Umstrittenes Täufertum 1525–1575. Ed. by Hans-Jürgen Goertz. 2nd edn. Göttingen 1977, 50–78.

Hall, Thor: Possibilities of Erasmian Influence on Denck and Hubmaier. In: MQR 35, 1961, 149–170.

Hanauer, Auguste: Etudes économiques sur l'Alsace ancienne et moderne. Vol. 2: Denrées et salaires. Straßburg 1878.

Hannen, Gottfried von: Aus baltischer Vergangenheit. Miscellaneen aus dem Revaler Stadtarchiv. Reval 1894, 123f.

Hausammann, Susi: Realpräsenz in Luthers Abendmahlslehre. In: Studien zur Geschichte und Theologie der Reformation. Festschrift für Ernst Bizer. Ed. by L. Abramowski and J. F. G. Goeters. Neukirchen 1969, 157–173.

Headley, J. M.: Luther's View of Church History. New Haven and London 1963.

Henschel, Martin: Figuraldeutung und Geschichtlichkeit. In: Kerygma und Dogma. Vol. 5, 1959, 306f.

Hillerbrand, Hans-Joachim: Anabaptism and the Reformation: Another Look. In: Church History 29, 1960, 404–424.

——: The Origins of Sixteenth Century Anabaptism: Another Look. In: ARG 53, 1962, 152–180.

Hirsch, Emanuel: Schwenckfeld und Luther. In: E. Hirsch: Lutherstudien II, 1954, 35–67.

Hoffmann, Erich: Flensburg von der Reformation bis zum Ende des Nordischen Krieges 1721. In: Flensburg. Geschichte einer Grenzstadt. Ed. by Die Gesellschaft für Flensburger Stadtgeschichte. Flensburg 1966 = Schriften d. Gesellschaft für Flensburger Stadtgeschichte, vol. 17.

Holl, Karl: Luther und die Schwärmer. In: Gesammelte Aufsätze zur Kirchengeschichte. Vol. 1: Luther. Tübingen 1932, 420–467.

Holmquist, Hjalmar: Die schwedische Reformation von 1523–31. Leipzig 1925 = Schriften des Vereins f. Reformationsgeschichte 43/2.

Horst, Irvin Buckwalter: The Radical Brethren. Anabaptism and the English Reformation to 1558. Nieuwkoop 1972.

Hoyer, Siegfried: Häresien zwischen Hus und Luther. Habil. Schrift, Phil. Fak. Leipzig (MS), 1966.

——: Martin Reinhard und der erste Druck hussitischer Artikel in Deutschland. In: ZfG 18, 1970, 1597–1615.

——: Nicolaus Rutze und die Verbreitung hussitischer Gedanken im Hanseraum. In: Neue hansische Studien. Ed. by Konrad Fritze, Eckhard Müller-Mertens, Johannes Schildhauer, Erhard Voigt. Berlin 1970, 157–170 = Forschungen zur mittelalterlichen Geschichte 17.

Huizinga, Jan: Erasmus. Deutsch von Werner Kaegi. 4th edn. Basel 1951.

——: Herbst des Mittelalters. Deutsch von T. Wolff-Mönckeberg. 6th edn. Stuttgart 1952.

Hulshof, Abraham: Geschiedenis van de Doopsgezinden te Straatsburg van 1525 tot 1557. Amsterdam 1905.

Husner, Fritz: Zwei unbekannte Wiedertäuferdrucke. In: Stultifera Navis. Jg. 3, 1946, 84–88.

Jannasch, Wilhelm: Reformationsgeschichte Lübecks 1515–1530. Lübeck 1958.

Jensen, H. N. A. - Michelsen, L. J.: Schleswig-Holsteinische Kirchengeschichte. Vol. 3, Kiel 1877.

Jessen, Jens: Die Entstehung und Entwicklung der Gutswirtschaft in Schleswig-Holstein bis zum Beginn der Agrarreformen. In: Zeitschrift für Schleswig-Holsteinische Geschichte 51, 1922, 1–206.

Joest, Wilfried: Ontologie der Person bei Luther. Göttingen 1967.

Johannesson, Gösta: Die Kirchenreformation in den nordischen Ländern. In: XIᵉ Congrès International des Sciences Historiques (Stockholm 1960). Rapports. Vol. IV, Uppsala 1960, 48–61.

Kaminsky, Howard: The Free Spirit in the Hussite Revolution. In: Sylvia L. Thrupp: Millenial Dreams in Action. Den Haag 1962.

Kasch, August: Das Kloster Reinbek. In: Festschrift zur 700-Jahrfeier der Gemeinde Reinbek. 1938, 23–116.

Kaufmann, Georg: Geschichte der deutschen Universität. Vol. 2, 2nd edn., 1958.

Kawerau, Peter: Melchior Hoffman als religiöser Denker. Haarlem 1954.

Kirchhoff, Karl-Heinz: Gab es eine friedliche Täufergemeinde in Münster 1534? In: Jahrbuch des Vereins für Westfälische Kirchengeschichte 55/56, 1962/63, 7–21.

Kittelson, James M.: Martin Bucer and the Sacramentarian Controversy: the Origins of his Policy of Concord. In: ARG 64, 1973, 166–183.

——: Wolfgang Capito, the Council and Reform in Strasbourg. In: ARG 63, 1972, 126–141.

——: Wolfgang Capito. From Humanist to Reformer. Leiden 1975 = Studies in Medieval and Reformation Thought, vol. XVII.

Klaassen, Walter: Hans Hut und Thomas Müntzer. In: The Baptist Quarterly 19, 1962, 209–227.

Klassen, Herbert: The Life and Teachings of Hans Hut. In: MQR 33, 1959, 171–205; 267–304.

Klopp, Onno: Geschichte Ostfrieslands. Vol. 1, Hannover 1854.

Koch, Klaus: Ratlos vor der Apokalyptik. Gütersloh 1970.

Kochs, Ernst: Die Anfänge der ostfriesischen Reformation. In: Jb. d. Gesell. f. bildende Kunst und vaterländische Altertümer zu Emden. Parts I and II in vol. XIX, 1916/18, 109–273; Part III in vol. XX, 1920, 1–125.

——: Grundlinien der ostfriesischen Kirchengeschichte. Quakenbrück 1938.

Köhler, Walther: Zwingli und Luther. Ihr Streit über das Abendmahl. 2 vols., 1924/1953.

——: Dogmengeschichte als Geschichte des christlichen Selbstbewußtseins. Vol. 2, Zürich 1951.

Kofler, Leo: Zur Geschichte der bürgerlichen Gesellschaft. 4th edn., Neuwied and Berlin 1971 = Soziologische Texte, vol. 38.

Koolman, Anton and Wiemann, Harm: Ostfriesische Geschichte. Part 1. Leer 1951.

Krahn, Cornelius: Dutch Anabaptism. Origin, Life and Thought. 1450–1600. Den Haag 1968.

Kriechbaum, Friedel: Grundzüge der Theologie Karlstadts. Hamburg 1967.

Krohn, Barthold Nikolaus: Geschichte der fanatischen und enthusiastischen Wiedertäufer, vornehmlich in Niederdeutschland. Melchior Hofmann und die Sekte der Hofmannianer. Leipzig 1758.

Kruse, E. C.: Melchior Hofmann in Holstein. In: Neue Schleswig-Holsteinische Provinzialberichte. 3. Jg., 1813, 499–526, 636–653; 4. Jg., 1814, 18–39.

Kühler, W. J.: Geschiedenis der Nederlandschen Doopsgezinden in de zestiende eeuw. Haarlem 1932.

Küttler, Wolfgang: Patriziat, Bürgeropposition und Volksbewegung in Riga in der zweiten Hälfte des 16. Jahrhunderts. Diss. phil. Leipzig (MS), 1966.

——: Sozialer Inhalt und politische Triebkräfte der Reformation im

Ostbaltikum. In: Weltwirkung der Reformation. Vol. 2, (Ost-)Berlin 1969, 377–390.

Kuhles, Joachim: Studien zur sozialen Lage der Volksmassen und zu den Volksbewegungen zur Zeit der Reformation in Livland. Diss. phil. Leipzig (MS), 1966.

———: Zur ideologischen Differenzierung der reformatorischen Bewegung im Ostbaltikum. In: Weltwirkung der Reformation. (Ost-) Berlin, 1969, vol. 2, pp. 377–390.

Kurze, Dietrich: Pfarrerwahlen im Mittelalter. Ein Beitrag zur Geschichte der Gemeinde und des Niederkirchenwesens. Köln-Graz 1966.

Lackner, Martin: Von Thomas Münzer zum Münsterschen Aufstand. In: Jahrbuch des Vereins für Westfälische Kirchengeschichte, 53/54, 1960–61, pp. 9f.

Landfester, Rüdiger: Frühneuzeitliche Häresien und koloniale Protestkulte: Möglichkeiten eines historisch-komparativen Zugangs. In: ARG 67, 1976, 117–152.

Landgraf, Henning: Bevölkerung und Wirtschaft Kiels im 15. Jahrhundert. Neumünster 1959 = Quellen und Forschungen zur Geschichte Schleswig-Holsteins, vol. 39.

Lau, G. J. T.: Geschichte der Einführung und Verbreitung der Reformation in den Herzogtümern Schleswig-Holstein bis zum Ende des 16. Jahrhunderts. Hamburg 1867.

Leenderts, W. J.: Melchior Hofmann. Haarlem 1883.

Lienhard, Marc (ed.): The Origins and Characteristics of Anabaptism/ Les Débuts Et Les Caracteristiques De L'Anabaptisme. Den Haag, 1977.

———: Les autorités civiles et les anabaptistes: Attitudes du magistrat de Strasbourg (1526–1532). In: Marc Lienhard (ed.): The Origins and Characteristics of Anabaptism. Den Haag 1977. pp. 196–215.

Linden, Friedrich Otto zur: Melchior Hofmann, ein Prophet der Wiedertäufer, Haarlem 1885.

List, Günther: Chiliastische Utopie, München 1973.

Littell, Franklin Hamlin: The Anabaptist View of the Church. 2nd edn., Boston 1958.

Locher, Gottfried: Die theologische und politische Bedeutung des Abendmahlsstreites im Licht von Zwinglis Briefen. In: Zwingliana XIII (1970–72), 281–304.

Lohse, Bernhard: Die Stellung der "Schwärmer" und "Täufer" in der Reformationsgeschichte. In: ARG 60, 1969, 5–26.

———: Hans Denck und der "linke Flügel" der Reformation. In: Humanitas – Christianitas. Festschrift Walter v. Loewenich. Witten 1968, 74–83.

Lubac, Henri de: Geist aus der Geschichte. Das Schriftverständnis des Origenes. Übertragen und eingeleitet von Hans Urs v. Balthasar. Einsiedeln 1968.

Lukács, Georg: Geschichte und Klassenbewußtsein. 2nd edn., Neuwied and Berlin 1970 = Sammlung Luchterhand, vol. 11.

Maurer, Wilhelm: Luther und die Schwärmer. 1952 = Schriften des Theol. Konvents Augsburg. Bekenntnisses VI.

Meihuizen, H. W.: The Concept of Restitution in the Anabaptism of Northwestern Europe. In: MQR 44, 1970, 141–158.

Mellink, A. F.: De Wederdopers in de Noordelijke Nederlanden. 1531–1544. Groningen 1953.

——: The Mutual Relations between the Munster Anabaptists and the Netherlands. In: ARG 50, 1959, 16–33.

——: Das niederländisch-westfälische Täufertum im 16. Jahrhundert. In: H.-J. Goertz (ed.): Umstrittenes Täufertum. Göttingen, 2nd edn., 1977, 206–222.

Meyer, Christian: Zur Geschichte der Wiedertäufer in Oberschwaben. Part I. Die Anfänge des Wiedertäufertums in Augsburg. In: Zeitschrift des Historischen Vereins für Schwaben und Neuburg. Vol. 1, 1874, 207–253.

Moeller, Bernd: Reichsstadt und Reformation. Gütersloh 1962 = Schriften des Vereins für Reformationsgeschichte 180.

Mühlen, Heinz von zur: Versuch einer soziologischen Erfassung der Bevölkerung Revals im Spätmittelalter. In: Hansische Geschichtsblätter 75, 1957, 48–69.

Mühlmann, Wilhelm E. (ed.): Chiliasmus und Nativismus. Studien zur Psychologie, Soziologie und historischen Kasuistik der Umsturzbewegungen. 2nd edn., Berlin 1964.

Müller, Johannes: Martin Bucers Hermeneutik. Gütersloh 1965 = Quellen u. Forschungen zur Reformationsgeschichte 32.

Müntzer, Thomas: Schriften und Briefe. Ed. by Günther Franz. Gütersloh 1968.

Müsing, Hans-Werner: Karlstadt und die Entstehung der Straßburger Täufergemeinde. In: Marc Lienhard (ed.): The Origins and Characteristics of Anabaptism. Den Haag 1977. pp. 169–195.

Neumann, Gerhard J.: Eschatologische und chiliastische Gedanken in der Reformationszeit, besonders bei den Täufern. In: Welt als Geschichte 19, 1959, 58–66.

Neuser, Wilhelm H.: Die Abendmahlslehre Melanchthons in ihrer geschichtlichen Entwicklung (1519–1530). Neukirchen-Vluyn, 1968.

Niitema, Vilho: Die undeutsche Frage in der Politik der livländischen Städte im Mittelalter. Helsinki 1949 = Annales Academiae Scientiarum Fennicae, vol. 64.

——: Der Binnenhandel in der Politik der livländischen Städte im Mittelalter. Helsinki 1952 = Annales Academiae Scientiarum Fennicae, vol. 76/2.

Nippold, Friedrich: David Joris van Delft. In: Zeitschrift für historische Theologie 33, 1863, 3–166; 34, 1864, 483–673; 38, 1868, 475–591.

Noll, M. A.: Luther Defends Melchior Hoffman. In: The Sixteenth Century Journal 4, 1973, 47–60.

Oberman, Heiko A.: The Shape of Late Medieval Thought: the Birthpangs of the Modern Era. In: ARG 64, 1973, 13–33.

Ohling, Gerhard: Junker Ulrich von Dornum. Aurich 1955.

Oyer, J. S.: Lutheran Reformers against Anabaptists. Den Haag 1965.

Ozment, Steven E.: Mysticism and Dissent: Religious Ideology and Social Protest in the Sixteenth Century. New Haven and London 1973.

Pater, Calvin Augustine: Melchior Hoffman's Explication of the Songs(!) of Songs. In: ARG 68, 1977, 173–191.

Peter, Rodolphe: Le Jardinier Clément Ziegler. Diss. Fac. theol. prot. Strasbourg (MS), 1954.

——: Le Maraîcher Clément Ziegler. L'homme et son œuvre. In: Revue d'Histoire et de Philosophie Religieuses 34, 1954, 255–282.

Peuckert, Will-Erich: Die große Wende. Das apokalyptische Saeculum und Luther. 2 vols., 2nd edn., Darmstadt 1966.

Plümper, Hans-Dieter: Die Gütergemeinschaft bei den Täufern des 16. Jahrhunderts. Göppingen 1972.

Pohrt, Otto: Zur Frömmigkeitsgeschichte Livlands zu Beginn der Reformationszeit. Riga 1925 = Abhandlungen des Herder-Instituts zu Riga I/4.

——: Reformationsgeschichte Livlands. Leipzig 1928 = Schriften des Vereins für Reformationsgeschichte 46/2.

Post, R. R.: The Modern Devotion. Confrontation with Reformation and Humanism. Leiden 1968.

Prange, Wolfgang: Die Anfänge der großen Agrarreform in Schleswig-Holstein bis um 1771. Neumünster 1971 = Quellen und Forschungen zur Geschichte Schleswig-Holsteins, vol. 60.

Preus, James S.: From Shadow to Promise. Old Testament Interpretation from Augustine to the Young Luther. Cambridge, Mass. 1969.

Preuß, Hans: Die Vorstellung vom Antichrist im späten Mittelalter, bei Luther und in der konfessionellen Polemik. Leipzig 1906.

Quanbeck, Warren A.: Luther and the Apocalyptic. In: Luther und Melanchthon. Ed. by Vilmos Vatja. Göttingen 1961, 119–128 = Referate und Berichte des Zweiten Internationalen Kongresses für Lutherforschung (1960).

Rammstedt, Otthein: Sekte und soziale Bewegung. Soziologische Analyse der Täufer in Münster (1534/35). Köln und Opladen 1966 = Dortmunder Schriften zur Sozialforschung, vol. 34.

Rapp, Francis: Réformes et Reformation à Strasbourg. Paris 1974 = Associations des Publications près des Universités de Strasbourg. Collection de l'Institut des Hautes Etudes Alsaciennes. Tom. XXIII.

Reimers, H.: Die Säkularisation der Klöster in Ostfriesland. 1908 = Abhandlungen und Vorträge zur Geschichte Ostfrieslands, H. 13/14.

——: Die Gestaltung der Reformation in Ostfriesland. 1917.

Ritter, F.: Zur Geschichte des Ostfriesischen Reformators Georg Aportanus. In: Jb. d. Gesellschaft f. bildende Kunst und vaterländische Altertümer zu Emden. Vol XVIII, 1913, 142–156.

——: Ein Gegenreformationsversuch Graf Ennos II. In: Jb. d. Gesellschaft f. bildende Kunst und vaterländische Altertümer zu Emden. Vol. XXI, 1925, 197–215.

Ritter, Fr.: Elsässische Buchdrucker im Dienst der Straßburger Sektenbewegungen zur Zeit der Reformation. In: Gutenberg-Jahrbuch 1962, 225–333; 1963, 97–108.

Röhrich, Timotheus Wilhelm: Zur Geschichte der Straßburgischen Wiedertäufer in den Jahren 1527 bis 1543: Aus den Vergichtbüchern und anderen archivalischen Quellen mitgeteilt. In: Zeitschrift für historische Theologie, vol. 30, 1860, 3–121.

——: Mitteilungen aus der Geschichte der evangelischen Kirche des Elsasses. Vol. 1, 1855.

Rosenkranz, Albert: Der Bundschuh. Vol. 2. Heidelberg 1927.

Roth, Friedrich: Augsburgs Reformationsgeschichte. Vol. 1, München 1881.

——: Zur Geschichte der Wiedertäufer in Oberschwaben. III: Der Höhepunkt der Bewegung in Augsburg und der Niedergang im Jahre 1528. In: Zeitschrift des Historischen Vereins für Schwaben und Neuburg. Vol. 28, 1901, 1–154.

Rott, Jean: Bucer et les débuts de la querrelle sacramentaire: L'instruction donnée à Gregoire Caselius pour sa mission auprès de Luther (octobre 1525). In: Revue d'histoire et de philosophie religieuses 34, 1954, 234–254.

——: Artisanat et mouvements sociaux à Strasbourg autour de 1525. In: Artisans et Ouvriers d'Alsace. Strasbourg 1965, 139ff. = Publications de la Société savante d'Alsace et des Régions de l'Est. Vol. 9.

——: Un Recueil de Correspondances Strasbourgeoises du XVIe siècle à la Bibliothèque de Copenhague. In: Bulletin Philologique et Historique publié par la Ministère de l'Education Nationale. Année 1968, Paris 1971, 749–818.

Ruether, R.: The Reformer and the Radical in the 16th Century Reformation. In: Journal of Ecumenical Studies 1972, 271–284.

Rupp, E. Gordon: Patterns of Reformation. London 1969.

Sandblad, Henrik: Kring Konflikten Mellan Gustav Vasa och Reformatorerna. Ett par Idéhistoriske Bidrag. In: Lychnos. Jg. 1941, 127–146.

——: De eskatologiska Föreställningarna i Sverige under Reformation och Motreformation. Uppsala 1942 = Lychnosbibliothek 5.

Schanz, Georg: Zur Geschichte der deutschen Gesellenverbände. Leipzig 1877.

Scheib, Otto: Die Religionsgespräche in Norddeutschland in der Neuzeit und ihre Entwicklung. In: Jb. d. Gesell. für Niedersächsische Kirchengeschichte 75, 1977, pp. 39–88.

Schieche, Emil: Die Anfänge der deutschen St. Gertrudis-Gemeinde zu Stockholm im 16. Jahrhundert. Münster/Köln 1952 = Pfingstblätter des Hansischen Geschichtsvereins. Blatt XXVII.

Schild, Maurice E.: Abendländische Bibelvorreden bis zur Lutherbibel. Gütersloh 1970 = Quellen und Forschungen zur Reformationsgeschichte, vol. XXXIX.

Schmaltz, Karl: Kirchengeschichte Mecklenburgs. Vol. 2, 1936.

Schmid, Hans-Dieter: Das Hutsche Täufertum. In: Historisches Jahrbuch der Görres-Gesellschaft 91, 1971, 327–344.

Schmidt, Heinrich: Die Reformation in Ostfriesland. In: Jb. der Gesellschaft f. Niedersächsische Kirchengeschichte 69, 1971, 7–31.

——: Politische Geschichte Ostfrieslands. Leer 1975 = Ostfriesland in Schutze des Deiches, vol. V.

Schmithals, Walter: Die Apokalyptik. Einführung und Deutung. Göttingen 1973 = Sammlung Vandenhoeck.

Schmoller, Gustav: Die Straßburger Tucher- und Weberzunft. Straßburg 1879.

Schoeps, Hans-Joachim: Vom himmlischen Fleisch Christi. 1951.

Schubert, Hans von: Der Kommunismus der Wiedertäufer in Münster und seine Quellen. Heidelberg 1919 = Sb. der Heidelberger Akad. d. Wiss. Phil.-Hist. Klasse 1919, Abh. 11.

Schwarz-Lausten, M.: Melchior Hoffman og de lutherske praedikanten i Sleswig-Holsten 1527–1529. In: Kirkehistoriske Samlinger 7. R. 5, 1963/64.

Schwarze, Nikolaus Hermann: Desselben Nikolaus Hermann Schwarze gesammelte Nachrichten von der Stadt Kiel im Holsteinischen. Ed. by M. Joh. Heinrich Fehse. Flensburg 1775.

Seebaß, Gottfried: Müntzers Erbe. Werk, Leben und Theologie des Hans Hut. Theol. habil. (MS), Erlangen 1972.

——: Bauernkrieg und Täufertum in Franken. In: Zeitschrift für Kirchengeschichte 85, 1974, 140–156.

Sider, Ronald J.: Andreas Bodenstein von Karlstadt. The Development of His Thought 1517–1525. Leiden 1974.

Skinner, Quentin: Meaning and Understanding in the History of Ideas. In: History and Theory, vol. VII, 1969, 3–53.

Smid, Menno: Ostfriesische Kirchengeschichte. (Pewsum), 1974. = Ostfriesland im Schutz des Deiches, vol. VI.

Spitz, Lewis W.: The Religious Renaissance of the German Humanists. Harvard University Press, Cambridge/Mass. 1963.

Spliet, H.: Die Schwarzen Häupter in ihrem Verhältnis zur deutschen kolonialen Ständegeschichte in Livland. In: Zeitschrift für Ostforschung 3, 1954, 233–247.

Sprengler-Ruppental, A.: Zur reformatorischen Kirchenrechtsbildung in Ostfriesland. In: Zeitschrift für evangelischen Kirchenrecht 10, 1963–64, 314–367.

Stadelmann, Rudolf: Vom Geist des ausgehenden Mittelalters. Studien zur Geschichte der Weltanschauung von N. Cusanus bis S. Franck. Halle 1929.

Stayer, James M.: Eine fanatische Täuferbewegung in Eßlingen und Reutlingen? In: Blätter für Württembergische Kirchengeschichte, Jg. 68/69, 1968/69, 53–59.

——: Melchior Hofmann and the Sword. In: MQR 45, 1971, 265–277.

——: Anabaptists and the Sword. Lawrence, Kansas 1972. 2nd edn. 1976.

——: Die Anfänge des schweizerischen Täufertums im reformierten Kongregationalismus. In: Hans-Jürgen Goertz (ed.): Umstrittenes Täufertum. Göttingen 1977, 19–49.

——: - Packull, Werner - Deppermann, Klaus: From Monogenesis to Polygenesis: The Historical Discussion of Anabaptist Origins. In: MQR 49, 1975, 83–122.

——: Die Schweizer Brüder. Versuch einer historischen Definition. In: Mennonitische Geschichtsblätter NF 29, 1977, 7–34.

——: Reflections and Retractions on "Anabaptists and the Sword". In: Mennonite Quarterly Review 51, 1977, 196–212 (identical with the preface to the second amended edition of "Anabaptists and the Sword", Lawrence Kansas, Coronado Press, 1976).

——: Reublin and Brötli, the revolutionary beginnings of Swiss Anabaptism. In: Marc Lienhard (ed.): The Origins And Characteristics Of Anabaptism. Den Haag 1977. pp. 83–104.

——: Oldeklooster and Menno. In: Sixteenth Century Journal IX, 1978, 51–67.

Steck, Karl Gerhard: Luther und die Schwärmer. Zollikon/Zürich 1955.

Steinmetz, David C.: Scholasticism and Radical Reform: Nominalist Motifs in the Theology of Balthasar Hubmaier. In: MQR 45, 1971, 123–144.

Stille, Hans: Nikolaus von Amsdorf. Sein Leben bis zu seiner Einweisung als Bischof von Naumburg (1483–1542). Diss. phil. Leipzig 1937.

Strasser, Otto Erich: Capitos Behiehungen zu Bern. Leipzig 1928.

Strobel, Georg Theodor: Melchior Hofmanns "Dialogus" von der Disputation zu Flensburg 1529. In: Georg Theodor Strobel: Beyträge zur Literatur, besonders des 16. Jahrhunderts. Vol. II, 1787.

Stupperich, Robert: Straßburgs Stellung zu Beginn des Sakramentsstreites 1524–25. In. ARG 38, 1941, 249f.

——: Das münsterische Täufertum. Münster 1958.

——: Straßburg und Münster in ihren Beziehungen 1531- 1534. In: Revue d'histoire et de philosophie religieuses LIV, 1974, 69–77.

Taubes, Jakob: Abendländische Eschatologie. Bern 1947 = Beiträge zur Soziologie und Sozialpsychologie 3.

Thrupp, Sylvia (ed.): Millenial Dreams in Action. Den Haag 1962.

Tillich, Paul: Protestantische Vision – katholische Substanz – sozialistische Entscheidung. 1952.

Torrance, T. F.: Die Eschatologie der Reformation. In: Evangelische Theologie, Jg. 1954, 334–358.

Transehe-Roseneck, A. v.: Die Entstehung der Schollenpflichtigkeit in Livland. In: Mitteilungen aus der livländischen Geschichte 23, 1924/26, 485–574.

Troeltsch, Ernst: Die Soziallehren der christlichen Kirchen und Gruppen. Tübingen 1912.

Tschackert, Paul: Dr. Eberhard Weidensee, Leben und Schriften. Berlin 1911.

Tschistoswonow, A. N.: Die soziale Basis und der historische Ort des revolutionären Täufertums. In: Wissenschaftliche Zeitschrift der Karl-

Marx-Universität Leipzig, Gesellschaftswiss. und sprachwiss. Reihe, Vol. 14, 1965, 407–418.

Usteri, J.: Die Stellung der Straßburger Reformatoren Butzer und Capito zur Tauffrage. In: Theologische Studien und Kritiken 57, 1884, 456–525.

Visser, C. Ch. G.: Luthers Geschriften in de Nederlanden tot 1546. Assen 1969 = Van Gorcum's Theologische Bibliothek, vol. 53.

Volbehr, Friedrich: Zur Geschichte der ehemaligen Kieler Stadtdörfer. In: Mitteilungen der Gesellschaft für Kieler Stadtgeschichte. H.2, Kiel 1879, 5–7.

——: Kieler Prediger Geschichte seit der Reformation. In: Mitteilungen der Gesellschaft für Kieler Stadtgeschichte. H. 6, Kiel 1884, 6–13.

Vos, Karel: Revolutionnaire Hervorming. In: De Gids (Amsterdam), Jg. 1920, 433–450.

——: Menno Simons, 1496–1561. Leiden 1914.

Waitz, Georg: Schleswig-Holsteins Geschichte. Vol. 2/2, Göttingen-Leipzig 1852.

Wallace, Anthony F. C.: Revitalization Movements. In: American Anthropologist 58, 1956, 264–281.

Walton, Robert C.: Was there a Turning Point of the Zwinglian Reformation? In: MQR 42, 1968, 45–56.

Wappler, Paul: Thomas Müntzer in Zwickau und die Zwickauer Propheten. Zwickau 1908. Reprinted: Gütersloh 1966.

——: Die Täuferbewegung in Thüringen von 1526 bis 1584. Jena 1913 = Beiträge zur neueren Geschichte Thüringens, vol. 2.

Wee, Hermann van der: La Réforme Protestante dans l'optique de la conjoncture économique et sociale des Pays-Bas meridionaux au XVI^c siècle. In: Sources de l'histoire religieuse de la Belgique. Moyen Age et Temps Moderne. Louvain 1968.

Weerda, J.: Das ostfriesische Experiment. In: Zeitschrift für evangelisches Kirchenrecht, Jg. 1956, 159f.

Weidling, Julius: Schwedische Geschichte im Zeitalter der Reformation. Gotha 1882.

Weigelt, Horst: Spiritualistische Tradition im Protestantismus. Die Geschichte des Schwenckfeldertums in Schlesien. Berlin-New York 1973 = Arbeiten zur Kirchengeschichte, vol. 43.

Weiß, Ruth: Die Herkunft der osthessischen Täufer. In: ARG 50, 1959, 1–16; 182–199.

——: Herkunft und Sozialanschauungen der Täufergemeinden im westlichen Hessen. In: ARG 52/53, 1961–62, 162–187.

Wendel, François: L'Eglise de Strasbourg. Sa constitution et son organisation. Paris 1942.

Westman, Knut B.: Reformationens Genombrottsår J Sverige. Stockholm 1918.

Wiarda, Tilemann Dothias: Ostfriesische Geschichte. Vol. 2, Aurich 1792.

Williams, George Huntston: The Radical Reformation. Philadelphia 1962.

——: Popularized German Mysticism as a Factor in the Rise of Anabaptist Communism. In: Glaube, Geist, Geschichte: Festschrift für Ernst Benz, ed. by G. Müller and W. Zeller. Leiden 1967, 290–312.

——: Sanctification in the Testimony of Several So-Called Schwärmer. In: MQR 42, 1968, 5–25.

——: German Mysticism in the Polarization of Ethical Behavior in Luther and the Anabaptists. In: MQR 48, 1974, 275–304.

Winckelmann, Otto: Der Schmalkaldische Bund. 1892.

——: Das Fürsorgewesen der Stadt Straßburg vor und nach der Reformation bis zum Ausgang des 16. Jahrhunderts. 2 vols. Leipzig 1922 = Quellen und Forschungen zur Reformationsgeschichte, vol. 5.

Windhorst, Christof: Täuferisches Taufverständnis. Balthasar Hubmaiers Lehre zwischen traditioneller und reformatorischer Theologie. Leiden 1976 = Studies in Medieval and Reformation Thought, vol. XVI.

Wittram, Reinhard: Die Reformation in Livland. In: Baltische Kirchengeschichte. Ed. by R. Wittram. Göttingen 1956, 35–36.

Wunder, Gerd: Über die Verwandtschaft des Wiedertäufers Melchior Hoffman. In: Der Haalquell. Blätter für Heimatkunde des Haller Landes. 23. Jg. Nr. 6, April 1971, pp. 21–23.

Yoder, John Howard: The Turning Point in the Zwinglian Reformation. In: MQR 32, 1958, 95–112.

——: Täufertum und Reformation in der Schweitz. Part 1: Die Gespräche zwischen Täufern und Reformatoren 1523–1528. Karlsruhe 1962 = Schriftenreihe des Mennonitischen Geschichtsvereins, vol. 6.

——: Täufertum und Reformation im Gespräch. Dogmengeschichtliche Untersuchung der frühen Gespräche zwischen schweizerischen Täufern und Reformatoren. Zürich 1968 = Basler Studien zur historischen und systematischen Theologie, vol. 13.

——: The Evolution of the Zwinglian Reformation. In: MQR 43, 1969, 95–122.

——: Der Kristallisationspunkt des Täufertums. In: MGB N.F. 24, 1972, 35–47.

Zijpp, N. van der: Geschiedenis der Doopsgezinden in Nederland. Arnheim 1952.

Zschäbitz, Gerhard: Zur mitteldeutschen Täuferbewegung nach dem großen Bauernkrieg. (Ost-)Berlin 1958.

——: Die Stellung der Täuferbewegung im Spannungsbogen der deutschen frühbürgerlichen Revolution. In: Gerhard Brendler (ed.): Die frühbürgerliche Revolution in Deutschland. (Ost-)Berlin 1961, 152–162.

Zur Mühlen, Karl-Heinz: Nos extra nos. Luthers Theologie zwischen Mystik und Scholastik. Tübingen 1972.

Abbreviations

Acta	Acta der Disputation zu Flensburg ... Ed. by Johannes Bugenhagen. Wittenberg 1529
AR III	Arbusov, Leonid iun. (Bearbeiter): Akten und Rezesse der livländischen Ständetage. Vol. III. 1495–1535. Riga 1910
ARG	Archiv für Reformationsgeschichte
BRN	Bibliotheca Reformatoria Neerlandica
CR	Corpus Reformatorum
CS	Corpus Schwenckfeldianorum. Ed. by Ch. D. Hartranft et al., vols. 3, 4, 5. Leipzig 1913/1914/1916
Dialogus	Anonymus [i.e. Hoffman, Melchior and Andreas Bodenstein von Karlstadt]: Dialogus und grundtliche berichtung gehaltner disputation im land zu Holsten ... Straßburg, Balthasar Beck, 1529
Jb	Jahrbuch (= yearbook)
Luther WA	Martin Luthers Werke. Kritische Gesamtausgabe. Weimar 1883f
MGB N.F.	Mennonitische Geschichtsblätter, Neue Folge
MQR	Mennonite Quarterly Review
N.F.	Neue Folge (= new series)
QFR	Quellen und Forschungen zur Reformationsgeschichte
Sb	Sitzungsberichte
Str StA	Straßburg, Stadtarchiv
Str ThA	Straßburg, Thomas-Archiv
SVRG	Schriften des Vereins für Reformationsgeschichte
TA	Täuferakten
TAE I	Quellen zur Geschichte der Täufer. Vol. 7: Elsaß I. Stadt Straßburg 1522–1532. Ed. by Manfred Krebs and Hans Georg Rott. Gütersloh 1959 = QFR XXVI
TAE II	Quellen zur Geschichte der Täufer. Vol. 8: Elsaß II. Stadt Straßburg 1533–1535. Ed. by Manfred Krebs and Hans Georg Rott. Gütersloh 1960 = QFR XXVII
UB	Universitätsbibliothek (= University Library)
ZfG	Zeitschrift für Geschichtswissenschaft
ZKG	Zeitschrift für Kirchengeschichte
ZSRg, KA	Zeitschrift der Savigny-Stiftung für Rechtsgeschichte, Kanonistische Abteilung
Zwingli, Werke	Huldreich Zwinglis Sämtliche Werke. Ed. by Emil Egli and others. Berlin 1905f. = Corpus Reformatorum vol. 88f.

List of Illustrations

Frontispiece: Melchior Hoffman in prison at Strasbourg. Print by Christoph van Sichem, early seventeenth-century; imaginary picture by the artist. Reproduction of the picture in Barthold Nikolaus Krohn: Geschichte der Fanatischen und Enthusiastischen Wiedertäufer. Leipzig, 1758. Provincial archives at Aurich. (The same motif was used for the dust-cover).

Plate 1: John Bugenhagen. Engraving by Theodore de Bry. Kupferstich-Kabinett Basel.

Plate 2: Specimen of Melchior Hoffman's handwriting from: Worhafftige zeuknus gegen die nachtwechter und sternen (Schriftenverzeichnis Nr. 24). The only surviving autograph of Hoffman. Strasbourg, Thomas-Archiv, Sign. 76, Nr. 39, Hoffmaniana 2.

Plate 3: Martin Bucer. Woodcut, dating 1586. Plate 7 in Johannes Ficker: Bildnisse der Strassburger Reformation. Strasbourg 1914. Original in the Strasbourg University Library. Bucer aged 53. Bibliothèque Nationale, Strasbourg.

Plate 4: Wolfgang Capito. Print by Peter Aubry. Ficker, Plate 6. Original at Strasbourg, Städtische Kupferstichsammlung.

Plate 5: Clemens Ziegler: The birth of the new man.

Plate 6: Clemens Ziegler: The struggle of the new man with the serpent.

Plate 7: Clemens Ziegler: The woman as the serpent from which the angels of death go forth.

Plate 8: Clemens Ziegler: The old, ailing man. Autograph drawings by Clemens Ziegler (coloured), prepared for the illustration of an unpublished MS: Ein mercklichen verstant über das geschriben biechlein von der sellickeit aller menschen selen wirt hier eigentlich angezeigt mit sigtbarlichen figuren durch Clemens zieler (sic!), gartner zu Strasbourg, vollendet am XII. dag christmond XXXII. December 1532. Strasbourg, Thomas-Archiv. Nr. 76.

Plate 9: Caspar Hedio: woodcut after the silver-point drawing by Baldung, dating 1543. In: Caspar Hedio: Eine ausserlesene Chronick von anfang der welt bis auf das jar 1543. Strasbourg 1543. Source also in Ficker, Plate 9.

Plate 10: Caspar Schwenckfeld von Ossig. Engraving by Theodor de Bry. Kupferstich-Kabinett Basel.

Plate 11: Otto Brunfels. Woodcut by Hans Weiditz, dating 1535. Ficker, Plate 11. Original in the Strasbourg University Library.

Plate 12: Jan van Leiden. Woodcut by Heinrich Aldegrever. 1535. Reprint: Max Geisberg: Die Wiedertäufer in Münster. Velen 1930. Plate 11 = illustrations of selected sources and documents for the history of Westphalia, Folder no. 4. Original in the British Museum, London. (Top right: the coat of arms, the globe pierced by two swords, the sword of the Spirit and the sword of revenge).

Plate 13: Coins of the Anabaptists: the ten-guilder piece. (Gold). Legend: IM REICH GOTTIS EIN KONIG AUFGERICHT VBER A: (LLE)X:. EIN GOT/EIN GLAUB/EIN TAUEE (TAUF). GOT. – ZU MVNSTER 1534. – WER NIT GEBOREN IST AUS DEM WASSE(R) Y(ND) H(EILIGEN) G(EIST) MAG NIT EINGEHEN (IN DAS REICH GOTTES). X. DAS WORT IST FLEIS(CH) WORDEN YND WONET IN UNS!

Plate 14: David Joris: The breaking-forth of the Holy Spirit.

Plate 15: David Joris: The restoration of the true Church, or the Bride of Christ.

Plate 16: David Joris: The figure of the new man. From David Joris: Wonderboeck, 1551 edition.

Folding Map at the end: Strasbourg, 1548. Print by Konrad Morand, Strasbourg, Municipal Archives.

Index

Author's Note
Names which occur in the footnotes are in general not included in the Index; neither are "Hoffman", "Melchiorites".
I give my best thanks to Miss Renate Böker, M.A., for her painstaking work on the Index.

Editor's Note
Variant spellings of names (e.g. Jacob/Jakob, Conrad/Konrad, Lucas/Lukas) have *not* been noted in the Index.

Ahlefeld, Benedikt von, 97
Ahlefeld, Gottschalk von, Bishop
  of Schleswig, 97, 98
Alba, 317
Alberts, Martyn, 331
Albrecht, Duke of Prussia, 97
Alckmaar, 335
Allstedt, 389
Alsace, 165, 170, 200, 253, 270,
  273, 310, 351, 365
Altbiesser, Symphorian, 288
Altdorf, 175
Altona, 23
America, 25
Amsdorf, Nikolaus von, 23, 101,
  110–12, 113–19, 122, 123,
  125–6, 250, 386
Amsterdam, 291, 323, 324, 327,
  328, 329, 330, 332, 335–6, 340,
  341, 374
Andreae, Laurentius, 91, 93
Ansbach-Bayreuth, 291
Aportanus (Jürgen van der Daere),
  154, 155, 319
Appenzell, 182
Aristotle, 224
Arnold, Gottfried, 137
Assyria, 346
Augsburg, 12, 14, 164–5, 191–2,

198–9, 202–3, 205, 212, 268,
  274, 275, 282
Augsburg, Confession of, 279,
  281, 371
Augsburg, Diet of (1530), 279
Augustine, St., 135
Aurich, 154, 156
Austria, 310

Baden-Baden, 290
Bader, Augustin, 19, 282
Bader, Sabina, 282
Balk, Matthijs van, 359
Baltic, 325
Bangarten, Diebolt, 378
Barse, Johannes, 135
Bartscherer, Lukas, 91
Basel, 279, 282, 283
Bastian, Hermann, 369, 371
Batenburg, Jan van, 29, 237, 317,
  339, 358, 360–1, 363, 367, 372
Bauman, Clarence, 1–2
Beck, Balthasar, 160, 206, 218,
  277, 351
Beck, Caspar (Melchior Hoffman),
  350–2
Bender, Harold S., 1–2
Benfeld, 297
Beninga, 316

422

Benninck, Cornelis, 330
Benoit, Andry, 376
Benscop, Drostin von, 327
Benzing, Josef, 32–3
Berchem, Joachim van, 327
Berne, 215, 279, 282, 283, 290
Berner, Alexander, 272, 277, 296
Berum, 158, 314
Betschold, Martin, 169
Beukels, Jan, 334–5, 337
Bibliander, 302
Biel, Gabriel, 222–3, 224
Biestermann, Hermann, 101–2
Björnsen, Björn, 93
"Black-Headed Guild", 43, 47, 48,
  52, 58, 59, 79, 87, 382
Blanke, Fritz, 1–2
Blankenfeld, Johannes, Archbishop
  of Riga, 36, 40, 47–8, 50,
  51–5, 59
Blaurer, Ambrosius, 196, 277–8,
  302, 304, 306
Blesdijk, 338
Bloch, Ernst, 20–1, 22
Blum, Wilhelm the elder, 206
Blum, Wilhelm the younger, 206,
  355, 356, 357, 378
Bocholt, 359–61
Böcklin, Wolfgang, 169
Boekbinder, Bartholomeus, 329,
  336–7, 341–2
Boekbinder, Gerrit, 334–5
Bohemia, 81
Bohemian Brethren, 249–50
Boie, Nicolaus, 127, 132
Bokman, Hans, 91, 93
Bomeromenus, Johannes, 376
Bomhower, Antonius, 47
Bordesholm, 101, 120
Bouma, Gellius Faber de, 154
Bramus, Thomas, 154
Bremen, 155, 157, 312–13
Bremen, Church Ordinance of
  (1530), 313, 314, 318
Brendler, Gerhard, 13
Den Briel, 334–5
Briessmann, Johannes, 78, 85

Brötli, Johannes, 6, 36
Brunfels, Otto, 168, 172, 277, 290
Brunt, Reynier, 327, 329, 332
Brussels, 315, 332, 333
Bucer, Martin, 30–1, 145, 146,
  160, 166, 168, 170–4, 181–2,
  184–5, 187, 195–7, 202–3, 212,
  234, 236, 250, 269, 279–80,
  282–5, 288–9, 294–6, 298–302,
  304–7, 351–3, 357, 369–72,
  374–6, 378
Bugenhagen, Johannes, 23, 45,
  60–1, 69, 112–13, 115, 126–9,
  132–7, 138, 143–4, 146, 155,
  157, 250, 386
Bühl, Konrad von, 378–9
Bullinger, 302
Bünderlin, Hans, 165, 174
Burckhardt, Jakob, 32
Büren, Idelette van, 377
Burgundy, 315

Calais, 326
Calvin, John, 12, 77, 376–7
Calvinism, 384
Cammerlander, Jakob, 277
Campanus, Johannes, 367
Campen, Jacob van, 134–6, 242,
  340, 342
Campen, Johannes van, 99, 127
Cankena, Heddo, 157–8
Canter, Jacobus, 154
Canz, Lübbert, 154, 319
Capito, Wolfgang, 167–73, 178,
  179, 182, 184, 187, 192–7, 203,
  277–8, 281–3, 285, 294–5,
  306–7, 350–1, 353, 355, 357,
  372, 374, 376, 378
Cathari, 262
Cellarius, Martin (Borrhaus), 165,
  180, 192–3, 196
Charles V, Emperor, 73, 121, 157,
  200, 211, 242, 248, 278, 279,
  298–9, 312, 325, 332, 357, 381,
  388
Christian II, King of Denmark, 89,
  93, 96, 121, 325

Christian III, King of Denmark, 28, 97, 118–19, 121–3, 125–9, 131–2, 137, 325
Clasen, Claus-Peter, 9, 10–12, 198
Clement VII, Pope, 47
Cohn, Norman, 15–16
Colijn, Pieter, 330, 332
Cologne, 306
Conrat (church administrator), 285
Constance, 283, 302
Constance, Council of, 249
Constantine, Emperor, 248
Copenhagen, 96, 107
Cornelius, Carl Adolf, 23
Crete, 199
Cyprus, 199

Daere, Jürgen van der (Aportanus), 154, 155, 319
Dagma, Regnerus (Reiner), 154, 319
Dalarne, 92
Danzig, 127, 135
Davis, Kenneth R., 8
Delft, 324
Delft, Maria van, 378
Denck, Hans, 3, 7–9, 25, 26, 31, 160–1, 165, 167, 180, 182, 184–92, 199, 202, 218, 219, 221, 222, 224, 229, 243, 257, 260, 262, 274–6, 286, 321–2, 387–9
Denmark, 96, 99, 106–7, 121
Deventer, 327, 332
"Devotio Moderna", 321–2
Diewer ("Queen Divara"), 335, 338
Dionysius Areopagita, 378
Dithmarschen, 127
Domizlaff, Helmuth, 33
Dornum, Essa von, 317
Dornum, Imele von, 317
Dornum, Margarete von, 317
Dornum, Ulrich von, 30, 153, 155, 157, 158, 314, 317, 319, 382, 383
Dorothea, Princess of Denmark, 97

Dorpat, 36–40, 42, 44, 46, 49–55, 59, 63, 69, 79, 84–8, 249, 382, 383
Drübel, Eckhard zum, 276
Dufft, Valentin, 206, 291, 292, 356, 357, 375
Duntzenheim, Konrad von, 169

Echsel, Wilhelm, 181, 184
Eckboldsheim, 356
Eckhardt, Meister, 7
Edam, 341
Edzard the Great, Count, 153, 154
Egenolf, Christian, 218
Eisenach, 79
Eisenburg, Johannes, 206, 291, 297, 306, 355, 362–6, 368–9, 371–5, 378–9
Emden, 154, 156, 157, 304, 312–14, 316–17, 328
Emmius, Ubbo, 317
Enckhuizen, 335, 341
Engelbrecht, Anton, 277, 288–90, 307
England, 12, 25, 81, 228, 325–6, 358, 363, 370
Enno II, Count of Frisia, 153, 156, 312–16, 318–20, 328, 382–3
Ensisheim, 310
Epicureans, 277, 287, 288–90, 295, 303
Erasmus, 6, 8, 224, 321–3, 343
Erb, Sebastian, 284
Esen, Balthasar, von, 315–16
Esslingen, 205
Estonia, 42–3
Ewsum, Christoffer von, 317, 327

Faber, Gellius, 324
Fabricius, Dionysius, 55–6
Fabritius, 370
Fälber, Leonhard, 369, 371
Farel, 377
Fast, Heinold, 1, 9, 32, 228–9
Ferdinand I, King of Austria, 211, 263, 310
Firn, Anton, 168

Fischer, Laux, 199
Flanders, 164–5, 312
Flensburg, 99, 107, 218
Flensburg Disputation, 126–36, 144, 158, 160, 386
France, 270
Francis, St., 211, 249
Franck, Margarethe, 277
Franck, Sebastian, 164, 165, 166, 167, 174, 186, 216, 243, 277
Franconia, 292
Frankfurt, 164, 371
Frederick I, King of Denmark, 30, 96–100, 106–7, 118–19, 121, 126–7, 135–7, 254, 325, 382, 383, 386
Frey, Claus, 291–3, 294, 335, 350, 351
Frisch, Hans, 267
Frisia, 153–9, 312–20, 327, 328, 331, 332, 336, 358, 381, 382–3
Fuggers, 199
Fuht, Hans, 254

Gansfort, Wessel, 321, 323
Gardeners, 274, 276
Geelen, Jan van, 340
Geldenhaur, 324
Geldern, Duke Karl von, 157, 312, 315, 317–18, 332, 333
Gemünden an der Wohrd, 369
Gendern, Karl von the younger, 332, 333
Genemuiden, 341
Geneva, 376
Gerbel, Nikolaus, 168, 173, 184
Gerber, Erasmus, 164, 170, 175
Gerbihan, Hermann van, 376, 377
Gerdsma, Johann, 317
Gerfalk, 355, 372
Germany, 228
Ginderich, Matthaus, 318
Gnapheus, 324
Goertz, Hans-Jürgen, 7, 33
Goeters, J. F. G., 5
Gottesheim, Conrad von, 169
Gottesheim, Friedrich von, 169

Götze, Melchior, 23
"Great Exodus", 341–2
"Great Guild", 43–4, 48
Grebel, Konrad, 3, 4, 6, 9, 10, 68, 179, 218, 321
Greece, 346
Gregory, 378
Gresbeck, Heinrich, 348
Groningen, 157, 321, 324, 327, 332, 333
Gross, Jakob, 181, 184, 199
Grüningen, 6
Gulik, Jan van, 359
Gustavus I Wasa, King of Sweden, 89, 90–4, 381, 382

Haarlem, 324, 332
Haas, Martin, 5
Habsburgs, 328
Hackfurt, Lucas, 168, 272, 277
Hadersleben, 122
Hadersleben, Ecclesiastical Ordinance of (1528), 122, 123
Hadrian VI, Pope, 47
Hage, Meinardus, 157–8
Hagenau, 277
The Hague, 324, 329, 330, 332
Hallau, 6, 179, 182
Hamburg, 98, 113, 115, 126, 127, 136, 157
Hanseatic League, 37–8, 44, 59–60, 89
Harge, Paul, 120
Harlingen, 154
Harlingerland, 315
Harrien-Wierland, 39–40, 55, 56–9, 85
Hasselt, 341
Hätzer, Ludwig, 3, 165, 180, 188, 197, 199, 202
Hechtlin, 288
Hedio, Caspar, 168, 169, 197, 202–3, 250, 305, 306–7, 351–2, 353, 357, 374, 378
Hedwig, Princess, 90
Hegge, Jakob, 127, 134–6
Heidelberg, 3–4

Heilbronn, 35
Herlin, Martin, 169, 284
Hermans, Jan, 329–30
Hesse, 121, 161, 358, 363, 369–72, 375
Hesse, Philipp, Landgrave of, 302, 314, 316, 369–72
Heymann, 332
Hilarius, 187
Hiller, Mathis, 181, 184
Hillerbrand, Hans J., 6–7
Hilten, Johannes, 79
Hoen, Cornelis, 143, 147–9, 172, 321, 323–4, 324
Holl, Karl, 3
Holland, 12, 13–14, 22, 25, 161, 164–5, 228, 333, 363, 383, 384
Holst, Gorius, 91, 92, 93
Holstein, 105, 106, 107, 113, 126–7, 382, 383
Hondebeeke, 324
Hoogstraten, Count, 332, 333
Horb, 184
Horn, 335
Houtzager, Pieter de, 329, 336, 341–2
Howerda, Hicco, 157, 314
Hoyer, Siegfried, 8
Hoyte, Hermann, 48
Hubmaier, Balthasar, 3, 6, 7, 10, 179, 182, 197, 222, 223, 224, 232, 321–2, 340
Hubrechts, Jan, 329, 330, 333
Hus, Jan, 24, 73, 79, 80, 137, 249
Hussites, 8, 79–80, 143, 248, 249, 262
Husum, 99, 106
Hut, Hans, 4, 8, 9, 10, 13, 16, 19–20, 36, 78, 180, 191, 198, 199–203, 205, 209, 212, 213, 218, 240, 275, 276, 340, 389
Hutterites, 3, 7, 9, 14

Iderhoff, Jeltko, 157
Ignatius, 378
Ingolt, Friedrich, 184
Innocent I, Pope, 248

Innocent III, Pope, 48
Irenaeus, 373
Isenbroeck, Wilhelm von, 47
Italy, 81, 270
Itzehoe, 99, 134
Ivan III, Czar, 37, 53, 54

Jacobs, Heymann, 333
Jans, Anneken, 361, 362
Jans, Ruysch, 330
Jemgum, 156
Jemgum, battle of, 315
Jever, Maria von, 315
John the Apostle, 158
Joris, David, 242, 311, 323, 327, 342, 357, 360–9
Jost, Agnes, 206, 369
Jost, Elizabeth, 206
Jost, Lienhard, 160, 168, 205, 206, 211, 212, 257, 260, 291, 297, 298, 311, 333, 356–7, 363–4, 366, 368, 369, 388
Jost, Ursula, 160, 168, 205, 206–10, 226, 298, 333, 355, 357, 388
Jubele, Jörg, 354
Juchsen, Jörg Haug von, 240
Jud, 302
Jungingen, Konrad von, 39
Jutland, 107

Kaffmeister, Hans the younger, 79
Kaffmeister, Heinrich, 79
Kappel, battle of, 280
Karlstadt, Andrew, 3, 4, 6, 8, 9, 24, 35, 46–7, 69–72, 84, 100, 112, 119, 127, 129, 135, 139, 141, 147, 149–51, 153, 157–9, 165, 172–4, 179, 215, 222, 247, 251, 279, 314, 318
Kautz, Jakob, 165, 167, 185, 187–8, 190–1, 269, 274–5
Kawerau, Peter, 25–27, 28, 31
Kemberg, 127
Kempe, Stephan, 127, 128, 132, 135
Kiel, 96, 100–16, 120–1, 136, 382
Kiel, Diet of (1526), 97–8

Kievel, Johannes IV, Bishop of Ösel-Wiek, 40
Kirchholm, Treaty of (1452), 38
Klaiber, Andreas, 204
Klopriss, Johannes, 337, 348
Kniebis, Nikolaus, 169, 170
Knipperdolling, Bernd, 337, 338, 353–4
Knopken, Andreas, 45–6, 47, 54
Kobian, Valentin, 277, 351
Kofler, Leo, 21–2
Kokenhusen, 50
Königsberg, 78, 85
Krahn, Cornelius, 29
Krechting, Bernd, 338, 354
Krechting, Heinrich, 361
Krohn, Barthold Nikolaus, 22–3, 121
Kron, Jakob, 297, 350, 352
Krüsi, Hans, 6, 36
Krutenau, 167, 356
Kühler, W. J., 28–9, 339
Kuhles, Joachim, 27–8
Kurland, 38
Kuyper, Willem de, 336–7, 341–2

La Roche, Alain de, 226
Landfester, Rüdiger, 18–19
Langenmantel, Eitelhans, 199
Larrelt, 156
Latvian Guild of Beer-Carriers, 48–9
Leendertz, W. J., 24, 25
Leer, 154, 156
Leeuwarden, 324, 328, 336–7
Leiden, 326, 335
Leiden, Jan van, 3, 29, 338, 339, 341, 343, 346, 348, 353–4
Leipzig, 46
Lessing, Gotthold Ephraim, 23
Lichtenberg, Johann, 245
Linde, Jasper, Archbishop of Riga, 40
Linden, Friedrich Otto zur, 24–5
Lindenfels (church administrator), 285
List, Günther, 19–20

Listinex, Aefgen, 327
Littell, Franklin H., 1–2
"Little Guild", 44
Livonia, 27–8, 30, 35–63, 66–7, 75, 78–81, 84–8, 152, 266, 325, 381–5, 389
Logum, Treaty of, 317–18
Loher (Leuber), Julius, 291
Lohmüller, Johannes, 38–9, 45–6
Lollards, 81
Lorenz, Gertrud, 206, 355
Lorenz, Josef, 206
Lose, Peter, 369, 371
Lostadt, Elsa van, 327
Lübeck, 60, 89, 95, 164, 325, 381
Lübeck, Law of, 41
Ludwig V, Elector Palatine, 268, 281
Lukácz, Georg, 21
Lüneburg, 157, 318, 369
Lüneburg, Church Ordinance of, 318–19
Lüneburg, Ernst, Duke of, 280
Luther, Martin, 2, 6–7, 10, 24, 30–1, 35, 36, 45, 50, 54, 57, 60–2, 68–9, 71, 75–8, 83–4, 86, 88, 92, 97, 99, 104, 110–15, 117–20, 125–6, 128–9, 134, 138–47, 150, 155, 156, 160–1, 171–4, 182, 183, 185, 195, 211, 214, 220–3, 226, 230, 238, 240, 245, 249–53, 256, 264, 280, 282, 296, 314, 317, 324–5, 343, 381, 383, 384, 388–9

Maastricht, 321
"Mad Friedrich", 99–100, 104
Magdeburg, 110–11, 113, 116–17, 122, 123
Mainz, Elector of, 281
Malmö, 107
Manhuss, 95
Maninga, Poppo, 154
Mantz, Felix, 6, 68, 355
Marbeck, Pilgram, 9, 10, 165, 191, 263, 267, 269–70, 274, 275

Marburg, 369, 370
Marburg, Colloquy of (1529),
　142, 278, 312–13
Marburg Articles (1529), 312–13
Maria of Hungary, 327
Marienburg, 44
Marienhafe, 154
Mark, St., 177
Marsow, Hermann, 52
Martin I, Pope, 248
"Martyr's Synod of Augsburg"
　(1527), 191–2
Matthew, St., 107–8
Matthijs, Jan, 3, 20, 22–4, 29, 232,
　261, 323, 334–40, 343, 345,
　347, 359–61, 390–1
Meiger, Fridolin, 184
Melanchthon, Philipp, 86, 112,
　118–19, 238, 250, 279–81, 302
Mellink, A. F., 28, 339
Memmingen, 282, 283
Menno Simons, 10, 22, 29, 32,
　228, 322, 380
Mennonites, 3, 4, 5, 9, 22–3, 321
Metz, 376
Meyger, Fridolin, 170–1
Michaelsdotter, Kristina, 90
Mieg, Andreas, 284
Miller, Haug, 199
Molsheim, 175
Molsheim, Diets of (1535), 310
Monnickendam, 341
Moscow, 53
Mueg, Daniel, 169
Mühlhausen, 200, 213
Mühlmann, Wilhelm E., 16–18,
　19
Mundolsheim, 356
Münster, 10, 13, 14, 16, 19, 22,
　24, 28–9, 31, 154, 161, 227–8,
　257, 259, 261, 273, 274, 302,
　307–8, 310, 321, 332, 335,
　337–42, 348, 353–4, 356, 358,
　363, 371, 379, 384, 390–1
Müntzer, Thomas, 3, 4, 6–7, 9,
　10, 16, 20–1, 27, 67, 78, 105,
　134, 139, 156, 174, 193, 196,

198, 199, 200, 202, 209, 213,
　240, 345, 383

Narva, 44, 50, 55
Nespitzer, Jörg, 205
Nessel, Valentin, 206
Netherlands, 28, 30, 139, 142,
　205, 237, 242, 261, 268, 298,
　302, 311, 312, 321–42, 356,
　358, 359, 372, 381, 382
Norden, 154, 156, 158, 314
Norden, Brixius ten, 302
Norden, Colloquy of (1527), 155
Norlinger, Jörg, 378
Novatian the Donatist, 301
Novgorod, 44
Noviomagus, Professor, 370
Nuremberg, 164
"Nuremberg Truce" (1532), 281

Obbenites, 358–9
Oberehnheim, 175
Oecolampadius, Johannes, 158,
　196, 282
Oldeguil, Johann, 154, 314, 317,
　319
Oldenburg, 157, 358, 359, 363
Oldersum, 156
Omken, Hero, 157
Origen, 373
Orlamünde, 35
Ösel-Wiek, 38, 39–40, 50, 86
Ossenbrügge, 95
Ottrott, 356
Overijssel, 332, 341
Ozment, Stephen E., 7–8

Paeuw, Jan, 340
Panner, Andreas, 274
Parper, Johannes, 98
Pastor, Adam, 228
Paul, St., 35, 39, 67, 70, 76, 100,
　102, 104, 107, 114, 186, 221,
　222, 236, 247, 248, 253, 373
Pelagius, 301
Pellikan, Konrad, 196, 302
Pelt, Johann, 157, 313

Persia, 346
Peter, St., 236, 300
Petri, Olavus, 89–90, 91, 93
Pfarrer, Mathis, 169, 304, 306, 352
Pfau, Hans, 205
Pfeiffer, Heinrich, 200, 213
Pfersfelder (Gross), Elisabeth, 292
Pfersfelder (Gross), Georg, 292
Pfitzer, Georg, 352, 355, 372
Philip, Landgrave of Hesse, 173
Philipp, Margrave of Baden, 268
Philips, Dirk, 32, 228, 242, 328–9, 342, 361
Philips, Obbe, 29, 206, 242, 260, 316–17, 328–9, 342, 358, 360, 361
Pilsen, 157
Piper, Kort, 91
Platter, Johannes, 38
Plettenberg, Wolter von, 36, 37, 38–9, 51, 57–9
Pliny, 225–6
Plümper, Hans-Dieter, 14
Pogwisch, Wulf, 97
Poland, 37, 325
Poldermann, Cornelis, 206, 257, 277, 297, 304–5, 331, 335, 338, 352, 390
Porten, Alidt ter, 327
Pravest, Wilhelm, 92, 101, 102, 119–21
Pskov, 37, 44, 53
Puritans, 12, 25, 358
Purvey, John, 78–9

Rantzau, Johann von, 97, 126, 129, 132, 134–6
Rebstock, Barbara, 205, 206, 212, 292, 333, 353, 355, 356–7, 363–6, 368
Rebstock, Hans, 205, 354
Reecalf, 332
Regel, Georg, 199
Reinbeck, 126
Reinbek, 98
Reinhart, Martin, 79–80

Rendsburg, 105
Rese, Hinrich, 155, 314
Ressem, Hylle van, 327
Reublin, Wilhelm, 6, 165, 179, 188, 190, 191, 263, 267, 269, 274, 275
Reval, 36, 38, 41–2, 44, 49–50, 53, 55–7, 85
Reval, Diet of (1524), 50
Reventlov, Detlev, 98, 126
Rhine, River, 176, 358, 363
Riga, 38, 39–40, 42, 44, 45–50, 53–4, 59, 79, 86
Riga Consistory, 86
Rinck, Melchior, 3, 36, 367
Ringenberg, Gerhard, 54
Rode, Hinne, 154, 157, 172, 314, 321, 324
Roll, Heinrich, 337, 369
Rome, 47, 346
Ronneburg, 54
Rosenblatt, Wibrandis, 282
Rostock, 79
Rothenburg, Hans von, 367
Rothmann, Bernd (Bernhard), 3, 20, 247, 232, 302, 337, 342–8, 363
Rott, Hans-Georg, 33
Rottenburg, 184
Rotterdam, 334–5
Ruprechtsau, 167, 175
Russia, 37, 38, 86, 381
Russian Orthodox Church, 249
Rutze, Nikolaus, 79

Sacramentarians, 314, 316, 321, 323, 325, 331
St. Gallen, 6, 182
Salzman, Thomas, 166
Sapidus, Johannes, 277, 288–9, 295
Sattler, Michael, 10, 165, 179, 180–4, 188–90, 274, 340, 383
Savonarola, Hieronymus, 81
Saxon Visitation (1528), 122
Saxony, 9, 36, 121, 127
Saxony, George, Duke of, 74

Saxony, John, Elector of, 278, 279–80, 313
Schaffhausen, 182
Scharnschlager, Leopold, 269–70, 274
Scheerder, Hans, 242
Schiltigheim, 356
Schleitheim, 389
Schleitheim Confession (1527), 3, 4, 68, 83, 182, 202, 263
Schleswig, 99–100, 106, 122
Schleswig-Holstein, 28, 96–121, 126–7, 129, 138, 152, 153, 381, 382, 384, 386
Schmalkalden, League of, 278, 280–1
Schnabel, Georg, 369, 371
Schneider, Jörgen, 354
Schnepfer, Hans, 354
Schoonhoven, Jan van, 359
Schramm, Gottfried, 33
Schreiber, Brand, 91, 93
Schubert, Hans von, 7
Schuhmacher, Heinrich, 367
Schuldorp, Hans, 104
Schuldorp, Marquard, 99, 101, 102–5, 107, 109–10, 113, 115–18, 121, 127, 386
Schultheiss, Wolfgang, 277, 288–90, 307
Schwabach Articles, 278
Schwäbisch-Hall, 35
Schwarz, Ruprecht, 274, 375
Schwarz, Theobald, 295
Schwarz-Lausten, M., 28
Schwebel, Johannes, 166, 168
Schweblin, 288
Schweinfurt, 281
Schwenckfeld, Caspar, 165, 167, 174, 177, 213–17, 219, 257, 272, 275, 276, 284, 286–7, 292, 295–7, 304, 355, 387
Seebass, Gottfried, 9, 33
Seid, Katharina, 204, 356, 357
Servetus, Michael, 165
Sigismund I, King of Poland, 74, 90

Silesia, 213, 304
Slegel, Adam, 274
Smirin, M. M., 27
Sneek, Tjaard van, 359
Snijder, Sikke Freerks, 328–9
Sophia, Queen of Denmark, 109
Sotteren, Jürgen von, 91
Spaarndam, 341, 342
Speyer, 319, 356, 357, 363
Speyer, First Diet of (1526), 97
Speyer, Second Diet of (1529), 268, 278, 312–13
Stackelberg, Peter, 52–3
Stayer, James M., 5, 9–10, 29, 33
Stecker, Nikolaus, 89–90, 92
Steinmetz, Max, 13
Steltz Guild, 184
Stevens, Johann, 158, 313–14
Stewert, Gert, 99
Stockholm, 30, 89–94, 381, 382, 383
Stodewescher, Silvester, Archbishop of Riga, 39–40
Storch, Nikolaus, 112
Stordeur, Jean, 376, 377
Stralen, Gottfried, 337, 348
Strasbourg, 12, 23, 25, 26, 31, 153, 158, 160–219, 220, 223, 258, 263–7, 268–311, 333–4, 339, 351–8, 362–9, 372, 374–80, 382, 383–4
Strasbourg Prophets, 160, 204–6, 210–13, 218–19, 257, 266, 388, 389
Strauss, Jakob, 4
Stübner, Markus, 112
Stumpf, Simon, 6
Sturm, Jakob, 169, 279, 284, 289, 302
Suave, Peter, 97, 118–19
Svenstrup, 107
Swabian League, 268
Swart, Peder, 91
Swarte Water, 341
Sweden, 37, 89–94
Swiss Brethren, 3, 4, 5–6, 9, 10, 23, 83, 181–2, 195, 196, 202,

274–5, 287, 292, 371, 375, 388–9

Taborites, 13, 143
Tasch, Peter, 363, 365, 366–75, 378–9
Tast, Hermann, 99, 126, 130, 132
Tauler, Johannes, 7
Tausen, Hans, 99
Tegetmeier, Sylvester, 46, 47, 49, 53–4, 57–8, 63, 69, 250
Teutonic Order, 35, 36, 38–40, 48, 53–5, 58–9, 86
Teylers Godgeleerd Genootschap, 24, 25
Theophilus, Master, 127
Thuringia, 9, 156, 200
Thyatira, 250
Tiemann, Johann, 157, 313
Törning, 122
Treptow, 45
Tricht, Jan van, 359
Troeltsch, Ernst, 2, 3
Tübingen, 369
Tucher, Jörg, 181
Turks, 81–2, 175, 176, 177, 200, 209, 210, 211–12, 213, 254, 261
"Twenty Articles", 318–19

Ubben(a), Wilhelm, 154
Ulm, 283, 369
Undermarck, Martin, 318
Uphusen, 157
Uppland, 92
Utenhoven, Wolfgang von, 97, 100
Utrecht, 332

Valentinus the Gnostic, 301
Västerås, Diet of (1527), 90
Venturinus, 211–12, 356
Vienna, 209, 261
Vinne, Dionysius, 337
Vlaming, Cornelis de, 327
Volkerts Trijpmaker, Jan, 232, 328–9, 330

Volz, Hugo, 277
Vos, Karel, 339

Wachter, Michael, 351, 352
Wacker, Bernhard, 286
Waldensians, 13
Waldis, Burckhard, 47
Waldshut, 6, 179, 181
Walhof, Johannes, 95
Warendorf, 348
Wassenberg, 337
Waterland, 332
Weber, Max, 3
Weidensee, Eberhard, 122–5, 147–8, 250
Weilersbach, 292
Wencker, Jakob II, 354
Wendt, Johann (Slavus), 122
Wesenberg, 55
Wesselburen, 127
Westphalia, 237, 261, 321, 323, 338, 353–4, 358, 359, 379, 383
Wetzel, Jakob, 378
Widholz, Endris, 199
Wieck, Johann van der, 302
Wijntgen, Philip, 331
Williams, George Huntston, 3–4, 7, 9
Wilmsen, Andreas, 95
Windsheim, 291, 322
Winter, Adolf, 378
Wirdum, 157
Wittenberg, 6, 54, 60–2, 90, 101, 110, 112, 113, 119, 122, 169, 237, 279, 280, 302, 314, 325, 369, 381, 384, 389
Wittenberg Concorde (1536), 146, 173–4
Wittenberg Reformers, 2, 8, 13, 27, 36, 62, 68, 136–7
Wolff, Hans, 179–80
Wolkersdorf, 369, 370
Wolmar, 35, 36, 45, 50
Wolmar, Diet of (1525), 57
Wolmar, Diet of (1533), 85
Wolsey, Cardinal, 326
Wolthusen, 314

Worms, 185, 187
Worms, Diet of (1521), 97
Worms, Edict of, 168, 332
Wulff, Konrad, 120
Wurmser, Bernhard, 169, 353
Wycliffe, John, 78
Wynssem, Jakob van, 327, 332
Wynssem, Lubbe van, 327

Yoder John Howard, 1–2

Zabern, 175
Zeeland, 331, 333
Zell, Katharina, 304
Zell Matthäus (Mathis), 168, 170, 179, 202–3, 204, 305, 306–7, 352, 374
Zelst, Johann, 317
Ziegenhagen, 113
Ziegler, Clemens, 24, 36, 165, 167, 172, 174–8, 179, 217, 227, 274, 275, 276, 284, 285, 308
Ziegler, Jakob, 277, 284, 289–90
Ziegler, Jörg, 179, 181
Zijpp, N. van der, 339
Zuber, Hans, 205
Zuider Sea, 325
Zürich, 2, 6, 9, 13, 68, 127–8, 237, 279, 280, 282, 302, 381, 389
Zutphen, Christoffel van, 359
Zutphen, Hendrik van, 359
Zwick, Johannes, 302
Zwickau Prophets, 3, 9, 16, 78, 112, 139, 174, 192, 209
Zwingli, Huldrych, 2, 5–6, 10, 77, 141–2, 145, 147, 148, 150, 151, 155, 157, 158, 173, 174, 196, 214, 217, 280, 282, 314, 343, 355, 379, 381

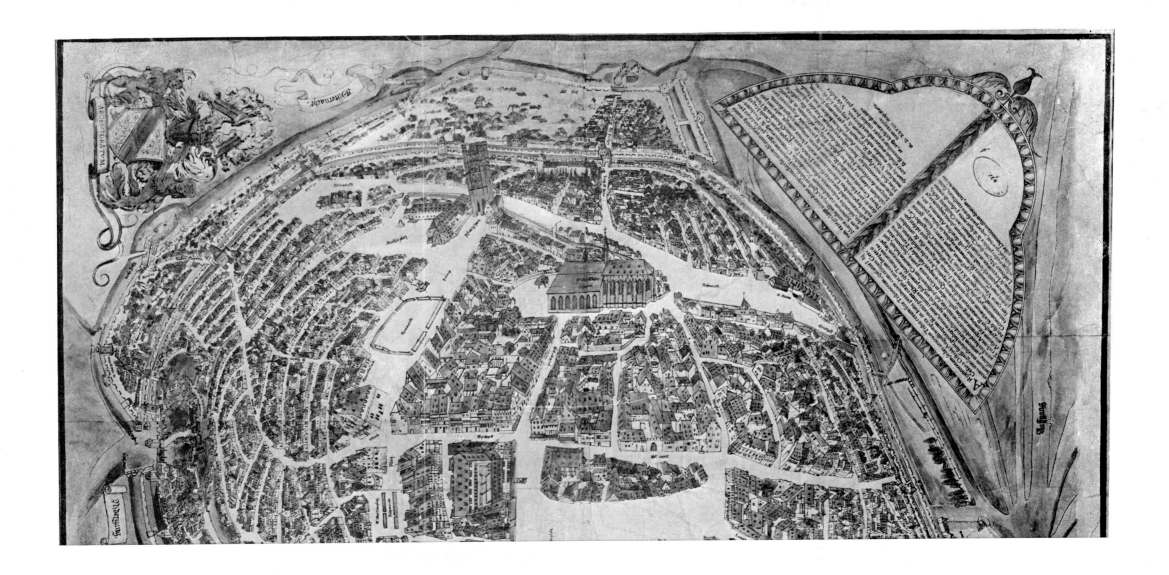